A Journal Briefing

Whitewater

From the Editorial Pages of
The Wall Street Journal.

Edited by Robert L. Bartley
with Micah Morrison
and the Editorial Page staff

Library of Congress Catalog Card Number:
94-79762

ISBN 1-881944-02-6

Printed in the United States of America

The Wall Street Journal.
Dow Jones & Company, Inc.
200 Liberty Street
New York, N.Y. 10281

TABLE OF CONTENTS

Roiling Rapids   257

Hearings   *451*

Introduction

The Whitewater affair has reached a punctuation mark. Congressional hearings are over, and looming ahead are a new special counsel, the fall elections and a new session of Congress. Clearly it remains too early for a final assessment, but just as clearly the imbroglio has taken a toll on the Clinton Administration. It's an apt time to review what we've learned.

Whitewater Development Co. was a failed Arkansas real estate speculation in which Bill and Hillary Clinton were partners, but by the fall of 1994 the name had come to signify more-broad-ranging questions about the character of the President and his circle. "Friends of Bill" seemed beset on every side by conflicts of interest and charges of ethical lapses. The Congressional hearings led to the resignation of Roger Altman, the deputy treasury secretary who had known the President since Georgetown University. David Watkins, an old Arkansas friend, resigned his White House position over a helicopter ride to a golf course. Webster Hubbell, former law partner of the First Lady, resigned as Associate Attorney General over billing questions at the Rose Law Firm. Bernard Nussbaum, who had met Hillary Clinton on the staff of the Watergate investigation, resigned as White House Counsel amid controversy over his handling of the papers belonging to Deputy Counsel Vincent Foster after his suicide. Meanwhile special counsel Robert Fiske had probed for legal violations both in Arkansas and Washington, only to be replaced by Kenneth Starr when a panel of judges decided it wanted its own man.

The swirling story is surely confusing to the public. Even the most informed and literate citizens understandably have trouble following the twists and turns and the personalities so fascinating to the cognoscenti. And of course, as the hearings closed the story was far from ended, with a great many loose ends. No one can confidently predict where Whitewater will ultimately lead, and the ordinary citizen is perplexed over even what questions to ask.

It is in the hope of giving readers some bearings that we have compiled a selection of materials published by The Wall Street Journal. One quick way to catch up on a rapidly developing story is to trace how it looked to editors and writers heavily involved. While our commentary on Whitewater has its fans and its critics, neither doubt that we've consistently been in the forefront of the story. Early on we raised questions about Administration figures from the Rose Law Firm, and were widely criticized for suggesting that Mr. Foster's death deserved a thorough investigation. As the Whitewater story started to break, it was of course not the work of opinion writers but investigative reporters, amply acknowledged both here and in our articles at the time. But our commentary has compiled the revelations of various investigators and, we hope, drawn the story into a whole not readily available elsewhere.

This is a collection of informed opinion about Whitewater broadly defined, including commentary on the BCCI scandal that in some ways seems to overlap. News articles and excerpts from documents have been included at key points. They are arrayed chronologically, with narrative added at chapter headings to provide some measure of continuity. A previously unpublished chronology is added. This collection is designed to provide a factual base and develop themes that advance understanding and illuminate outstanding questions. A reader who reviews the chronicle here will understand what has happened so far, and be alert and prepared for future turns in the tale.

ROBERT L. BARTLEY
Editor
The Wall Street Journal
September 6, 1994

Setting the Stage

1992 opened with President George Bush drifting in his re-election campaign, Pat Buchanan mounting an insurgent run at the GOP nomination, and Ross Perot grabbing headlines. Bill Clinton was merely one of a pack of Democratic Party hopefuls chasing their party's nomination—and not a very promising one at that. By the time of the New Hampshire primary in February, Gov. Clinton was struggling against reports of sexual escapades and draft-dodging.

On March 8, as the Clinton campaign pulled into the primary lead, The New York Times published a story by investigative reporter Jeff Gerth on the Clintons' links to Madison Guaranty Savings & Loan and the Whitewater Development Company. Mr. Gerth's article established a number of key facts: the Clintons appeared to have put little money into the Whitewater company, which seemed to have been heavily subsidized by their partner, James McDougal, although the 1978 partnership was structured on a 50-50 basis; Madison Guaranty, taken over by Mr. McDougal in 1982, grew rapidly but ran into trouble and faced closure by the state; Madison then was represented by Hillary Rodham Clinton, the governor's wife and a partner in the Rose Law Firm, before the new state securities commissioner, who recently had been appointed by her husband.

The Clintons' business relationships, Mr. Gerth wrote, raised "questions of whether a governor should be involved in a business deal with the owner of a business regulated by the state and whether, having done so, the governor's wife through her law firm should be receiving legal fees for work done for the business." On March 20, Jerry Seper of The Washington Times reported that Mrs. Clinton had been paid $2,000 per month for fifteen months to represent Madison before the Arkansas Securities Commission.

The Clinton campaign quickly produced a report by Denver lawyer James Lyons, a Clinton supporter, stating that no improprieties had taken place and that the Clintons had lost $68,000 on Whitewater. The issue faded away.

Many reasons have been advanced for the press's failure to pursue Whitewater for the eighteen months following the publication of the Lyons Report. In "Why the Press Quit on Whitewater in 1992," Forbes MediaCritic editor Terry Eastland cites the complexity of Mr. Gerth's story and its reliance on fragmented financial records, many of them over a decade old; a lack of investigative resources at major news organizations, or an unwillingness to invest those resources in the story; the hostile response of the Clinton campaign to Mr. Gerth's article, as well as its emergence in the middle of a tumultuous primary season.

Mr. Eastland also indicates that Whitewater may not have been the sort of story the press wanted to hear about. The "reporting on the journalists who covered the 1992 campaign suggests that they were tired of George Bush and liked Bill Clinton," Mr. Eastland writes. "On February 2, 1992, the New York Times's Howell Raines remarked on 'an extraordinary burst of journalistic fawning' over Clinton. Later that month, then New Republic senior editor Rick Hertzberg, reporting on his 'informal poll' of the campaign press corps, found that 'the real reason members of The Press like Clinton is . . . [that] they think he would make a very good, perhaps great, President."

As Election Day neared, The Wall Street Journal broke stories about important aspects of Bill Clinton's draft record. It also examined the financial empire run in Little Rock by Jackson Stephens, which had exerted a powerful influence on Arkansas politics. In early litigation involving the Bank of Credit and Commerce International, Stephens properties were represented by the Rose Law Firm, with Hillary Rodham appearing in a peripheral role. After the election, questions about Mrs. Clinton and her Rose Law Firm partners would soon emerge.

REVIEW & OUTLOOK

Who Is Bill Clinton?

We doubt that what the United States needs now is an easy re-election for George Bush. The President was talking yesterday about how it'd be great if he were running unopposed for the Republican nomination, free of the Buchanan insurgency. Then he could concentrate on the mercurial Governor from Arkansas. Instead, what this President and the country very much need right now is some serious political competition among serious candidates with serious ideas. For now, we seem headed in the other direction. No wonder voters are surly.

Bill Clinton

Operation Desert Storm was a grand achievement for the U.S., but it did have the effect of driving relatively strong and familiar Democrats such as Al Gore and Bill Bradley from the field. With Bill Clinton now regnant, the system must once again come to grips at the presidential level with more Democratic mystery and weirdness.

Every four years the Democrats send us another Governor we have to get to know. Getting to know Jimmy Carter took more than a few months. The first time we ran a two-name editorial to get at the mind of a confused policy maker was February 8, 1977, "Jimmy McGovern." It commented on the Carter appointment of Paul Warnke, chief apologist for George McGovern's $30 billion cut in the Pentagon budget, as head of the Arms Control and Disarmament Agency. This was somewhat surprising from an Annapolis graduate who'd run an anti-Washington campaign, and we noted: "But if he intended to follow the foreign and defense policies so roundly rejected by the voters four years ago, it would have been nice if he had told us so during the campaign." By 1980, everyone in the country knew what was meant by the phrase, "There you go again." In 1984 we had to go through the experience of getting to know Geraldine Ferraro and John Zaccaro, who copped a plea. But Fritz Mondale was a known quantity and made no attempt to hide it, pledging to raise taxes and saying that Ronald Reagan would too but wasn't honest about it. Senator Mondale carried Minnesota and the District of Columbia, and in 1986 the top marginal tax rate was cut to 28%.

So in 1988 it was back to Michael Dukakis, and Kitty. By this time the voters were savvier about getting to know people. They got a quick fix on Governor Dukakis, in no small part thanks to Roger Ailes's revolving-door ad (which contrary to popular mythology never included Willie Horton; that ad was put on the air by an independent group spending its own money). The ride in the tank also helped. Such are the straws voters must stay alert for while watching modern Democrats campaign for the presidency.

So it now appears we will get to know, or try to get to know, Bill Clinton and Hillary. The Gennifer Flowers tank has already rumbled by. But where's the rest of them? We seem to have a distant memory of Governor Clinton riding onto the scene with talk of a "New Covenant," which had something to do with emphasizing economic growth, honest work, redesigning welfare and other lurches toward the center; even Orange County Republicans seemed taken with it. Then two weeks ago it turns out that the Governor's campaign is actually about "populism," with something called "the rich" being chased down to "pay their fair share." And when do we get an honest fix on how Hillary's politics fit into all this?

The real question is why the party that dominates Congress has to keep putting up unknowns to contest the world's most powerful political office. Why is Washington such dead ground for growing Democratic presidential timber? About this there is no mystery. It is because the political positions of the Democratic House Caucus are rigorously enforced on Congresspeople. Encumbered with this awful political baggage, none of them can win a presidential election.

Senator Bob Kerrey, who could make legitimate claims to being a person of some substance, dutifully carried the Beltway Democratic baggage of protectionism and national health into his campaign. He went down in flames. Tom Harkin, an even more hard-core carrier of the Caucus's politics, was the 4% man.

So once again it comes to this: Is there any real reason to trust an unknown Governor when he says he's different? We'll find out eventually, and with any luck at all, revelation will come before November.

Letters to the Editor

Hillary. And Bill

In regard to your March 12 editorial "Who Is Bill Clinton?": To me, Bill Clinton comes across as an LBJ-type cowboy. Surely one—the original—was enough. Mr. Clinton shares with George Bush the principle: Do anything, say anything, whatever it takes to get elected." Let the voter beware.

MAURICE KEMP

Aurora, Colo.

REVIEW & OUTLOOK

Clinton's Baggage

In his acceptance speech tonight, Bill Clinton will look and sound free as a bird. In public appearances, he's been confident, healthy, eager to talk, eager to please. But just off camera, you can see the men and women who have to deal with Clinton's baggage. In politics, baggage is the concerns, worries, unexploded rumors or nagging negatives that dog politicians. Baggage alone doesn't necessarily kill a candidacy. The danger of baggage is that it creates doubts.

How heavy is Bill Clinton's baggage?

Everyone who's read the polls will start with the "character issue." As we watch delegates wearing T-shirts proclaiming "I Believe Anita," we wonder whether it's really forbidden to utter the name Gennifer Flowers. Maybe in the long run it's best that the prestige press never ran the transcripts of the tapes she offered, though the test will be whether the same delicacy pertains to a future Robert Bork, Clarence Thomas or Dan Quayle. This and other disconcerting episodes have been submerged by talk of his humble origins, but they have not really been answered. In particular, we wonder whether a mature Bill Clinton still feels the same way about Vietnam as the young Bill Clinton did.

There is a second problem labeled Hillary. Mrs. Clinton was appealing in a CNN interview this week, but the problem is not her home life but her public life. Since it is so clear that Governor Clinton is a lifelong pol, we look for clues as to what he really believes. His wife's beliefs seem firm and clear. She is an activist lawyer and leading intellectual theorist for the "legal rights" movement, which seeks "change" through the courts. Mrs. Clinton's personal interest has been to expand the legal rights of children against their parents, an agenda at which voters are entitled to take pause. For that matter, how would a President Clinton stand on the broader issue of litigiousness, when, for example, our non-Yalie Vice President calls for less of it?

None of these personal handbags, though, will burden Mr. Clinton as much as the double steamer trunk of a party he starts to carry tonight. Tuesday, hidden behind the All-Star game, some of us saw the Not for Primetime Players. Rep. Pat Schroeder, a liberal icon, presided over an evening of Jimmy Carter and Jesse Jackson. President Carter faulted the foreign policy that won the Cold War as too tough. The Rev. Jackson broke new theological ground with the observation that Jesus "was the child of a single mother," adding, "It was Herod — the Quayle of his day — who put no value on the family." An AIDS mother, meanwhile, said that her daughter did not "survive the Reagan administration."

The second party trunk is, as we've already observed, the Democratic Congress. The attitudes on display Tuesday, having repeatedly proved a failure in presidential politics, didn't prevail in this year's presidential nomination. But they have consistently prevailed in the Congressional caucuses. The votes of the Democratic Leadership Council, Mr. Clinton's base, have kept the Democrats as the majority party. But the caucuses have served to enslave the DLC to the liberal agenda. Nor, as the Carter administration showed, can a Democratic president necessarily break this grip.

The conventional view is that this year the Democratic Party has finally changed, that the liberals were delivering their swan songs. But this is politics. No one retires to the crypt voluntarily. Liberals still lead virtually every committee of Congress; the key staffers are liberals; the liberals give the Democratic Party its elan, not to mention a good share of its money.

Nominee Clinton's target voters, the Reagan Democrats, deserted the party over this liberal agenda. They're patriotic, and don't care for the suggestion that America is a force for evil in the world. They think "fairness" is a code word for handouts to the poor. While increasingly accepting of blacks and other minorities, they see themselves suffering from quasi-quotas in jobs and promotions. They are pro-family and certainly pro-child, though they don't understand what this has to do with the courts. They currently are also very much upset with the pain and uncertainty caused by the recession coinciding with the Bush administration, which opens the opportunity for the Democrats to win them back.

In his address tonight, possibly Governor Clinton will deal with some of these other concerns. If the voters this year are volatile and angry, it's in large part because they've been paying attention, and there are some important aspects of Bill Clinton's candidacy that need a lot more clarification. Though the convention's goal has been to avoid disputes, we don't see how it's possible to hide the Clinton baggage from the voters indefinitely.

REVIEW & OUTLOOK

Beyond BCCI, SMERSH?

Asked last week about the possibility of an independent counsel to probe the BCCI scandal, Senator John Kerry replied, "There already is an independent counsel, Bob Morgenthau." This strikes us as a capital idea, if only the federal government makes sure that the Manhattan District Attorney has the resources and authority to do the whole job.

Clearly there is plenty left to investigate, despite the 800-page report by Senator Kerry and Senator Hank Brown, compiling public knowledge of the massive international financial scandal. An appendix to the report lists some 20 further trails to explore, but even these are but suggestions of much larger questions never made quite explicit.

To take one particular, it's important to recognize the intimate relation between the two financial scandals in current headlines — BCCI and BNL, the financing of the Iraqi armament program by the Atlanta branch of Italy's Banca Nazionale del Lavoro. Swiss banker Alfred Hartmann was on the board of both institutions, and there were numerous cross-dealings. As the Kerry report details, the two banks worked hand-in-glove, with BCCI milking its international connections to make overnight loans to BNL to finance Iraqi weapons.

In addition, BCCI had a rich collection of other financial connections. The Kerry report raises the suspicion that BCCI helped Charles Keating move funds abroad in the midst of his Savings and Loans depredations. The report calls for further investigations of David Paul of CenTrust, and also raises questions about figures such as Marc Rich, the fugitive commodities giant, and William Casey, former Director of Central Intelligence.

Running through these connections is the suggestion of something out of a James Bond novel — SMERSH, a vast international criminal network in many ways more powerful than individual governments. The large question is: What are we dealing with here? Was BCCI really, in the Kerry report's words, "an elaborate corporate spider-web with BCCI's founder, Agha Hasan Abedi and his assistant, Swaleh Naqvi, in the middle?" Or was BCCI a part of an even wider web?

We know, too, that BCCI's modus operandi around the world was bribery and subversion of government officials. We know its attempts to penetrate the U.S. financial system benefited from a remarkable series of regulatory blunders and oversights. So another large question, perhaps beyond the ken of a Senate committee, is whether any U.S. officials were bribed, and if so who and how?

Similarly, the whole arms-to-Iraq episode was an incredible blunder. These columns, among others, warned repeatedly that the coddling of Saddam Hussein was folly. Was this policy merely State Department fantasy (quite conceivable), or was there something more sinister involved? And how did regulators manage to miss the financial transfers to Iraq?

And how do you explain the Justice Department's bizarre handling of the case against BNL Atlanta head Christopher Drogoul? Prosecutors have now abandoned the plea bargain they'd reached with Mr. Drogoul, after weeks of searing skepticism from his lawyer and the judge about prosecutors' insistence that no one higher in BNL was involved. Mr. Drogoul will now go to trial, after the elections.

Vice presidential nominee Al Gore recently raised the arming-Iraq issue against President Bush, of course. But the BCCI side of the scandal is littered with Democrats like Clark Clifford and Bert Lance. On the Republican side suspicions fall on Clifford protege Robert Altman and Senator Orrin Hatch, who almost escaped in the Kerry report while an aide was cited, and who may get the powder puff of the Senate Ethics Committee. Bill Clinton and Ross Perot have not yet been vetted for SMERSH connections. Senator Kerry himself had close contribution-raising connections with Mr. Paul. Can anyone be trusted?

Columnist William Safire, who's done yeoman work in spotlighting the implications of the BNL case, has been calling for an independent counsel. When the Justice Department is at least part of the investigation, it makes sense to have someone else investigate. The problem is that it doesn't work; by definition, Lawrence Walsh and his ilk are amateurs — useful for political persecutions, but not for serious investigation.

Mr. Morgenthau's leadership in the BCCI case shows the virtues of professionalism and experience. He has true independence, and a big start in investigating the case. But to do the whole job, he needs money and authority. His budget for enforcing the law in Manhattan is $56 million, as compared with the $32 million to $40 million spent by Mr. Walsh over such crimes as lying to Congress. He has considerable authority — the Atlanta branch of BNL was subsidiary to a New York branch, for example — but in the end is only a county DA.

Even without an independent counsel law, procedures exist for solving these difficulties. Local law enforcement authorities routinely receive federal grants for special purposes such as anti-drug efforts. And there is plenty of precedent for cross-designating federal and state prosecutors. So Mr. Morgenthau can be granted some money, for example to hire the investigative services of Kroll Associates, and be cross-designated as an assistant U.S. attorney to enforce federal law if necessary.

There is no great mystery about how best to proceed. The only mystery is whether the Kerry Committee, the Congress and the U.S. government are serious about getting to the bottom of the BCCI-BNL scandal.

News Story

Wide Net:
Arkansas's Stephenses, Hedging Bets, Help Both Bush and Clinton

Investment-Banking Family With Interests to Protect Warms Up to Governor

Flap Over a State Bond Issue

By THOMAS PETZINGER JR.

Staff Reporter of THE WALL STREET JOURNAL

LITTLE ROCK, Ark. – No matter who comes out on top on Election Day, Jackson Stephens should be a winner.

The billionaire investment banker is part of President Bush's Team 100, a group of $100,000 GOP contributors who can count on special White House access. His son and business partner, Warren Stephens, carries his own impressive Republican credentials, once having played host to a fund-raiser at which Mr. Bush mingled with Arkansas GOP leaders.

Jackson Stephens

But the Stephens empire also bankrolls Bill Clinton. Jack Stephens is the leading stockholder in a bank that gave Mr. Clinton's campaign a $3.5 million line of credit, helping him overcome a cash crunch and rekindle his candidacy in the Super Tuesday primaries last March. And as of the latest count, contributions from employees at Stephens Inc. made the family-owned investment-banking firm the Democratic ticket's third largest source of cash in corporate America.

What does Jack Stephens want from government? At the state and local level, the answer is obvious: He wants business. So far this year, his firm has underwritten fully half the bond issues here in Arkansas. On occasion, the company has even provided services to both sides of the same bond transaction, collecting big fees in the process.

At the federal level, Mr. Stephens may want something different. The Arkansan — who played a central role in bringing Bank of Credit and Commerce International to America — sits atop an empire that could well raise questions with an aggressive financial regulator. What Jack Stephens wants from the U.S. government is to be left alone.

Though they appear to meet the letter of the law, his business holdings fly in the face of the 60-year-old federal doctrine that is supposed to keep banking and securities as separate as church and state. Mr. Stephens and his family own 36.8% of Worthen Banking Corp., Arkansas's largest banking company. He is barred by law from "controlling" the bank, but it pays fees to his other firms, finances his deals at below the prime rate — and now serves as his instrument of political clout.

"They found years ago that to protect themselves, they had to have influence in the seats of power, in Washington and here," says the state's auditor, Julia Hughes Jones, of the Stephenses. "The operation of government is nowhere near what we were taught in civics class. They knew that before a lot of people did."

Mr. Stephens is hardly the first tycoon to help both sides in a political contest, but anyone hoping to hear him expound on his intentions is in for a disappointment. The 69-year-old Mr. Stephens hides his point of view behind a slow drawl, thick tinted glasses, a cocked eyebrow and a cloud of cigarette smoke.

Even getting in to see him is tricky; the elevator to Mr. Stephens's penthouse office suite is a kind of combination lock, so visitors must know a coded sequence of floor numbers to get there.

While waving off questions he doesn't want to hear, Mr. Stephens defends his business practices and expresses ambivalence about politics and politicians — most notably about Bill Clinton. Asked for an appraisal, Mr. Stephens smirks and draws on his cigarette. "No comment," he says.

Much of his antipathy is ideological. Mr. Stephens, like many other members of his organization, has a passion for the fervently capitalist, anti-government writings of the late Ayn Rand. He can cite the page number at which a character in the novel "Atlas Shrugged" begins a soliloquy on money as the root of all good. Gov. Clinton's willingness to tax and to rely on government solutions doesn't go over well with Mr. Stephens. Mr. Clinton has also centralized much of the state's bonding authority, loosening the Stephenses' grip on underwriting.

The Stephens organization not only has contributed to a number of Gov. Clinton's political opponents over the years, it also gave some of them jobs when they lost. In 1986, when the Stephenses were underwriting his opponent's candidacy, Mr. Clinton essentially accused them of trying to buy influence. "After you have a billion dollars and a house in Florida," he told a local newspaper, "what else can you buy but a governor?"

But despite their past animosity, political and commercial necessity in recent years has pushed the Stephens family and Mr. Clinton into each other's arms. "They the Stephenses don't particularly like Clinton, but they want to hedge both sides," says Roy Drew, a bond analyst here and a former Stephens Inc. stockbroker who has become a critic of the company's dealings with the state. Although Worthen Banking and Mr. Stephens both deny that he had any role in the big line of credit to the Clinton campaign, there's little doubt that much of the political gratitude flowing from a Clinton presidency would be directed at Jack Stephens.

Mr. Stephens, though professing disaffection with politics and politicians today, was steeped in them as a young man. The son of an Arkansas legislator, he worked throughout his teens as a statehouse page, fetching Cokes and watching deals unfold. Years later, having made it big in natural-gas production and investment banking with his brother, the late Witt Stephens, he again jumped into politics as a fund-raiser for his Naval Academy classmate Jimmy Carter. Later, President Carter appointed a member of the Stephens organization, Vernon Weaver, to head the Small Business Administration.

As the family fortune swelled, Jack Stephens became enamored of banking, acquiring interests amounting to 4.9% (just below the level requiring public disclosure) in a number of financial institutions across the South. One was the predecessor of First American Bankshares Inc., of Washington, D.C., which ultimately fell under the secret and unlawful control of BCCI Holdings (Luxembourg) S.A.

In his dealings with the principals of BCCI, back in 1977, Mr. Stephens was assisted by Curt Bradbury, then a 26-year-old financial analyst at Stephens Inc. Mr. Bradbury played a role in trying to persuade BCCI to buy shares in the Washington bank. Mr. Bradbury is now the chairman of Worthen Banking, which makes him the chief banker to the Clinton campaign.

Mr. Bradbury argues strenuously that his leading shareholder had nothing to do with the $3.5 million line of credit to the Clinton campaign ($2 million of which was drawn down). "I did that, he didn't," Mr. Bradbury says of the loan, one of the biggest of its kind ever made in a presidential campaign. "And he didn't know I was doing it."

Messrs. Bradbury and Stephens are sensitive on that point. It would be illegal for Mr. Stephens to exercise any control over Worthen Bank — much less to have a hand in a huge loan to a presidential candidate. But a visit to the bank and an examination of some of its records suggest that even if he doesn't control Worthen, he has plenty of influence.

A computer terminal emblazoned "Stephens Link" is the first thing you see walking into the lobby of the main branch here. Touching the screen, you learn that you can open a trading account at Stephens right there from the floor of Worthen Bank. The computer provides investment reports on several "stocks of interest," many of them companies in which the Stephens family owns shares or to which Stephens Inc. provides investment-banking services. Stephens Link is hooked up to many other banks as well, but Worthen was the customer that got it off the ground.

The insider relationship is also evident in Worthen's loan book. When Mr. Stephens assumes a line of credit for his personal investments — often at $5 million a crack — it's generally at a quarter of a percentage point below the prime rate. Likewise, the family investment-banking company takes out credit of as much as $7 million, the house limit, at the broker loan rate minus a quarter-point. A number of other family-owned entities borrow at prime. Sometimes the borrowings are unsecured, although that happens less often than in years past, according to Worthen's disclosures in proxy statements on file at the Securities and Exchange Commission.

Worthen's Mr. Bradbury says the favorable rates reflect the family's triple-A credit-worthiness. "The Stephenses borrow here on no better terms than they borrow anywhere else," he says. Actually, a family-owned crafts-marketing concern, Leisure Holding Co., has long borrowed from a Dallas bank at 1 1/4 points above prime, but Mr. Bradbury says this is because the Stephenses didn't provide a personal guarantee.

In addition, Stephens companies collect a variety of fees from Worthen. In the decade since the Stephenses bought into the bank, it has paid more than $30 million to Systematics Inc., a Stephens-founded data-processing firm. Stephens Inc. provides investment-banking services to Worthen, although at discount rates — something it agreed to do to settle a shareholder lawsuit alleging self-dealing. Worthen also lends to the investment-banking clients of Stephens Inc., as it did with $5 million it kicked in to a syndicate that helped finance the Stephens-managed hostile takeover of Holly Farms by Tyson Foods Inc.

In a case pending in federal bankruptcy court, Worthen came up with some of the money that helped the Stephens family unload a struggling business it owned. The company, Hollis & Co., once had a sweet arrangement selling industrial equipment to Arkla Inc., a publicly held natural-gas utility that brother Witt Stephens, who died in 1991, had headed for years. But new management at Arkla eventually began putting purchases out for competitive bid. By 1984, the Stephenses decided to sell Hollis.

The buyers turned to Worthen Bank for financing, and, to their surprise, got the cold shoulder from loan officers. A member of the purchasing group claimed that he later brought the problem to Jack Stephens's attention. "Take care of that," Mr. Stephens told an aide, according to the buyer's deposition filed with the U.S. District Court in Little Rock.

Within hours, Worthen had assigned a team to the account. "We had a loan approved for $4 million the next day, or shortly thereafter," the purchaser testified.

Alas for Worthen, Hollis went into Chapter 11 bankruptcy court proceedings almost immediately, causing the bank to charge off at least $1.6 million of the loan. In the bankruptcy case, the trustee claims the business was insolvent when Worthen financed the sale by the Stephens family.

"The Stephenses got their money out, and Worthen took the hit," says Sheffield Nelson, who says that, as the president of Arkla, he began the competitive bidding that set Hollis on its downward path. Mr. Nelson's management decisions in his years at Arkla became a major irritant to the Stephens family, causing a bitter split. Warren Stephens says no one at Stephens Inc. ever pressured Worthen to finance the transaction.

Although, in 1987, the comptroller of the currency gave Worthen a slap on the wrist for a number of self-dealing transactions involving Jack Stephens, the Federal Reserve Board, which has responsibility for keeping banks and brokerage firms separate, has never laid a finger on the Stephens empire. "Mr. Stephens can own stock in the bank so long as he doesn't have more than 50%," says Virgil Mattingly, the Fed's general counsel in Washington. In fact, the Stephenses' interest, combined with the Worthen stock held by Stephens partners in a number of overseas financial-service ventures, once reached 51%. The Fed says that wasn't unlawful because the partners weren't themselves investment bankers.

Whether a Clinton administration would look askance at the situation can't be predicted, but Mr. Bradbury (another Ayn Rand devotee) is counting on the kind of access to a President Clinton that would help him communicate his views. "I would like to be in a position to think I could call the president of the United States," he recently told an interviewer for the weekly Arkansas Times, "and give him my views — on the Federal Reserve, for example." Mr. Bradbury now adds that he was only referring to his views on economic policy in general.

Over the years, the law firm of which Hillary Clinton was a member played a major role in representing Worthen and the Stephenses' other interests. Ms. Clinton herself once represented a Stephens affiliate. As for the governor, however, relations with the Stephens empire remained icy until the late 1980s.

By that time, a younger generation of management — Bill Clinton's contemporaries — was ascending in the Stephens organization, led by Jack's son Warren at the investment bank company and by Mr. Bradbury at Worthen Bank. Meanwhile, Witt Stephens, whose politics were Democratic to the extent that his brother's were Republican, began getting courtesy calls from Gov. Clinton.

The governor began looking more favorably on some of the Stephens family's deals. In the late 1980s, Mr. Clinton helped to clear the way for at least $100 million in complex bond issues underwritten by Stephens Inc. Using state pension funds, Stephens Inc. arranged for a group of state and local agencies — a port authority, a student-loan agency and a cultural commission — to earn a total of nearly $4 million through a series of arbitrage transactions. Stephens got $1.6 million in fees.

In carrying through the transactions, Stephens provided investment-banking services to the buyers as well as to the sellers of the bonds, although Warren Stephens says the company was acting in a fiduciary capacity solely on the sell side of the deal. Critics of the fees, he says, "had no concept of how hard we'd worked on the concept." Betsey Wright, a Clinton campaign official, says the governor's actions were intended to benefit the state, not Stephens Inc.

After relations between the Stephenses and Gov. Clinton warmed, there was much controversy here over the Stephenses' effort to get state aid in a nursing-home deal. Working as the investment banker, Stephens Inc., in 1989, was trying to engineer the sale of 32 Arkansas facilities by Beverly Enterprises Inc., the nation's largest nursing-home operator, which badly needed cash to stave off failure. The Stephenses had more at stake in the sale than their investment-banking fee. They owned an issue of preferred stock convertible into 10% of Beverly's common. Worthen's Mr. Bradbury sits on Beverly's board. Mr. Stephens's personal lawyer also represented Beverly in the proposed transaction.

Beverly sought approval for a $75 million state bond issue to provide the Texas company buying the nursing homes with tax-exempt financing; that way, the buyer could pay a higher price, benefiting the Stephenses and other Beverly shareholders.

Among the members of the state agency voting to give preliminary approval to the bond issue was a Clinton appointee who happened to be one of Mr. Bradbury's lieutenants at Worthen Bank. ("He probably shouldn't have voted on it," Mr. Bradbury says.)

Gov. Clinton, too, said he would consider backing the securities sale. The Clinton campaign says the governor feared that Beverly would otherwise go out of business, leaving patients homeless.

At the last minute, however, the bond issue encountered opposition from Steve Clark, the state attorney general. Then, with the issue scheduled for a final vote by the state bonding agency, one of the lobbyists promoting the deal mentioned that he was working to raise some political contributions for Mr. Clark, who at the time was contemplating a run for governor. "I think I can get you $100,000, if you can just be neutral" on the bond issue, the lobbyist said, according to the attorney general's court testimony in the lobbyist's subsequent municipal court trial on bribery charges.

Among those from whom the lobbyist had already solicited cash:

The lawyer for Jack Stephens, a lawyer who at that moment was trying to push through the Beverly bond issue.

The whole deal was scuttled by Gov. Clinton in December 1989, when the attorney general went public with the purported bribery offer. The lobbyist was acquitted after telling the judge the campaign contribution had nothing to do with the bond deal, which was a different "track" in the same conversation.

Jack Stephens will say little about the whole affair. "It was just a big mess," he says.

The Stephenses' relations with Gov. Clinton reached a critical stage in 1990, when Mr. Nelson, the dreaded former head of the Arkla gas utility, won the Republican nomination for governor, defeating a candidate strongly backed by the Stephens clan. Mr. Nelson ran against Gov. Clinton in the general election. The Stephenses threw in their lot with the incumbent Democrat.

Four days before the general election, Warren Stephens says Mr. Clinton telephoned him at home in a panic over a series of ads in which his opponent was attacking him as a tax-and-spend liberal. Could Mr. Stephens raise $10,000 in 11th-hour campaign funds? Mr. Clinton asked. Warren Stephens agreed. Based on the assurances from him and four other fund-raisers, Mr. Clinton immediately borrowed $50,000 for a media counterattack. Mr. Clinton won the election handily, although he probably would have anyway.

Controversy such as the Beverly affair faded from memory here as White House fever swept Little Rock. Worthen's Mr. Bradbury certainly has a case of that. He says he responded eagerly when officials of the Clinton campaign approached him last December about the line of credit. A golfing companion of Mr. Clinton, Mr. Bradbury played host to a Clinton fund-raising dinner in August at which guests included the actors Chevy Chase and Cybill Shepherd, the jazz artist Herbie Hancock and several senators, congressmen and governors.

"It's an interesting experience to have a personal friend not only running for president, but maybe going to make it," says Mr. Bradbury.

REVIEW & OUTLOOK

Offstage Spectacle

As the Presidential candidates take the stage for tonight's debate, another spectacle offstage may engulf the next presidency. Unless someone can get to the bottom of the matter, the next President may find his administration spending its energy not on the economy or other campaign issues, but on loans to Iraq by the Banca Nazionale del Lavoro.

This would be especially true in a second Bush administration, given the handling of the BNL prosecution in Atlanta. The prosecutors first struck and then withdrew a plea bargain with the head of the local bank, Christopher Drogoul. Judge Marvin Shoob withdrew from further handling of the case, professing himself unable to believe the Justice Department's contention that Mr. Drogoul loaned Iraq some $2.1 billion without the knowledge of anyone higher in the bank. By now the CIA has admitted it wrote a misleading letter to the prosecutor. The CIA and the Justice Department are pointing fingers at each other over the blame. The FBI is investigating, but the Justice Department has launched what appears to be a counterprobe of whether FBI head William Sessions committed "crimes" like billing the government for personal phone calls.

As Senator Alan Simpson makes clear alongside, however, Congressional Democrats also have much to answer for in their support of the BNL loans. As is typical of Congressional witch hunts, some of the most culpable are now leading the charge to assign blame elsewhere. And coming in the last weeks of a presidential campaign, the cries of scandal could be mistaken for the kind of interbranch mudslinging the Democratic Congress has so often directed at the Republican presidency.

As defenders of the presidency in most of these matters, though, we find the Iraqi loans and the bungled BNL prosecution a far more serious matter. The BNL scandal, for one thing, is intimately related to the BCCI scandal, as the Kerry report on BCCI makes clear. The same report also details the role of Little Rock billionaire Jackson Stephens, whose empire helped bankroll both the Bush and Clinton campaigns, in the early days of BCCI's U.S. ventures.

While of course these associations prove nothing, they do provide food for thought and reason for investigation. We know that BCCI worked through bribery, and would like to be assured that the Iraqi loans and BNL prosecution were at worst a mistaken policy and a subsequent cover-up.

Yesterday, Senator David Boren, head of the intelligence committee, renewed a demand that Attorney General William Barr appoint an independent counsel to investigate the case. Senator Boren is certainly right that the matter requires a "truly independent investigation." But given the Lawrence Walsh fiasco and other uses of the independent counsel statute to turn policy differences into criminal violations, invocation of this device is scarcely reassuring.

There once was a tradition of independent prosecutors within the Justice Department, including Archibald Cox and then Leon Jaworski during Watergate. While a President might interfere, he had to pay a heavy political price. This tradition, like the Senate's advise and consent powers on court appointments, has been a casualty of the partisan and interbranch warfare of recent years. Happily, however, a highly suitable substitute is available.

As we have pointed out before, and as Senator Kerry suggested in the BCCI case, we already have an independent prosecutor, Manhattan District Attorney Robert Morgenthau. Unlike some new prosecutor, he would not have to start from scratch. During his BCCI investigations, for example, he has already moved to subpoena BNL documents. With his background as a U.S. Attorney, he has the experience to know when prosecutorial discretion may indeed be necessary and when it is an abuse of power. Most important of all, his BCCI work has already established that he is truly independent, of the Justice Department, the Congress, and the whole Beltway. No other conceivable prosecutor could match these qualifications.

Putting Mr. Morgenthau on the case would not require unprecedented laws or procedures. He would need some money, a special grant of the type routinely given to local law enforcement authorities for special purposes. He would need a cross-designation as an assistant U.S. Attorney, a step with ample precedent, and the cooperation of the FBI and other federal authorities. This would give the Republic a truly independent investigator without the usual fuss.

These steps would give us the best possible assurance that the truth would eventually be known, after a full, thorough and patient investigation. And thus they would also ensure that the BNL matter is neither exploded nor buried in the excitement of a presidential campaign.

Letters to the Editor

Stephens Answers Allegations

Editor's Note: The letter is reprinted as the author sent it to The Wall Street Journal. A condensed version appeared in the newspaper.

I have been a regular reader and strong admirer of The Wall Street Journal for nearly five decades. That, among other reasons, made my disappointment all the more acute observing the repetitive pattern of negative comments about me, my family and my company during the course of this year. Thus, it is with genuine sadness and regret that I am finally compelled to write and protest the latest episodes exhibited in Thomas Petzinger, Jr.'s article on Page A1 of The Wall Street Journal of Monday, October 12, 1992, and in the editorial entitled Offstage Spectacle appearing on page A14 of the Thursday, October 15, 1992, edition of the Journal, which I regard as reckless, irresponsible journalism. The Petzinger article is especially unfortunate and distressing because it is riddled with numerous inaccuracies and misstatements despite the substantial time and effort we at Stephens Inc. spent trying to educate Mr. Petzinger to the true facts. At this point, I have no alternative but to acquaint you directly with the facts and to insist that you promptly correct the numerous misstatements and inaccuracies.

The inaccuracies in the article are too numerous to permit extensive individual treatment. Nevertheless, I am compelled to address specifically the most malicious of the false statements and innuendos.

BCCI. The repeated suggestions by your newspaper that Stephens

Inc. or I had any role in 1977-78 with respect to the illegal activities of BCCI revealed 14 years later in 1991 are baseless and obviously intended to do harm. The suggestion that I "played a central role in bringing [BCCI] to America" or that I or anyone else at Stephens"played a role in trying to persuade BCCI to buy shares" in Financial General is reckless and irresponsible.

As your reporter was emphatically informed and as the record of the Financial General episode in 1977-78 unequivocally demonstrates, BCCI representatives were introduced to me by associates—not as people with an interest in Financial General but rather as people with a third party client interested in Financial General. Having no reason at that time—15 years ago—to doubt what I was told, I proceeded as any other businessman in my position would have done. First, Stephens Inc. opened a brokerage account for the clients who were interested in purchasing Financial General shares—which is, after all, the business we are in. Stephens was paid normal brokerage fees for this service. Second, Stephens sold approximately 13,000 shares in Financial General which it owned for approximately $165,000 to an American lawyer who represented to us that he was acting as an agent on behalf of individual clients. We made a 13 cent per share profit on that sale before deducting interest costs which very likely turned it into a loss.

Neither I nor anyone else at Stephens has knowingly had any contact or involvement with anyone representing, affiliated with, or otherwise involved with BCCI since 1978. The 1977-78 encounter was brief, fleeting, and most assuredly, an ordinary business transaction. These people were introduced to us; our contacts were strictly ordinary course of business; and when our business was concluded we had no further contact with them. Your newspaper's persistent characterization of me as a "central figure in the BCCI investigation" is baseless and false and your reporter willfully refused to reflect the facts.

Compliance with Law. Mr. Petzinger is especially malicious and defamatory in his statement that I sit "atop an empire that could well raise questions with an aggressive financial regulator" and that "though they may appear to meet the letter of the law [my] business holdings fly in the face of the 60-year old doctrine that is supposed to keep banking and securities as separate as church and state." What questions? And what conceivable basis could he have for the implication that our business is not subject to aggressive financial regulation? In fact, it is subject to rigorous regulatory scrutiny. I am bound to say that journalism by innuendo is by definition irresponsible, as well as libelous in this case—and I have no doubt that the reporter in question knows it.

As for the 60-year-old "church and state" doctrine that he so piously cites, someone should bring it to the attention of Citibank, Chase Manhattan, Morgan, First Chicago, Bank of America and dozens of other banks in America which are engaged in the securities business—with the blessing of the Federal Reserve Board. Someone should also bring it to the attention of Credit Suisse which controls a U.S. bulge bracket securities firm. Someone should also bring it to the attention of Merrill Lynch which owns Merrill Lynch Bank and Trust Co. and to Shearson Lehman which owns Boston Safe Deposit and Trust Co. and is under common control with the American Express Centurion Bank. Indeed, one might bring it to the attention of the Federal Reserve Board itself which seems to be ignorant of the doctrinal shrine at which The Wall Street Journal and at least one of its staff reporters apparently worship.

In truth, there is no such doctrine, and your contrary assertion which, at a minimum, implies unethical or possibly illegal conduct is reprehensible and per se defamatory. As your know or should know, there is a tremendously complex set of laws and regulations which are administered by experts in various agencies and which can be complied with only with the daily, unstinting and expert assistance of highly trained, specialized lawyers—for which we at Stephens (and others at similar firms) pay dearly. Your reporter has none of these qualifications, and I find it reprehensible that he has the temerity, nevertheless, to be suggestive through innuendo and implication that our business conduct is somehow legally improper or should be called to task. Indeed, I find it especially irresponsible and malicious when the General Counsel of the Federal Reserve Board is willing to be quoted to the effect that there is no law against my ownership of stock in Worthen, so long as it is less than 50%, but your reporter persists with his defamatory innuendo on the subject.

Worthen Bank. Wholly apart from the legal infirmities of the various comments relating to our involvement with Worthen Bank, the editorial policy reflected in the Journal's treatment of these issues is, at best, disingenuous. This is a bank which in 1985 was virtually certain of becoming a $200 plus million failure for which the FDIC (and the U.S. taxpayers) would have been responsible. We could just as well have let it go on the corporate welfare rolls. We did not. We stepped in and risked our own capital to prevent that result, and we assisted in locating and providing the human capital necessary to complete the turnaround. As a result, the following improvements have been achieved by the management of Worthen from the end of 1986 to June 30, 1992.

| | | ($'s in thousands) | |
CATEGORY	1986	1991	6/30/1992
Nonperforming loans	$105,315	$18,663	$22,407
Ending equity	83,459	143,604	174,103
Equity/assets	3.87%	5.88%	6.38%
Classified loans/equity	221.6%	31.9%	28.7%
Net income	($37,537)	$22,884	$14,185*

*For the 6 months ended June 30, 1992

This is a private enterprise success story which should command the admiration of a newspaper like The Wall Street Journal, especially in light of the public burden which the alternative would have created. The fact that your reporter apparently is looking for any excuse to slander our efforts is strong evidence that someone there has an ulterior motive.

Worthen Bank Relationship. Your reporter repeatedly attempts to suggest that Stephens and I receive favorable treatment from Worthen Bank due to various factors which he implies are improper. Once again he is wrong—grossly so. All transactions between Worthern and me, my company or an affiliate or client have occurred in the open light of day without pressure of any kind and with the approval of Worthen's management and independent Board of Directors and have been reviewed by bank regulators in their annual audits of Worthen. In the teeth of this fact, the article is riddled with falsehoods and misstatements regarding our relationship to Worthen.

• When I or my family borrow money—whether from Worthen or elsewhere—we generally do so at less than the prime rate. We made this clear to your reporter, but he apparently is more interested in creating the false impression that at Worthen this is due to something other than our creditworthiness.

• While it is true Stephens agreed to perform investment banking services at a discount to help settle class action litigation arising out of the near failure of the bank in 1985, Stephens had always provided these services at a reduced rate. This is done in an effort to remain competitive and keep the business. Even so, Worthen does use other investment banks from time to time.

• Worthen was the first bank to subscribe to the Stephens Link service, but was quickly followed by others. Worthen Investments is now a significant profit center for Worthen and there are 240 other banks in 22 states that are now customers. To create the impression that Worthen is the bellwether for the service ignores both the sheer number and size of some of the other customers (like Wells Fargo and NationsBank). To imply that the system would not be successful without Worthen is an obvious and blatant distortion.

• The statement by your reporter that the Comptroller of the Currency "gave Worthen a slap on the wrist for a number of self-dealing transactions involving Jack Stephens" is totally false and has no basis in fact.

• The allegations about Stephens putting pressure on Worthen to loan money to the purchaser of Hollis is perhaps the most malicious piece of the article. Mr. Petzinger was told that the top officers of the bank at the time of the Hollis purchase had testified under oath that no one at Stephens had pressured them to make the loan. At the time of their testimony they were no longer officers of Worthen, having been replaced after the Bevel Bressler Schulman collapse. Your reporter, however, completely omitted this critical fact from the article. Instead, he presented a one-sided view that is entirely inaccurate and could only be described as deliberately biased.

• The assertion that Worthen was the lead source of financing which facilitated our sale of Hollis is also false. Bank of New England provided $11.5 million of the funds for the acquisition of Hollis. Worthen provided $5 million.

Beverly Enterprises. The allegations about Beverly Enterprises are in the same vein. In simple terms, your reporter claims Beverly was failing—which it did not—and that Stephens was seeking to engineer a sale of Beverly's Arkansas assets—which never happened—to benefit Stephens. The reason the sale did not occur according to your reporter was opposition from Steve Clark, the Arkansas state attorney general, who claimed to have been offered what amounted to a bribe by a lobbyist who your reporter tries to tie to me by saying the lobbyist had solicited my unnamed lawyer for contributions. The article acknowledges that the lobbyist was acquitted in a trial on bribery charges in which Steve Clark testified against him—which presumably means the jury did not believe Clark. What it maliciously fails to say, however, is that in a separate subsequent case Steve Clark was indicted and convicted on felony charges for theft of property and had his license to practice law revoked by the Arkansas Supreme Court. Why, I want know, is he presented as the only credible, reliable source on the subject of Beverly Enterprises?

Apart from the specific inaccuracies, misstatements and falsehoods detailed above, I am further disturbed by the overall attitude reflected by your newspaper's coverage of Stephens Inc., my family and myself. There appears to be an overriding preconception about us which stubbornly refuses to yield to any contrary factual information, or even to accept the possibility that it could be mistaken. Under these circumstances, I am driven to the conclusion that the Journal is engaged in a vendetta to discredit me and my family as part of some separate and hidden agenda which has nothing directly to do with us. In conclusion, as I said at the outset, I must insist that you correct the false and distorted picture of me, my family and my business which the Petzinger article and reference to me in your editorial have created—which you can easily do by publishing this letter.

JACKSON T. STEPHENS
Chairman
Stephens Inc.

Little Rock, Ark.

REVIEW & OUTLOOK

Bill Meets the Bond Traders

Bill Clinton offers himself as a different kind of Democrat, part of a new generation that doesn't "think the way the old Democratic Party did." Perhaps he actually means it. How would you ever know?

This newspaper's editorials, however outspoken, are not written from a partisan agenda. We are not tied to a political party or to particular candidates, let alone interested in trying to tell our independent-minded readers how to vote. We are interested in issues, measuring our life and times from the perspective of a philosophy that might be described as free men and free markets. In that cause, we take support where we find it.

Bill Clinton

Accordingly, we've had some favorable things to say about Mr. Clinton's economic program and his "new Democrat" theme. We find it commendable that the Clinton economic plan is focused on growth. We agree that the key to growth in the 1990s will be investment; we would stress incentives for private, market-driven investment. Mr. Clinton's almost-endorsement of the North American Free Trade Agreement suggests he understands that open trade is vital in today's interlinked global economy. If these themes were adopted by the Democratic Party, it would be a big step forward for the intellectual causes we champion.

Problem is, on the other side of these issues you also find Bill

Clinton. He wants to provide incentives for growth, but also to raise taxes, at least on incomes above $200,000. He wants Nafta, but with reservations. He wants an open economy, but with a tax on foreign firms at the risk of starting a beggar-thy-neighbor cycle around the world. He wants investment, but with bureaucrats in Washington deciding where and how. He doesn't favor Keynesian pump-priming, except maybe just now. And so on.

All of the pressures of his constituency will be forcing him toward the latter agenda rather than the first. George Mitchell trying to use

FRUSTRATING CANDIDATES

SECOND IN A SERIES

the tax system to level incomes. The labor unions trying to block foreign competition to keep unskilled wages high. The environmentalists seeking to run the world. The plaintiff lawyers after their cut. The teachers' unions seeking higher salaries, and the construction unions wanting to build bullet trains from nowhere to nowhere. Can we really expect him to Sister Souljah them all; what kind of a strong man has emerged from Arkansas?

What's more, the numbers don't add up. There simply are not enough people making $200,000 or enough profits by foreign firms to provide the revenues Mr. Clinton proposes to spend. He promises large savings on health care, but he isn't willing to face the two ways to ration scarce resources: prices or queuing. In a Clinton Presidency, which would give: his spending programs, his tax pledges or his promise to reduce the deficit?

This question has been dogging the bond markets as they contemplate a Clinton victory. The campaign had to send out advisers to batten down headlines about spending stimuli, because bond markets are so sensitive to hints of inflation. The market's verdict is hard to ignore; interest rates directly affect investment and also the government deficit. We're certain that as President, Bill Clinton would get to know the bond traders even better. Unlike the electorate, they vote every day, if not every minute. And they constantly will be asking, will the real Bill Clinton please stand up?

* * *

Which brings us to the character issue. It is certainly a tribute to Mr. Clinton's persistence and audacity as a campaigner that he now poses as a victim. The truth is that by the standards applied to Robert Bork, John Tower, Clarence Thomas and others, Mr. Clinton has had a free ride.

There are, of course, valid privacy concerns about passport files and other government records, but it is also true that the accounts of Mr. Clinton's draft problems emerged so grudgingly that they invited intense scrutiny. Our judgment is that to get his ROTC deferment, young Bill Clinton lied deliberately with malice aforethought about his intention to attend the University of Arkansas. And our suspicion is that the full extent of his anti-war activities at Oxford has still not been revealed, which says something not only about Bill Clinton's actions 20 years ago but about Bill Clinton's promises today.

The epitome of Mr. Clinton's free ride is Charlotte Perry, an Arkansas woman who filed a grievance about not getting a state job that went to Gennifer Flowers. The tapes of Ms. Flowers's conversations with Governor Clinton make it clear enough that she was trying to set him up, but he has never denied it was his voice that was recorded. At one point the following exchange occurs:

FLOWERS: The only thing that concerns me at this point is the state job.

CLINTON: Yeah, I've never thought about that, but as long as you say you've been looking for one, you'd check on it — if they ever ask if you've talked to me about it, you can just say no.

If Anita Hill had offered this tape, would Clarence Thomas have been asked to account for this answer?

* * *

Even laying aside the issue of the real Bill Clinton, the optimistic one gives pause enough. Yes, we need investment, certainly we need better education, and infrastructure is always nice. But how do we achieve these wonderful things?

Alongside, John Rutledge captures the spirit of the Clinton approach, the dark side of supply-side thinking. Manipulate incentives to achieve nonmarket outcomes. Emulate the Japanese and German industrial planners. At this moment, the Japanese miracle reminds us of the Massachusetts miracle that vanished immediately after the last presidential campaign. The Germans aren't far behind.

Perhaps there's room to ask just how much new infrastructure — as opposed to simple maintenance of roads and bridges — we can profitably use. After all, world competition will not favor those with the most infrastructure, but those with the most efficient infrastructure. And can we best get a fiber-optic network by having the government build it, or by changing the regulation of phone companies so they can build it? Just why do per-pupil expenditures reach $9,240 a year in Jersey City, where the state seized the schools when only 16% of ninth-graders could pass proficiency tests?

Even at its best, the Clinton program has an answer for every economic problem except problem Number One: The government does not work. Instead of trying to figure out how to fix the blasted thing, Mr. Clinton would load it down with more and more responsibilities.

Now, the Republic would survive a President Clinton. It survived Jimmy Carter, and Mr. Clinton strikes us as smarter, much better prepared and tougher at least in his single-minded focus on winning elections. There are worse things to be than a highly competent politician, and a President Clinton would find himself disciplined not only by the exigencies of re-election but by the eternal vigilance of the financial markets.

Still, we question whether something new and different is on the ballot this year. At the end of the day, Bill Clinton stands for bigger government. Sure sounds to us just the way the old Democratic Party used to think.

REVIEW & OUTLOOK

Mack the S&L 'Crook'

Perhaps the best point of the Little Rock summit was the recurring theme of getting the lending machinery restarted in an era of regulatory overkill. For some insight on what's gone wrong, President-elect Clinton might ask his new chief of staff and one of his earliest friends, Thomas "Mack" McLarty III. He would no doubt get an earful about the economic effects of the jihad against Savings and Loans "crooks."

Until last Monday, Mr. McLarty was chief executive of Arkla, a natural gas company with offices in Little Rock. He recently wrote his shareholders explaining why the government is suing them for $535 million over a belly-up Texas S&L. Mr. McLarty called it "another case where the Resolution Trust Corp. is chasing 'deep pockets' in response to political pressure." As another company executive says, the hunt for thrift villains long ago transcended "hot tubs and hookers."

Arkla wasn't even in the S&L business. But nowadays almost anybody out there can become a target of opportunity for the government's lawyers. While making the usual noises about "vigorously" defending itself, Arkla began trying to settle before the case was filed. With the RTC's official complaint, its stock plummeted 20% and Moody's put its debt on the watch list.

A little history: In 1989, University Federal Savings of Houston went spectacularly bust, taking $2 billion in taxpayer money with it. University had once belonged to Entex, a Houston gas company, but had been bought out by its managers two years earlier. Entex itself was later bought by Arkla. The RTC is arguing that Entex bears responsibility for University, and as Entex's parent, Arkla's liable too.

The real nut is University's management buyout. By 1989, like most Texas S&Ls, it was bleeding from multiple real-estate wounds, and a sale was possible only because of "supervisory goodwill." This is a fanciful form of capital invented by the Federal Home Loan Bank Board precisely so ailing S&Ls like University could stay open and the government wouldn't have to pay off their depositors.

Mack McLarty

Having shed University, Entex then sold itself to Arkla, but only after the Bank Board had certified that Entex had no further responsibility for the S&L. The Bank Board itself is now defunct, and the RTC argues that Entex was wrong to avail itself of an escape route designed and approved by federal regulators. Arkla is the deep-pocket defendant on the hook for $535 million, even though it never made a dime in the thrift business.

Now, the "political pressure" Mr. McLarty mentioned to his shareholders emanates primarily from Congress, and particularly from the Congressmen who protected truly bad S&Ls from regulators. The prime suspect is Senate Banking Chairman Don Riegle, a charter member of the Keating Five. They want to catch some "crooks" to blame. Better yet if the "crooks" have prominent names like Neil Bush, so in accepting high office Mr. McLarty is a brave man.

After his chat with Mr. McLarty, Mr. Clinton might have a word with Stephen Trafton. He's the CEO of Glendale Federal Bank of California, hired as a cleanup specialist to deal with one of the thrift industry's biggest remaining messes.

Glendale is also in trouble over "supervisory goodwill." In 1981 it took over a weaker S&L at the behest of regulators who promised it could count "goodwill" against its capital requirements. But in 1989, Congress decided that supervisory goodwill was a blunder and wrote down the S&L industry's capital by $18 billion overnight. At the stroke of a pen, Glendale became subject to being closed.

Glendale took to the U.S. Court of Claims, contending it had a contract with regulators, and if they changed their minds they had to pay restitution. It is the biggest of some 40 plaintiffs presenting similar claims. And this past summer, Chief Judge Loren Smith ruled that Glendale's agreement with regulators was a binding contract on which the government reneged, and that Glendale was due damages, with the amount to be determined by further litigation.

Whatever happens next in court, it may be too late for Glendale. Unless it can replace the capital Congress wiped out (mission impossible in California's sagging economy), regulators will turn it into a pumpkin on June 30. No doubt RTC lawyers will then argue that the Court of Claims case is moot, since Glendale no longer exists. Closing the bank will probably cost the government about $2.5 billion. Glendale says it could settle for $1 billion, enough to meet its capital requirements and stay in business.

Something's rotten somewhere. The RTC legal offensive is destroying value and undermining confidence throughout the economy. You'll never get a vigorous recovery with the government in court with companies like Mr. McLarty's Arkla and people like Mr. Trafton. Indeed, RTC litigiousness probably cost George Bush the presidency. As one of his first acts, Mr. Clinton should rein it in before it does the same for him.

REVIEW & OUTLOOK

Hillary's Job

It was good to read in the Journal yesterday that President Clinton is thinking of giving his wife, Hillary, the job of health-care reform czar. The assignment hasn't been confirmed yet, but it would be good for a number of reasons, some of which bear directly on Hillary Clinton's role and some more generally on the role, or multiple roles, of women in our times.

The consequence of not giving Hillary a real job doesn't look attractive. The idea that Mrs. Clinton would have an office in the West Wing (the heavy hitters' wing), would have her own staff, would carry no official title or assignment but would sit in a corner of the Cabinet meetings taking down names is a recipe for a full-core meltdown of the Clinton administration.

Hillary Clinton

The first time it became known that Mrs. Clinton had overruled a Cabinet Secretary, the new Cabinet would collapse as a functioning instrument of discussion and advice. The inherent intimidation factor is overwhelming. How would this be different than to have had Nancy Reagan sitting in on Cabinet meetings?

But Hillary doesn't do teas. And why should she? She is undoubtedly, as her many Boswells have written, a forceful, intelligent woman of independent accomplishment. It may well be that the time has come to rethink the First Lady model that we've lived with for some 200 years. Hillary Clinton is hardly unique. A President Dick Cheney would come with Lynne Cheney. Phil Gramm comes with Wendy Gramm. As a force of nature, both are Hillary's equal (at the very least).

Wendy Gramm

Once the lawyers figure a way around the Bobby Kennedy rule, putting Hillary at the head of an interagency task force on health care makes considerable sense. Certainly it is possible that the dark night of the progressives would descend on us all, that Mrs. Clinton, HHS's Donna Shalala and Clinton aide Ira Magaziner would conspire to truly nationalize health care. But if our reading of the many recent media hagiographies of the First Lady are correct, Hillary Rodham's animating life force has been to succeed. Success in health-care reform is going to require, most of all, a maturity of judgment about how best to handle the issue's endless, often contradictory forces. Simply tying a ribbon around some progressive pipe dream would ensure a large and very public failure.

Deciphering the health-care puzzle is a serious, complex job — just like the jobs that all the other serious people in the Clinton administration are taking on. If Mrs. Clinton is going to revise the way we think about First Ladies, better it should be in an assignment like this, as a public equal of her administration peers, than as a figure in the shadows. That said, we think Mrs. Clinton's boosters ought to consider the possibility that they are distorting public understanding of their own cause — elevating the role of women in public life.

It is hard not to notice that when what Hillary Clinton represents is written about, the one group of women who merit no mention are the women who have served in the Bush administration. Our

Lynne Cheney

list would include: Carla Hills (the Trade Representative), Lynn Martin (Labor Secretary), Lynne Cheney (the Humanities Endowment), Wendy Gramm (Chairman of the Commodity Futures Trading Commission), Connie Horner (director of White House personnel), Gail Wilensky (who ran Medicaid and Medicare), Diane Ravitch (policy at Education) and Lee Liberman (deputy White House counsel).

You could elect any one of these women to the Oval Office and stock the Cabinet with the rest of them, and the country would run like clockwork. But they are Republican women, and solidarity of some sort says they don't count (an exclusionary practice one might have thought abandoned back around the eighth grade).

Carla Hills

Such silent blacklisting of accomplished women in public life is going to confuse many less-political women, and perhaps cause some unfortunate casualties. Zoe Baird, one of the few people who seems to have been President Clinton's personal choice, has now fallen into some sort of politically incorrect gray area. Many of the women who are pressing Hillary's cause seem content to let Ms. Baird bleed to death in front of Joe Biden's humiliating committee ("Right now, Zoe Baird is his nominee," was the White House's semi-support yesterday). Hillary Clinton is being asked to carry a heavy load for a lot of other people. It wouldn't be so heavy or risky if her supporters long ago had more honestly dispersed the burden.

The Rose Partners

For most of 1993, the Whitewater Development Co. and Madison Guaranty were absent from the news. But the Journal focused on the four Rose Law Firm partners who took influential positions in the Administration:

Mrs. Clinton, presiding over the health care task force from the West Wing of the White House; Vincent Foster, White House Deputy Counsel; William Kennedy III, White House Associate Counsel; and Webster Hubbell, Associate Attorney General. The Rose alumni soon became engulfed in controversies involving the Justice Department position in a Congressional corruption trial, the seige of David Koresh and his followers in Waco, Texas, the secrecy under which Mrs. Clinton was operating her health care task force, and the firing of members of the White House travel office at the instigation of Clinton cronies.

Those controversies were overshadowed on July 20, when Vincent Foster drove to Fort Marcy Park in Virginia and committed suicide. In the weeks before his death, Mr. Foster had been the subject of two Journal editorials critical of his handling of freedom of information and secrecy issues surrounding Mrs. Clinton's task force. The Journal called for a "serious investigation" into Mr. Foster's "sad and troubling" death. Following Mr. Foster's death, the Journal was attacked by some commentators, particularly after an unsigned, torn-up note that included a complaint about the newspaper was found in his briefcase. But as the weeks and months rolled by, the suggestion of a thorough investigation seemed increasingly prescient, with growing suspicions about the death and growing questions about the handling of the investigation and Mr. Foster's office papers. Eventually, a more adequate if belated investigation was conducted under special counsel Robert Fiske.

REVIEW & OUTLOOK

Who Is Webster Hubbell?

Well, Webster Hubbell is a close friend of Bill Clinton and a former law partner of Hillary Rodham Clinton in Little Rock's Rose law firm. During the past five weeks he's taken up an office in the Justice Department; in the absence of an Attorney General, he's described as the department's "liaison" to the White House. Now his intervention in a corruption trial of a Congressman has led to the resignation of a U.S. Attorney and a stinging rebuke from a federal judge.

Webster Hubbell

The case concerns Rep. Harold Ford, who has represented Memphis, Tennessee, for 18 years and sits on the House Ways and Means Committee that will pass on the Clinton economic program. He was indicted by a federal grand jury in 1987 on charges that he accepted $1.2 million in improper payments from the corrupt Butcher banking empire. He launched a successful political campaign to have the trial moved from Knoxville to Memphis, where his family has a machinelike grip. Memphis is a black-majority city, and Rep. Ford is a prominent member of the Congressional Black Caucus. His brother sits in the State Senate and holds a court post that controls some city pensions. During his trial, Rep. Ford constantly accused prosecutors and witnesses of racism and orchestrated frequent and vocal demonstrations outside the courtroom.

In 1990, after 10 weeks of testimony, the jury deadlocked with eight whites voting to convict Mr. Ford and four blacks voting for acquittal. The trial judge, U.S. District Judge Odell Horton, ruled that the trial had been flawed by Mr. Ford's incendiary appeals to racial solidarity. Judge Horton, a black appointed to the bench by Jimmy Carter, noted that two members of the jury were determined to acquit Mr. Ford regardless of the government's evidence. "Juror misconduct permeated the trial of this case," Judge Horton ruled. He ordered that jurors for the second trial should be selected from a nearby city that is 20% black. He then stepped down from the case due to illness.

Jury selection for the retrial produced a jury of 11 whites and one black. Rep. Ford cried foul and began lobbying the Clinton White House to have it dismissed. Jesse Jackson intervened with White House officials, and Mr. Ford spoke in mid-February with President Clinton himself. A few days later, Mr. Hubbell arranged for the Black Caucus to press Mr. Ford's case with Stuart Gerson, a Bush holdover who is Acting Attorney General. The next day, just before the trial was to begin, Mr. Gerson renounced the Justice Department's long-standing support for Judge Horton's order and demanded the new jury be dismissed.

Court officials in Tennessee went ballistic. Ed Bryant, U.S. Attorney for the Western District of Tennessee, resigned; two Justice lawyers quit the case. The new trial judge, Jerome Turner, denied the department's motion in a blistering statement: "A white man, as three of the defendants are in this case, is not entitled to a white jury. Likewise, a black man, as one of the defendants is, is not entitled to a given number of black jurors." Chastened, Justice reversed itself. Mr. Ford's retrial will now proceed; the issue of biased juries is a real one, but it should be settled at the trial level and not in back-room Washington meetings.

Yet the case stirs doubts about the administration of justice, and indeed about the paths of accountability, in the new administration. While the White House denies that it asked Justice to interfere with the jury-selection process, career Justice officials are outraged at the perception that political muscle led to the reversal of the department's position. William Greenhalgh, a Georgetown University law professor, says he has never heard of such an attempt. "Just bluntly, it's wild," he says. Republicans want an investigation. Before her withdrawal, Zoe Baird said her top priority would be to take politics out of the Justice Department, as if Ed Meese had demanded a new jury for Bob Wallach. No doubt Attorney General-designate Janet Reno will come to her confirmation hearings prepared for the issue.

After all, we seem to have the spectacle of Hillary Clinton's former law partner fixing meetings between Justice officials and demand-waving pols, with the pols getting Justice to do their bidding. And of Webster Hubbell, a temporary appointee not subject to confirmation proceedings, apparently running the Justice Department as a partner of the First Lady. We are left to wonder what kind of Justice Department this will be, and what kind of administration.

REVIEW & OUTLOOK

Who Is Webster Hubbell?—II

While the court takes no pleasure in determining that one of the first actions taken by a new President is in direct violation of a statute enacted by Congress, the court's duty is to apply the law to all individuals.

So said U.S. District Court Judge Royce C. Lamberth yesterday in ruling on the Federal Advisory Committee Act's application to Hillary Rodham Clinton's Health Commission; he decided that the act's requirement of open meetings and other formalities applied to some meetings of the commission and its subgroups, but that for other meetings these requirements were unconstitutional. The White House now seems to be saying that there were no formal meetings, that the much heralded commission doesn't exist. The administration has, however, dropped its former contention that Mrs. Clinton is "the functional equivalent of a federal employee."

No doubt Mrs. Clinton's legal tangles – which involve not only the judge's mixed ruling on FACA but also the historic Anti-Deficiency Act and the Kennedy anti-nepotism bill – can and should somehow be set straight. Yet it could scarcely be clearer that the Clinton crew has been engaged in the kind of legal corner-cutting that leads to trouble. Attorney General Nicholas Katzenbach once offered the famous declaration that the Gulf of Tonkin Resolution was the "functional equivalent of a declaration of war," apparently back when today's administration lawyers were politically prepubescent. And we wonder how Zoe Baird and Judge Kimba Wood take the suggestion that in keeping the public in the dark about her deliberations, Mrs. Clinton has *vio-*

lated the law?

Clearly this administration needs some legal advice, which brings us to Janet Reno, whose nomination as Attorney General is rolling through a Senate glad to be rid of so vexsome a matter. In the cloistered existence of the home her mother built with her own hands, Ms. Reno has never hired an illegal alien. Her views aren't exacty our cup of tea, but we believe Presidents get to appoint their own officials, so we see no particular reason to oppose her. Indeed, we'd be a lot more comfortable if we were really sure that once confirmed she'll be running the Justice Department.

On this score, we were far from reassured by Ms. Reno's responses to questions about the peculiar behavior of the Justice Department in the corruption trial of Rep. Harold Ford in Memphis. As we described March 2, a U.S. attorney resigned and the presiding judge issued a blistering denial when Justice switched its position to ask that the jury be dismissed. Acting Attorney General Stuart Gerson ordered the reversal after a meeting with the Congressional Black Caucus. While Mr. Gerson is a Bush administration holdover, the meeting was engineered by the Justice Department's spanking-new "liaison" with the White House, Webster L. Hubbell.

Mr. Hubbell is a former mayor of Little Rock, and a partner with Mrs. Clinton in the Rose Law Firm there. At one point in his career, at the appointment of Governor Clinton, he served one year as chief justice of the Arkansas Supreme Court. While he apparently plans to stay on at Justice, we will not have an opportunity to learn if he's hired an illegal alien, since his appointment is not subject to Senate confirmation.

Asked about the Justice switch in the Memphis trial, Ms. Reno said she'd talked to Mr. Gerson and Mr. Hubbell, and thought they were both wonderful men. No one tried to influence anyone, they told her; the Justice Department's switch, quickly reversed, was an impartial reading of the law. In other words, there's no one here but us chickens. And Ms. Reno has concluded, "I don't see any further action to be taken on it."

The further action needed, if we can be blunter than is couth for Senators, is to choose between two respectable alternatives. One, get Webster Hubbell out of the corridors of Justice. Or two, get him out in the light of day through nomination for a confirmable post. In prior administrations, without the patina of "diversity" or the inconvenience of ethics laws, Mr. Hubbell would surely be Bill Clinton's Attorney General. But in an era when Zoe Baird and Kimba Wood are too suspicious-looking to hold office, a Webster Hubbell is better off pulling strings behind the scenes. Our incumbent moralists somehow see nothing untoward here, though they surely would have turned apoplectic if instead of being nominated as Attorney General Ed Meese had been appointed to look over the Attorney General's shoulder (let alone if he had set up meetings that turned around Justice's position on a corruption trial).

So to state the obvious, the issue with Mr. Hubbell, and the issue with Mrs. Clinton, is called accountability. If you are going to wield power, you have to follow procedures set up to ensure you take public responsibility for your actions and decisions. It's a principle, we take it, none too scrupulously observed by mores conditioned in Arkansas.

Editorial Feature

Reno (or Someone) Stages a Tuesday Noon Massacre

"I keep politics out of what I do, Senator."

So said Janet Reno, America's new attorney general, at her confirmation hearing this month. Most Americans would like to believe her. But now, just two weeks later, she has dismissed all 93 U.S. attorneys in one unclean sweep. If Ms. Reno isn't playing politics, then who is?

Potomac Watch

By Paul A. Gigot

Every president deserves his own appointees, but Ms. Reno's Tuesday noon massacre is extraordinary in scope and speed. U.S. attorneys are the federal government's top prosecutors. They arrest the mobsters and political crooks. Spread out around the country, they typically serve four-year terms.

That's why recent presidents have replaced U.S. attorneys only gradually, one at a time, as their terms expire or successors are ready. President Clinton said yesterday he's only following precedent, but he's way out-of-date.

Only last November, New York Democratic Sen. Daniel Patrick Moynihan said he would "recommend that the current U.S. attorneys be allowed to complete the remainder of their terms" to stay above politics. He said this has "become the norm" since 1977. In Washington, D.C., the Ford-era U.S. attorney stayed on for 18 months under Jimmy Carter. And the Carter-appointed attorney, (Clinton friend) Charles Ruff, stayed on for 13 months under Ronald Reagan.

Clinton transition officials were saying for weeks they'd do the same. Then General Reno rides in to give the attorneys just 10 days to make way for "interim" replacements. Send in your resignations. Clear out your desks. The Clinton team is here. Except that it really isn't. Ms. Reno is the only Justice official the White House has even nominated. Yet she thinks it's wise to remove 93 managers from the front lines. Maybe she's a recluse.

Janet Reno

Sensitive cases are going to stagnate or suffer, especially because "interim" officials rarely risk their careers by making the tough calls often required of U.S. attorneys. Michael Chertoff, the U.S. attorney from New Jersey, has to begin the celebrity case of Republican former Judge Sol Wachtler soon, but now is supposed to leave office next week.

"At best it's a bush league exercise," says one prominent Democrat and former U.S. attorney. "What you're saying is this is a political job, to the victors go the spoils, so get out. It's a terrible signal."

Reagan-era Attorney General Ed Meese adds that "my recollection is that we kept the attorneys on until we replaced each one. It seems a dumb idea to leave a bunch of empty offices." Perhaps Ms. Reno should consult Mr. Meese for ethics and management advice.

The illogic of the dismissals has people wondering about other motives — such as saving Chicago Rep. Dan Rostenkowski. Jay Stephens, the U.S. attorney here, has been investigating the titan of Ways and Means as part of the House post-office probe. After he got his 10-day notice, Mr. Stephens held his own press conference to say he was "within 30 days" of a decision on Rosty. (After this public riposte, Justice backed off and said some attorneys may be able to stay longer than 10 days, but not apparently Mr. Stephens.)

I like Rosty, a brusque but candid politician of the old school, and I hope there's no cause for indictment. Rosty himself says Mr. Stephens, a Republican, is on a fishing trip. But it's also true that the indictment of the Ways and Means chairman would cost Mr. Clinton his field general in getting his tax-and-spend program through Congress.

The suspicion is especially acute because it follows White House meddling on behalf of another Ways and Means member, Harold Ford of Tennessee. A member of the Black Caucus, Mr. Ford is accused of taking $1.2 million from the corrupt Butcher banking empire. After jury selection produced a panel of 11 whites and one black, he and Jesse Jackson protested to the White House.

Then-acting Attorney General (and Bush holdover) Stuart Gerson met with the Black Caucus and later demanded that the jury be dismissed. The U.S. attorney and two lawyers quit the case in protest. The Gerson-Black Caucus meeting was arranged by Webster Hubbell, a former Little Rock mayor and $310,000-a-year law partner of Hillary Clinton who is now Justice's "liaison" with the White House (a.k.a., Mr. Clinton's Hubbell Telescope).

All of which raises the deeper issue of who is really running Justice. Ms. Reno says dismissing the 93 attorneys was a "joint decision" with the White House — which means the White House decided and she announced it. Her letter asked the U.S. attorneys to send their resignation letters "care of John Podesta, assistant to the president and staff secretary, with a copy to me." Independent justice?

General Reno's spokeswoman adds that Mr. Hubbell was an "adviser" on the dismissals, though he hasn't even subjected himself to Senate confirmation. Perhaps in another era Mr. Hubbell would be Mr. Clinton's attorney general. But in this age of "diversity" and ethical appearances, a presidential crony from Arkansas seems to need a skirt to hide behind.

It all smacks not of "American renewal" but of an administration that is the most secretive and deeply political since Richard Nixon's.

REVIEW & OUTLOOK

Worth a Closer Look

Last week the Federal Reserve Board approved Worthen Banking Corp.'s acquisition of another Arkansas bank, Union National Bank. At the same time, Worthen announced that the Board had ordered an investigation of whether Worthen's ownership complied with the Bank Holding Company Act. The curious approval-first, investigation-later procedure caught our attention, especially given the identity of the parties involved.

Jackson Stephens

Worthen Bank, after all, came up with the loan that kept Bill Clinton's campaign going when it was running out of cash during the New York primary. More than 36% of its stock is held by Arkansas billionaire Jackson Stephens and his family. Through a family corporation, Stephens Group Inc., they also control Stephens Inc., often cited as the biggest investment bank off Wall Street.

Perhaps not surprisingly, given such a large financial empire in relatively small Arkansas, the Stephens ties reach deep into the Clinton administration. Hillary Clinton, for example, represented Stephens in some matters when she was at the Rose Law Firm. White House Chief of Staff Thomas F. "Mack" McLarty was chairman of the natural gas utility Arkla Inc., also historically and financially connected with the Stephens family.

The Stephens interests were among the few largest sources of Clinton campaign cash, and Worthen stock jumped to a 52-week high on the date after the Clinton victory. The Stephens empire, attracting more attention with the rise of Mr. Clinton, is an unusual if not unique one. The Glass-Steagall Act is intended to separate investment banking and commercial banking, and other banking legislation imposes close scrutiny of dealings between banks and their affiliated companies. In addition, Stephens Inc. played a role in the purchase of the First American Bank by the Bank of Credit and Commerce International; in a letter to the editor of this newspaper on November 18, Jackson Stephens explained that the only link was that the BCCI figures showed up in Little Rock and opened brokerage accounts.

The Federal Reserve order approving Worthen's acquisition said it was "specifically conditioned upon compliance with all the commitments given in connection with these applications," but did not spell out the commitments or mention the investigation. The Worthen press release said the investigation was intended "to review the ownership and control of Worthen Banking Corp. for compliance with the Bank Holding Company Act, including the nature and extent of the relationships between Worthen Banking Corp. and Stephens Group Inc. and its subsidiaries." It also spelled out three sets of conditions.

First, approval was granted "in reliance upon representations and commitments to the effect that Stephens Group and its subsidiaries do not and will not exert control over the management or policies of Worthen Banking Corp." – which is to say, precisely what is to be investigated. Also, that Stephens Group will comply with Sections 23A and 23B of the Federal Reserve Act, which regulate transactions between a bank and affiliates to preclude self-dealing. And finally, that "Stephens family members will cooperate with the management of Investark Bankshares Inc. to promptly achieve a conversion of First National Bank of Stuttgart from a national bank to a state, non-member bank." The apparent significance of this stipulation is that a state bank that does not join the Federal Reserve system is not subject to Glass-Steagall.

This strikes us as a heavy load of regulatory reservations, a feeling we have been discussing this week with the Fed's General Counsel and press offices. The Fed wanted to investigate the "talk" of de facto Stephens control of Worthen, its spokesman explained, but in the absence of a clear violation of law "there didn't seem to be any reason to hold up the merger." Despite a nine- or 10-month investigation by the St. Louis Federal Reserve, he added, "we just couldn't find any violation of the law."

As a precedent for simultaneously approving and investigating, the Fed cites the acquisition of the failed Bank of New England by Fleet/Norstar Financial Group. The Fed approved the acquisition while setting up an investigation of charges that a Fleet mortgage subsidiary had violated the Truth in Lending Act. But unlike the Worthen order, the Fleet one detailed both the charges to be investigated and the reason for urgent approval, namely that the Federal Deposit Insurance Corp. wanted to stanch the bleeding at the failed bank. In the Worthen case, the urgency was that the merger contract was about to expire, and the Fed had imposed a deadline on itself for acting on merger applications.

* * *

Now, it is not in itself of national moment whether Worthen buys another bank to grow from 11.1% of Arkansas deposits to 13.6%. We have no doubt the Stephens interests have excellent lawyers who can find the best ways around the likes of Glass-Steagall; the Worthen stockholdings are individual rather than corporate, for example, and Worthen Chairman Curt Bradbury is a former Stephens executive rather than a present one. Perhaps Glass-Steagall is overly restrictive and never should have been enacted in the first place. In light of Mr. Stephens's charges that we are picking on him, we should add that Stephens Inc. has done a lot of valuable investment banking for its clients.

It's also true that the Federal Reserve is an independent body to which the Clinton administration has made no appointments. And that the Stephens family also contributes to Republicans and was not exactly without influence in prior administrations.

Still, banking regulations do matter, especially in the wake of concerns raised by the BCCI and Savings and Loan scandals. And in our own view, it could scarcely be clearer that Worthen and Stephens are parts of the same financial empire. Perhaps legal maneuvering has kept them within the edge of the law, but it seems to us that in one way or another the Stephens interests have managed to stake out a privileged position regulators preclude for other financial firms.

* * *

We recently used the phrase "mores conditioned in Arkansas," and a letter from a justice of the state's Supreme Court berated us for a gratuitous swipe. Without insulting everyone in the state, though, that is precisely the point. States do have their political and business cultures, and Arkansas mores have moved to Washington. We used the offending phrase in an editorial about former Rose partner Webster Hubbell and his "White House liaison" role at the Justice Department, where he has just been made Associate Attorney General-designate. We also note reports that the race for FDIC chairman is between two Arkansas bankers, one of them backed by Worthen.

So if the Fed feels it must give permission for Worthen to expand, we certainly hope that its promised investigation actually eventuates. Given the broad significance, we further hope the Fed will tell us what it learns about the way things are done in Arkansas. Indeed, if the district bank inquiry has so far exonerated the Worthen-Stephens links, the Board could calm our concerns by sharing with us the St. Louis findings.

REVIEW & OUTLOOK

Who Is Webster Hubbell?—III

We've asked about Webster Hubbell's role twice before, so we'll ask again. What was his contribution to the Waco-related events of the past three days? Some inside the Beltway find inquiries about Mr. Hubbell amusing, as in the April 3 Washington Post account depicting Mr. Hubbell "smiling softly, like a shy child." It added: "When the Journal alleged further dark doings at the Justice Department, the headline read: Who Is Webster Hubbell? – II."

Webster Hubbell

We're back, this time with company. This is the text of a fascinating exchange between NBC's Tom Brokaw and Attorney General Janet Reno, which was broadcast about 11:42 Monday night.

Brokaw: Once the fire broke out, what did you tell President Clinton?

Reno: I haven't talked to President Clinton yet, because I have other [sic] with me, have been talking to the White House while I've been talking with the FBI. And as I have said, this is my responsibility, I'm accountable for it, and I've been trying to respond to questions from you and others in the media.

Brokaw: With all due respect, General Reno, you mean that the President has not had a direct conversation with you, has not expressed curiosity?

Reno: The President has expressed extensive curiosity. He has had a direct conversation with Webb Hubbell, who was with me as I was talking to the FBI.

Brokaw: And what did he tell Webb Hubbell?

Reno: You would have, I should say, as I understand, he was talking with Webb Hubbell. But you would have to check and see.

Brokaw: Webb Hubbell did not share with you what the President was saying?

Reno: Again, I have been trying to respond to the people. Trying to be accountable to the people. Trying to take your request and the request of others for information as to what happened. And as soon as I'm through this, I'm gonna talk to the President.

REVIEW & OUTLOOK

Who is Webster Hubbell?—IV

So Webster Hubbell faces opposition to his nomination as associate attorney general, ostensibly because he belongs to a country club that until recently had no black members. We don't think this good reason to reject a nominee, and continue to believe Presidents should get the advisers they want. So, having made Webster Hubbell a word in some households, we hereby tender our endorsement.

Webster Hubbell

We do not jest; our offer is subject only to the usual caveat that no landmines explode as his record is explored. The serious point here is that no chief executive is going to be silly enough to surrender control over Justice. The Founders put Justice under the President precisely because they understood the importance of what the Federalist Papers call the "unitary" executive. A system of checks and balances requires an executive strong enough to resist the encroachments of Congress. While the risk of "politicizing" Justice is always there, the voters are a better check on abuse than is some mythical "independence."

Mr. Clinton presumably knows this, which is why he wants his friend and former Little Rock mayor at Justice. A more candid President might have named Mr. Hubbell as attorney general, just as Jimmy Carter put trusted friend and lawyer Griffin Bell in the job. But Mr. Clinton felt bound by his pledges of diversity and instead named in succession three women he didn't know. Yet during the Waco crisis Mr. Clinton's Justice contact was Mr. Hubbell, as even Ms. Reno has publicly admitted. Especially in a crisis, Presidents need advisers they know they can trust.

Mr. Hubbell's opponents are an odd union. On the right, Paul Weyrich's Coalitions for America wants to expose the "hypocrisy" of Democrats who lambasted Republican nominees for belonging to all-white clubs. This publicity has in turn coaxed the liberal moralists from their holy places. Senator St. Paul Simon of Illinois says Mr. Hubbell "is going to have to clarify the situation before the committee," adding that, "ideally, I would have preferred that he not belong to a club that has not been admitting blacks." No doubt Ralph Neas and Anthony Lewis will weigh in soon.

The critics of hypocrisy have a point, since Mr. Simon would be asking for more than a clarification if Mr. Hubbell were a Republican. The country club standard wasn't even on the table until Mr. Simon and Howard Metzenbaum decided it was a good way to block Republican nominees in the late 1980s. Some sincere critics from the Arkansas NAACP have also spoken up, though there's no evidence that Mr. Hubbell discriminated against anyone.

Senate Republicans might better aim their guns at the far stranger crowd now settling in elsewhere at Justice. Lani Guinier, Mr. Clinton's choice for the civil rights post, wants to Balkanize America by race. Walter Dellinger, the nominee for office of legal counsel, which is supposed to protect presidential power, sided with Congressional claims throughout the 1980s. And someone should ask Gerald Torres, the environmental nominee, if he thinks property rights are even protected by the Constitution. Drew Days, the solicitor general-designate, comes out of the Larry Tribe school of exotic legal activism.

These nominees are "political" not because they are friends with a President but in a much more dangerous sense. They're the sort of law school professors/activists who want to visit their strange theories on the rest of us. This seems to be the legal-political community that advises Hillary, and we suspect Bill felt obliged to name such people to appease his party's left. And that he expects Mr. Hubbell to temper their activism with political reality; someone has to provide adult supervision.

Now that Mr. Hubbell has our endorsement, we would like to ask two favors in return. One, he set the President straight on the independent counsel issue, with exactly the same executive-powers arguments we have just recited in backing his nomination. Two, again for exactly the same reasons, he ought to get up a letter of apology to Ed Meese.

Throughout the Reagan years, Mr. Meese was pilloried by Democrats and their media acolytes as a presidential crony who "politicized" the Justice Department. President Clinton and Attorney General Reno also picked up the refrain. Perhaps Mr. Hubbell, a presidential golfing buddy and former law partner of Hillary Clinton, can now get them to sign up for the principle that a President needs his own man at Justice after all. Mr. Meese in turn could offer pointers on how to survive Paul Simon, Howard Metzenbaum and the rest of Joe Biden's Senate Judiciary Committee.

Mr. Hubbell can send the apology to Mr. Meese c/o the Heritage Foundation, 214 Massachusetts Ave., N.E., Washington, D.C., 20002.

REVIEW & OUTLOOK

Who Is Vincent Foster?

In its first few months, the Clinton White House has proved itself to be careless about many things, from Presidential haircuts to appointing a government. But most disturbing is its carelessness about following the law.

While we have our own complaint that we will presently explain, we hasten to point out that our concern is shared by at least two federal judges. Indeed, they're exploring the largely uncharted legal ground of use of the contempt power to get the Clinton Crowd to obey the law.

In a suit over preservation of computer tapes from the Reagan-Bush era, Judge Charles R. Richey has already issued a contempt order because the administration "dillydallied" in following his earlier order, and threatens $50,000-a-day fines against the White House and National Archives. Now Judge Royce Lamberth has threatened contempt unless the Hillary Clinton health task force takes steps to follow his order to preserve materials relating to its activities.

Quite frankly, we have mixed emotions about these developments. We think that in the post-Watergate era, the executive branch has been on the short end of the balance of powers, and that the government would work better if this were redressed. We find Judge Richey's order more than a little presumptuous, and tend to think the law before Judge Lamberth is a legislative intrusion on executive power. But we can understand that both judges reacted to a certain lack of seriousness − contempt in its most basic meaning − toward legal rulings.

Judge Lamberth's case, for example, concerned whether the

Hillary task force had to follow the Federal Advisory Committee Act, in which Congress prescribed hoops Presidents have to jump through in appointing outside commissions. Judge Lamberth held much of the law unconstitutional and laid out what might be seen as accommodating requirements, but dismissed the argument that this was not an outside commission because Mrs. Clinton was "the functional equivalent" of a government employee.

The government appealed the latter finding in a still-pending case; in the oral arguments Judge Laurence Silberman asked whether she took an oath of office or could be impeached. Meanwhile, the task force simply ignored the rest of Judge Lamberth's rulings, for example holding meetings without adequate notice.

We've been having a similar problem with Vincent Foster, deputy White House counsel and one of Mrs. Clinton's former partners in the Rose Law Firm in Little Rock. After we succeeded in making Webster Hubbell famous, it occurred to us we might have occasion to repeat the favor for other Rose partners, and requested photographs of Mr. Foster and associate White House counsel William Kennedy. Eventually some subaltern in the counsel's office relayed the message, "Mr. Foster sees no reason why he should supply the Journal with a photo."

Vincent Foster

Given this encouragement, we filed a request for photos of Mr. Foster and Mr. Kennedy under the Freedom of Information Act. The act requires officials to respond within 10 business days, a deadline that expired May 21. Despite repeated inquiries with those officials who return our calls, the White House still owes us either some photographs or an explanation of why our request has been refused.

At one point, we were told it ought to be worked out, and were referred to deputy press spokesperson Ricki Seidman, who seems not to return calls from our editorial page staff. David Gergen was not exactly overjoyed that we held up public complaint until he arrived, noting that our artists have already converted his photograph into a dot-drawing. But he seems to have jolted the matter off dead center; we're now told there's a draft letter somewhere in the bureaucracy saying the FOI Act does not apply to the White House counsel's office, but the press office can give us photos if it chooses. So we're back to the Seidman black hole, but the letter should be interesting reading.

No doubt Mr. Foster and company consider us mischievous (at best). Of course the Clinton administration has little reason to love us. Back when the rest of the press was in its pre-Waco honeymoon, we were already pulling the loose strings of the basic "New Democrat" lie. Still, we remain supportive when Mr. Clinton returns to that campaign theme, as with Nafta. Indeed, when Mr. Hubbell proved man enough to face public hearings on his appointment as associate attorney general, we saw no reason he should be denied confirmation. Even if we were as uniformly hostile as sometimes charged, there are larger points here. How an administration deals with critics is a basic test of its character and mores, and how scrupulously it follows the law is even more directly significant.

Does the law mean one thing for critics and another for friends? Will we in the end have to go to court to get a reply, or will even that work? Does it take a $50,000-a-day fine to get this mule's attention? Will a task force bearing the First Lady's name blithely ignore a district court order even as its appeal is being heard by the D.C. Circuit? Judge Lamberth demanded, "I want a name and address of who's going to be accountable, who's going to be held in contempt if there are documents destroyed."

Who ensures that this administration follows the law, or explains why not? A good question. While Constitutional law may not have been the big part of the Rose firm's practice, it seems to us that a good man for the job would be Deputy Counsel Foster.

Editor's Note: The following day The Journal printed the item below.

PHOTOS ON WAY

The White House Counsel's office tells us that the photographs we discussed in yesterday's editorial are now on the way. Indeed, it turns out that a fax to that effect arrived in our offices just before publishing deadline Wednesday night. We're a bit abashed that it didn't promptly come to the attention of the responsible editors, but not too abashed given the already extensive delay in the White House response. We look forward to sharing with readers the likeness of associate counsel William Kennedy III and deputy counsel Vincent Foster.

REVIEW & OUTLOOK

Vincent Foster's Victory

Meet Vincent Foster, movement conservative.

Vincent Foster is one of the White House lawyers from the Rose Law Firm, whose picture we've been seeking through the alleys and byways of the Freedom of Information Act. The picture arrived in time this week for us to celebrate Mr. Foster's victory yesterday in the battle over Hillary Clinton's status as head of the Clintons' health care task force.

Vincent Foster

An appeals court ruled Tuesday that, as Mr. Foster had been arguing, Mrs. Clinton is indeed the "functional equivalent" of a federal employee, at least as concerns compliance with the Federal Advisory Committee Act, or FACA (as in "focka").

The FACA Fight, initiated by various health and doctors' groups, was over whether the Hillary Clinton Health Task Force had to hold its meetings in public, which is what FACA requires when private citizens are serving on a President's advisory committees. Or whether Hillary, the functional federal equivalent, could hold her meetings in secret, as she desired. The appeals court said, sure, go ahead and meet in secret if you want. That's a win for the White House.

However, the court also said it didn't have a clue as to what exactly the task force's so-called "working groups" were all about, or whether

FACA applied to their members. The White House said those are all federal employees, too, so they can hold secret meetings. But the appeals court said the legal status of these people isn't at all clear, and ordered the district court to revisit the FACA netherworld to explore such issues as whether some of Hillary's helpers are "special government employees" or "full time" or "intermittent" or "consultants."

Finally, the court said the plaintiff doctors groups get to look at the almost football-field's worth of paper and documentation that the working groups have piled up by now.

As we say, for achieving these outcomes we think Mr. Foster deserves a salute from conservatives. With one mighty sweep he has struck a blow for separation of powers, executive authority, critics of the litigation explosion, and we dare say, even for the formulators of the Reagan White House's off-the-books Iran-Contra operation.

Conservatives have worried out loud for years about inroads against the President's ability to carry out the functions of his office. In particular, conservatives have noted Congress's instinct to usurp presidential authority, tipping the balance of powers in the legislature's favor. Thus, particular or parochial interests subsume any national interest that a President is elected to represent.

Judge Laurence Silberman, writing for the appeals court (and alluding to Alexander Hamilton along the way), noted: "The ability to discuss matters confidentially is surely an important condition to the exercise of executive power. Without it, the President's performance of any of his duties . . . would be made more difficult. In designing the Constitution, the Framers vested the executive power in one man for the very reason that he might maintain secrecy in executive operations."

Alas, the Clintonites, as is their wont, again allowed hubris to smother mere principle. Instead of a more well-defined operation, they went secret over changing the entire American health care system. Even defenders of executive authority would blanch at such imperial overstretch.

And so now the Clintons will discover the pleasures of the litigation explosion as defined by former Vice President Dan Quayle. Instead of doing productive work, they will spend days bringing forth box after box of documentation, while arguing with a judge about "intermittent" vs. "full-time" — just the way private companies do for the federal prosecutors and agency bureaucrats who enforce the kinds of vague laws that the Clintons' political philosophy favors. Dan Quayle has further details.

As for Iran-Contra, we suspect that Vincent Foster and Ollie North might hit it off. After all, we're supposed to believe that the health task force "officially" disbanded on May 30, and so FACA's requirements are moot. That is, we're supposed to believe that Mrs. Clinton and her associates will never ever hold off-the-books meetings with "non-government" advisers to get the reform plan finished.

Mr. Foster's boss, Bill Clinton, often rails against the gridlock of the "last 12 years." For that reason, we're glad that the case of *Association of American Physicians and Surgeons v. Hillary Rodham Clinton, et al.* has given a Democratic administration the opportunity to explore the questions of presidential authority discussed by Judge Silberman and his colleagues in their decision for the White House.

REVIEW & OUTLOOK

Who Is William Kennedy III?

The White House report on its travel office scandal, Gergened out into the void of the July 4 weekend, would have you believe that William Kennedy III is just one of four White House aides who will have letters of reprimand put in their personnel files. In fact, the associate White House counsel is also the former managing partner of Little Rock's Rose Law Firm, which is to say Hillary Rodham Clinton's number one legal partner.

Friday's limited, modified hangout does establish a basic factual record, but obviously puts a defensive gloss on the travel office shenanigans. Even at its most innocent level, it's a chortle-chucked portrait of court intrigue. But the titillation should not obscure the chilling reality: One of the First Lady's closest associates invoked the White House in calling the FBI to instigate a criminal investigation of functionaries who'd incurred the displeasure of the Clinton inner circle.

William Kennedy III

The origins of this displeasure seem to lie with Catherine Cornelius, the distant Clinton cousin appointed to head the travel office when seven employees were fired, and Harry Thomason, the First Couple's filmmaker crony, who also has a pecuniary interest in TRM, an air charter firm inquiring after White House business. It soon spread to Deputy Communications Director Jeff Eller, with whom Ms.

Cornelius had "a personal relationship," the report reports. And to David Watkins, major-domo for personnel, and High Chamberlain Thomas "Mack" McLarty.

And soon the word was up to the Queen herself. Mrs. Clinton was inquiring about the travel office with Deputy White House Counsel Vincent Foster and Chief of Staff McLarty, received updates from Mr. Watkins and was carboned on crucial memos.

Mr. Kennedy, however, did the heavy lifting. He called the FBI — because, the report states, he couldn't figure out where else to get some auditing expertise. When the FBI was slow to respond, he said he'd call the IRS instead. A week later, IRS auditors did show up at UltrAir, the TRM competitor usually used by the travel office; an IRS statement denies there was any contact with the White House. According to press reports, the agents told UltrAir officials they'd read about the controversy in the press.

In any event, auditors from Peat Marwick were soon swarming over the travel office accounts, quite plausibly finding the records a mess and identifying $18,000 in disbursements not accounted for. The seven employees were fired, and the White House announced that the FBI had started an investigation, and the FBI's spokesman was summoned to the White House for "inquiries" about his impending press statement. As a result of their roles, Mr. Kennedy, Mr. Watkins, Mr. Eller and Ms. Cornelius were reprimanded, but no further action was taken.

Now, the travel office snafu was so complete it's tempting to ring it up to inexperience. Unhappily, it seems part of a law enforcement pattern centering on the Rose clique. Remember Webster Hubbell, the former Rose partner who was "White House liaison" to the Justice Department and now associate attorney general; he set up the meetings that led to the Justice Department reversing its position in a corruption trial of a member of Congress. Mr. Foster is also a former Rose partner. His defense of Mrs. Rodham Clinton's health care task force did succeed in getting her declared a federal employee, but cut some legal corners along the way.

We've been particularly interested in the Rose firm's four-partner implant in the administration because of its representation of the Arkansas financial empire headed by Jackson Stephens. Our interest in the Stephens companies, in turn, was piqued because they handled the deal when proxies for BCCI bought Washington's First American Bank. Mr. Stephens says there has been no further contact with the BCCI figures.

Stephens executives were an important source of contributions for the Clinton campaign, and its primary-season finances were salvaged by a timely loan from Worthen Banking Corp., more than 36% owned by Stephens interests. Mr. McLarty, by the way, was chief executive of Arkla Inc. — the Arkansas Louisiana Gas Co. that was the original cornerstone of the Stephens fortune. Unhappily for Stephens, its new influence brought increased scrutiny of an ongoing concern about whether it complies with laws mandating the separation of investment banking and commercial banking. The Fed found one holding, in the First National Bank of Stuttgart, in violation of the Glass-Steagall Act. Papers putting the holding at 43% instead of 60% were filed, according to Jeff Gerth's report in the New York Times, by the Rose firm's William Kennedy III.

Now, we wouldn't want to make too much of all this. Lawyers are paid to take positions in defense of their clients. The Stephens companies have done a lot of economic good, and we're not sure we agree with Glass-Steagall in the first place. Any administration will reach back to home-state roots in appointing key personnel, and we think conflict-of-interest concerns have been carried to the point where people of stature shun government.

Still, the early indications of the Rose view of the law are certainly disconcerting, displaying a lot of cornercutting and casual abuse of power. If these are the people in position to start FBI investigations and sway the administration of justice, they are going to bear a lot of watching.

REVIEW & OUTLOOK

FBI Director Rose?

All of Washington wants to know when poor, beleaguered William Sessions will resign as FBI director — a sure indication that this is the wrong issue. We'd rather know who is going to select the next successor to J. Edgar Hoover.

President Clinton will have the final word, but as with all appointments it will matter whose advice his choice reflects. Will it be that of Janet Reno, the ostensible attorney general? Or will Mr. Clinton listen to his legal cronies from Little Rock who are already placed at the heart of his administration? We know who would better reassure Americans about the prospects for apolitical justice.

Hillary Clinton

Ms. Reno is of course the latest media darling, and we might even join the praise if she ever really gets control of the Justice Department. For the evidence so far is that control has in fact rested with appointees from Little Rock's Rose Law Firm, which happens to be Hillary Rodham Clinton's former firm.

On the day of the Waco crisis, for example, Mr. Clinton spoke not with Ms. Reno but with his golfing pal, Webster Hubbell, by then nominated to be "associate attorney general." Earlier, as "White House liaison," Mr. Hubbell was the one who set up the meetings that led to Justice reversing itself on a corruption trial of a Democratic congressman. And the same Mr. Hubbell met with Congressional baron John Dingell before Ms. Reno agreed to the highly unusual move of letting the Dingell staff investigate career Justice attorneys about prosecutorial judgments. It's fair to ask if these incidents are just the tip of the Hubbell telescope at Justice.

Vincent Foster

Then there are the two former Rose partners in the White House counsel's office. Vincent Foster, the deputy White House counsel, serves as all-purpose adviser to Hillary Clinton on health reform thickets and other matters. (His sister, Sheila Foster Anthony, is slated to run Justice's legislative office.) And William Kennedy III, the number three White House counsel, somehow felt no qualms about asking the FBI to investigate the White House travel office without so much as informing Ms. Reno. This is the same White House that also ordered Ms. Reno to fire every sitting U.S. attorney, another break with longtime practice.

And don't forget the fourth and most powerful former Rose partner, the First Lady. We now know Mrs. Clinton inquired about the travel office affair with Mr. Foster, and that she was prominently carboned on copies of crucial memos. She also handpicked old friend Bernard Nussbaum for the top White House counsel position, so in a sense the entire counsel's office reports to her, if not officially at least informally.

Mrs. Clinton's friends keep showing up for crucial Justice posts, too. Eleanor Acheson, the nominee for chief judge picker, roomed with her at Wellesley. Gerald Torres, who is slated to run the environmental crimes division, once worked at the Children's Defense Fund, where Mrs. Clinton was chairman of the board. And Mrs. Clinton had attended the wedding of her longtime friend, Lani Guinier.

Webster Hubbell

Now, we've always believed Presidents deserve the nominees they want, even a President (and First Lady) who used to denounce Ed Meese as a political crony of Ronald Reagan. But hypocrisy aside, cronyism is a lot more serious when it begins to involve criminal prosecution, and especially the FBI. The FBI's police power is arguably the most easily abused in Washington, as the revelations about the late Mr. Hoover prove.

So it's a good sign that Ms. Reno succeeded in getting her own choice, Carter-era veteran Jo Ann Harris, to run Justice's criminal division. It's even better that in the process she had to beat back another Hillary crony, New York lawyer Susan Thomases, who wanted the job for her law partner Benito Romano, a former aide to political prosecutor Rudy Giuliani.

But the bigger test will be the FBI post. The best name that has so far surfaced in public is Louis Freeh, a respected New York judge. In any event, the choice should be someone with enough independence to be able to refuse the next time William Kennedy III asks the FBI to investigate some political enemy. A Rose clique from Little Rock that has already shown a willingness to cut many legal corners needs adult supervision.

William Kennedy III

REVIEW & OUTLOOK

What's the Rush?

So the gang that pulled the great travel office caper is now hell-bent on firing the head of the FBI. The news reports say that William Sessions has already offered to resign pending approval of a successor; we wish someone would explain to us the hurry.

William Sessions

The FBI director, whatever the incumbent's shortcomings, was given a 10-year term to provide some measure of political independence. To be sure, the President has a right to fire the director, as President Truman fired General MacArthur. But that is not to say every incoming president is justified in firing an incumbent and appointing his own director. We do not want law enforcement put at the disposal of this or that political faction.

If Mr. Sessions is fired it will of course be for ostensible cause, as the travel office firings were over expense records. His sin was to take his wife on his government airplane, and to claim for tax purposes that his limousine was a law enforcement vehicle because he carried firearms in the trunk. Even if he did not use the plane for haircuts, this is apparently deemed reason for summary dismissal. In the travel office case, by contrast, Associate White House Counsel William Kennedy III earned a meaningless letter of reprimand for misusing the FBI's investigative powers.

We hope Mr. Sessions pointed this out to White House Counsel

Bernard Nussbaum, who sat in with Attorney General Janet Reno and Deputy Attorney General Philip Heymann in the shoot-out with Mr. Sessions on Saturday. Also present was Associate Attorney General Webster Hubbell, the man who brokered a meeting that resulted in the Justice Department reversing its position in the corruption trial of a member of Congress. Mr. Hubbell and Mr. Kennedy are alumni of Little Rock's Rose Law Firm, as are Mrs. Clinton and Deputy White House Counsel Vincent Foster, both of whom were also involved in the travel-office affair.

The leaks on Saturday's meeting are that Webb Hubbell et al. told Mr. Sessions to resign or be fired, probably today; on the way out he stumbled on a curb and broke his elbow. Presumably Mr. Sessions is leaving sooner or later; the conventional wisdom within the Washington Beltway has certainly run against him, for whatever that's worth. He has apparently alienated important subordinates, perhaps because he's a poor administrator. Or perhaps, as he claims, because of his efforts to promote blacks and women. The opposition has a bipartisan patina, since the charges against him were originally leveled by Bush Attorney General William Barr on his last day in office.

The original Bush administration investigation, it should be carefully noted, was announced immediately after it became public that the FBI had launched an investigation into the controversial prosecution of the head of the Atlanta branch of the Banca Nazionale del Lavoro over illicit loans to Iraq. Mr. Barr's own investigator, a prominent former judge, exonerated the Justice Department handling of the BNL case, but we're not sure the final word has been heard.

President Clinton met Friday with Federal Judge Louis J. Freeh of New York, reportedly the leading contender as Mr. Sessions' successor. Judge Freeh is fine by us, but his meeting with the President only deepens the mystery over the hurry. If the choice of a successor really is imminent, why not get him nominated? If Mr. Sessions resigns we worry that Judge Freeh, given the record of the Clinton appointments process, may trip over a Kimba problem or somesuch. The agency would be left adrift and the appointment up for grabs.

Our Washington bureau reported in March that the administration was intent on getting rid of Mr. Sessions in order to replace him with Richard Stearns, a judge on the Massachusetts Superior Court. Judge Stearns and President Clinton were war protesters together as Rhodes Scholars at Oxford. Judge Stearns was also a deputy campaign manager in George McGovern's 1972 presidential race, as well as national director of delegates in Sen. Edward Kennedy's 1980 presidential nomination bid.

This kind of appointment would be another matter indeed. We are far enough along toward making the FBI job a political football. Mr. Sessions is leaving under attack from various quarters; his predecessor, William Webster, left to become Director of Central Intelligence, only to resign that job rather abruptly. Strange things are going on in law enforcement, as the BNL and BCCI cases show. The mores on display from the Rose alumni are far from confidence-building. It seems to us Mr. Sessions would do the nation and his agency a favor to stand by his position, leaving when a successor is ready or letting the President take full responsibility for a firing.

Why don't serious people understand this immediately? What kind of a political culture do we have where the big issue is not whether the FBI director fairly enforces the law, but whether he takes his wife on an airplane?

REVIEW & OUTLOOK

A Washington Death

The death by gunshot wound Tuesday of deputy White House counsel Vincent Foster is an event both sad and troubling. Mr. Foster's body was discovered Tuesday at Fort Marcy, a Civil War era fort in Virginia that overlooks the Potomac River. U.S. Park police said yesterday that Mr. Foster was found about 200 yards from his car, slumped against a cannon, with a gun in his hand.

Vincent Foster

Mr. Foster, 48, left a wife and three children; one can only grieve for them and for his friends in the White House and elsewhere. While the cause of death had not been conclusively established as of yesterday, the park service was presuming it a suicide by gunshot wound to the head, though it would not say whether a note was found.

Suicides are a special sort of personal tragedy, but perhaps more so in public life. The responsibilities of a high public official are enormous, and of course their activities are always subject to the scrutiny and criticism of political foes, the public, the press and sometimes even their own allies. The cumulative pressure of those responsibilities and the attention may not always be apparent on the surface.

As readers of this page are aware, we have devoted considerable space to inquiring after the precise nature of the activities of the four Rose Law Firm partners from Little Rock working in the Clinton

Administration — Mr. Foster, Webster Hubbell, William Kennedy III and of course First Lady Hillary Clinton. We think these issues are entirely appropriate, and presume there will be occasion to return to them in the future. All Americans have a legitimate interest in the inner workings of an administration governing them.

If anything, Mr. Foster's tragic death adds to the curiosity. Those who knew him consider him an unlikely suicide. We're told he had no history of depression. His legal specialty was litigation, which is to say he was scarcely a stranger to stress. He seemed devoted to his children, and was after all at the pinnacle of nearly any career. As of yesterday, no one was able to offer a persuasive reason why he would have taken his own life.

The death by gunshot of a high White House official under mysterious circumstances is bound to be troubling. Mr. Foster was the Number 2 lawyer associated with the Oval Office, just behind Chief White House Counsel Bernard Nussbaum, and as a part of the Clinton inner circle was far more important than even his title indicated.

Appearing in the Rose Garden around midday, President Clinton said, "There is really no way to know why these things happen." The President added, "We'll just have to live with something else we can't understand." The President had known Mr. Foster since kindergarten in Hope, of course, and on a human level this reaction was entirely appropriate.

Later in the day, however, the White House announced that the Justice Department will nonetheless investigate, under the direction of Attorney General Janet Reno and Deputy Attorney General Philip Heymann. That investigation is important and necessary. We hope it is thorough and convincing. There is likely to be a problem coordinating the FBI, now in a leadership transition, the park police, local authorities in Virginia and so on. A direct appointment such as special counsel within Justice would make clear who is in charge and directly responsible.

We had our disagreements with Mr. Foster during his short term in Washington, but we do not think that in death he deserves to disappear into a cloud of mystery that we are somehow ordained never to understand. The American public is entitled to know if Mr. Foster's death was somehow connected to his high office. If he was driven to take his life by purely personal despair, a serious investigation should share this conclusion so that he can be appropriately mourned.

REVIEW & OUTLOOK

Self-Fulfilling Prophecy

In our initial comments on the death of Vincent Foster, we remarked that "the death by gunshot of a high White House official is bound to be troubling" and commended the announced Justice Department investigation. We added, "A direct appointment such as special counsel within Justice would make clear who is in charge and directly responsible."

No such appointment was made, of course, and it now seems the investigation has fizzled out for want of direction and responsibility. "There is no investigation being conducted by the Justice Department," spokesman Carl Stern said Monday. Deputy Attorney General Philip Heymann, previously announced as the official coordinating the effort, says only that he's receiving "regular reports" from the federal Park Police, who discovered the body in Fort Marcy Park on the Virginia side of the Potomac. This is quite a change from the earlier statement of another Justice spokesman that the probe would seek "to find out what the factors were — if it was a suicide — that led to him killing himself." Now, Mr. Foster was a member of the inner circle of the President of the United States. In his eulogy for his boyhood friend, the President said Mr. Foster's friends found him a "great protector." The White House counsel's office handles sensitive presidential issues, for example the still-uncompleted blind trust for the first couple's financial assets.

Mr. Foster, a first-rate lawyer and steeled litigator, was suddenly found dead, apparently killed with an antique handgun. He left no suicide note. His Arkansas friends do not consider him a likely suicide. Since his death there have been reports that he was dispirited in his last few weeks. But the Washington Times reported that one anonymous source told it he'd discussed depression with his brother-in-law, former Rep. Beryl Anthony; and that Mr. Anthony responded, "There's not a damn thing to it. That's a bunch of crap."

"He was not 'chewed up' by Washington," Doug Buford, a Little Rock lawyer friend of Mr. Foster, told The Washington Post. "I resent that suggestion. Vince was such an able man. I think maybe the incredible pressure, the workload, exhausted him, and that was part of it. But ultimately, something was badly askew, something so wrong it could make him think his three kids could be better off without him."

These circumstances call for a serious investigation, going well beyond the Park Police's "routine" handling of a corpse. At least so it seems to us, and at least some others. In a column concentrating on the personal aspects of the suicide, the Post's Meg Greenfield took pains to observe, "I think it is both necessary and right that the death be investigated vigorously by police and Justice Department officials, as is being done, and also that the press not ignore the questions raised by the unaccountable violent death or turn away from the pursuit of the answers to them. For there are clearly identifiable public questions yet to be answered, one hopes in a way that will not needlessly or clumsily intensify public grief."

The vigorous investigation has not taken place, and apparently will not. White House counsel Bernard Nussbaum sorted through Mr. Foster's papers, removing any that fell under attorney-client privilege with the President, and gave us his word that nothing shed light on the suicide. So nothing will be done to tell the public why so sensitive an official took his own life, or for that matter, reassure us that he indeed did. The mystery, we suspect, will haunt the White House as further scandals pop up, as they do in most administrations.

But in most administrations Presidents do have their way. President Clinton's first reaction to the suicide was, "We'll just have to live with something else we can't understand." Despite second thoughts at Justice, it seems that the President's view will not only prevail, but become a self-fulfilling prophecy.

REVIEW & OUTLOOK

Re Vincent Foster

A torrent of news has overwhelmed the story of the suicide of Vincent Foster, deputy White House counsel and Clinton family friend. But we don't want to let the week expire without remarking that, yes, we did notice the amazing barrage of leaks and polemics suggesting we pulled the trigger.

Of course we were the only news organization to spotlight Mr. Foster prior to his suicide. We certainly did raise pointed questions in our commentary on the practices of the administration's Rose Law Firm partners – Mr. Foster, Mrs. Clinton, Associate Attorney General Webster Hubbell and Associate White House Counsel William Kennedy III. Our experience in reading between the lines of leaks tells us that we do at least appear in the torn-up note found at the bottom of his briefcase.

Yet there is no way to cover national government on the assumption that a high official and steeled litigator secretly suffers from depression, and may commit suicide if criticized. What we said about Mr. Foster was nothing compared to the abuse heaped on the likes of Ed Meese, Robert Bork and Clarence Thomas. We appreciate the remarks of William Safire of the New York Times and Doug Ireland of the Village Voice to the effect that we were merely doing our job.

In the Washington Post and the New Republic, of course, we have been instructed in manners and civility by Michael Kinsley, who makes his principal living as a participant in a TV screaming match. And in the New Yorker, Sidney Blumenthal, who during the presidential campaign trashed George Bush's record in World War II, tells us that we help make Washington a tough town. Naturally, those who resent our unapologetic views grabbed the occasion to beat up on us.

Yet it remains true that Mr. Hubbell brokered a meeting leading to a Justice Department intervention in a corruption trial. And that Mr. Kennedy called the FBI into the White House travel office, and back in Arkansas signed suspect papers for the Stephens empire. It is also true, though we didn't dwell on it earlier, that when Mrs. Clinton's health task force was under court order to give advance notice of meetings, Mr. Foster signed notices that appeared in the Federal Register after the meetings had already been held.

It is not true, Mr. Blumenthal to the contrary, that after the election Mr. Foster "helped set up a blind trust" for the Clintons. The failure to create this trust was the subject of critical editorials in Newsday and Money magazine; we're now told it was filed July 26.

One has to ponder, of course, whether these problems were the result or the cause of Mr. Foster's depression. Probably we will never know, especially given the way the investigation has been handled. There has been widespread criticism of the 30-hour delay in releasing the Foster note to the investigators, the confusion over who was investigating and the change in stories about Mr. Foster's impressions on associates. This is already leading to the wildest speculation; we even read one report suggesting Mr. Foster was murdered by a drug-dealing cabal of military officers.

We hope and trust that the White House will seek to repair some of this damage with more openness. We hope there's the fullest possible accounting in the blind trust, for example. And given the fingers pointed at us, we have a particular stake in seeing the full text of the Foster note.

Our critics were particularly upset by our suggestion that the administration turn the investigation of the suicide over to a "special counsel within Justice." (Not a special counsel of the Lawrence Walsh ilk, as Mr. Kinsley distorted it.) As we said at the time, the point was to coordinate the investigation. By now it ought to be clear that the White House would have served its own interests by taking our advice.

Editorial Feature

Corrupt Capital: The BCCIs Yet to Come

By JAMES RING ADAMS

The trial of Robert Altman is over. But the political pathology that produced the BCCI case and a host of other highly expensive financial debacles is thriving.

A jury decided that Mr. Altman didn't break a law when he acted as an interlocutor between Washington, D.C.'s largest bank chain and the colossal global fraud that was the Bank for Credit and Commerce International. That issue is probably settled for now, both for him and for his mentor, Washington superlawyer Clark Clifford. But the spate of second-guessing that followed Mr. Altman's acquittal largely overlooked a more serious issue. In the course of its career as central banker to the drug trade, international terrorism and the world's "gray market" in arms, BCCI also took in billions from third-world small businessmen and national treasuries. It lost, by current estimates, $12 billion of its $20 billion in deposits, and covered it up as long as it could.

Very few of BCCI's victims lived in the U.S., a problem for the prosecution of Mr. Altman and Mr. Clifford. Yet the financial pattern in Britain, for example, was much the same as the S&L debacle, where many average citizens have suffered, as investors, foreclosed borrowers, and, most broadly, taxpayers.

These disasters reached such proportions because the crooked bankers shunted some of their gain toward political friends and then used these friends to shield themselves from investigation. When

BCCI was first exposed as an agent for drug lords, in a money laundering indictment in Tampa, Mr. Altman used his influence in Washington to protect the reputation of its senior officers. He even, according to evidence undisputed even by the senator, drafted a statement delivered in the Senate by Utah's Orrin Hatch.

This wasn't breaking the law. But the pressure created a political climate that discouraged career bureaucrats from sticking out their necks to investigate crimes. Manhattan's District Attorney Robert Morgenthau frequently received little support from the Justice and State departments in his attempts to gather evidence for this wide-ranging case.

There have been a spate of articles this week about the "tarnished reputation" of Mr. Morgenthau for prosecuting Mr. Altman; these come in particular from those Washington "watchdogs" who shrugged off the many courtroom reversals of Iran-Contra special prosecutor Lawrence Walsh.

But it was Mr. Morgenthau who broke the BCCI case, when the federal government lost interest. Mr. Morgenthau is the wrong target of criticism when he faces so many leads that the federal government is less disposed than ever to follow. Criminal charges in the case, for instance, are still pending against Saudi businessmen Khalid bin-Mahfouz and Ghaith Pharaon, whose American partners have included a son of George Bush, the late John Connally and Miami S&L chairman David Paul. Regulators say BCCI helped prolong the life of Mr. Paul's CenTrust Savings Bank, whose collapse left U.S. taxpayers with a loss of at least $1.7 billion.

There are also questions about Mr. Pharaon's, and BCCI's, involvement in the takeover of Bert Lance's National Bank of Georgia, which became a unit of Messrs. Altman and Clifford's First American Bankshares. Mr. Lance became a salaried agent of BCCI right after he resigned as Jimmy Carter's budget director, and there are myriad questions about the access he gave that bank to Democratic political networks.

Mr. Lance worked with Little Rock broker Jackson Stephens to arrange the first, unsuccessful, BCCI run at the Washington bank that Messrs. Altman and Clifford later succeeded in taking over. Jack Stephens was the power behind Worthen Banking Corp. and Arkla Gas Co., whose officers (including the president's chief of staff) now line the White House; he was, and is, an important client of the Rose

Law Firm, which once employed Hillary Clinton. BCCI's influence spread through GOP networks as well—including business partners of George Walker Bush, the former president's son, and Sen. Hatch.

The mere fact that so many well-connected figures have been involved with the BCCI case goes far to explain why Washington was reluctant to pursue the case. The Manhattan district attorney picked up the investigation by default, when the Justice Department and even the Senate seemed willing to let it drop.

If President Clinton has made one thing clear, it is that he is less interested than even his predecessor in rooting out political corruption. That task was the weakest part of his attorney general's resume. Mr. Clinton has consistently sided with bankers against the regulators (some of whom have given Mr. Stephens quite a hard time). There is even an ominous tinge to the current proposal to unify federal law enforcement agencies under the Justice Department, since it would eliminate the interservice rivalry that has helped to keep some past investigations open.

To judge from the reaction to the Altman verdict, this permissive attitude toward corruption is now seeping into the press and the circles of "proper" opinion. But the questions from the BCCI case remain unanswered, and the possibility that Washington cronyism will further pervert representative government seems greater than ever.

Mr. Adams is business editor of the Waterbury (Conn.) Republican-American and the co-author, with Douglas Frantz, of "A Full Service Bank: How the BCCI Stole Billions Around the World" (Simon & Schuster, 1992).

Letters to the Editor

Arkla and Stephens

James Ring Adams, in his Aug. 20 editorial page piece "Corrupt Capital: The BCCIs Yet To Come," asserts that "Jack Stephens was the power behind . . . Arkla Gas Co. . . ." While the Stephens family did have a significant role at Arkla at one time, that ended years ago. Witt Stephens, Jack's late brother, retired as CEO of Arkla (then Arkansas Louisiana Gas Co.) in 1973 and had no role, formal or informal, after that. In the nine years I have been with Arkla, we have never identified Stephens-related stock ownership that exceeded 100,000 shares. Arkla currently has 122 million shares outstanding.

I also would be grateful if Mr. Adams would identify the numerous Arkla officers who "now line the White House."

MICHAEL B. BRACY
Executive Vice President
Arkla Inc.

Shreveport, La.

Review & Outlook

More to Hear

So, we have a solution after all to regulating an international banking system grown too complicated for authorities in the U.S. or U.K. The Luxembourg court of appeal decided that someone has to do the job, and turned thumbs down on proposals to let the BCCI case die with a whimper.

The court rejected the proposed settlement between liquidators and shareholders of the Bank of Credit and Commerce International. Under its terms, the emirate of Abu Dhabi, the principal shareholder, would pony up $1.7 billion, but would receive half of previously recovered assets and also be allowed to submit its own creditor claims on the settlement pool. The depositors, out more than $10 billion, would receive payments of some 30 cents on the dollar.

Depositors receiving restitution would have to agree not to bring further suits alleging that Abu Dhabi was a party to the fraud by the bank it owned. But Abu Dhabi is sheltering—under "house arrest" — many of the bank's executives, and its records. The Luxembourg liquidator, Brian Smouha of Touche Ross in London, gave a deposition describing a warehouse of records some 60 yards long to which he was not permitted access.

The liquidators, however, expressed their regret at the court's rejection of the settlement they'd negotiated. Much of the coverage of the decision treated it as a blow to the creditors, on the grounds they'd receive no money until after further litigation reaching into the next century. The Washington PR firm of Robinson, Lake, Lerer

& Montgomery issued a statement on behalf of Abu Dhabi saying that creditors "have lost their only opportunity for a timely payment."

No one writing about the Luxembourg decision, though, happened to notice a filing with the court by Harry W. Albright Jr., the trustee for Washington's First American Corp. He objected to the settlement on some interesting grounds. For example that its terms "do not obtain from Abu Dhabi compensation that adequately reflects Abu Dhabi's involvement and culpability for the fraud." He said the settlements might have seemed reasonable when first negotiated, but asserted that "the role of the Abu Dhabi defendants in BCCI wrongdoing has become increasingly clear."

Mr. Albright pointed out that First American has an active civil suit in Washington, D.C., district court, asserting damages that if collected would redound to the benefit of a world-wide settlement pool. The suit cites as defendants Sheikh Zayed bin Sultan Al-Nahyan, the ruler of Abu Dhabi, along with his family, retainers and holding companies, including the Abu Dhabi Investment Authority. Also various prominent shareholders of and fronts for BCCI, as well as Clark Clifford and Robert Altman, who ran the First American Bank while it was owned by BCCI.

These worthies, it might be noted, own assets all over the world that would be subject to seizure to satisfy any judgment Mr. Albright might obtain. Mr. Altman was acquitted in a recent criminal trial, of course, but the standards of proof will be much lower in the civil action.

Also, the outcome of a trial just might be affected by those 60 yards of documents in Abu Dhabi, and the witnesses. In his letter to the court, Mr. Albright complained that the proposed settlement "as currently drafted will impede First American's efforts to prosecute." The liquidators have conducted investigations that presumably have uncovered information that might be helpful in the First American suit, but revealing any such information "may be inconsistent with their obligations under the proposed settlement agreements."

Judge Raul Gretsch pondered all this, and decided that while the settlement had already been approved in the United Kingdom and the Cayman Islands, in Luxembourg it smelled like a cover-up. The liquidators have "no right to sign" the settlement, he said, because it "creates a creditor privileged to the detriment of others."

Clearly some of the creditors would prefer to take what they can get now rather than take their chances with further litigation against well-financed defendants. But some of the parties dispute the claim that 93% of creditors approved the settlement, saying that most creditors did not vote and most of those who did are in Abu Dhabi. Most creditors have already written off their money, we suspect, but there seem to be at least a few who feel it was bad enough to be taken by the original fraud without being taken again in its settlement.

The same division seems to appear among the regulators who missed the world's biggest bank heist. Mostly they would like it to go away so they can forget. For our part, we'd like to have some answer to the question Mr. Altman's acquittal has only heightened. To wit, how did it all happen anyway? We're glad to know that Harry Albright and Raul Gretsch share our curiosity.

Whitewater Breaks

From April 1992 through September 1993, questions about the Clintons' relationship with Madison Guaranty almost entirely vanished from the national news. But in Arkansas, in the summer of 1993, another level was being added to the Whitewater story.

On July 20, the day Vincent Foster committed suicide in Washington, the FBI obtained a warrant to search the Little Rock offices of David Hale, a former Clinton-appointed municipal judge and the head of Capital Management Services, an investment company chartered by the Small Business Administration. Indicted on fraud charges unrelated to the Clintons, Mr. Hale offered the U.S. Attorney in Little Rock, Paula Casey, a deal: He would provide information about the banking practices of the Arkansas political elite in exchange for leniency. Ms. Casey, a longtime associate of Gov. Clinton, refused. Mr. Hale then went public with a claim that James McDougal and Gov. Clinton had pressured him into making a $300,000 loan to a company affiliated with Madison Guaranty and run by Mr. McDougal's wife; $100,000 of that loan apparently ended up in a Whitewater Development Co. account.

By October, reports of a Resolution Trust Corp. probe into Madison Guaranty were creeping into the news. In November, Ms. Casey and Associate Attorney General Webster Hubbell abruptly recused themselves from Whitewater matters. On Capitol Hill, Rep. Jim Leach (R. Iowa), the ranking minority member of the House Banking Committee, began pressing for hearings into events surrounding

Madison Guaranty. He was rebuffed by committee chairman Henry Gonzalez (D. Texas), who criticized the request as a "purely political fishing expedition" —a theme that would be heard with increasing frequency in the weeks and months ahead.

In the final days of 1993, the American Spectator magazine and Los Angeles Times published new allegations of the President's sexual infidelities while governor, and Washington Times reporter Jerry Seper broke the news that Whitewater files had been removed from the office of Vincent Foster. Whitewater was back on the front pages, and pressure for a special counsel and Congressional hearings was mounting. The Journal published two long editorials providing a framework for these revelations by sketching the fundamental outlines of what had been reported and what concerns were involved.

News Story

U.S. Investigating S&L Chief's '85 Check To Clinton, SBA-Backed Loan to Friend

By Bruce Ingersoll and Paul M. Barrett

Staff Reporters of The Wall Street Journal

WASHINGTON — Federal prosecutors are investigating whether money from a now-defunct Arkansas thrift was illegally diverted in the mid-1980s to local politicians, including a re-election campaign of then-Gov. Bill Clinton.

The probe is the latest development in a larger federal investigation of Madison Guaranty Savings & Loan, which was taken over by federal regulators after it failed in 1989. In addition, prosecutors are investigating an alleged defrauding of the Small Business Administration by the head of a Little Rock small-business investment company, which lent money to the wife of James McDougal, a Clinton business associate and owner of Madison Guaranty. Both the political contributions and the fraud allegations are being handled by the U.S. attorney in Little Rock, Paula Casey.

Federal officials familiar with the inquiries said the Resolution Trust Corp. recently referred to Ms. Casey the matter of possibly illegal campaign contributions. The U.S. attorney's office is examining, among other questions, whether checks drawn on Madison accounts went into a Clinton campaign fund. Ms. Casey, a Clinton appointee, declined to comment.

White House aides said yesterday that in 1985 Mr. Clinton had received a $3,000 personal check from Mr. McDougal. The contribution was part of a larger effort to retire debts from Mr. Clinton's 1984 gubernatorial campaign.

Mr. McDougal is a longtime friend of Bill and Hillary Rodham Clinton, and in 1978, he and his wife invested with the Clintons in an Ozark Mountains real-estate venture known as Whitewater Development Corp. The U.S. attorney's office is looking at Whitewater's dealings with Madison Guaranty. The Clintons have described Whitewater as a money-losing venture.

The McDougals also figure in the small-business fraud investigation. One of the investment-company transactions being scrutinized is a $300,000 loan in 1986 to a firm owned by Susan McDougal. "We're looking at all the financial dealings of the company," said Martin Teckler, the SBA's deputy general counsel.

Yesterday, White House aides sought to distance the president from the investigations. As for the $3,000 check from Mr. McDougal, they said that neither Mr. Clinton nor his staff had any reason at the time to suspect there was anything improper about the 1985 contribution.

"The first we heard about the investigation into political contributions was from press calls," said White House spokesman Jeff Eller. The Washington Post yesterday reported the RTC referral to the U.S. attorney.

"The investigation will just take its course," Mr. Eller added.

An RTC spokeswoman said the cause of Madison Guaranty's collapse has been under investigation, but she wouldn't confirm or deny that the RTC had asked the U.S. attorney to make a further criminal inquiry of possibly improper campaign contributions.

"With all failed savings and loans, we do an investigation," said RTC spokeswoman Felisa Neuringer. "If we find something that goes beyond our realm" of civil enforcement measures, "then we can and do make referrals to the Justice Department."

A federal official familiar with the matter said Ms. Casey, the federal prosecutor, will have to determine whether allegations related to transactions in the mid-1980s can still be prosecuted. Two obstacles could be the expiration of the statute of limitations and the disappearance of records.

Ms. Casey was also asked to look into Madison Guaranty's dealings with Arkansas Gov. Jim Guy Tucker, according to the Washington Post. The thrift lent more than $1 million to Mr. Tucker's companies for real estate and other ventures in the mid-1980s, while he was a member of a Little Rock law firm that represented Madison. The thrift sustained large losses on some of the loans, the Post reported.

Last night, Mr. Tucker's press secretary said that the governor denies any wrongdoing in connection with loans to himself or partnerships in which he has an interest, and added that there are no outstanding loans.

On a parallel track, federal prosecutors in Little Rock are pursuing a criminal case against a former local judge, David Hale, and two other men involved in the collapse of Capital Management Services Inc., a SBA-funded investment company. In September, a federal grand jury indicted Mr. Hale, owner of Capital Management, and the others on fraud charges, and the SBA took over the undercapitalized investment company.

Capital Management made loans to companies in which Mr. Tucker had large stakes as well as the $300,000 loan to Master Marketing, a real estate firm owned by Susan McDougal, according to loan documents. Mr. Hale said that losses on these loans were partly to blame for Capital Management's downfall.

Mr. Hale tried to stave off his indictment by offering to cooperate with federal prosecutors in an investigation of Madison Guaranty, including possible misuse of funds for political purposes. Ms. Casey declined to comment on why Mr. Hale's offer was turned down.

Mr. McDougal, who was acquitted in 1990 of fraud charges stemming from Madison Guaranty's collapse, couldn't be reached yesterday for comment. James Henley, father of Susan McDougal, said last night: "She has no wish to comment at all."

News Story

Loans for Disadvantaged Go to the Advantaged

By JOHN R. EMSHWILLER and BRUCE INGERSOLL

Staff Reporters of THE WALL STREET JOURNAL

Can the governor of Arkansas and a former star National Football League quarterback borrow money under a government-backed loan program designed for disadvantaged business people?

When it comes to the federal Small Business Investment Company program, the answer is yes.

Under the SBIC program, a company that was supposed to lend only to the disadvantaged made a $150,000 loan in 1986 to a business controlled by Jim Guy Tucker, who became the governor of Arkansas last year after President Clinton's election. The same SBIC firm also made a loan to Arkansas businesswoman Susan McDougal. She and her husband James were friends and onetime business partners of the Clintons in a real-estate development venture.

In a similar but unrelated set of transactions, an Alabama SBIC lender to the disadvantaged made hundreds of thousands of dollars of loans to possibly unqualified borrowers, including former NFL star Ken Stabler.

Gov. Tucker and Mr. Stabler deny any wrongdoing or even any knowledge that they were receiving funds reserved for disadvantaged business people. Mrs. McDougal couldn't be reached for comment, but her father has said she doesn't want to discuss the $300,000 loan she obtained.

The questions raised by the loans to Mr. Tucker and the others help explain why the Small Business Administration is in the process of overhauling the SBIC program, which has been plagued by financial problems and scandals in the past several years.

Under the SBIC program, hundreds of privately owned companies have been set up to help finance small businesses with a combination of private capital and federal funds. Currently, that pool of funds stands at about $3.2 billion. About $900 million of that has been raised by selling public debentures that are guaranteed by the federal government.

A big chunk of the SBIC money — nearly $550 million — is supposed to go only to citizens who are "socially or economically disadvantaged." That money is handled by "specialized" SBICs, whose sole function is to lend or invest money in small businesses owned by disadvantaged business people.

Traditionally, in the federal lexicon, "disadvantaged" has almost always referred to nonwhites. But SBA rules allow specialized SBICs to lend to whites, if the whites can prove economic disadvantage.

However, the SBA definition of that condition is murky. For instance, one criterion says the person should be "low income" but isn't more specific. "Inability to compete effectively . . . because of current or past restrictive practices" is another test with no further definition. Somewhere among these fuzzy definitions is the place where the quarterback, the governor and a number of other well-to-do white people can be found.

In Arkansas, SBA and other federal investigators are poking through the rubble of a failed specialized SBIC known as Capital Management Services Inc. Firms in which Mr. Tucker had an ownership interest received at least $300,000 in loans from Capital Management. In February 1986, one firm controlled by Mr. Tucker, Castle Sewer & Water Corp., obtained a $150,000 loan to buy a suburban Little Rock sewer and water system from Madison Financial Corp., a unit of Madison Guaranty Savings & Loan, a now-defunct thrift that was headed by James McDougal, the Clinton associate.

Gov. Tucker insists that he never applied for a loan as a disadvantaged person, and that he never knew that such loan was the only type that Capital Management could legally make. At the time of the loan, Mr. Tucker, a graduate of Harvard College and the University of Arkansas law school, was practicing law and pursuing various business interests. He had already been state attorney general and served a term in Congress in the 1970s. He was elected lieutenant governor in 1990.

"If there was any rule violated, I'm unaware of it," says Gov. Tucker. "I have never heard the term specialized SBIC in my life." He blames any irregularities on David Hale, who at the time was president of Capital Management. Mr. Hale was recently indicted on federal fraud charges unrelated to the loans.

Capital Management's $300,000 loan to Mrs. McDougal's business, a real-estate firm called Master Marketing, also occurred in 1986. It isn't known how those funds were used, though the Washington Post reported earlier this week that some of the money went to buy land for Whitewater Development Corp., the Clinton/McDougal Ozark Mountains real-estate venture. After a few months, the land was transferred to a McDougal-controlled company.

Capital Management's Mr. Hale claims he made the Tucker and McDougal loans as favors to friends — and in the case of Mrs. McDougal, after lobbying by Mr. Clinton. White House officials say the president doesn't recall ever discussing the loan with Mr. Hale.

"It was obvious they didn't qualify" for disadvantaged status, says Mr. Hale. "But they were in deep trouble, and if you've got a friend, you've got to save him."

Mr. Hale, a municipal judge in Little Rock until his indictment in September, denies defrauding the SBA. He blames Capital Management's downfall partly on the loan to Susan McDougal and on two Tucker loans. Aides to President Clinton and Gov. Tucker have suggested that Mr. Hale has been raising questions about their respective financial dealings in a quest for a plea bargain.

Martin Teckler, deputy general counsel for the SBA, says the agency is trying to trace the flow of Capital Management's funds and is scrutinizing loan documents to determine whether borrowers actually qualified as "socially or economically disadvantaged." He says that SBA officials haven't yet come to any conclusions on Gov. Tucker or Mrs. McDougal.

Rule violations can lead to a suspension or revocation of an SBIC's operating license. Criminal penalties can be imposed on borrowers if they willfully misrepresent themselves as being disadvantaged, SBA officials say.

The SBA also has raised questions about the loans made by Alabama Capital Corp. to Mr. Stabler and other white business owners. Mr. Stabler, who for years was a star quarterback with the Oakland Raiders and other pro teams, is currently a television sports commentator and a celebrity spokesperson for various companies.

He's also a budding entrepreneur with plans to open a small restaurant in an old Victorian house in Mobile, Ala. In March 1992, Mr. Stabler's company, Stabler Co., received a $75,000 loan toward that project from Alabama Capital, a specialized SBIC based in Mobile. Last January, Mr. Stabler received two more loans, totaling $100,000, from Alabama Capital. One loan was used to pay off a $75,000 Internal Revenue Service tax lien.

Mr. Stabler says he isn't familiar with the SBIC program, but doesn't consider himself disadvantaged, economically or otherwise. "I wasn't aware it was a program for disadvantaged people," says Mr. Stabler. He says he simply needed financing and was introduced to Alabama Capital by his accountant.

An SBA examination report of Alabama Capital dated Sept. 14 raised questions about the propriety of the loans to Mr. Stabler and several other business people — including one white man who, the examination report said, had a personal financial statement showing a net worth of more than $1 million.

According to the SBA report, Alabama Capital justified the Stabler loans partly on the grounds that Mr. Stabler was burdened by the IRS tax lien.

Michael De Laney, vice president of Alabama Capital, says he couldn't comment on the loans. However, in a letter late last year to the SBA, the company's president, David De Laney, Michael's brother, staunchly defended the company's lending practices. He argued that because small businesses have difficulty borrowing money, many entrepreneurs are in a disadvantaged status.

As part of its SBIC reforms, the SBA is reconsidering its definition of economically disadvantaged, says an agency spokesman. He says the SBA has several times in the past asked Congress for more specific guidance but has never gotten it.

News Story

Justice Department Takes Over Probe of Thrift Owned by Clinton Associate

By BRUCE INGERSOLL

Staff Reporter of THE WALL STREET JOURNAL

WASHINGTON — The Justice Department's criminal division has taken over the investigation of an Arkansas thrift owned by a business associate of President Clinton's after the U.S. attorney in Little Rock took herself out of the case.

The department said U.S. Attorney Paula Casey and her staff decided to recuse themselves because of their familiarity with some of the people involved with Madison Guaranty Savings & Loan Association, which failed in 1989, and another defunct Little Rock lender, Capital Management Services Inc.

Last month, the Resolution Trust Corp. asked Ms. Casey to investigate whether more than $250,000 in business loans may have been diverted from Madison Guaranty for improper purposes, including retiring debts from Mr. Clinton's 1984 gubernatorial campaign. Until it was taken over by federal regulators, the thrift was owned by James McDougal, a friend and business partner of Mr. Clinton who also raised funds for his campaigns.

Mr. McDougal and his wife, Susan, were partners with Bill and Hillary Rodham Clinton in a money-losing real-estate venture known as Whitewater Development Corp.

Ms. Casey's office also has been investigating loans made by Capital Management, an investment company, to Susan McDougal and Arkansas Gov. Jim Guy Tucker, among others, during the mid-

1980s. The company had been chartered and funded by the Small Business Administration to lend money to the disadvantaged.

The owner of Capital Management, David Hale, has been indicted on federal fraud charges unrelated to the loans. Mr. Hale, a former municipal judge in Little Rock, blames his company's downfall partly on the $300,000 loan to Susan McDougal and two Tucker loans. He says he made the loans as favors to friends—and in the case of Mrs. McDougal, after lobbying by Mr. Clinton. White House officials say the president doesn't recall ever discussing the loan with Mr. Hale.

Ms. Casey is an appointee of President Clinton's and a friend of the Clintons. Her husband, a lawyer, has a state-government post.

The recusal was intended "to ensure that there be no misperceptions about the impartiality" of the parallel Madison Guaranty and Capital Management investigations, John Keeney, acting assistant attorney general, said.

Donald Mackay, a senior trial attorney in the criminal-fraud section in Washington, is taking charge of the investigations. He will be assisted by two other Washington-based prosecutors.

Separately, Republican lawmakers asked House Banking Committee Chairman Henry Gonzalez to hold hearings on Madison Guaranty. Minority members on the panel expect Rep. Gonzalez, a Texas Democrat known to be a political maverick, to heed their request, even though an inquiry into the thrift's financial dealings isn't likely to please the White House.

Meanwhile, at the request of House Small Business Committee Chairman John LaFalce, the SBA is looking into the Capital Management case, including the loan to Susan McDougal and loans to companies in which Mr. Tucker had an ownership interest. SBA officials are to report back to Rep. LaFalce, a New York Democrat, by Monday.

Mr. Hale, who denies any wrongdoing, has offered to testify about the loans. Messrs. McDougal and Tucker deny Mr. Hale's claims that he was pressured into making the loans.

News Story

House Panel to Study Thrift Owned by Clinton Associate

WASHINGTON—The House Banking Committee is beginning to look into the financial dealings of an Arkansas thrift owned by a business associate of President Clinton.

Committee Chairman Henry Gonzalez won't decide whether to hold hearings on Madison Guaranty Savings & Loan Association until the preliminary inquiry is completed, a spokesman for the Texas Democrat said.

Republican members of the panel had requested a full-scale investigation of the now-defunct Little Rock thrift Nov. 9, after the Resolution Trust Corp. asked federal prosecutors to conduct a criminal investigation. Until it failed in 1989 and was taken over by the RTC, Madison Guaranty had been owned by James McDougal, a longtime friend and business partner of Mr. Clinton who also raised funds for his campaigns.

A Justice Department criminal-fraud team is looking into several matters, including whether more than $250,000 in business loans may have been diverted for improper purposes, including retiring debts from Mr. Clinton's 1984 gubernatorial campaign.

REVIEW & OUTLOOK

Arkansas Anxieties

House Banking Chairman Henry Gonzalez is one of the most independent Democrats on Capitol Hill, but we now learn that even he will not press an investigation likely to embarrass a Democratic White House. So past Congressional investigations — Iran-Contra, for example, or Chairman Gonzalez's own hearings on the failed S&L whose directors included a son of President Bush — seem more hypocritical than ever.

The current issue involves another failed S&L, owned by a former  business partner of President and Mrs. Clinton. Anyone who doubts that there is much to investigate should read the letter nearby by Rep. Jim Leach, the banking committee's ranking Republican and one of the most independent members of his party. There is a rich cast of characters: James B. McDougal and his Madison Guaranty Savings & Loan. Former municipal Judge David Hale and his Capital Management Services Inc., a failed small-business investment company. Whitewater Development Corp., an Ozark real-estate fling owned by Mr. McDougal, his wife and Hillary and Bill Clinton.

The narrow issue is simply put: Where did the money go when taxpayers were forced to pick up the tab for the failure of Madison and Capital Management? Were these institutions run as piggy banks for a self-dealing circle in Little Rock? Did some of the taxpayers' money go to cut the loss in Whitewater, or to fuel Bill's political ambitions?

Why were state and federal regulators slow to curb the abuse?

The Resolution Trust Corp. made criminal referrals of some of these issues. Judge Hale is currently under indictment for fraud, and in attempting to plea bargain is pointing fingers directly at Bill Clinton. Mr. McDougal was acquitted in his fraud trial but is subject to new investigation. Clearly the issue needs an airing. After expressing initial sympathy for a bipartisan investigation, Rep. Gonzalez refused to sign letters requesting documents from federal regulators.

The narrow issue of scandal is especially pertinent given the broader issue of the Clinton Administration proposal to "unify" banking regulation under a presidential umbrella, also discussed nearby by Federal Reserve Chairman Alan Greenspan.

* * *

We've been watching the Madison-Capital Management-Whitewater story with avid interest as it's been reported elsewhere, by now widely if not especially loudly. But we've not joined the fray, even as some of our left-wing compatriots branded us as mean scandal-mongers who drove Clinton aide Vincent Foster to suicide. We're taken aback by Rep. Gonzalez's apparent suggestion that Mr. Foster's death bestowed an indulgence on all past sins by himself and his clients. So before going any further with the story of Madison, etc., it is perhaps an apt moment to review our editorials on Mr. Foster and the Rose Law Firm partners; what were they all about?

These editorials pressed two points: What we dared to call Arkansas mores, that is, the habits and ethical standards that prevail in Arkansas government and permeate much of the state's business and legal community. Arkansas judges, remember, are required to swear a loyalty oath to the Democratic Party. The Rose Law Firm's most prominent client was Jackson Stephens's financial empire, parts of which helped bring BCCI to the U.S., and other parts of which provided key financing for Bill Clinton's presidential primaries. The Rose partners included Mr. Foster, Hillary Clinton, Associate Attorney General Webster Hubbell and Associate White House Counsel William Kennedy III.

The second point concerned the administration of justice; would Arkansas mores infect law enforcement? We somehow thought it untoward that Mr. Hubbell brokered a change in the Justice Department position in an ongoing corruption trial. We looked askance as Mr. Kennedy called the FBI into the White House travel office, with Mr. Foster reporting on handling of the scandal to Mrs. Clinton. We raised questions about Mr. Foster's attitude toward the Freedom of Information law, and his handling of litigation over secrecy in Mrs. Clinton's health task force.

These seem to us legitimate issues then and now. More: While no proof is possible, we would like to think that our willingness to raise them early and vigorously had a real impact on the justice system. At least despite early reports, Massachusetts Judge Richard Stearns, an Oxford war-protest buddy of the President, was not appointed to head the FBI. Judge Louis Freeh instead was a commendable appointment.

* * *

When the Clinton Justice Department fired all 32 U.S. attorneys, the cynics thought it was to remove Jay Stephens from his seat in the District of Columbia, where he was pursuing the House Post Office scandal involving House Ways and Means Chairman Danny Rostenkowski. The grand jury that originally heard the Rostenkowski evidence was allowed to expire as its term ended. But even the cynics failed to notice that when the incumbent U.S. attorney left Little Rock the appointment went to Paula Casey, a long-time associate of Bill and Hillary Clinton and other Arkansas pols. She has now been forced to recuse herself from Madison, etc. So has Associate Attorney General Hubbell, he says.

Janet Reno has sent some career types down to Little Rock to poke around. The Republican minority on the Banking Committee has now requested documents from the Resolution Trust Corp., the Office of Thrift Supervision, the Small Business Administration, the Arkansas Securities Department and the Federal Deposit Insurance Corp. We shall see how they respond. Mr. Hubbell is still entrenched at Justice and Rep. Gonzalez is balking in Congress.

So let us break our silence on Madison, etc., to point out that it raises two issues that strike us as familiar. One: Could it be that a suspicious set of mores has been carried from Arkansas to the White House? And two: Will the law be administered equally? The final check is the electorate, we suppose, but how will it learn the truth?

Editorial Feature

Will Congress Touch Arkansas Banking?

The following is an exchange of letters between Reps. Jim Leach and Henry Gonzalez, respectively the ranking minority member and the chairman of the House Banking Committee, on a potential investigation of a failed Little Rock savings and loan owned by a former business partner of President and Mrs. Clinton. A related editorial appears nearby.

Dear Henry:

I am in receipt of your letter dated Dec. 9, 1993, regarding Madison Guaranty Savings & Loan and would like to take this opportunity to respond respectfully to your point that Madison's "failure follows a familiar pattern and there is no information suggesting it was a unique case or one that presents legislative issues not previously addressed or any issues now pending before the committee." I would disagree with that assessment and emphasize the exceptional circumstances concerning both the failure and resolution of Madison which appear atypical and call out for congressional review.

Jim Leach

One of the most important constitutional roles of the Congress is to provide oversight and I was encouraged by your statement at this morning's hearing that the committee has not completed its review of the thrift debacle. Of the greatest governmental failures of the last 20 years, one that stands out is that oversight has been too lax, not too vigorous. If we fail to pursue our constitutionally given oversight responsibilities, we are in effect giving a permissive green light to those who want to fudge the law or set aside ethics.

The minority feels strongly that there are a number of legislative aspects that relate directly to the failure and resolution of Madison Guaranty. First, reorganization of the banking regulatory structure has received high priority on the administration's and the commit-

Henry Gonzalez

tee's agenda. Based on news accounts alone, the abuse of state powers and failure of state regulation that appear to exist in the Madison case warrant investigation in the context of addressing reform of the regulatory structure.

Second, as you know, Congress recently approved what is hoped to be the final installment to shore up the deposit insurance system for savings and loans. Although the overall cost to the taxpayers for Madison's failure is relatively small, the percentage of dollar loss to total assets is unusually high. In fact, the cost of Madison's failure equaled nearly 50% of the institution's total assets.

Third, it is apparent that Madison was allowed to continue in existence as a private piggy bank despite its insolvent condition. Here Madison bears direct relevance to whether Congress insists on early intervention and resolution of troubled institutions as well as issues related to financial institution insolvency. As you know, Congress is now considering the repeal or modification of many of the early intervention and safety and soundness provisions of [the Federal Deposit Insurance Corp. Improvement Act]. In your letter, you state that "Madison Guaranty was placed under regulatory surveillance early on, appropriate disciplinary measures were put in place, and the institution closed when conservation efforts failed." Unfortunately, this is not the case. Federal regulators noted severe problems with Madison's condition in 1984. Yet from 1984 to 1986, Madison grew from a $49 million institution to a $125 million institution.

Fourth, as in the case of BNL, government guarantees of private loans were reportedly abused, with allegations that [Small Business Administration] guarantees were improperly obtained and used by Madison officials. It is my understanding that the Small Business

Committee has found this issue alone sufficient to conduct a committee investigation. I believe the Banking Committee has a greater legislative interest in the Madison case than our sister committee.

Fifth, during Mr. James McDougal's tenure at Madison, it was reported that loans to officers, directors and executives increased from $500,000 to $17 million. With such a dramatic growth in loans to insiders, the committee should investigate whether spurts in growth of an institution's loans to insiders should be a legislative concern or at least serve as a warning to the regulators. Moreover, absent an investigation, the committee will not be permitted to know how the regulators responded to this issue during their examinations of Madison.

Sixth, it appears Madison paid its real estate subsidiary substantial commissions for land sales, including payments of more than $712,000 during a three year period to Mr. McDougal's wife, Susan, and two of her brothers, James and William. The committee should determine whether insider financial arrangements should be subject to greater scrutiny. Again, absent a review of regulatory documents, the committee will not be permitted to know how the regulators responded to this issue during their examinations of Madison.

Seventh, it appears that Madison's legal documents were so poor that in many cases examiners could not determine the "real nature" of the transactions. The committee needs to determine if there should be a base standard for an institution in keeping adequate legal documents.

Eighth, it appears improper accounting techniques were used to disguise solvency problems. The committee needs to determine if these accounting practices are still being used by some financial institutions.

Ninth, after Madison's failure, the late Vince Foster of the Rose law firm solicited legal work from the FDIC to sue Madison. Rose was selected to pursue Madison's accountants, Frost & Co. Rose settled the $60 million suit for $1 million. Sources claim that the $1 million was below Frost's insurance coverage. Rose billed the government $400,000 for its work. Webster Hubbell, now associate attorney general, was the lead attorney in the case. His father-in-law was an officer of a subsidiary of Madison and, in fact, was one of Madison's largest borrowers. Hubbell's father-in-law did not repay $587,793 in loans to Madison. FDIC officials have said that they were not aware of the

Rose law firm's work on behalf of Madison before it was hired.

The committee must examine the lack of internal controls at the FDIC with respect to its enforcement of conflict of interest rules in the hiring of outside attorneys. Not only had Rose worked for Madison, but the lead attorney had a relative deeply in debt to the institution. How could this have escaped the knowledge of FDIC officials? Without a committee investigation, we cannot determine the adequacy of the FDIC's past and current procedures for disqualifying firms with conflicts.

Tenth, the [Resolution Trust Corp.] has made a criminal referral to the Justice Department which includes allegations that corporate funds may have been used by Madison for political purposes. As you know, corporate contributions by federally chartered institutions are barred by federal election law. The Madison case raises the issue of whether state chartered, federally insured institutions should also have the same restriction.

Finally, the Frost & Co. audit, that was used by the Rose firm to help keep Madison in business in 1985, failed to disclose that Frost's chief auditor of Madison, James Alford, had two outstanding loans at Madison at the time of the audit. The committee needs to determine whether or not federal banking regulators should be barred from accepting an audit from an individual or firm indebted to the institution.

So much more is needed to be known about Madison and as you have said so often, the public has a right to know. The above list is not an exhaustive outline of the issues presented by the Madison case which bear relevance to the committee's jurisdiction, but is a cursory overview of circumstances based on news reports which indicate a direct link to the committee's legislative interests.

Above all, Congress has an obligation to the American public to ensure that no American, whatever his or her position, is above public accountability and the rule of the law.

JAMES A. LEACH

* * *

Dear Jim:

I have perused your lengthy letter of Dec. 9, 1993, slipped under my door late last evening.

Let me reiterate that I fully understand that political operatives within your party are exerting tremendous pressure on you to link the failure [of] Madison Bank directly to the president, even to the point of raising an insensitive reference to the sad case of the late Vince Foster.

Since the very first day of my chairmanship I have strived, on a bipartisan basis, to study and rectify the types of regulatory abuse issues identified in your letter. I do not believe I need to detail how the Banking Committee, under my chairmanship, has successfully addressed, through oversight and legislation, the issues you raise, regardless of the political affiliation of the individuals involved.

However, I will never permit the Banking Committee to become an instrument of any party's desire to conduct a purely political fishing expedition. Rest assured, the committee will continue to review this matter but, again, I will not permit Republican political operatives to set the agenda of the House Banking Committee.

HENRY B. GONZALEZ

REVIEW & OUTLOOK

Whitewater: A Primer

At holiday gatherings across the land, heads are shaking with worry over our President. Amid the likes of Vincent Foster's death and Arkansas state troopers' allegations of what amounts to satyriasis, the President won a moment of relative serenity by promising to give Justice Department investigators his files on Whitewater Development Corp. So it's time for a Whitewater primer, laying aside sex and suicide to follow the money.

The essential suspicion to be investigated is this: That in return for campaign contributions and other financial favors, Governor Clinton used political influence to keep a shaky savings and loan afloat while it was milked of money, sticking taxpayers with the tab through federal deposit insurance. The Madison Guaranty S&L was owned by James McDougal while the McDougal and Clinton families were partners in  Whitewater. In essence, the issue is whether Governor Clinton did for Madison and McDougal what five Senators did for Lincoln Savings and Charlie Keating.

A great deal has already been published on Whitewater, though it wasn't making headlines when we offered our December 15 editorial "Arkansas Anxieties." The issue was raised during the 1992 presidential campaign by Jeff Gerth of the New York Times, but was put to rest when the campaign produced a report by Denver attorney James Lyons. It was boosted back in the news this year by reports that the Resolution Trust Corp. had referred Madison Guaranty for criminal investigation, and especially by the indictment of former Judge David Hale, who charged that Governor Clinton had urged him to make a loan partly responsible for the related failure of Capital-Management Services Inc., a small-business investment company.

The following items have been reported by responsible papers, and are drawn together here in what we hope will be a comprehensible whole:

* * *

Mr. Clinton and Mr. McDougal met while both worked for Senator William Fulbright. In 1978, when Mr. Clinton was Arkansas Attorney General, they and their wives joined in Whitewater, a land-development venture along the White River in the Ozarks. Like a lot of other ventures of the time, the idea ran afoul of the end of easy money and the 1980-1982 recessions. The Lyons report said the Clintons lost $69,000; Mr. Lyons described the Clintons as "passive shareholders."

The Washington Times, however, has uncovered a letter in which Hillary Clinton asks Mr. McDougal for full power of attorney over Whitewater, with authority to execute "checks, notes, deeds, agreements, certificates, receipts or any other instruments." It is not known whether this request was implemented.

Whitewater's finances were intermingled with its principals'. For example, in what the Clintons' attorneys said was a pure error, both Whitewater and the Clintons took tax deductions for payments by Whitewater on a loan Mrs. Clinton took out on the corporation's behalf. Many important Whitewater records are missing, which frustrated Mr. Gerth's 1992 investigation and a recent probe by federal prosecutors. Mr. McDougal claims, and the Clintons deny, that the records were delivered to the Arkansas Governor's mansion at the behest of Mrs. Clinton.

Reporters who have examined the Clintons' tax returns say no Whitewater loss was claimed for tax purposes. Indeed, they reported a $1,000 capital gain when they disposed of their interest in the venture by reselling it to Mr. McDougal. Chris Wade, an Arkansas real estate agent who managed Whitewater, recently told the Washington Post that he does not believe the venture lost money. The Post also reported that in the mid-1980s, "tens of thousands of dollars were passing through Whitewater's account" and that "the transactions seemed to bear no direct connection to Whitewater's lot sales or home development activity."

* * *

Whitewater's accounts, often overdrawn, were located at Madison Guaranty, which Mr. McDougal bought in 1979, with the help of a loan from Worthen Bank, which held a lien on his interest. Madison's assets grew to $107 million in 1985 from $6 million in 1982. Loans to its own officers and directors grew to $17 million from $500,000. Loans were also extended to Senator Fulbright and various Arkansas political figures. The Los Angeles Times has reported that current Arkansas Governor Jim Guy Tucker negotiated a 50% reduction in his debt of more than $1 million, while Seth Ward, father-in-law of current Associate Attorney General Webster Hubbell, defaulted on $587,793.

Mr. McDougal drove a Bentley around Little Rock, while his wife Susan advertised real estate projects by appearing on television in hot pants while riding a white horse. A Post profile reported that "In their heyday in Little Rock, it seemed the Clintons and McDougals couldn't get enough of each other." McDougal was said to have easy access to the Governor's office. He has since undergone the collapse of Madison (at a cost to taxpayers reported as $47 million to $60 million), hospitalization in a manic episode, acquittal in a 1990 fraud trial, divorce and personal bankruptcy.

In 1985, Mr. McDougal held a fund-raiser in the Madison Guaranty lobby to retire Governor Clinton's 1984 campaign debts. The Times' Mr. Gerth has reported that the debt consisted of $50,000 the campaign owed to Mr. Clinton personally, which he in turned owed to another small Arkansas bank owned by one of his senior aides. Several of the $3,000 donations were cashier's checks drawn on Madison. One of them was issued in the name of Ken Peacock, an Arkansas businessman who was then a 24-year-old son of a Madison director. He told the Post he was baffled by the check: "I don't know anything about it."

Shortly after the fund-raiser, Madison received approval from Beverly Bassett Schaffer, Mr. Clinton's newly appointed financial regulator, for a plan to meet its capital requirements by selling preferred stock. Mrs. Schaffer had earlier briefly served as a lawyer for Madison, and Mr. McDougal said he had urged her appointment. The Arkansas Democrat Gazette recently reported that she said she'd never met Mr. McDougal and that "it was her relationship with Mr.

Clinton — not James McDougal — that helped her land the job as securities commissioner."

Mrs. Schaffer denies any favoritism to Madison, and there is no evidence that Governor Clinton urged her to go easy. However, the attorney representing Madison was Hillary Clinton. One of Mrs. Schaffer's letters on the issue is addressed to the Rose Law Firm and opens, "Dear Hillary." Mrs. Clinton received a $2,000-a-month retainer from Madison. In an account denied by the White House press office, Mr. McDougal told the Los Angeles Times, "I hired Hillary because Bill came in whimpering they needed help."

* * *

David Hale was another prominent Arkansas Democrat and Clinton supporter. When Governor Clinton formed the state's first municipal claims court, he appointed Mr. Hale as its first judge. By early 1986, the Los Angeles Times reported, he was running the largest court in the state. He was also the head of Capital-Management Services Inc., an investment company chartered by the Small Business Administration. Last September a federal grand jury indicted Mr. Hale on charges of defrauding the SBA, which took over the failing company. As Journal news stories have reported, the SBIC was legally permitted to loan only to "socially or economically disadvantaged" proprietors.

Prior to his indictment, Mr. Hale made offers to implicate Governor Clinton in connection with a $300,000 loan from Capital Management to a real estate firm owned by Susan McDougal; investigators are trying to determine if part of this money made its way into Whitewater. In interviews with various newspapers, Mr. Hale said Mr. McDougal urged the loan to help "clean up" problems involving "the political family." When Governor Clinton personally urged the loan, he said, "I knew I had to help. There never was any question." The White House press office has said President Clinton has no recollection of such a conversation, and Mr. McDougal also denies the account.

Mr. Hale's plea-bargain attempts were made when the case was being supervised by Paula Casey, a former associate of both Bill and Hillary Clinton who was appointed to the Little Rock vacancy when the Clinton Administration dismissed all incumbent U.S. attorneys. She recused herself from the Madison-Whitewater case in early November, but also said she "concurred" in a decision by earlier prosecutors not to follow it when it was first referred. It has been referred a second time, and is now being handled by career Justice Department lawyers from Washington.

* * *

The facts recounted above contain no "smoking gun," but they surely arouse suspicion. Surely Hillary Clinton was disingenuous in saying during her year-end interview that she is "bewildered" that Whitewater remains "a topic of inquiry." The Clinton Administration has just proposed a sweeping change to give the President much more direct control over regulation of banks throughout the land. Before that happens, at the very least, some of those involved in Whitewater should go up on oath somewhere to testify on what really happened when Bill Clinton presided over banking regulation in Arkansas.

Letters to the Editor

False Accusation Repeated as Fact

On Dec. 28, 1993, The Wall Street Journal claimed that Seth Ward, father-in-law of Webster Hubbell, had failed to repay large sums of money borrowed from Madison Guaranty Savings & Loan Association. The claim was based on a Washington Post story of Nov. 3, 1993. The problem is, the statement is totally false. After examining the claim, the Arkansas Democrat-Gazette wrote that the loans "were settled in 1986 and 1988 and were not in default."

The Washington Post has never printed a retraction or correction, and consequently this false statement has been republished by most of the English language publications in the world, including The Wall Street Journal.

Mr. Ward has been involved in protracted litigation with Madison Guaranty Savings & Loan Association and the Resolution Trust Corporation, as receiver for Madison Guaranty, and it has never been contended in that litigation that Mr. Ward had failed to repay any loans from Madison Guaranty.

The Wall Street Journal has published another statement to the effect that transactions involving Mr. Ward, among others, led to the insolvency and failure of Madison Guaranty in 1989. The undisputed testimony in the state court lawsuit between Mr. Ward and Madison Guaranty was that the transactions in which Mr. Ward was involved constituted "a pretty good deal for Madison."

It is obvious that the RTC would not have agreed on April 30, 1993, that Mr. Ward had no further obligation whatsoever to it or Madison

Guaranty if, in fact, Mr. Ward had defaulted on loans and had in any way contributed to the failure of Madison Guaranty.

In their zeal to tarnish Webb Hubbell and the Clinton administration, the media, including the Journal, have been most irresponsible and unfair to Seth Ward.

ALSTON JENNINGS

Little Rock, Ark.

Editorial Feature

Clinton Allegations
Cause GOP Memory Loss

"We ought to have confidence in our nation's attorney general — con-fidence that she [Janet Reno] can conduct criminal investigations with independence and without the intrusion of politics."
> — Sen. Robert Dole on the Senate floor, Nov. 18, 1993

"She's [Ms. Reno's] wasted a lot of time dragging her feet, and it's time she moved and appointed an independent counsel."
> — Sen. Dole on "Meet the Press," Jan. 2, 1994

The year isn't even a week old and Bob Dole already is a candidate for the political hypocrisy award of 1994. What transpired in 45 days was that President Clinton and Ms. Clinton's relationship with a failed savings and loan in the 1980s began to dominate the headlines; Bob Dole, who blocked extending the independent counsel legislation in 1992 when a Republican was in the White House, smelled blood.

The political context is Washington returning from the holidays

Politics & People

By Albert R. Hunt

readying for a rough year while a couple potential scandals circle the first family. Some early conclusions from all this are:

— The Clinton sex scandal is dying a well-deserved death, but the financial allegations may have legs.

The public, to the surprise of cynics, has much less interest than the press in stories about Bill Clinton's alleged infidelities as governor of Arkansas. The story was seamy, if not specious, from the start.

The essence, as most everyone knows by now, involved several former Arkansas state troopers, represented by a Clinton-hating Republican politico, telling how the former Arkansas governor used them to facilitate sexual assignations.

Titillation aside, it seems obvious that a) the stories added little to the knowledge voters possessed during the 1992 election that Bill Clinton had a philandering past; b) the allegations, at the core true, were probably embellished to make a more marketable story; and c) the most serious charge — that the president may have tried to silence accusers with job offers — was flimsy at best.

By contrast, the S&L flap won't fade as easily. The central issue is: Did the now-defunct Madison Guaranty Savings & Loan illegally funnel political and personal funds to the Clintons in the 1980s? The head of Madison, James McDougal, and the Clintons were partners in a separate land development company, Whitewater Development Co., which also may have illicitly gotten money from a small business investment company run by David Hale, whom Gov. Clinton appointed a state judge. The plot thickened following the tragic suicide last July of Vince Foster, a White House counsel and the Clintons' former lawyer; within hours, presidential aides hastily spirited Whitewater files out of Mr. Foster's office.

The Clintons — the first lady once received a $2,000-a-month retainer as Madison's attorney — deny any improprieties and say they actually lost almost $69,000 from the Whitewater investment. Yet a report asserting this by a Clinton friend last year is flawed and there are key records missing. Meanwhile, Mr. Hale, under indictment himself, privately is trying to cut a deal claiming that he has some incriminating documents.

— This is exactly the sort of case for which the independent counsel measure was intended.

When interviewed, with promise of confidentiality, two top lawyers, both with criminal and financial expertise though not involved in this case, separately arrive at the same deduction: The Clintons may have engaged in ethical transgressions, but the possibility of any criminal violation is far-fetched. The Clintons should have avoided any deals with Mr. McDougal, a well-known hustler in Arkansas political circles, but the first family has no history of seeking big bucks or cutting shady deals.

But this is why a truly independent counsel, to investigate serious allegations by very top executive-branch, and sometimes congressional, figures, is necessary: to establish innocence as well as guilt. "The appearance of justice having been done is equally as important as justice having been done," says Sen. William Cohen (R., Maine), a champion of independent counsel legislation. Conservative critics forget it was their hero, Ed Meese, who requested an independent counsel back in 1984 and was cleared of any criminal conduct.

Legislation extending the law is essential. A measure has passed the Senate, and the House expects it to do likewise by early February. An undeniable problem is that the statute of limitations on some of the Madison allegations expires in March, but even the current investigation — being conducted by a highly respected career official — is unlikely to wrap up in two months.

What Sen. Dole proposes is for Attorney General Reno, on her own, to appoint a so-called "independent" counsel. That person, of course, would report to her and Associate Attorney General Webster Hubbell, whose father-in-law got a huge loan forgiveness from Madison. That's like setting up a blind trust that you can peek at. If a Justice Department-designated counsel issues a report exonerating the Clintons, one already can hear the Kansas Republican questioning the "independence" of the conclusion.

— With Democrats running the executive branch for the first time in a dozen years, Republican views on executive privileges and perquisites are in a metamorphic free fall.

Remember those days when Republicans passionately protested against any encroachment on executive authority? That started to end about 351 days ago — when Bill Clinton was sworn in.

Mainstay in the old argument was opposition to counsels truly independent of the executive branch. Now conservatives are calling for independent counsels to investigate allegations not only against the Clintons but separately against Commerce Secretary Ron Brown. Similarly, on foreign policy, remember those impassioned conservatives who protested against any efforts to tie the president's hands on Nicaragua or El Salvador or Beirut during the 1980s? Suddenly, for Bob Dole and others, the principles changed this year when it came to Somalia and a Democratic president.

"These Republicans don't even come up with an argument for changing their position," notes Rep. Barney Frank (D., Mass.). "They just figure the public doesn't have any memory."

In a variation on this separation-of-powers issue, here's one more prediction: If the GOP picks up 20 or 25 House seats this year and a half-dozen Senate seats — putting them within striking distance of congressional control — watch all the conservative clamor for term limits follow the same fate as worries about encroaching on executive authority with measures like independent counsels.

Letters to the Editor

Here's the Way I Remember It

The only memory loss in Al Hunt's Jan. 6 column is his own ("Clinton Allegations Cause GOP Memory Loss," op-ed, Politics & People).

Mr. Hunt argues that my request for the appointment of a "special counsel" to examine the burgeoning Whitewater controversy is somehow inconsistent with a statement I made last November opposing the re-authorization of the Independent Counsel Act. The statement Mr. Hunt cites as inconsistent is this: "We ought to have confidence in our nation's attorney general-confidence that she can conduct criminal investigations with independence and without the intrusion of politics."

Now, here's what Mr. Hunt forgot. The very next sentences of my remarks make this point: "In fact, the attorney general already has the authority to appoint special counsels in cases that merit an independent review. This authority exists with or without an independent counsel statute, and it has been invoked by past attorneys general. . . ." It didn't fit Mr. Hunt's argument, but the fact is I opposed the independent counsel statute in part because the attorney general already has the authority to appoint special counsels, the same authority Republicans, Democrats and editorial writers for many of the nation's most respected newspapers have now urged Attorney General Reno to use.

Mr. Hunt then suggests I would be critical of any final report "exonerating the Clintons." In fact, I have provided Attorney General

Reno with a list of seven individuals, including such prominent Democrats as former Carter administration Attorneys General Griffin Bell and Benjamin Civiletti, whom I believe would be suitable for appointment as Whitewater special counsel. All seven individuals have reputations for integrity and competence that are unassailable, and whose conclusions wouldn't be second-guessed by me, or I believe most Republicans.

I hate to disappoint Al Hunt, but I'll have to decline his nomination for his political inconsistency award — the facts disqualify me.

SEN. BOB DOLE (R., KAN.)
Senate Republican Leader

Washington

Editorial Feature

On Arkansas Sex,
Not Inhaling,
And Whitewater

By ROBERT L. BARTLEY

When the Gennifer Flowers tapes hit the headlines during the 1992 campaign, our Albert Hunt wrote a column defending candidate Bill Clinton against her "sordid, sleazy story," and also laying out conditions that might make a candidate's sex life pertinent. For example, "One, if the candidate lies."

While most of us would instinctively agree, the exception is interesting. We don't care whether he did it, but we do care if he did and denies it. Why, precisely?

Well, we teach little children not to lie because it's wrong morally, but also because it often has serious practical consequences. If you tell one lie, you typically have to cover up by telling more. After a while you reach the completely implausible, and people stop believing you. And they don't believe you in the next pinch, even if then your story is true.

At the presidential level, we call this credibility. A leader who isn't believed is not likely to be effective; a president needs bonds of trust with the people. The shredding of these bonds, not some two-bit burglary, is why President Nixon had to leave office. Election as president gives you a birthright of credibility, but you can only go to the well so many times. And here is the real danger to President Clinton in the new sex allegations raised by state troopers in Arkansas. They erode credibility just when he needs all he can muster to deal with the financial questions we call the Whitewater issue.

* * *

Sexual issues are always problematical, of course. It is unseemly to gossip about the most private aspects of someone else's life, and there's no consensus on standards to apply to political leaders. While some would punish any infidelity, others scoff that rulers have always had concubines and even harems. Still others, starting here, would say that Dwight Eisenhower sleeping with his driver in the midst of World War II is one thing, while the wanton promiscuity the troopers allege in Arkansas is quite another.

These allegations were first detailed by David Brock in the American Spectator, and there was an initial attempt to impugn his scoop with the label "conservative," as if that were a dread disease. But the Los Angeles Times quickly confirmed the essence of the Brock report by publishing its own extensive investigation. The net is that two troopers told the same stories on the record to two publications, and were supported by two other troopers talking on a not-for-attribution basis. Among other things, they support Miss Flowers's original account. There are also her tapes, plus the L.A. Times study of official phone records supporting at least one part of the troopers' story.

Voters will have to make up their own minds on both truth and relevance. But with due respect for the problem of proving a negative, the presidential response has scarcely built confidence.

The White House branded the troopers' charges as "outrageous." But when a reporter asked, "So none of this ever happened?" the president suffered a fit of stammering. Mr. Brock makes the point that the original Gennifer Flowers denials also had a slippery quality. In confessing marijuana experiments, candidate Clinton protested that he didn't inhale. Are the present protests of the same ilk?

As the troopers' story spread, Betsey Wright, the sometime Clinton aide who popularized the phrase "bimbo eruption," decamped to Little Rock, along the way consulting her favorite private eye, San Francisco-based Jack Palladino. Soon stories began to appear about the troopers' warts. A sex harassment charge against one trooper turned out to have been dismissed. An insurance company litigator charged the two troopers lied in an insurance scam; it turns out they did get drunk and wreck a state car, but the litigation is about who should pay medical bills.

And Ms. Wright proudly displayed an affidavit from trooper Danny Ferguson saying, "President Clinton never offered or indicated a willingness to offer any trooper a job in exchange for silence or help in shaping their stories." Re-interviewed by the L.A. Times, Mr. Ferguson said, yes, the president called. Yes, they talked about what troopers were going to say about the sex charges. Yes, they talked about two different jobs. But the quid pro quo was never explicitly expressed. That is, he didn't inhale.

* * *

Getting into a spitting match with his own former security guards will surely deplete a president's reservoir of credibility. Worse, this amplifies all the doubts in the Whitewater case. Here the suspicion is that funds from a failing savings and loan were diverted into Whitewater Development, a real estate venture partly owned by the Clintons. Whatever else, the defensive themes sound familiar.

It's an "old story," we hear for example; is that a denial, or not? It was a "money-losing venture," as if it would be perfectly OK to float off your real estate investment loss on the taxpayer through deposit insurance so long as nothing new gets into your own pocket. The loss was never deducted for tax purposes, but was documented in an "accountant's report," though as the Journal's Bruce Ingersoll just demonstrated, the report ignores major transactions. The Clintons were "passive shareholders," though at one point Hillary requested a power of attorney over the whole business. The records from Vincent Foster's office will be released, though it turns out only to the Justice Department, and it further turns out, only after a delay for "inventory." And, of course, "we've said enough."

The damage from the troopers is contained by a natural, in this libertine age even touching, reluctance to traffic in sexual gossip. But in both cases the excuses are sounding increasingly lame. Whitewater could become Bill Clinton's credibility sinkhole, simply because no one is inhibited in talking about dirty money.

Mr. Bartley is editor of the Journal.

Letters to the Editor

Trooper Affidavit Is a Farce

Robert Bartley's Jan. 6 editorial-page article "On Arkansas Sex, Not Inhaling And Whitewater," justifying continued press coverage of the current scandals involving Bill and Hillary Clinton, answers the critics of press coverage, including your own Albert Hunt, clearly and forthrightly.

However, Mr. Bartley commits one error of fact that, had the truth been known to him, would have further bolstered his position. In his column, Mr. Bartley refers to "an affidavit from Trooper Danny Ferguson saying, 'President Clinton never offered or indicated a willingness to offer any trooper a job in exchange for silence or help in shaping their stories.'"

In fact, Trooper Danny Ferguson did not sign an affidavit, and made no such statement under oath. I am enclosing a photostatic copy of the actual affidavit in question, as it was published in the Arkansas Democrat-Gazette of Dec. 30. As you may see, the affidavit was not signed by Trooper Ferguson, but was signed by Robert Batton, who stated he was signing "on behalf of" his client. In a newspaper article accompanying the depiction of the affidavit, the Arkansas Democrat-Gazette report revealed that Betsey Wright had attempted to obtain such an affidavit directly from Mr. Ferguson, but was only able to obtain an affidavit signed by his attorney. The report further revealed that Bruce Lindsey, lawyer and White House aide to President Clinton, solicited and obtained the assistance of Little Rock lawyer Stephen Engstrom, in preparing the enclosed affidavit.

That is, the facts surrounding the affidavit are as follows: Betsey

Wright, Clinton's longtime henchman and fixer, came to Little Rock lawyer Stephen Engstrom, at the request of Bill Clinton, in an attempt to persuade Trooper Ferguson to recant his earlier claims made to the Los Angeles Times that he had been offered a job as a United States Marshal or with the Federal Emergency Management Agency, in exchange for his silence about Mr. Clinton's criminal abuse of power while governor of Arkansas. Trooper Ferguson refused to recant his story under oath, which could have subjected him to criminal penalties if the statement under oath proved to be false. Thereupon, the fixer and the two lawyers hit upon the idea of having Mr. Ferguson's lawyer execute an affidavit, under oath, which, as you may see, only states that Mr. Ferguson told the lawyer the contents of the affidavit. Therefore, neither Mr. Ferguson nor his lawyer has stated under oath that "President Clinton never offered or indicated a willingness to offer any trooper a job in exchange for silence or help in shaping their stories." No one has sworn to this statement.

Mr. Bartley could also have noted that the statement I have just quoted is not, as a matter of logic, one that anyone can swear to, other than President Clinton himself. Neither Trooper Ferguson, lawyer Batton, Stephen Engstrom nor Betsey Wright could possibly swear that President Clinton never offered a job to any trooper.

Bill Clinton, acting through Wright, Engstrom and Batton, has engaged in trickery and deception in the matter of the affidavit of Danny Ferguson. Bill Clinton is not known as Slick Willie for nothing.

The "affidavit" is a farce, and was evidently executed for the sole purpose of deceiving the public and the press. Your readers might want to know why this was done.

TIMOTHY F. WATSON SR.
Attorney

Newport, Ark.

Editorial Feature

What Did He Know, and When Did He Know It?

When the White House sacked every sitting U.S. attorney last March, this space hyperbolically deplored "the most secretive and deeply political" administration "since Richard Nixon's." By now that looks understated.

Whitewater may not be Watergate, but the Clinton White House's skill in handling the real estate-S&L suspicions has certainly earned

Potomac Watch

By Paul A. Gigot

it the right to be called Nixonian. Its gift for inspiring suspicion in reporters, its mastery of the self-inflicted wound, and its talent for seeming uncooperative and slippery are all qualities worthy of the master himself.

Having worked as staffers on the House committee to impeach Mr. Nixon, Hillary Clinton and White House counsel Bernie Nussbaum may have absorbed more political lessons than they ever imagined. As John Le Carre once wrote about the CIA and KGB, maybe they fought a "looking glass war." Let's examine how the Clintons have turned a seemingly small scandal into a potentially much bigger one involving the abuse of presidential power:

• *The non-denial denial.* This White House is adept at not giving a straight answer. So Whitewater was just "old stories" that were "already investigated." Naturally, these dismissals (non-denials) only raised suspicions when reporters discovered new stories — e.g., that the lawyer retained by the Clintons to "investigate" Whitewater in 1992 had ignored large transactions.

• *The coverup.* When Vincent Foster, the Clintons' personal lawyer, shot himself in secluded Fort Marcy last summer, the White House response was to blame the press. A chorus line of commentary accused this newspaper, in particular.

But we've since learned that the troubled Mr. Foster had more on his mind than tart editorials. As the lawyer putting together the Clintons' presidential blind trust, he handled the First Couple's personal finances. Yet he was well behind the pace of any recent presidency in establishing that blind trust, which was finally and quietly filed a week after he died. What took so long?

Richard Nixon

On the day he died, Mr. Foster received a phone call from James Lyons, the lawyer he'd hired to file the Clintons' 1992 Whitewater "report." On the same day, too, a subpoena was issued to search the Little Rock offices of David Hale. A former judge appointed by Mr. Clinton, Mr. Hale has since been indicted and has accused Mr. Clinton of benefiting from a $300,000 loan Mr. Hale made to a business partner of the Clintons.

Perhaps these are coincidences, but they raise doubts, especially because the White House has been so eager to blunt queries about Mr. Foster. The probe of his death was confined to the Park Police, who have no expertise in mysterious deaths. Their report also remains a secret, though the Justice Department promised to make it public.

And don't forget the early sacking of those U.S. attorneys: That meant Mr. Clinton could nominate Paula Casey, a former campaign worker of his, to the Little Rock U.S. attorney's post that would investigate Whitewater. She has since recused herself, but not before recommending to Washington that a criminal referral of the case to Justice by the Resolution Trust Corp. not be pursued.

• *A modified limited hangout.* Clinton spin-meisters know the Ziegleresque value of appearing to be forthcoming even while stonewalling. So a Dec. 23 decision to release Whitewater documents taken — in secret — from Mr. Foster's office was hailed by the likes of George Stephanopoulos as coming clean.

But now we learn that this disclosure was rigged by the White House so as to avoid having to make any documents public. By conspiring to have Justice issue a subpoena for the documents, the White House made sure nosy reporters can't obtain those documents under the Freedom of Information Act.

Bill Clinton has one advantage Richard Nixon never had — a Congress of his own party. House Banking Chairman Henry Gonzalez, who did yeoman work on the Keating Five, has suddenly lost interest in S&Ls. That's why even Iowa Republican Jim Leach, the least partisan member of Congress, has called for a "special counsel."

This is not, despite claims by Clinton partisans, the same thing as a Lawrence Walsh-type "independent counsel." Barney Frank (D., Mass.) wants to use Whitewater to revive that law, ramming it through the House without allowing a vote on whether it should cover Congress as well as the executive branch. But this could actually help a coverup, because a Whitewater Walsh could keep documents under wraps for years.

As scholar Terry Eastland reminds me, Watergate and even Teapot Dome were investigated by "special prosecutors" without the runaway, hair-trigger Walsh-type statute. Whitewater could be as well, if the counsel were someone with the proven integrity of Manhattan D.A. Robert Morgenthau. Such a counsel would at least be subject to political constraints, the way a Walsh-type counsel isn't. Even better would be a televised congressional hearing, a la the Keating Five, so voters could decide for themselves. With an administration as Nixonian as this one, how else is it going to restore its credibility?

REVIEW & OUTLOOK

A *Congressional* Responsibility

A good rule in politics is that when Barney Frank and Newt Gingrich agree on something, it's time for second thoughts. So with everyone shouting for an "independent counsel" to investigate President and Hillary Clinton's Whitewater mess, we'd like to explain our doubts.

We bow to no one in our concern over Whitewater, and, more broadly, over the Arkansas political mores that have migrated to Washington. Surely this is a subject that needs to be investigated by someone with the power of subpoena. The press is doing a good job on Whitewater at the moment, but cannot subpoena documents or force people to testify under oath. We also understand why, given the current  state of our political culture, people clamor for an "independent" archangel to solve political problems. But independent counsels are troubling precisely because they have become a device for letting our political institutions shirk their constitutional responsibilities.

In particular, where is the Congress? The Whitewater episode is made to order for Congress's constitutional role of oversight. Yet the Banking Committees that were all over Neil Bush and Charlie Keating are suddenly silent about a failed S&L that was owned by a business partner of the President and paid his wife $2,000 a month for legal work. Surely Congress ought to be playing its role of educating the public.

It's fair, of course, to ask who in Congress has the credibility to do it. The sight of Senate Banking Chairman and Keating Fiver Don Riegle investigating anyone is, we admit, fodder for "Saturday Night Live." The Judiciary Committee could explore Mr. Clinton's firing of 93 U.S. attorneys last March, an act that let him appoint a crony in Little Rock, but this would again highlight the Anita Hill gang.

Yet sometimes Congress has been up to the job. Henry Gonzalez's Keating Five hearings helped the public understand what happened to the S&Ls, amplified later by special counsel Bob Bennett's ethics probe. For that matter, there is plenty of precedent, ranging from Mr. Bennett to Arthur Liman and back at least to Ferdinand Pecora, for Congress to appoint its own "special counsel," not only providing investigatory expertise but absorbing political heat.

Another constitutional option, first suggested by Sen. Lauch Faircloth and since picked up by both Bob Dole and Jim Leach, is for the attorney general to appoint a "special counsel" within the executive branch. Indeed, we ourselves suggested this after Vincent Foster's death, if only to assign responsibility and accountability for its investigation. This is different from the independent counsel law, because such a "special counsel" remains accountable to the attorney general. A President could always fire him, a threat that makes the counsel accountable to someone. But this threat cannot be carried out without a heavy political price, as Richard Nixon learned when he dismissed Archibald Cox during Watergate.

Washington has seen a lot of scandals over 200 years, after all, and the country somehow coped before the independent counsel law was passed in 1978. Teapot Dome and Watergate were both exposed without such a law. The Pecora hearings in the 1930s probed financial and political ties that embarrassed both Republicans and Democrats. Any peek at history shows the system worked better before the independent counsel law was enacted.

This is because the institution is an invitation to dodge responsibility, if indeed that is not its very purpose. Along the way it manages a fatal confusion of the roles of educating the public and enforcing the law. When Democrats in Congress lost their showdown with Ollie North in public hearings, they tried to criminalize their differences via Lawrence Walsh. Because he has been outside political control, Mr. Walsh could take six years, spend $35 million and still face no discipline. The courts are even now cleaning up after his blunders, by awarding legal fees to individuals Mr. Walsh has unfairly harassed.

We now seem on course to have this law reinstated – without even, as Barney Frank hopes, a vote on whether miscreant Congressmen should face a similar institution. Then Ms. Reno can appoint a counsel and wash her hands of the matter. Democrats in Congress will also claim they've done everything they could, insulating themselves from any responsibility before the voter. A Whitewater investigator might of course turn into another Lawrence Walsh; he might even find a crime worse than accepting a security fence. He might also swallow all of the documents and silence the issue for years.

If Congress is to create some "independent" body, let it be one worthy of the task. Whitewater, after all, is merely the latest episode in the S&L disaster, the House post office, the ongoing Rostenkowski probe, the hints of political influence via BCCI (of which we may learn a great deal more through the settlement Bob Morgenthau & Co. have won from Abu Dhabi). Why not a special commission, with the power of subpoena and public hearings, to explore the corruption of the political process? Our candidate to head it would be retired Supreme Court Justice "Whizzer" White.

The point is that while laws may have indeed been broken in Whitewater, the more important point is to find out what happened. An independent counsel poring over the statute books looking for a crime that might fit the facts – this is a trap. Instead, Republicans should have the gumption to force Democratic leadership to face up to a full and public investigation. By obstructing the work of Congress if that proves necessary, a committed minority can force a Congress to do its duty.

The Democrats may object, just as Janet Reno may prove she lacks the independence to investigate her President. But the Founders provided a ready solution to such a political impasse. The solution is democracy, and as Congress very well understands, the next elections are scheduled for November.

Editorial Feature

Reno's Madison Problem—and How She Can Solve It

In recent weeks, Attorney General Janet Reno has said repeatedly that it's pointless for her to name a special counsel to investigate matters involving the failed Madison Guaranty Savings & Loan.

Because she would be the person appointing such a lawyer, she has explained, she still would be related to the investigation and it would be questioned on that account. Only an independent counsel statute,

Rule of Law

By Terry Eastland

which she has strongly supported, could eliminate this problem, she says, since under such a law a special court would select the counsel. But because there is no such law, she will keep to herself the Madison case, with lawyers at the main Justice Department—the building at 10th and Constitution in Washington—handling it and reporting to her.

Ms. Reno made basically the same argument in explaining why the probe of Commerce Secretary Ron Brown was not handed off to a special counsel but kept within main Justice. For Ms. Reno, apparently, it's either the independent counsel of the independent counsel law or main Justice with herself in charge. There is no "third way" for handling exceptional cases—those in which top executive officers are accused of criminal wrongdoing or in which an investigation of friends or relatives of top officers might result in a conflict of interest.

Ms. Reno's position on how to handle exceptional cases is eccentric, to say the least. She is the first attorney general since before Watergate to say, in effect, that exceptional cases should be handled within main Justice and no place else. More important, her position is unpersuasive. First, it's illogical to say the public should trust her to handle the case but not to make a good choice of someone to take it over. Second, it's not necessarily pointless to handle a case like the Madison probe by putting it outside main Justice.

Janet Reno

In 1979, Jimmy Carter's first attorney general, Griffin Bell, found himself in a situation similar to Ms. Reno's. Justice was investigating allegations that the president's family peanut business had received questionable loans from the National Bank of Georgia, operated by Mr. Carter's friend Bert Lance, and that some of the loan money had been illegally diverted into his 1976 presidential campaign. Mr. Bell's Justice Department decided that the newly passed independent counsel law did not reach allegations made before its enactment.

Mr. Bell did not insist on keeping the case within main Justice but named New York lawyer Paul Curran as special counsel to conduct the investigation, ultimately giving him the full powers previously granted to Archibald Cox and Leon Jaworski, the Watergate special prosecutors, both appointed by the attorney general. Lasting almost eight months and finding no grounds for prosecution, Mr. Curran's investigation was widely regarded as thorough and, in the words of the Washington Post, "entirely persuasive." Here is evidence that an outside lawyer chosen by the attorney general can do a good job of handling the exceptional case.

A Curran-style appointment is but one of several kinds of special-counsel arrangements used in the recent past that are available to Ms. Reno. Nor is a special-counsel option the only alternative she has. When the U.S. attorney in Denver recused himself in 1990 from the fraud investigation of the Silverado thrift—a case involving the president's son, Neil Bush—then-Attorney General Richard Thornburgh had the case forwarded to the U.S. attorney in Dallas, Marvin Collins, the most experienced bank fraud prosecutor available. His work on the case has been widely accepted.

By taking their respective cases outside main Justice, Mr. Bell and

Mr. Thornburgh managed to allay concerns that political appointees in Washington might somehow manipulate the investigative process.

Ms. Reno has not lacked for opportunity to put the Madison case where it probably belongs. Last October the Resolution Trust Corp., having intensified its investigation of possible bank fraud, sent an expanded referral to the Clinton-appointed U.S. attorney in Little Rock, Paula Casey. The Clintons were named in the referral—how is unclear—but Ms. Casey, a law student of Bill Clinton's at the University of Arkansas and a 1992 campaign volunteer, declined to pursue the recommended investigation. Later, she recused herself—something she should have done earlier. There was "a need to ensure that there be no misperceptions about the impartiality of the investigation," according to the department's press release.

Ms. Reno could have adhered to department policy and reassigned the case to another U.S. attorney, as Mr. Thornburgh had done in the Silverado case. Instead, she pulled the case into main Justice.

As it happens, there is a law enforcement theory under which Ms. Reno's insistence on keeping the case inside her own building might make sense. Assume that the White House spinmasters are wrong, that there are "specific, credible allegations" of wrongdoing on the part of the Clintons, and Ms. Reno knows what they are.

Given her belief that an independent counsel bill is soon to become law, it would make sense for her to treat such allegations as if the independent counsel law had already been passed. Under the law, "specific, credible allegations" trigger what is called a "preliminary investigation." Handled by the criminal division, such an inquiry may lead to a court-appointed counsel. On this theory, Ms. Reno could be running a de facto preliminary investigation in anticipation of a new law.

Again, this theory assumes a certain set of facts. As matters now stand, Ms. Reno's insistence on keeping the case within main Justice is only creating political pressure for her to dispose of it in perhaps the worst way—by handing it off to an independent counsel (once the independent counsel law is passed) on another basis.

The new law, like the previous one, will include a provision whereby the attorney general may seek a court-appointed counsel when an investigation of criminal charges could result in a personal, financial or political conflict of interest for the attorney general or other Justice officers. The independent counsel law has not before been used in cases of conflicts involving the president, and were Ms. Reno to employ it here, she would create a precedent that in similar circumstances could lead to the appointment of other independent counsels, for this president and future ones.

This would certainly be one way for Ms. Reno to get rid of her Madison problem. But it would not be required by the law, and it would hardly serve the best interests of the presidency or the country.

Mr. Eastland is editor of Forbes MediaCritic and a fellow at the Ethics and Public Policy Center in Washington.

REVIEW & OUTLOOK

The Foster Test

In an independent investigation of the Whitewater mess, the purpose has to be reassurance that no major scandal lies hidden. Auditing financial deals from 1985 will not be enough. The test of a serious probe will be: Does it illuminate events surrounding Vincent Foster's death last July 20?

We suggested this same investigation immediately after the apparent suicide of the Deputy White House Counsel and Clinton friend, of course, and were castigated for cruelty toward the deceased and the presidency. Even last week, White House stonewaller Paul Begala complained about trying "to politicize the tragic death of a talented public servant." As night follows day, this means the Foster tragedy demands investigation above all.

ON ETHICS

Revelations about the handling of Mr. Foster's office papers, remember, is what brought Whitewater to a boil. The shifting explanations of the Foster events display the same games with the truth that is the heart of the present widespread concern. Until the Foster death is seriously studied, a Banquo's ghost will stalk not only the independent investigation but the next three years of the Clinton Administration.

* * *

By now, of course, we know that Mr. Foster was working on Whitewater shortly before his death. He had served as the Clintons' lawyer when, in December 1992, they severed their ties with Whitewater Development Co. by selling their interest to James McDougal for $1,000. Mr. Foster also directed the preparation of delinquent tax returns for Whitewater itself, which he delivered to Mr. McDougal's lawyer last June 21.

This was part of Mr. Foster's more general work on the Clinton finances. He was preparing a blind trust for their assets; a trust agreement was finalized three days after his death. Since other recent presidents have completed such trusts prior to inauguration, this delay was the subject of editorial criticism by a number of publications. The Des Moines Register, for example, wrote that Mrs. Clinton's health-care stocks should have been put in trust; Dennis Ryerson, editor of the Register's editorial pages, tells us he received a polite phone call from Mr. Foster elaborating reasons for delay.

It's doubtful that the Foster files will be a Rosetta stone for Whitewater, if only because many essential files were known to be missing as early as the first stories by Jeff Gerth of the New York Times during the 1992 campaign. Mr. McDougal says, and the Clintons deny, that the missing files were delivered to the Arkansas Governor's mansion. Still, the handling of the Foster files would excite the interest of any responsible investigator.

The White House says that, after a July 22 review by White House Counsel Bernard Nussbaum, files on the first couple were sent to their private lawyer, Foster's personal papers to his family's lawyer, and items pertaining to his official duties were shown to investigators probing his death.

But it's been widely reported, most recently in yesterday's New York Times, that the Whitewater papers were removed on July 20, not July 22. Robert Langston, chief of the Park Police investigating the death, was quoted to this effect as early as August 10. His press spokesman told the Times that either Mr. Nussbaum or an assistant had removed a carton of files and later returned it; "I don't have any idea whether they were all brought back or not. I could only trust that they were, but I would never bet money on it or say for sure."

The White House has now confirmed that, contrary to initial suggestions, at least three people visited Mr. Foster's office within hours of his death: Mr. Nussbaum, Maggie Williams and Patsy Thomasson. Ms. Williams is chief of staff to Mrs. Clinton, who was at the time in Little Rock, and Miss Thomasson is a special assistant to the president. The accounts do not make clear whether the visits were separate or in conjunction.

The Washington Times has detailed the backgrounds of the two additional aides. Ms. Williams had been communications director at the Children's Defense Fund and press deputy at the Democratic National Committee. Miss Thomasson, a longtime Arkansas political figure, was once executive vice president at Lasater & Co., which earned some $1.6 million in commissions for handling Arkansas state bond issues. The state contracts were awarded while Dan R. Lasater, head of the firm and a heavy financial contributor to Clinton campaigns, was under investigation for cocaine distribution. He was convicted and sentenced to 30 months in prison in 1986; an unindicted co-conspirator was Roger Clinton, the president's brother and a Lasater employee, who pleaded guilty in an earlier cocaine case. Miss Thomasson wasn't implicated in the drug cases, and Governor Clinton named her to the politically powerful post of chairman of the Arkansas Highway Commission.

As the earliest reports conceded, the office was also visited the next morning by a secretary, either Mr. Foster's or Mr. Nussbaum's. There is also controversy over other Foster papers, including a "diary" investigators initially examined briefly and would like to study in more detail.

* * *

Mr. Foster's death and accompanying events came at a curious juncture in the Clinton Administration. The Zoe Baird and Kimba Wood nominations had collapsed. David Gergen had joined the administration on May 29. Mr. Foster was involved in litigation over the secrecy of the First Lady's health task force. The White House report on the travel office fiasco was issued July 2, in the holiday lull, but Congressman Jack Brooks suggested an investigation. Mr. Foster sought a personal lawyer, and a lengthy New York Times report said he told his wife they might be better off in Little Rock.

On his way back from a vacation in Hawaii, President Clinton spent the July 17-18 weekend in Little Rock. His itinerary there, so curious it was recorded in a page-one story in the New York Times on Monday, July 19, included a four-hour dinner with David Edwards, a friend from his time in England and now a Little Rock investment adviser. Mr. Edwards is known for his gourmet cooking and Arab connections, having been instrumental in a $23 million contribution from the king of

Saudi Arabia to establish a Middle Eastern studies program at the University of Arkansas. Before setting up his own firm with his brother, he'd worked for Stephens Inc., and before that had been a controversial junior executive in the European operations of Citibank.

That Monday the President spoke to Mr. Foster for 20 minutes; the White House says the Deputy Counsel declined the President's invitation to a movie in the family quarters. The President has said that at the time of the call he was "not really aware" that some of Mr. Foster's associates had come to consider him "quite distressed."

Mr. Foster had spent the weekend at the Maryland shore with his wife. For most of Saturday and Sunday they joined with two other couples, Associate Attorney General and former Rose partner Webster Hubbell and former Deputy White House Counsel Michael Cardozo and their wives. Mr. Hubbell joined the gathering after a Saturday morning meeting to fire William Sessions as director of the FBI.

Hillary Clinton and Chelsea had remained behind in Hawaii and California, but stopped to visit Little Rock on their way back. Mrs. Clinton's plane landed on July 20 at 7:30 p.m. Central time, or shortly after Mr. Foster's body was discovered at Fort Marcy. The visit was something of a surprise; the Arkansas Democrat-Gazette attributed its story to the charter service at the local airport. She learned of the death at 9:45 Eastern time in a phone call from White House Chief of Staff "Mack" McLarty, who had been notified at 9:15 and told the President when he finished the Larry King show at 10.

* * *

On Tuesday, the day of Mr. Foster's death, the White House announced the appointment of Louis Freeh as FBI director. The same day back in Little Rock, the Chicago Tribune reported, a federal magistrate issued a search warrant for the offices of David Hale, who later tried to plea bargain by implicating the President in a suspect loan, thus reopening the Whitewater issue. Denver lawyer James Lyons, whose report put the issue to rest during the campaign, told the Tribune he'd talked several times to Mr. Foster shortly before his death, but denied it was about Whitewater. The Washington Times has reported that Mr. Foster's phone logs on the morning of his death include calls from Mr. Lyons and from someone at the Rose Law Firm in Little Rock.

On July 26, nearly a week after the death, a member of the counsel's office found torn-up scraps, apparently overlooked in an earlier search, at the bottom of Mr. Foster's briefcase. They are pieced together into a note listing a series of things troubling Mr. Foster. Only one smudged palm-print was found on the paper, and it was held 30 hours by the White House before official investigators were notified. The note complained that "WSJ editors lie without consequence" and specified controversies such as expenses for redecorating the White House, but contained no allusion to Whitewater.

* * *

Let us specify, lest compiling these facts gets us accused of the dread crime of innuendo, that we do not know what to make of all this. But we do think it's high time someone found out. We also think that back on July 21, when President Clinton said, "We'll just have to live with something else we can't understand," he already knew a great deal that you probably have just learned.

REVIEW & OUTLOOK

Fountain of Trust?

One of the most dramatic themes of our era is a world-wide confrontation with corruption. Governments have fallen in the midst of money scandals in Italy, Japan and France. BCCI represents the biggest bank robbery in history, victimizing Pakistani immigrants in London and equally innocent central banks. In South America, governments are consumed in pitched wars with gangs of drug lords.

This global background should be kept in mind in appointing — or assessing — a special prosecutor to investigate the President of the United States. For our own part, as we've said  before, the Whitewater issue ought to be the subject of a Congressional investigation rather than a criminal inquiry. A special prosecutor will have irreconcilable mandates; if he sticks too strictly to the law the public will remain unsatisfied and skeptical; but if he exposes everything of legitimate public concern he will look abusive by normal prosecutorial standards. Only a public airing, the purview of Congress, can settle the ultimate issue, which is whether Bill Clinton has breached his claim to our trust.

By the same token, if some lonely Diogenes does undertake this search, there is no telling where it may lead. Even if Bill and Hillary Clinton are eventually seen as somehow culpable in Whitewater, of course, it was penny-ante on the scale of global scams. Still, Mr. Clinton does hold the most powerful and most complicated office on the globe. He comes from a state, it becomes increasingly evident, not well attuned to contemporary standards of conflicts of interest. And at the same time, the tentacles of global corruption seem to reach nearly everywhere.

We may yet get a dramatic lesson on this latter point from the remarkable settlement just reached in the BCCI case. The sheik of Abu Dhabi has finally agreed to extradite the former BCCI chief executive, Swaleh Naqvi, and to give U.S. investigators access to BCCI records spirited out of London to the gulf emirate. The settlement represents a singular achievement for New York District Attorney Robert Morgenthau and Harry Albright, the court-appointed trustee who took over Washington's First American Bank when it was severed from BCCI ownership. They were once told by eminences of the establishment that further Abu Dhabi investment was the only recourse for First American. And after the acquittal of Clark Clifford acolyte Robert Altman, that the whole BCCI matter should be dropped.

Yet the investigations are already rolling forward with the new records, which can be cross-checked against newly uncovered records in Luxembourg. Mr. Altman's acquittal leaves us without an answer to the question of how a clan of crooks came to own the biggest bank in Washington. The hot-button question in the search of the newly available records will be whether American regulators or politicians got payoffs.

It's a long way from the Persian Gulf to the Ozarks, of course, but then, on their way to buying First American the BCCI surrogates found their way to Little Rock, where Stephens Inc. handled their brokerage. Worthen Bank, controlled by the Stephens family, also was the most important source of loans for the Clinton campaign, and also held a lien on James McDougal's interest in Madison Guaranty Savings & Loan.

Oh, by the way, the BCCI case is also related to the BNL case, a major embarrassment for the Republican Justice Department. In that case, remember, the Atlanta branch of Italy's Banca Nazionale del Lavoro made loans, backed by the U.S. Department of Agriculture, that funded Iraq's war machine. BCCI lent a friendly hand with overnight deposits. When the judge wanted to know why the branch manager was prosecuted without much study of whether anyone back in Rome knew, the Bush Justice Department chartered its own special investigator. Judge Frederick Lacey concluded that BCCI was involved, but only through the local manager. But this has not stilled suspicion, especially since it seems implausible that the bank headquarters wouldn't find out what was happening with more than $2 billion in loans.

So, where will Floridian Janet Reno now look for her fountain of trust? The Attorney General must find someone prominent enough to command immediate respect, and Clark Clifford is no longer available. She has to look for someone who has no Democratic Party conflicts of interest, but no Republican Party ones either. She has to look for someone untainted by the least connection with any of the scandals around the globe, the full extent of which are still under investigation. And the duty of this Diogenes will be either (1) to impugn the President, or (2) tell the people: take my word and stop asking questions.

Somehow it seems to us that an open Congressional probe, for all its predictable imbecilities, is a more viable alternative.

Letters to the Editor

Worthen Disputes Implied Linkages

Your Jan. 18 lead editorial "Fountain of Trust?" states that Worthen is controlled by the Stephens family. This statement is false. Several Stephens family members and trusts, if aggregated, currently own approximately 26% of the outstanding shares. However, they do not control the management policies, lending or operations of Worthen. No Stephens family members or nominees sit on Worthen's board of directors or hold any officer position with Worthen. All directors of Worthen are elected by the stockholders at large and represent all stockholders. Fourteen of Worthen's 15 directors are outside, independent directors; only one Worthen director also serves as an officer of Worthen. This group of distinguished and accomplished individuals repudiates the suggestion that any attempt has been made by any Stephens family member to inappropriately influence the activities of Worthen.

In the same sentence in which your editorial inaccurately attributes control of Worthen to the Stephens family, you also state that Worthen made loans to President Clinton's campaign committee and held a lien on James McDougal's Madison Guaranty stock, in a thinly veiled attempt to imply that the two loan transactions were related to each other. In fact, these loan transactions are not related to each other and are separated in time by a period of 10 years.

Furthermore, the loan to Mr. McDougal and the attendant taking of the lien was initiated in 1982, prior to the time that any Stephens family member owned any shares in Worthen. Additionally, no current member of Worthen's executive management team was in executive management of Worthen when that loan was approved or made. For the sake of perspective, the outstanding balance of Mr. McDougal's loan never exceeded $250,000. The value of Worthen's lien on the Madison Guaranty stock was irretrievably destroyed in 1987 when Madison Guaranty was taken over by the regulators.

The loan extended to President Clinton's campaign committee was originated long after Madison Guaranty had ceased to exist. The campaign loan was approved and made by current management on a sound banking basis, secured by campaign matching funds payable by the U.S. Treasury and was paid in full as agreed, in July of 1992. The interest rate charged to the campaign committee was the maximum rate allowed by Arkansas law. Ten years elapsed between the making of these two loans. Contrary to the intended implications of your editorial, absolutely no relationship exists between the loan to President Clinton's campaign committee and the loan to Mr. McDougal — or for that matter, between either of those loans and the Stephens family's ownership interest in Worthen.

We disagree with the thought that such inaccuracies, innuendoes and phantom linkages can continue to be made without consequence. Future publications that assert or imply the existence between Worthen and Stephens family members of relationships that do not in fact exist or that suggest a linkage between the 1992 loan to the Clinton campaign committee and a 1982 loan to Mr. McDougal will be viewed as attempts to intentionally mislead the public and damage the reputation of Worthen.

WILLIAM B. KEISLER
General Counsel
Worthen Banking Corp.

Little Rock, Ark.

Letters to the Editor

Stephens Responds to Editorial

Editor's note: This letter is reprinted here as the author sent it to the Wall Street Journal. The Journal printed a condensed version.

How speculative does something have to be before you fail to mention it in your editorials? The latest attempt to somehow link BCCI, Whitewater, and James McDougal to Stephens is absurd. Since no one has bothered to ask, I thought I would give you the time frame in which these events occurred.

The stock purchases in First American Bank, by what we (and everyone else) thought were four individuals acting on their own behalf, occurred in 1977. That was the last we heard from them. Apparently, in 1982 and 1983 Worthen Bank loaned James McDougal a total of $250,000 to first buy into and then acquire control in Madison Guaranty. These loans occurred BEFORE our investment in Worthen in November of 1983. I am informed Worthen subsequently charged off $100,000 of these loans in 1987, closing its books on the subject. The Worthen loan to the Clinton campaign, which as I have explained before, was secured by receivables from the Federal Election Commission, was made in 1992. We first learned of this loan from local newspaper accounts.

How you can possibly suggest there is a connection between these totally unrelated events is beyond me. Linking them together in one paragraph (as you have now done twice) is truly a modern journalistic feat. You are deliberately compressing this time line to suit your views. We expected that you would try, but we never dreamed you would ignore the total time frame and the elapsed time between these events. Your deliberate creation of the false impression that these events overlap, and are connected, just continues the malicious pattern of The Wall Street Journal toward our firm and family.

We would appreciate your setting the record straight. Given your pattern, I expect this should be done by publishing this letter.

WARREN A. STEPHENS
President
Stephens Inc.

Little Rock, Ark.

A Prosecutor

On January 20, 1994, amid mounting political pressure, Attorney General Janet Reno appointed Robert Fiske as special counsel to investigate Whitewater. Mr. Fiske was a Manhattan lawyer of good reputation, but the editorial pages of the Journal were disturbed by his representation of BCCI figure Clark Clifford. Many were skeptical of such suspicions; Warren Stephens of Stephens, Inc. described them as "malicious." But the Journal felt suspicion was justified pending a full explanation of the BCCI affair.

As Mr. Fiske began to put together an investigative team, Dow Jones & Co., the publisher of The Wall Street Journal, and Journal editor Robert L. Bartley filed a lawsuit over a Freedom of Information request for the U.S. Park Police and FBI reports on the Foster death. Release of these reports had been promised at a Justice Department press conference and repeatedly delayed. The Journal was drawn into a Freedom of Information battle with the Justice Department over U.S. Park Police and FBI reports on Vincent Foster's death.

Whitewater had begun to spin into a bewildering array of facts, allegations and rumors. But by mid-February, The Wall Street Journal and other publications were turning to what appeared to be a new level of the affair, one that had little to do with a long ago land deal—a pattern of interference with key government and regulatory agencies.

REVIEW & OUTLOOK

Too Much Baggage

So the gang that gave us Defense Secretary Inman now offers us, as special counsel to investigate possible impropriety by the President, Clark Clifford's lawyer.

Do not misunderstand (though we suppose that asks too much); this is not intended as a personal attack on Robert Fiske Jr. Lawyers are entitled to have clients, and in the legal maneuvering Mr. Clifford switched to another lawyer. Unquestionably, Mr. Fiske carries a reputation as an upstanding member of the New York bar. On the basis of what we know about him, for most posts he would be an outstanding choice.

Indeed, we ourselves strongly supported his nomination as Deputy Attorney General when he was attacked by 14 U.S. Senators. The Senate's conservative faction sent a letter to President

Robert Fiske

Bush opposing Mr. Fiske on the grounds that he had been chairman of the American Bar Association judicial selection committee. While we agreed with their criticism of the increasingly politicized committee, we observed that within the committee Mr. Fiske had been a force for the good. And on the basis of his own tenure as U.S. Attorney in Manhattan, that he would be a salutary restraining hand on federal prosecutors on issues such as the application of RICO, the racketeering statute being applied to financial institutions. ("Why

Justice Needs Fiske," June 22, 1989.) We failed to persuade the Senators, and Mr. Fiske eventually withdrew.

Mr. Fiske's new appointment, however, is far from an ordinary post, as we elaborated earlier in the week ("Fountain of Trust?" January 18). The whole idea is to find someone whose word most Americans would be inclined to take on trust, which surely means someone not in the least connected to the scandals circling the globe. There are even certain speculative but still possible connections between Whitewater and the BCCI scandal. Little Rock's Stephens financial empire helped bankroll Bill Clinton's presidential campaign, and also held a lien on James McDougal's interest in Madison Guaranty Savings & Loan. Another part of the same empire handled the brokerage when BCCI surrogates bought Washington's First American Bank — and installed Mr. Clifford as its head.

Now of course, Mr. Clifford escaped trial in New York on health grounds, perhaps a testimony to Mr. Fiske's efforts on his behalf. And his acolyte Robert Altman was acquitted of misleading regulators, leaving the intriguing question of how it was BCCI came to own the biggest bank in Washington. But investigators now have access to a passel of BCCI documents not available during this trial. In any event, knowingly or not, Mr. Clifford and Mr. Altman indisputably worked for BCCI.

Given the extreme sensitivity of the special counsel post, surely it would have been possible to find someone other than a prominent member of Mr. Clifford's defense team. Yes, Mr. Fiske is widely seen as upstanding; his list of character witnesses would be almost as long as his client's. But such a list is cool comfort to the growing number of Americans who think that something is wrong in high places.

Why, for that matter, select someone who'd attracted the written opposition of 14 Senators? If the object is to build trust in the investigation, why then pick someone with prepackaged enemies?

In all, a very curious selection. Why did Janet Reno make this choice, if she did? Why did Davis, Polk & Wardwell consent to have an active partner in this role, and what does its client list look like? (Lawrence Walsh had retired from Davis, Polk before mounting his crusade.) And since Mr. Fiske must know what baggage he rightly or wrongly carries, why would someone of his integrity accept the appointment?

The ultimate point of these questions, we suppose, is that the very notion of special prosecutors asks too much. Mr. Fiske promises that at the end of his investigation he will issue a public report. Why, is that what he did as a U.S. Attorney? No, either he indicted and put the decision before a judge and jury, or he shut up; that is the way the criminal process is supposed to work. We clearly do need a public report, but that is the purview of an investigation by the legislative branch, which operates by give and take in the light of day. We wish Mr. Fiske the best of luck with his investigation, but his curriculum vitae makes a Congressional probe of Whitewater all the more necessary.

Has this Republic really reached the point that a Democratic Congress cannot be expected to openly investigate suspicions involving a Democratic President? Have we reached the point where it is unreasonable even to ask? For one guess, not necessarily; but if we have, what we need is a new Congress.

News Story

Dow Jones, Editor
Seek to Get Reports
On Foster's Death

By JOE DAVIDSON

Staff Reporter of THE WALL STREET JOURNAL

Dow Jones & Co., publisher of The Wall Street Journal, and Robert Bartley, editor of the newspaper, asked a federal court to force the release of reports on White House lawyer Vincent Foster's death.

In a lawsuit against the Justice Department filed Friday in U.S. District Court in New York, Dow Jones and Mr. Bartley, who oversees the editorial and related pages, said the agency has "constructively and improperly denied" their Freedom of Information Act request for the documents.

Mr. Foster was deputy White House counsel when he apparently shot himself in a park outside Washington on July 20. The U.S. Park Police ruled it a suicide. Using the FOIA, Mr. Bartley on Aug. 18 requested reports prepared by the police and the Federal Bureau of Investigation.

The reports are "records of substantial public interest and should be available to the press and public for review and discussion," the suit contends.

Last week, the New York Post reported that emergency personnel responding to Mr. Foster's death said the way they found him — how he was lying, the location of the gun and the amount of blood — wasn't necessarily consistent with suicide.

Federal officials said the death was probed by the police, and a torn-up note, apparently written by Mr. Foster and found in his briefcase, was investigated by the FBI. That note, which showed Mr. Foster upset by a variety of things, included the sentence "The WSJ editors lie without consequence." The Journal had run several editorials criticizing Mr. Foster's role in the White House.

Since his death, White House officials have revealed that his office contained papers concerning the Whitewater Development Corp. investment by Bill and Hillary Rodham Clinton. Those papers have been subpoenaed by the Justice Department, and matters relating to the investment are being investigated by an independent counsel appointed by the attorney general.

Justice Department spokesman Carl Stern said the agency is "doing the best we can" to comply with FOIA requests. "Some of the material was close to being released," Mr. Stern said, "but the appointment of an independent counsel required us to ascertain from him whether the material might be evidence in his investigation and whether its release would interfere with his work."

REVIEW & OUTLOOK

Release the Foster Report

An excerpt from the Aug. 10 press conference at the Justice Department discussing the Park Service Police report on the death of Deputy White House Counsel Vincent Foster. Carl Stern is the department's Director of Public Affairs; FOIA refers to the Freedom of Information Act.

. . . .

Mr. Stern: Thank you. Thanks a lot.

Q: Wait a minute, sir!

Q: From which office are we getting the report?

Mr. Stern: The report —

Q: When is it being released?

Mr. Stern: As soon as the FOIA section processes the report, it'll be available to you. That has already started before this meeting even took place.

Q: Do you have to file a request or is it going to be released to everybody at once?

Mr. Stern: The normal practice of the FOIA section is to call the people who have requested it and let them know that it's available and to ask them whether they would like it mailed or would they like to pick it up. (Laughter.)

Q: Who do we tell?

Mr. Stern: If you'll send an FOIA to Philip Heymann, the deputy attorney general, or to me, we'll make sure that it gets up to that section.

Q: The question is to both of these gentlemen here. You say this man was in great depression and he'd been dissatisfied with the government. Therefore we certainly need to know what departments and what agencies of government he talked with recently, and that would be in the telephone log, and you're not going to make that public?

Mr. Stern: Sarah, if you put in a Freedom of Information Act request, we'll make sure that it's handled.

Q: (Off mike) — Freedom of Information Act — (off mike). I want to know what

Mr. Stern: Sarah, I don't think we have that available at this — at this point.

Q: Well, why don't you?

Mr. Stern: You want some special servicing? Is that it? You're not content to wait and do it the normal way, through a Freedom of Information Act request?

Q: No. Hell, no I'm not

Mr. Stern: Okay

Q: — going to wait on that.

Mr. Stern: Thank you very much.

Upon reading this exchange, we did what we thought we were being asked to do, submit a FOI request to Mr. Heymann. We received a letter dated Aug. 25 from Charlene Wright, Deputy Chief of the Initial Request Union of the Office of Information and Privacy at the Justice Department, acknowledging receipt of our letter on Aug. 18 and explaining:

This Office has a backlog of initial requests, as well as limited personnel resources. As you may be aware, documents responsive to your request will require consultations with other Department of Justice components and agencies. Accordingly, I must inform you that we will be unable to comply with the statutory time requirement for processing of this request on behalf of the Office of the Deputy Attorney General.

In October, we visited Mr. Stern's office to take up the invitation, also issued at the Aug. 10 press conference, to view an actual copy of the note discovered at the bottom of Mr. Foster's briefcase. The text had been released but copies had been withheld "to respect the family's wishes." To the untrained eye, the handwriting on the note corresponded well enough with a sample of Mr. Foster's writing we had independently obtained. At that time Mr. Stern predicted the FOI request would be honored within the month.

It is now the last day of January. An independent counsel has specified that Mr. Foster's apparent suicide must be part of his inquiry into the activities surrounding Whitewater Development Corp. Yet the report the FOIA section started work on prior to the Aug. 10 press conference has not yet been released.

What's more, the New York Post enterprised its own report, based for example on interviews with George Gonzalez, a Fairfax County paramedic who says he was the first rescue worker to view the body; Kory Ashford, a technician who helped put the body into a body bag; and Park Policeman Kevin Fornshill, the first police officer at the scene. According to the Post, they found the body in a neat condition, still clutching the revolver with arms peacefully at its side, and with only slight traces of blood. Homicide detectives interviewed by the Post uniformly said that when someone puts a revolver in his mouth and pulls the trigger, the result is "a mess."

The Post reports of last Thursday and Friday, which also detail apparent discrepancies over ballistic testing of the revolver, are either wrong or right. If they are wrong, it's a great pity the complete Park Service Police report has not been released to still such speculation. If they are right, the Justice Department and the Park Service Police have had a great deal to hide. Either alternative suggests that the report should be released forthwith.

Accordingly, we filed suit in Federal District Court in Manhattan Friday in an attempt to get the government to comply with the requirements of the Freedom of Information Act. We have also sent Mr. Heymann an additional FOI request for an actual copy of the Foster note; given what we now know about previously secret visits to his office the night of his death and the removal of papers, it's time the handwriting were studied by more than an untrained eye.

Strange things are happening at the Justice Department. Mr. Heymann has just announced his resignation. On the same day, Janet Reno's personal aide Lula Rodriguez departed amid an investigation of abuse of absentee ballots in a relative's Florida election campaign. Associate Attorney General Webster Hubbell has had to recuse himself from Whitewater, the department's most serious and sensitive business. The Park Police are now telling the Post that if it wants further information on Mr. Foster it should use the FOI process. The White House is refusing to comment on the Post stories on the grounds that the special counsel, Robert Fiske, "has now included that in the scope of his investigation."

While of course we have not polled all major news organizations, those our counsel has queried report that they did not go through the FOI formalities on the Park Service Police report, relying instead on private assurances it would routinely be released. We might suggest, however, that they take some note of our lawsuit. With all the backing and filling, we are starting to smell the issue of whether FOIA, and for that matter special counsels, can be invoked as part of a coverup.

Editorial Feature

A Question of Independence

*The following is excerpted from an exchange Tuesday at the Senate
Banking Committee confirmation hearings of the nominee to chair the
Federal Deposit Insurance Corp., Ricki Tigert:*

Sen. Lauch Faircloth (R., N.C.): I had the opportunity last week
to visit with Ms. Tigert very briefly, but there are a lot of issues that
are going to be confronting the FDIC in the next few years. But since
there have been no hearings on the Whitewater fiasco, I wanted to
talk to Miss Tigert today about Madison Guaranty Savings & Loan.
And unless and until Congress holds hearings, forums such as this
are about the only opportunity we have to ask the questions the
American people want answered.

If you would tend to as short an answer as possible, Ms. Tigert, I
would appreciate it.

Ricki Tigert: Of course, Senator.

Faircloth: In looking at the news stories published, I see you are a
personal friend – and I did not know this in the meeting the other day
– of President and Mrs. Clinton. I see in Time magazine (Jan. 17 edition) one of Mrs. Clinton's statements was that her favorite activity
at Renaissance weekend was "hanging out with Ricki Tigert." That
was her favorite activity. Is it accurate to say that you are a personal friend of both Mrs. Clinton and President Clinton?

Tigert: I've known the president and Mrs. Clinton for eight years,
and I respect and admire both of them, Senator.

Faircloth: Did you know Associate Attorney General Webster

Hubbell?

Tigert: I've never met Mr. Hubbell.

Faircloth: Did you ever meet Vince Foster?

Tigert: I've never met, I did not meet, Mr. Foster.

Faircloth: Were these both not attendants at Renaissance weekend?

Tigert: To my knowledge, they never attended.

Faircloth: The FDIC has an ongoing investigation into the millions of dollars that Madison Guaranty lost that the taxpayers picked up. Very briefly, what is the status of the investigation, and what have you learned about the involvement of Webster Hubbell and the Rose law firm.

Tigert: Senator, I know nothing about this matter other than what I've read in the newspaper. I consider myself to be a private citizen until and if I am confirmed by the U.S. Senate. . . .

Faircloth: If you are confirmed, you are going to be head of what is supposed to be an independent agency. You are also a very close friend of the Clintons and many others who are implicated in the Whitewater scandal. Now every other friend of the Clintons that has been appointed to government has been discouraging congressional investigations into the Whitewater and Madison Savings & Loan scandals.

Ms. Reno was here Nov. 7 and I asked her very straightforward to appoint an independent investigator to take a look at it. She was quite adamant in her statement that she was handling it, she would decide when to appoint an investigator, and that the buck stopped with her.

I was really impressed by what she had to say, but I find out three months, or two and a half months, later that she decides that she needs to appoint an investigator when the "investigatees" (i.e., President Clinton and Ms. Clinton) say it is fine to appoint somebody to investigate us. She never moved until the president said, "Yes, it looks like now we better appoint an investigator." And up she comes with an investigator.

Is that the kind of independence we can expect from you, or will there be another kind?

Tigert: Senator, I've spent most of my career in public service in nonpolitical jobs. I spent seven of those years at the Federal Reserve. I know what independence is. I've served at an independent agency. I believe in the credibility of the regulatory process, and I think it is essential that the FDIC continue its strong history of independence and if I'm confirmed by the Senate, I can assure you that the FDIC will be independent.

Faircloth: Well, doesn't it present an almost impossible situation when this very, very close friendship with Mrs. Clinton (she says she enjoys "hanging out" with you) — doesn't that present almost an impossible situation that here you are investigating and in charge of any possible criminal violations, and certainly extreme embarrassment, of your favorite "hanging out friend"? And she being the First Lady, that would present a problem to me.

Tigert: Senator, with respect to any issue that comes before the FDIC during my tenure, if I am confirmed by the U.S. Senate, I will be extremely sensitive to issues of potential conflicts of interest or any appearance of conflict of interest. As I've indicated, I know nothing about this matter other than reading a few newspaper articles, but I am absolutely committed to assuring the credibility of every regulatory undertaking of the FDIC.

Should an occasion arise with respect to any issue where the issue of an appearance of conflict of interest could come up, I will consult with the ethics officials of the FDIC and with the Office of Government Ethics, and take the appropriate steps.

Faircloth: Well don't we almost go in with an inevitable conflict, when your closest personal friend — you are responsible for investigating! Wouldn't you almost have to withdraw before you . . .

Sen. Alfonse D'Amato (R., N.Y.): Would the senator yield for a point on that?

Faircloth: I will.

D'Amato: Miss Tigert, let me ask you this: If indeed you found yourself in a situation where you are confirmed, and you have an ongoing investigation and it might possibly involve the president or Mrs. Clinton, would you recuse yourself?

Tigert: As I've indicated, Senator, with respect to any matter where there is an appearance of conflict of interest, after consultation with the appropriate ethics officials, I will take the necessary steps to assure the credibility of the regulatory and enforcement process.

D'Amato: I think what Sen. Faircloth is really coming to is that it would be, and would appear to be, extremely difficult — if not impossible — as it relates to any actions that the FDIC might have to take or decide to take one way or the other, that you would be in a position, in a just absolutely untenable position, if you were a person who had to make that decision. I believe that what we are getting to is,

How would you handle that? Would you recuse yourself? And I don't think you'd have to look to ethics people, I think anybody might tell you that — you might want some time to think about this — but it would seem that a recusal would be most obvious in this kind of situation. In anything, in any dealings with Whitewater, or with the possible review, or with bringing any actions as it relates to Madison, etc., you would be in this position — and anyone else in your position would do the same. Good faith would probably require you to recuse yourself. I couldn't see how you could get around this.

I do not mean to be argumentative, or to put you on the spot. I'm trying to help you out.

Tigert: I appreciate that, Sen. D'Amato.

Faircloth: From what Mrs. Clinton has said, and from what you said, you are talking about avoiding a conflict, and if I have any sensitivity as to where we are headed, it is as straight into one as you can go! Because from everything we have read — and I certainly have no knowledge other than what I have read in every publication out — that there is an investigation of Whitewater, Rose law firm, Madison Savings & Loan. Many aspects of it involve Mrs. Clinton and President Clinton.

Now the FDIC is in the middle of the investigation, and the investigation involves your two closest personal friends. What are you going to ask somebody — the ethics committee — what are you going to ask them? Are they really your close, personal friends? I don't even see . . . it seems inevitable. . . .

D'Amato: I don't think it's above question, and I think what we're attempting to get from you — straight up or down — will you recuse yourself in any matter as it relates to Madison and Whitewater?

Sen. Donald Riegle (D., Mich.): . . . As I hear your answer, what you've said is that you don't know anything beyond what you've seen in the newspapers; you're about to assume this job, if confirmed, and that if you find that in the course of the way that issue is being handled within the FDIC — or for that matter anything else — but specifically on this one, if you find anything that suggests to you any conflict or appearance of conflict, you'll act on that. You'll talk to the ethics officials and you'll take whatever steps are appropriate.

Editorial Feature

Bank Job: Nobody Here But Us Friends

Say what you will about President and Mrs. Clinton, they don't lack for brass. The couple who appointed a protegee and friend to supervise Madison Guaranty S&L in Little Rock now want a chum of the First Lady to regulate American banks. Does anyone else find this odd?

In Arkansas, Beverly Bassett Schaffer was the Clinton appointee who gave Madison a regulatory pass, informing Mrs. Clinton with a "Dear Hillary" letter. In Washington, Ricki Tigert is Mr. Clinton's nominee to lead the Federal Deposit Insurance Corp. Time magazine has reported that "Hillary's favorite activity" at Renaissance Weekend each year is "hanging out with friends, including FDIC nominee Ricki Tigert."

Potomac Watch

By Paul A. Gigot

Every president appoints pals, but this nomination is notable because it fits a pattern of Clinton regulatory cronyism that produced Whitewater-Madison in Arkansas and is now migrating to the Beltway. Combine this pattern with the Clinton Treasury's remarkable proposal to unite all U.S. bank regulation under one agency, thus grabbing power from the independent Federal Reserve, and at least some questions deserve to be asked. For starters, what's going on here?

Perhaps Ms. Tigert will turn out to be a tiger of independence. But the Beltway attorney sounded more like a White Housecat at her Senate confirmation hearings on Tuesday. North Carolina's Lauch Faircloth and New York's Al D'Amato gave her several chances to say she'd recuse herself from any matter involving the Clintons. Ms. Tigert refused to recuse, offering lawyer-like evasions. And she wasn't even asked tough questions, such as what role she played in monitoring BCCI during her seven years as a Federal Reserve lawyer. Ms. Tigert was "associate general counsel" when that corrupt banking empire infiltrated the U.S. financial system.

Moreover, Ms. Tigert was slavish in endorsing the Clinton administration's bank regulatory heist. This is the proposal to consolidate all regulatory powers into one new agency, ostensibly "independent" but in practice beholden to Treasury. The new banking czar would in effect be another Clinton pal from their Oxford and Yale days, Eugene Ludwig, the current comptroller of the currency. This power grab is being sold as more "reinventing government," and some streamlining is desirable. But maybe politics also explains a lot.

One big supporter is Senate Banking Chairman Don Riegle, who perfected the link between politics and regulation with his exertions for Charlie Keating. Mr. Riegle, who doesn't dare stand for re-election this year, wants to go down in history for something more than being Charlie's angel.

Two former Riegle aides are now pushing "consolidation" from key positions at Treasury and the comptroller's office. The Treasury aide, Richard Carnell, actually wrote much of the burdensome financial regulation of recent years. So now he is flacking a proposal that would in effect give him more power, all in the name of easing the overregulation he helped create! He's not short of brass either.

Having a single, all-powerful regulator would also enhance the, well, opportunities for political mediation. Last week Mr. Carnell exulted in public that "the proposal will give consumer interests something they have never had before: a federal regulator that takes them seriously." Parse that sentence: By "consumer interests" he means not Joe Depositor but interest groups and Nader-type lobbies trying to allocate bank lending via politics.

Fear of such power is one reason bankers are resisting all of this, or at least most of them are. One laggard so far is the American Bankers Association (ABA), a fact that has raised eyebrows because of the presence of Curt Bradbury on the 23-member ABA board. Mr. Bradbury is the CEO of Arkansas's Worthen Banking Corp., which lent Mr. Clinton's campaign cash at a time of need in 1992. Worthen has been in a spat with the Fed, which has been tougher on Worthen than the comptroller and would lose clout under the Clinton proposal. Donald Ogilvie, the ABA's man in Washington, says Mr. Bradbury hasn't dictated ABA policy, which he expects will be decided next week. If the ABA blinks, eyebrows will stay raised.

The biggest political play here, however, is the slap at the Fed, one Beltway institution the Clinton team doesn't yet dominate. Fed Chairman Alan Greenspan and his colleagues are fighting the Riegle-Clinton power grab, and in unusually blunt terms. This, along with banker resistance, means Congress probably won't go along.

Unless, that is, Mr. Clinton can change the Fed. At least that's the message sent by Frank Newman, a senior Treasury aide, when he, Mr. Carnell and Mr. Ludwig met last month with the executive committee of the Independent Bankers Association of America, which is fighting the Clinton plan. Mr. Newman said the administration will get three Fed appointments in the coming years. "The message was, if we don't get you now, we'll get you later," says a witness. With Fed Vice Chairman David Mullins's surprise departure this week, that later could be even sooner.

Every president needs pals in high places, but maybe not in regulatory places if you've taken on as much Whitewater as this president has. If Mr. Clinton is going to insist on naming cronies as the nation's top financial regulators, then maybe he can at least stop trying to give them all of the regulatory power. People might get the wrong idea.

Editorial Feature

New Independent Counsel Law Should Apply to First Lady

Today Congress will resume debate over the lapsed independent counsel law, and the arguments no doubt will be colored by President and Mrs. Clinton's controversial financial dealings in Whitewater Development Corp. I am against reauthorization of the statute in any form, but since it soon may be reauthorized, Congress might as well ensure that the statute fulfills its asserted purposes and applies in a fair and consistent manner.

Congress thus ought to resolve a question of increasingly pressing importance: Should a president's spouse be covered by the independent counsel statute? In light of

Rule of Law

By Theodore J. Boutrous Jr.

dent counsel statute? In light of Whitewater, and Hillary Rodham Clinton's deep involvement in the politics and policy of her husband's presidency, the answer to that question is clearly yes.

Everyone now seems to agree that special procedures are necessary in cases involving possible claims of high-level, executive-branch wrongdoing. Whitewater is such a case. Republicans, led by Senate Minority Leader Bob Dole and joined by numerous Senate Democrats, persuaded the White House to request that Attorney General Janet Reno appoint an outside "special counsel" — who will be insulated by Justice Department regulations from political pressures — to investigate the Whitewater affair.

Even as she announced the appointment of Robert Fiske, however,

Ms. Reno reiterated her position that only a truly independent counsel appointed by the courts pursuant to the statute would instill public confidence in the Whitewater investigation. But this preference poses a problem that goes beyond Whitewater.

The independent counsel statute has never explicitly covered the president's spouse, and neither the House nor the Senate proposals pending in Congress would do so either. The statutory mandate for an

Hillary Clinton

independent counsel has always applied only to certain specifically identified high-ranking executive-branch officials, including the president. Neither the first lady nor any other executive-branch spouse has ever been included.

Whitewater shows why this makes no sense. As virtually everyone must know by now, the Whitewater controversy, fairly or unfairly, focuses as much on Mrs. Clinton as on the president. According to Time magazine, "compared with the President, the First Lady was a central player." Both were investors in the failed land deal. Mrs. Clinton's conduct also allegedly included: her securing of a $30,000 loan to purchase a model home for the development property and the subsequent sale of the home; her legal representation of Madison Guaranty S&L; the involvement of her law partners in various other Whitewater events; and her 1988 letter asking for power of attorney for the company.

The position of first lady no longer can be characterized as simply ceremonial — particularly since the office's policy-making function has now been made explicit. In its recent decision concerning the legal status of Mrs. Clinton and the Health Care Task Force over which she presided, the federal appeals court in Washington had little trouble concluding that the "President's spouse acts as the functional equivalent of an assistant to the President" and that the first lady is a "full-time officer or employee of the government."

Mrs. Clinton has been repeatedly characterized as the president's closest adviser. She was charged by the president with the responsibility of formulating and implementing the most far-reaching policy initiative of his administration, health care reform, and she recently testified before five congressional committees on the president's plan. The first lady also reportedly played a key role in choosing the president's cabinet, including Attorney General Reno.

During the recent Senate hearings concerning reauthorization of the independent counsel statute, Ms. Reno testified: "The reason I support the concept of an Independent Counsel, with statutory independence, is that there is an inherent conflict whenever senior Executive Branch officials are to be investigated by the Department of Justice and its appointed head, the Attorney General. . . . The Independent Counsel Act was designed to avoid even the appearance of impropriety in the consideration of allegations of misconduct by high-level Executive Branch officials."

I believe that the Justice Department special-counsel process is fully adequate to address these concerns. But if one agrees with the attorney general's assertions, I do not see any way to dispute that the president's spouse should be subjected to mandatory coverage under any new independent counsel statute.

The "inherent conflict" and appearance problems identified by Ms. Reno would exist just as clearly if the attorney general and her subordinates retained responsibility for investigating allegations of misconduct against a first lady. Moreover, investigation and prosecution of a first lady would, in many ways, raise far more sensitive issues than cases involving other top presidential aides and advisers.

In fact, an attorney general would likely recoil in horror from the idea of targeting and pursuing the boss's spouse in connection with a criminal inquiry. Members of Congress (and some members of the press) cannot even bring themselves to ask Mrs. Clinton tough policy questions. This makes it especially difficult to imagine the attorney general and career prosecutors tenaciously investigating or bringing charges against a first lady.

Except in the most extreme circumstances, such factors would also create enormous political and practical obstacles for the attorney general that would rule out the discretionary appointment of an independent counsel to prosecute a first lady. Only mandatory coverage will fulfill the purposes offered to justify the independent counsel law.

As a matter of principle, any new independent counsel law should apply to presidential spouses (and Congress), or it should not be passed at all. Mrs. Clinton's role as policy and political adviser to the president is not likely to be an isolated incident in the history of the presidency. Nor can mandatory application of the independent counsel law to presidential spouses be challenged by the Democrats as a partisan issue.

Sen. Dole has fully endorsed Mrs. Clinton's policy activities as entirely appropriate. He often remarks amiably that he plans to fulfill a similar role when his wife, Elizabeth, is elected president. What better reason could there be for the Democratic Congress to vote to ensure that the president's spouse is covered by the independent counsel law?

Mr. Boutrous is an attorney in Washington who has represented parties in independent counsel matters.

Editorial Feature

The Clinton Two vs. the Keating Five

By DAVID I. THOMPSON

As one who lived through the myriad investigations launched as a result of the failure of Charles Keating's Lincoln Savings in 1989, I have more than a passing interest in the allegations surrounding the Clintons' involvement with Whitewater Development Corp. and Madison Guaranty Savings & Loan.

The Clintons and their defenders repeatedly argue that because the Clintons (allegedly) suffered a loss on their investment in Whitewater, they could not have engaged in any wrongdoing. Yet even if the Clintons did lose money on the specific Whitewater investment, the relationship they developed with their business partner and Madison owner, Jim McDougal, profited them handsomely in terms of campaign contributions, handshake loans and access to powerful people. More important, the cozy relationship between the Clintons and Madison may have kept Madison alive longer than it should have, magnifying the bill to the taxpayers.

Indeed, many of the issues that appear relevant to Madison and Whitewater are identical to those scrutinized so exhaustively with respect to Lincoln. Here are a few comparisons that merit scrutiny by the special counsel appointed by Janet Reno to investigate the case:

• *Unfair influence.* Charlie Keating was pilloried for his generous donations to politicians, including the "Keating Five" in the Senate, who went to bat for him in dealing with zealous regulators. Without diminishing the significance of the political pressure those senators could impose upon the regulators, ultimately it was only pressure they could bring; the Keating Five had no direct control over Lincoln's supervision, and the regulators eventually triumphed over both Lincoln and the senators, ruining a few careers in the process.

In contrast, Bill Clinton as governor had the power to hire and fire the Arkansas securities commissioner, responsible for supervising all state-chartered thrifts. In 1985, shortly after Madison had received a negative regulatory audit noting its "unsafe and unsound" practices, and shortly after Mr. McDougal raised $35,000 to "knock out" a personal debt Bill and Hillary Clinton owed from the latest gubernatorial race, Mr. Clinton fired the sitting commissioner and replaced him with a longtime friend and political supporter.

Thus, Mr. Clinton had life-and-death power over the bureaucrat with life-and-death power over Madison. Never mind the Clintons' small investment with Whitewater. Mr. McDougal had just proved his usefulness to Mr. Clinton in other ways. How useful would he be if his S&L were taken over? The Clintons at the very least had an incentive to provide as sympathetic an ear as possible to Mr. McDougal and Madison, and they seem to have done it.

• *Cronyism.* Another of Mr. Keating's actions that outraged the public was the hiring, on a monthly retainer, of a California law firm whose senior partner was one of Gov. George Deukmejian's closest political advisers. This firm represented Mr. Keating's interests before the California Securities Commission, headed by a lawyer formerly employed by the same firm. After Lincoln was seized, the firm and its lawyers were accused of using their connections with the Deukmejian administration to prop up a tottering institution. They, along with other Keating lawyers, were sued and ultimately settled for several million dollars.

Mr. McDougal went Mr. Keating one better, taking a belt-and-suspenders approach to the state regulatory process. Not content with the knowledge that a Friend of Bill's was now the securities commissioner, he went to Hillary Rodham Clinton for his legal representation, placing her on a monthly retainer. Mrs. Clinton's assignment was to represent Madison before the Arkansas securities commissioner after the Federal Deposit Insurance Corp. issued its report of Madison's "unsafe and unsound" practices. Mrs. Clinton's lobbying apparently succeeded: Armed with an independent audit, she persuaded her friend the state regulator to keep Madison open. During the next year, Madison more than doubled in size and left a bigger crater for the taxpayers to fill when it was finally seized.

• *Misleading the regulators.* One of Charlie Keating's biggest sins was allegedly misleading the regulators by "file-stuffing" — creating documents that, although created after the fact, were written in the present tense to leave the impression that loan- and real-estate underwriting was thorough and complete at the time a particular transaction was entered into. In the Keating case, such conduct involved criminal penalties, since making "false entries" and misleading the regulators are strictly forbidden.

Yet Hillary Rodham Clinton's law firm, which had represented Madison for several years before it failed, flagrantly misled the FDIC after the agency seized Madison in 1986. The FDIC elected to sue the accounting firm that had pronounced Madison healthy and whose report Mrs. Clinton had vouched for in arguing for Madison's continued existence.

The FDIC lawsuit against the accountants should have been a big deal; Madison's failure cost $60 million against reported total assets of $120 million, meaning that 50 cents of every dollar held by Madison and allegedly examined by the auditors was phony. As with Lincoln's accountants, Madison's accounting firm represented a deep pocket with which to cover some of the losses to the taxpayers. Amazingly, Mrs. Clinton's law firm bid for and was awarded the representation to sue the accounting firm.

How could a law firm that only a year earlier had used the accountants' report to help keep Madison alive now sue the accountants for the report? Normally, in the S&L carnage that resulted from deregulation and then reregulation, legal counsel to institutions that failed as spectacularly as Madison (at least equal, on a percentage-of-assets basis, to Lincoln's failure) expected to find themselves on the receiving end of major litigation almost as a matter of course. Mrs. Clinton's law firm, in fact, was an "institution-affiliated party" as defined in section 901 of FIRREA, and thus its own dealings with Madison should have been scrutinized closely.

Mrs. Clinton's law firm escaped such a fate the old-fashioned way, apparently flagrantly misrepresenting prior ties to Madison. Late White House Deputy Counsel Vincent Foster, Mrs. Clinton's partner at the law firm, wrote to the FDIC in an effort to get the representation against the accounting firm, stating, in pertinent part: "the firm does not represent any savings-and-loan association in state or federal regulatory matters."

The present tense chosen by Mr. Foster makes the statement literally accurate, but any first-year law student knows that fraud can arise when one omits material facts necessary to make a statement not misleading — i.e., that the law firm had represented Madison in the extremely recent past. Lincoln's lawyers got sued for hundreds of millions of dollars; Madison's lawyers not only got off scot-free, but also collected a $400,000 fee for suing the accountants and "winning" a paltry $1 million settlement.

Moreover, if it can be established that Whitewater or its partners received one dollar of benefit from Madison, indirectly or directly, diverted any business opportunity rightfully belonging to Madison, or otherwise profited at Madison's expense, then a whole new area of investigation opens wide, with possible prohibited affiliate transactions of the kind that were fatal to Mr. Keating.

It must be noted that the contributions to the Keating Five, the cozy relationships with state supervisors, the employing of influential law firms, and so on, did not, directly, convict Charles Keating. But those things did focus such widespread attention on Lincoln and its operations that the full power and wrath of the U.S. government eventually came down on Mr. Keating's head.

It would seem only logical that when the same, or more extreme, indicators of questionable conduct are present in a case involving the highest elected official in the country, the same standards of scrutiny be applied. Let's be fair: Applying the Lincoln test to Madison will show that we do have a government of laws, not men.

Mr. Thompson is a Cincinnati attorney who was a vice president and corporate counsel for Lincoln Savings from 1985 to 1989.

REVIEW & OUTLOOK

FOB Regulation

Today the Senate Banking Committee will vote on Ricki Tigert as head of the FDIC, she having agreed to recuse herself from issues involving the Clintons and Whitewater. Let us all pause to see who is running the rest of the bank regulatory apparatus. Why, Deputy Treasury Secretary Roger Altman, a presidential appointee as well as Georgetown friend, is running the ostensibly independent Resolution Trust Corp. And Eugene Ludwig, another college Buddy of Bill, has been installed as Comptroller of the Currency.

Why, the FOBs are taking over financial regulation, lock, stock and barrel. They haven't quite got the Federal Reserve yet, but they have a regulatory reform proposal that would take care of that. The Clinton folks aren't content to relegate cronies and pals to harmless backwaters like Commerce or Postmaster General or the alter ego of a presidential Counselor. They learned back in Arkansas that it was convenient to have a Beverly Bassett Schaffer sending "Dear Hillary" letters waving through a new capitalization plan for a financial institution.

We're glad to see that a couple of courageous Republicans are blowing the whistle.

North Carolina's Senator Lauch Faircloth, unlike some of his colleagues on Don Riegle's banking committee, isn't willing to let the matter drop with Ms. Tigert's recusal. In the FDIC nominee's first appearance before the committee, the Senator raised the issue of how someone who says she's known the Clintons for eight years and been a Renaissance Weekend regular could convincingly head an agency with an active investigation of the Madison S&L collapse. Ms. Tigert weasled, but later sent Senator Faircloth a recusal statement, which she said was written after consulting FDIC's ethics office. She promised she'll recuse herself from matters "concerning President or Mrs. Clinton in their personal capacities."

While consoling Ms. Tigert on the "unfortunate fate" surrounding her nomination, Senator Faircloth is now wondering about the caveat "personal." Does that remind you of "didn't inhale" or "no price controls?" Sen. Faircloth now wants Ms. Tigert to "expand your recusal" from matters involving the "personal" activities of President and Mrs. Clinton to include their public activities. More pointedly, he asks: "Will you recuse yourself from matters concerning Webster Hubbell, Vincent Foster, Dan Lasater, Frost and Company, Madison Guaranty Savings and Loan, the Worthen Bank Corporation" and onward through all the financial institutions now running under the Whitewater flag? How did we end up with an FDIC head going in recusing herself from the agency's most sensitive business?

Meanwhile, Rep. Jim Leach is wondering about Deputy Treasury Secretary/Interim RTC CEO Roger Altman. The Congressman wrote last week also seeking recusal commitments in matters involving the RTC's investigation of Madison's collapse and relationship to Whitewater. Mr. Leach's tone is cordial, but he thinks the inherent conflicts need to be faced:

"I have high regard for your personal integrity, but as you know, from the beginning, it has been an awkward situation to have a presidentially appointed and confirmed officer of the Treasury Department also head an independent federal agency, the RTC. When this prospect was first suggested at the beginning of the Clinton Administration, it did not strike the Minority as overly unreasonable for a month or two given the fact that no RTC head had been selected.

"However, it has been over a year since the administration has been in office and it can only be described as structurally unseemly for a political appointee of an Executive branch department to make what are, in effect, law enforcement decisions for an independent federal agency as they may touch upon the President."

Finally, we have Mr. Ludwig, appointed by Mr. Clinton to head the comptroller's office, which regulates and examines national banks. They attended Oxford and Yale together, and remain close. Just how close the American Banker described in its Jan. 31 edition, reporting on a videotape taken at a Renaissance Weekend by someone from "Saturday Night Live" who was also there: "The tape featured Mr. Clinton. But it was hard to miss Mr. Ludwig in a bright blue sweater and white shorts. Almost every shot of the President showed the beaming comptroller at his shoulder."

So we have three Friends of Bill or Hillary calling signals, amid a blizzard of recusals, at three traditionally independent bank regulatory agencies. Surely by now enough is known of the Clinton political mores to agree that we're past the point of simply passing all this through as of no consequence. After the Savings and Loan scandal, BCCI, the Keating Five and now whatever Whitewater is, it ought to be at least clear that federal financial regulators should be held to a Caesar's wife standard of propriety and independence. Instead, we get this.

We're quite used to the Clinton White House stonewalling or deriding anyone's inquiries or doubts about its behavior. But we're glad that Senator Faircloth and Rep. Leach are persisting with their questions about the administration's appointment practices. As we run the numbers, Renaissance Weekend plus Whitewater plus the RTC plus the Comptroller plus the FDIC plus regulatory independence does not compute.

REVIEW & OUTLOOK

Who Is Webster Hubbell?—V

Well, today Webster Hubbell settles in as regent at the Justice Department. Deputy Attorney General Philip Heymann headed back to Harvard Friday—a "pushee," in the words of a Washington Post

Webster Hubbell

editorial. Attorney General Janet Reno still sits on the throne, though uneasily, her halo askew over the departure of aide Lula Rodriguez amid vote-fraud suspicions, not to mention a stiff round of disparaging leaks. It could scarcely be clearer that the administration of justice is now dominated by the associate attorney general, former Rose Law Firm partner of the First Lady, Sugar Bowl tackle and big Friend of Bill.

Just in case anyone missed the point, when Mr. Heymann decided to go sooner rather than later, he told Mr. Hubbell, not Ms. Reno. Indeed, in explaining his conflict of "management style" with Ms. Reno, he told U.S. News, "When it comes to giving regular Justice input into administration policies, we have relied too exclusively on Webb Hubbell's free and comfortable access to the White House. And although Webb is effective, there are costs to such an informal and ad hoc approach." In our earlier scrutiny—Who Is Webster Hubbell-I, II, III and IV—we quoted Ms. Reno on ABC saying that during the Waco fiasco the President never spoke to her, only to Webb.

* * *

So it is of some moment that the regent has problems of his own, stemming not only from his friendship with the President and partnership with the First Lady, but his own actions in a Whitewater-related lawsuit.

The suit was against the Little Rock accounting firm of Frost and Co., over the audit the Rose Law Firm had used to help persuade regulators not to close Madison Guaranty, the thrift run by the Clintons' Whitewater partner James McDougal. The FDIC hired Rose on the basis of the representation by the late Vincent Foster that it "does not represent" any thrifts, Madison by that time being defunct.

So with Mr. Hubbell as lead attorney, Rose set out on behalf of the government to sue its former client's accountants. The most succinct report of these actions is in the New Yorker of Jan. 17, which added that Mr. Hubbell settled the case "for a reported one million dollars, which was considerably less than the accounting firm's insurance coverage"; and that Rose collected a fee of $400,000.

The FDIC is looking into this matter. Presumably it will eventually report that everything's OK, because back then Mr. Hubbell whispered into someone's ear that Rose had represented Madison. But the question still remains, how did Rose get on both sides of these issues? To put the sinister suspicion plainly: Could it be that Mr. Hubbell and Mr. Foster, recognizing that their friends and indeed their firm were implicated in Frost's deceptive audit, managed to insinuate themselves as the government's attorney so they could fix the ticket?

* * *

The Chicago Tribune has discovered two more cases in which Rose represented government regulators. Its Nov. 3 report discusses suits arising out of the failure of two Illinois thrifts, First American Savings and Loan Association of Oak Brook, and Home Federal Savings and Loan of Centralia. Each had started lawsuits, later continued by the government, against the Little Rock bond firm headed by Dan Lasater. They alleged that the Lasater firm had lost the thrifts' money in unauthorized trades, contributing to failures taxpayers had to redeem through deposit insurance.

Mr. Lasater was a big contributor to the Clinton gubernatorial campaigns and a big underwriter of Arkansas bond issues. Also a benefactor who provided Roger Clinton, the President's brother, a job and money for debts connected to his drug problem. Mr. Lasater was also the host of lavish parties, leading to his own conviction and jail-ing on cocaine charges.

The Rose firm landed the government's First American case shortly after taking on the Madison one. The Tribune reported that while Mr. Hubbell handled most of the S&L work, this case was assigned to Mr. Foster and Hillary Clinton. The Home Federal thrift had hired Rose before being seized by the government; but there is a controversy about Mr. Lasater being represented by a recently departed Rose lawyer who'd worked on the First American suit with Mrs. Clinton and Mr. Foster.

The Home Federal case, filed at $4.6 million, was settled for $250,000 on Mr. Foster's advice. The First American case, filed at $3.3 million, was settled for $200,000. An FDIC spokesman has reassured our reporter that so far as they have determined, the First Lady was not involved in the settlement. At the time of these settlements Mr. Lasater was in prison, having given legal authority to manage his affairs to a business associate, Patsy Thomasson. Those who keep at their bedside a Whitewater cast list will recognize her name as one of the three White House aides to visit Vincent Foster's office the night of his death.

* * *

Not to worry; the regent at Justice has recused himself. Indeed, the whole matter is in the hands of special counsel Robert Fiske, who can sort out the Rose partner's possible conflicts of interest.

Which reminds us, what about Mr. Fiske's own firm, Davis, Polk & Wardwell? Upon inquiry from Senator Arlen Specter, Ms. Reno said that Mr. Fiske has taken a full leave of absence, which means something other than resignation. Davis Polk is a sprawling firm with sprawling clients, Morgan Guaranty for starters. Seems to us there's a potential for conflict of interest with practically the whole world.

Again, not to worry: Ms. Reno told the Senator that Mr. Fiske gave assurances he was not aware of any Davis Polk client involved in Whitewater. Hmmm. When the special counsel gets around to learning something about Whitewater, he will discover its largest single transaction was a land deal with International Paper Co., which standard compilations list among Davis Polk's prominent clients.

Last week the Washington Times reported that anonymous sources at the Rose Law Firm said it was shredding documents relating to Whitewater. The Associated Press inquired at Mr. Fiske's Little Rock office and reported, "'Mr. Fiske is aware of the Washington Times report on shredding of documents. That will be investigated by his office,' said a staff assistant who would identify herself only as Joyce." Reuters also found Joyce while seeking Mr. Fiske in Little Rock, reporting that his office is unmarked but has a black electronic keypad beside the door.

But, not to worry. Reports say Mr. Fiske has leased his offices for three years. Which is to say, beyond the next Presidential election.

* * *

What all of these issues need is a good airing and explanation, not to a court but to the American public. While Congressional Democrats are hesitant, the vehicle for such an airing will soon be available. There will have to be confirmation hearings for Mr. Heymann's successor; the rumored designee is Pentagon counsel Jamie Gorelick, who shares with Mr. Fiske the distinction of having been one of Clark Clifford's lawyers in the BCCI case.

As a deputy is considered, Mr. Hubbell's regency at Justice is surely relevant. All that's necessary is for the Republican minority on Judiciary to follow the example freshman Senator Lauch Faircloth is setting on the Banking Committee, and start asking the obvious questions.

Regulators

By February 1994, new evidence was emerging of what appeared to be Clinton Administration attempts to influence federal probes of Madison Guaranty. On February 24, Deputy Treasury Secretary Roger Altman told the Senate Banking Committee that he and other Treasury officials went to the White House to give a "heads-up" briefing on the Resolution Trust Corp.'s investigation of Madison and Whitewater Development Co. At the time, Mr. Altman also was serving as acting head of the RTC, an independent federal agency. Over the next five months, Mr. Altman would repeatedly amend his recollection of events. On March 5, White House Counsel Bernard Nussbaum resigned amid controversy over the improper contacts.

Meanwhile, concerns were raised over events at the Federal Deposit Insurance Corp., where Renaissance Weekend participant Ricki Tigert was about to take over as chairman, with influence over aspects of the Whitewater probe. The FDIC that month had determined that Webster Hubbell and the Rose Law Firm had violated no conflict-of-interest rules in representing Madison Guaranty in 1985, then suing it on behalf of the FDIC in 1989.

In Little Rock, new facts were coming to light about U.S. Attorney Paula Casey's handling of the David Hale plea bargain; Ms. Casey was a longtime political ally of the Clintons. Calls for Congressional hearings mounted. Mr. Fiske opposed hearings, arguing they would interfere with his investigation. In "The Fiske Coverup II," the Journal noted that "the main public interest here is not in putting the likes of

Roger Altman in jail but in finding out what the Clinton/Little Rock/Rose presidency is all about."

REVIEW & OUTLOOK

Arkansas Forbearance

So the Federal Deposit Insurance Corp. has determined that Webb Hubbell and the Rose Law firm violated no conflict-of-interest rules when they worked both sides of the street regarding Madison Guaranty S&L of Little Rock in the 1980s. The FDIC's eight-page opinion makes some facts clear: Rose had previously represented Madison before state securities regulators. In doing so it had presented audits prepared by Frost & Co. Then Rose and Mr. Hubbell signed up to represent the government in a suit against Frost over its Madison audits. There is no record that Rose told the FDIC about its previous representation of Madison. Mr. Hubbell and another Rose partner say they remember oral disclosures, but the FDIC personnel involved have no recollection of them.

Webster Hubbell

The FDIC verdict: No conflict here.

When Rose offered the Frost audit to regulators in 1985, the FDIC opinion says, "There is no indication in the records, or based on our review, that the Firm did anything more with respect to the audit in question than take it at face value." And "there is no evidence that the Firm had a close relationship with the S&L;" (To judge by the opinion, the Whitewater partnership between Rose partner Hillary Clinton and Madison owner James McDougal escaped the notice of the FDIC's legal eagles.) And since in 1985 Rose represented the S&L, and in 1989 represented the conservator who took over the S&L after seizure, the interests in the two cases are not "directly adverse."

Somehow it seems to us the interests of a conservator trying to clean up a mess are pretty much adverse to the interests of the folks responsible for making the mess. Indeed, who needs a legal opinion to explain what is clearly a conflict on its face? Having been involved itself, Rose might have an interest in bailing out its former business associates; Rose in fact settled the suit against Frost in 1991 for $1 million, according to several reports much less than the limit of Frost's insurance. Alternatively, Rose might have an interest in protecting itself by blaming other parties for all mistakes. If this isn't a conflict of interest, what is?

But we guess that Arkansas rules now apply at the FDIC, even before the advent of Hillary buddy Ricki Tigert. So it only seems fair that everyone caught up in the S&L maelstrom of the 1980s gets the benefit of these new, more forgiving Arkansas standards of ethics.

A different set of rules applied to law firms that had represented wayward S&Ls, remember, before FOBs started turning up in headlines. Candidate Clinton proclaimed in his 1991 announcement speech that, "When the ripoff artists looted our S&Ls, the president was silent. In a Clinton Administration, when people sell their companies and their workers and their country down the river, they'll get called on the carpet."

And indeed, word of a new, relaxed standard has spread slowly. The day before the FDIC exonerated Rose over Madison, the Resolution Trust Corp. filed a $400 million suit against Streich Lang, a prominent Phoenix law firm that had represented Western Savings and Loan Association. Some of its partners, the RTC alleged, personally profited from the fake sale of some of its properties. The firm's managing director pointed out that the RTC has sued "some of the finest law firms across the country," and that the Phoenix suit "is consistent with the government litigation strategy regarding RTC takeovers."

The granddaddy of these cases concerned Kaye, Scholer, a New York firm that represented Charlie Keating's Lincoln S&L: It was coerced into a $41 million settlement in 1991 when the government froze its assets. The Kaye, Scholer case raised interesting questions in how far a firm can go in making representations for a client the firm does not itself believe. Regulators believe the firm lied to them, but a disciplinary committee of the New York bar has since looked into the case and found no evidence that any Kaye, Scholer partner violated ethical rules. Yet the firm was not allowed to defend itself. John Feerick, dean of Fordham School of Law, says the asset seizure was a "gross abuse of power." This action, he adds, "effectively took away the ability of the law firm to defend itself and forced it into a settlement."

Now that the FDIC has cleared the Rose Firm and Webb Hubbell, we hope it plans to give Kaye, Scholer its money back. Otherwise the lesson of the FDIC memo is that Arkansas forbearance applies only to firms that included the Associate Attorney General and the First Lady. But the same old ferocious rules will apply to ordinary mortals.

REVIEW & OUTLOOK

The FDIC Clears Another

As we reported yesterday, the Federal Deposit Insurance Corp. decided Webster Hubbell had no conflict of interest representing the government suing auditors over the failure of Madison Guaranty Savings and Loan, though the Rose Law Firm had itself presented the

said audit to regulators in representing the said thrift. Not to rest on its laurels, the FDIC has also cleared Hillary Clinton of conflict in representing the government against Dan Lasater, her drug-felony friend.

Mrs. Clinton's case first came to light in the Chicago Tribune earlier this month. In a story that received less attention than it deserved, the Tribune reported that while at the Rose Firm she had represented federal regulators in a 1980s lawsuit against Mr. Lasater arising out of the failure of First American Savings and Loan

Hillary Clinton

Association of Oak Brook, Ill.

Mr. Lasater was a Clinton family friend and political ally, a one-time Arkansas high-flyer like Whitewater figure James McDougal. Mr. Lasater gave a job to Mr. Clinton's half-brother, Roger, helped the younger Clinton pay off drug debts, and was a big contributer to Mr. Clinton's campaigns.

After he was elected governor, Mr. Clinton lobbied the Arkansas legislature to let Lasater & Co. handle state bond issues. The deals earned the Lasater company millions in commissions, according to published reports. As it turned out, those contracts were awarded to Mr. Lasater while he was being investigated for cocaine distribution. He was convicted and sentenced to 30 months in prison in 1986. His business affairs were then handled by Patsy Thomasson, who was also one of the three White House aides who secretly searched Vincent Foster's office within hours of his death last year.

First American S&L sued the Lasater firm over the $361,000 it claims it lost in unauthorized trades in Treasury bond futures. The suit originally asked for $3.3 million in damages, and was eventually settled for $200,000 when the Federal Savings and Loan Insurance Corp. (FSLIC) continued it after the thrift's failure. The suit was handled by a Chicago law firm that in turn hired the Rose Firm, where the case has handled by the late Vincent Foster and Mrs. Clinton.

The FDIC, which absorbed duties of the now-defunct FSLIC, concludes that all of this is no big deal. All Mrs. Clinton did, it subsequently told the Tribune, was to sign an amended complaint reducing the damages sought to $1.3 million from the original $3.3 million. She was not involved in the final settlement for $200,000, it said, and under conflict-of-interest rules of the time had no obligation to disclose that she and the defendant were personal friends. FDIC spokesman Alan Whitney said that the FDIC people found that "Mrs. Clinton's involvement was confined to two hours reviewing the amended complaint." This was not extensive enough to be a conflict, the agency decided, though it did not interview Mrs. Clinton.

While none of this looks like a hanging offense, Ed Meese would no doubt have been hanged if he'd done something comparable. Imagine that as a private attorney he'd represented the government in signing papers slashing the damage claims against E. Bob Wallach. And even if Mr. Foster rather than Mrs. Clinton was the lead attorney, somehow the Rose Firm ended up handling the case against another member of the Clinton circle.

Much of what's going on at the FDIC, of course, is bureaucratic self-protection. In the Hubbell case, the agency's memo lamented the lack of developed procedures and the "enormous increase in workload due to the rapidly expanding duties of the FDIC." So "in hindsight documentation regarding the retention of the Firm is more limited than would ideally be hoped for." That is, the bureaucrats don't want to admit they might have missed one.

This bureaucratic instinct, though, corresponds directly with the personal interest of the First Lady, the Associate Attorney General and ultimately the President. We very much doubt that Hillary Clinton ever took Arkansas Securities Commissioner Beverly Bassett Schaffer aside to tell her to go easy on Madison, but after the Rose Firm invoked the name, the approval letter came back addressed "Dear Hillary." Mrs. Clinton's friend Ricki Tigert had not yet taken the reins at the FDIC, but when we see the agency going out of its way to make excuses for powerful political figures, we suspect it's got the message already.

REVIEW & OUTLOOK

Presumption of Rascality

"There is still a presumption of innocence in this country," President Clinton said in defending his campaign jaunt for criminal investigation target Danny Rostenkowski. The presumption of innocence certainly does pertain to criminal trials, when someone might go to jail. But yesterday the President was stumping for Rep. Rostenkowski in an election; the issue in the March 15 Chicago primary is whether the Ways and Means chairman is fit to be among the dozen or so most powerful men in our government. Voters are entitled to use whatever standard they want — presumed innocence, Caesar's wife or something in between — in deciding whether to throw the rascals out.

This confusion of the criminal process and the political process has become a bane of national life. In part because Congressional Democrats, unable to beat the Reaganites at the polls, undertook to criminalize policy differences through Lawrence Walsh and other special prosecutors. But perhaps in larger part because our Congresspersons have so managed to entrench themselves that the only way to turn them from office is to send them to jail.

By now the rascals have even learned to protect themselves from the judgment of the voters by invoking the criminal law. The notion is: unless my skullduggery is serious enough to rate a jail sentence, and provable beyond a reasonable doubt, voters aren't entitled to hold it against me at the voting booth. Indeed, if I'm clever and lucky enough to get everything subpoenaed, locked up in some prosecutor's file case and subject to investigations that reach beyond the next election, voters aren't even entitled to know the facts.

Rep. Rostenkowski is a certified pioneer of this ploy. The House Post Office scandal erupted in January 1992, and it was apparent from the first that the Ways and Means chairman was a suspect. Last year, Postmaster Robert Rota pleaded guilty to conspiring with "several" Members to embezzle money from the government, and court documents seem to implicate Rep. Rostenkowski. The prosecutor investigating him, Jay Stephens, was swept way when Hubbell & Reno fired all U.S. attorneys. With the switch, the grand jury conducting this investigation was allowed to expire. But his successor, Eric Holder, has by now convened another grand jury, where one of Mr. Rostenkowski's employees recently took the Fifth Amendment.

Rep. Ernest Istook, a freshman Republican, thinks it inexcusable the House hasn't conducted its own probe into who took what from the Post Office till. Last month, he and 54 co-sponsors demanded an investigation. Hours before a scheduled vote, House leaders produced a letter from Mr. Holder saying that a House investigation to inform the voters "could significantly damage" his probe. In other words, until we can determine if Danny is a thoroughgoing crook, voters being asked to perpetuate his extraordinary powers should be kept in the dark about his use of those powers.

In the Clinton Administration, this seems to have become the prevailing standard. Commerce Secretary Ron Brown was "cleared" when a grand jury decided there wasn't enough evidence to indict him for taking a bribe from a Vietnamese businessman. But why was Mr. Brown hanging around with the suspect businessman in the first place, and why did he lie about it? Lacking an indictment, the criminal law does not and should not answer these questions. But somehow or another, voters are entitled to an explanation.

Most spectacularly of all, of course, the President himself has Rosty-ployed his Whitewater vulnerability into the abyss of the Robert Fiske investigation. Yesterday we received Justice's answer to our Freedom of Information request for a copy of the Park Service's report on the death of Vincent Foster: We can't have it because Independent Counsel Fiske "has determined that the public release of all or any part of the records at this time would be detrimental" to his investigation. But voters are entitled to know right now what kind of corruption it is that seems to be metastasizing through the Justice

Department, the Little Rock U.S. attorney's office, the FDIC, the Treasury and Resolution Trust Corp. — where one after another Webster Hubbell, Paula Casey, Ricki Tigert and Roger Altman have grudgingly and belatedly recused themselves from important public business. While we're glad to see Mr. Fiske starting to show some life, he has no mandate to answer this question.

The body directly responsible to the voters is of course the Congress, which should have the responsibility for making a record the electorate can judge. But Congress has never met a responsibility it can't duck, and a Democratic majority is not about to investigate a Democratic presidency. Instead, we are treated to the hilarious spectacle of Don Riegle (of the Keating Five) and John Kerry (buddy of CenTrust crook David Paul) piously explaining they do not want to impede Mr. Fiske.

As for Congress policing its own Post Office, or Danny Rostenkowski or even lesser Congresspersons, forget it. Congress routinely and explicitly exempts itself from laws it applies to the rest of us, and its internal "ethics investigations" are neither ethical nor investigations. The House will likely vote this Wednesday not to investigate the Post Office scandal, just as it voted last month to exempt itself from the special prosecutor it was applying to the executive branch.

We're not keen on sending Members of Congress to jail. But so long as Congress puts itself above laws that apply to citizens and even Presidents, the presumption voters ought to apply in the voting booth is a presumption of rascality.

Letters to the Editor

It's Unfair to Presume Guilt by Association

Your March 1 editorial "Presumption of Rascality," on the Senate Banking Committee's hearings on the Resolution Trust Corporation, raised many serious, legitimate questions, but regrettably engaged in some unwarranted and inaccurate personal snipings.

During my years in the Senate I have proven my willingness to investigate unpopular matters. I was the first to expose Oliver North's private aid network; I exposed Manuel Noriega's drug connections and first uncovered the link to BCCI; I produced an unmatched record of the BCCI scandal; I sought full investigative powers from the very committee you encourage to investigate now, and received no support from the Republicans you defend.

Ironically, what you referred to as my "pious concern" that a partisan, political hearing is not the proper venue for a Whitewater investigation is shared by independent counsel Robert Fiske, a lifelong Republican who was nominated by President Bush to be second-in-command at the Justice Department.

As you may remember, Congress has proven its ability to interfere with and bumble ongoing investigations. Oliver North, John Poindexter and others had their convictions overturned precisely because of conflicts that arose directly from the congressional hearings into the Iran/Contra affair.

And finally, it's apparent that guilt by association is still alive at The Wall Street Journal. David Paul was no more my "buddy" than Mike Milken and Ivan Boesky were yours.

Sen. JOHN KERRY (D., Mass.)

Washington

Editorial Feature

A Whitewater Whitewash

By ALFONSE D'AMATO

The American people have a right to know the facts about the Whitewater/Madison affair. They also deserve to know that laws will be enforced impartially even if that enforcement may touch upon powerful public officials. Judging from the defensive reaction of Democratic political operatives in recent days, something may well be rotten in Little Rock — and Washington.

Some have claimed that Congress must sit by idly until special counsel Robert Fiske completes his investigation — an investigation that could take years. Their rationale: Congressional intervention would compromise the integrity of his investigation. On the contrary, I believe Congress must use its oversight capacity to protect the integrity of any Whitewater/Madison investigation.

Roger Altman

Last week, the Senate Banking Committee discovered a clear threat to the integrity of the Resolution Trust Corp.'s investigation — from top administration officials and political insiders.

The RTC's investigation may already have been compromised. In deeply disturbing testimony, Deputy Treasury Secretary Roger C. Altman confirmed that he and Treasury General Counsel Jean Hansen went to the White House to give a "heads-up" briefing. This briefing was attended by White House Counsel Bernard Nussbaum and an unnamed assistant, Deputy Chief of Staff Harold Ickes and the first lady's chief of staff, Margaret Williams.

Apparently, Mr. Altman believed that top White House legal and political advisers needed his guidance to understand "the legal and procedural framework within which the RTC was working" in connection with Madison. The White House now states falsely that Congress and the media also received such briefings. But at the time this group was meeting at the White House, I was speaking out on the Senate floor about the RTC's failure to provide our committee with any information about its activities on the Madison/Whitewater mess. And I have yet to encounter a reporter covering this story who says he was briefed by the RTC, let alone its acting CEO, Mr. Altman.

Mr. Altman's apparent lapse of judgment triggers serious questions. Why did Mr. Nussbaum, as White House counsel, need to be briefed on the RTC's investigation of Madison? This investigation does not touch upon the president in his official capacity.

And what about Mr. Ickes and Ms. Williams? Why would these political operatives need to be briefed by a top agency official on that agency's investigation into a matter that has nothing to do with the executive office of the president? Ms. Williams, a former Democratic National Committee operative, had earlier joined Mr. Nussbaum in searching Vincent Foster's office. Why was this briefing attended by the Treasury general counsel, Ms. Hansen, when it dealt with matters within the RTC's authority?

Mr. Altman has finally recused himself from the Whitewater/Madison matter. Unfortunately, that does not answer questions about the propriety of this meeting, and his recusal cannot ensure that a fair and impartial investigation will be conducted. These are legitimate issues that warrant a congressional hearing.

The RTC's deputy CEO, John Ryan, recently wrote to me that "it is standard operating procedure not to discuss any matter relating to the review of potential civil claims of any institution" and that it was "inappropriate" to provide any "specifics" or any "information relating to the status of our review. . . ." Apparently, different standards may apply to discussions with the White House.

Sen. D'Amato, of New York, is the ranking Republican on the Banking Committee.

Editorial Feature

Whitewater: It's the Coverup More Than the Deal

Call it the Whitewater conundrum.

The so-called Whitewater scandal will embarrass President Clinton, cost him some extra taxes, and raise substantive ethical questions about the first lady's conduct as a private lawyer. But the betting here is that there won't be any political smoking gun or certainly any findings of criminality involving the first family.

If the current performance continues, however, it's less than a longshot bet that one or two White House aides could end up in the slammer — not for what happened in Arkansas in the 1980s, but for the way matters are being

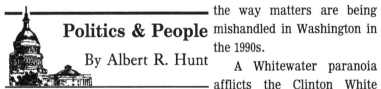

Politics & People

By Albert R. Hunt

mishandled in Washington in the 1990s.

A Whitewater paranoia afflicts the Clinton White House team. They've underreacted at the wrong times — on supplying information and the need for an outside investigation. They've overreacted at others — elevating critics with intemperate attacks. The presidential counsel, Bernard Nussbaum, supposedly the ethical gatekeeper in the White House, has caused more problems than he's prevented. White House aides, acting in a careless, ad hoc campaign-type manner, seem oblivious to the risks they face if they're ever deposed on this issue.

The result is a textbook case of the common observation of defense lawyers: What's done after an alleged offense creates more culpability than the act itself.

Why? One answer is that there has been no one in this White House with the independent judgment or standing to walk into the Oval Office on something this sensitive and tell the president how badly it's being botched.

The other, probably more important, answer is Hillary Clinton.

Previously, the first lady would take such bad news to her husband. But Whitewater may pose even more danger to her than to the president, and the bunker mentality at the White House is a reflection of Hillary Clinton.

Ms. Clinton is a strong woman who drives her ideological foes crazy; they resort to cheap shots like labeling her an ineffective left-wing zealot, or engaging in personal innuendo. In fact, she's a valuable public servant and perceptive political adviser. But not on the matters that affect her. Earlier this year, during the so-called Travelgate flap, White House aide John Podesta reportedly brought some bad news to the first lady and was slapped down. That story has spread, and it's produced a chilling reign of fear on Whitewater.

Hillary Clinton

In reality, the charge by some Nixon apologists that this is reminiscent of Watergate is preposterous. Whitewater involves relatively small dealings a decade ago, when Bill Clinton was governor of Arkansas, in contrast to the wholesale criminal mugging of the Constitution that the Nixon White House committed.

A good example of Whitewater hyperbole is the 1985 Clinton fundraiser hosted by Whitewater partner James McDougal that almost certainly involved some illicit funds. But it's extremely doubtful that Mr. Clinton would have known about that. An incumbent governor, especially in a state like Arkansas, has an easy time raising money legally, so there was no reason for him to countenance a shady fundraiser. The incentive for the influence-peddling Mr. McDougal was to tell his friend, the governor, what a successful event it was, not to confess that actually it was tainted.

Unlike some other politicians, money never has been a driving force for Bill Clinton. This was probably best put by the Washington Post's David Broder, who, on "Meet the Press" recently, said bluntly: "If you told me Bill Clinton was very horny or very ambitious, I would have no trouble believing it. If you told me he was money-hungry and was cutting corners for money, I'd say that doesn't sound like the Bill Clinton I know."

To be sure, when special counsel Robert Fiske is through, Whitewater will take a toll on the Clintons. There seems little doubt they will owe more taxes, although tax experts say it's unlikely that any fraud case could be brought against them. And Bill Clinton will be embarrassed by the highlighting of his terrible judgment in associating with the likes of James McDougal; Dan Lasater, an Arkansas investor and convicted cocaine distributor; and David Hale, a Clinton-appointed judge, now under indictment.

But the most lethal blows are likely to be directed against the first lady who, unwisely, was involved in a triangular conflict of interest: As the spouse of the governor and a Whitewater investor, she was representing Mr. McDougal before state regulators. And she was the family decision-maker on investments.

Ms. Clinton and her friends are determined to resist this. It won't work. Earlier, White House sources say, she opposed a special counsel because there was no damage control plan but then clung to that view when it was no longer tenable. Similarly, a good counsel today would advise her that a Whitewater hit is inevitable, but it's not the end of the world.

Other Clinton operatives need to understand their campaign-style tactics aren't working. When Paul Begala goes on CNN's "Inside Politics" and attacks Rep. Jim Leach — perhaps the most nonpartisan GOP member of the House — as a politically inspired hatchet man on this issue, it backfires. The same when other Clintonites go after New York Sen. Alfonse D'Amato.

(It's extraordinary that the Clinton tactics have provided even a semblance of credibility to this New York Republican on an ethics issue; given his sleazy past, Al D'Amato lecturing on ethics should be as credible as Louis Farrakhan preaching about tolerance.)

But the White House blunders on Whitewater are endless, the latest being Deputy Treasury Secretary and acting RTC head Roger Altman's meeting with three top White House aides to brief them on a Whitewater-related issue. Mr. Altman now has recused himself from any Whitewater dealings. But the briefing was attended by White House counsel Nussbaum — who not only shouldn't have participated, but should have stopped it before it started.

If Whitewater is to be only an embarrassment, rather than a cancer that eats away at the president's credibility, three steps are in order:

- Mr. Nussbaum, a nice man and an able Wall Street lawyer, must be replaced. He's out of his political depth at the White House.

- A small Whitewater team must be formed to deal with the intricacies of the scandal, as White House hopes that it would recede after the appointment of Mr. Fiske haven't materialized. A leading outside political adviser has suggested this; it should be headed by someone with no previous connections to the issue.

- Someone must tell Ms. Clinton that she's causing a lot of the problems, and a continuation threatens things far more important to her, such as her role in the health care deliberations. In short, the first lady needs a Hillary Clinton.

Letters to the Editor

Them Dry Bones

The charge that Whitewater is reminiscent of Watergate "is preposterous," says Al Hunt ("Whitewater: It's the Coverup More Than the Deal," Politics & People, March 3). Indeed, it was the coverup and lying plus assorted skeletons uncovered in the investigation that sank the Nixon presidency. But the "deal" was a "crime," in which nothing was stolen and no one was hurt.

In the case of Whitewater we do not know if anything was stolen nor what skeletons may still be uncovered. We do know that one of the participants committed suicide. Stay tuned.

HARRY LEE SMITH

Alpharetta, Ga.

REVIEW & OUTLOOK

Asides

Who Is Webster Hubbell?—VI

The War of the Roses seems to have erupted in Arkansas, with the Washington Post reporting that the Rose Law Firm is investigating billing irregularities by former partner Webster Hubbell, now associate attorney general and (well, you know the rest). The Justice Department yesterday issued Mr. Hubbell's statement declaring, "I did not overbill the RTC or other clients," and assuring curiosity-seekers that the inquiry is "in no way out of the ordinary."

Over at the White House, Press Secretary Dee Dee Myers described President Clinton's reaction: "He stands by Webb." She said Chief of Staff Mack McLarty had questioned Mr. Hubbell about the report and "received assurances from Webb that it wasn't true and the President is satisfied by that."

REVIEW & OUTLOOK

Poison, Then Recuse

Recusal is suddenly much in the news, with the disclosure that Treasury official and part-time regulator Roger Altman gave White House Counsel Bernard Nussbaum a "heads-up" about the statute of limitations. While Mr. Altman subsequently proferred a recusal in his post as head of the Resolution Trust Corp., some ask if the damage is already done.

Paula Casey

So this is perhaps an apt moment to take a closer look at the recusal of Paula Casey, U.S. Attorney in Little Rock, from the case against David Hale. Independent Counsel Robert Fiske Jr. is now supposed to determine whether the President and Mrs. Clinton did anything wrong in their involvement with Whitewater Development Corp., but as a result of Ms. Casey's handiwork and some decisions of his own, his first priority seems bizarre. He and three assistants were in court this week to press the prosecution of the most threatening witness so far against the President.

To review the basics: Mr. Hale is a former municipal judge appointed by Governor Clinton, and also head of Capital Management Services Inc., a small-business investment company. His SBIC failed, and he is now charged with fraud; search warrants in his case were issued the morning of Vincent Foster's suicide. Among his bad loans was $300,000 to a company controlled by Susan McDougal, a Whitewater partner with her husband and the Clintons; some $110,000 of this loan ended up in the Whitewater account. Mr. Hale has told reporters that the loan to Mrs. McDougal was made at Governor Clinton's behest.

Ms. Casey was appointed U.S. Attorney in Little Rock after the incoming Clinton Administration's unprecedented action of firing all sitting U.S. Attorneys at a swoop, without replacements ready for many. She is a former campaign worker for and law student of the President.

Reprinted nearby is some pre-indictment correspondence between Ms. Casey and Mr. Hale's lawyer, Randy Coleman, concerning a possible plea bargain just prior to his indictment. We would not render any judgment on the substance of the correspondence, which must be read as the pushing and shoving typical of such negotiation. Given the experience of the insider-trading prosecutions, the Wedtech case and the like, we'd be among the last to rely on uncorroborated plea-bargain testimony. The evidence that Mr. Hale made fraudulent loans seems strong, and Mr. Coleman, clearly no fool, is trying to posture him in the best light.

Still, it could scarcely be clearer that Ms. Casey had no business in the middle of these negotiations. Mr. Hale and Mr. Coleman were being asked to deliver their evidence to a longtime associate and appointee of someone it purported to implicate. Ultimately, Ms. Casey, like Mr. Altman, found it necessary to recuse herself, as Mr. Coleman suggested early on. But by then Mr. Hale had been publicly indicted, precluding the possibility of his being wired up in an undercover investigation into, as Mr. Coleman put it, "the banking and borrowing practices of some individuals in the elite political circles of the State of Arkansas."

When Mr. Fiske arrived on the scene, he had the Hale prosecution to deal with, and decided to press it as hard as possible, filing a superseding indictment. In court arguments this week, he won a ruling that Ms. Casey's involvement with the grand jury did not automatically taint the indictment; there was no smoking gun, and she recused herself only because of appearances, etc., etc. Also in these hearings, Mr. Hale's co-defendants won a separate trial; they will be tried in June while Mr. Hale's trial will start March 28.

"We consider Hale an essential witness, and the reason we asked for a prompt trial date is that it's necessary to resolve this pending indictment before he's available to us," Mr. Fiske says. Mr. Hale has never told his Clinton story to law-enforcement officials; Mr. Fiske's court filings say it's necessary to conclude his "dual status — as witness in the overall investigation and as defendant here."

Another law-enforcement official might see no reason why the trial could not be delayed while Mr. Hale's evidence was collected and tested. His defenders of course contend he is being singled out for prosecution and punishment precisely because he threatens to implicate others, including Mr. Clinton. The best result would be a plea bargain before the March 28 date, but Ms. Casey's pre-recusal maneuvering complicates the prospects. There is now of course no possibility of using Mr. Hale to gather fresh evidence. Also, he now has the conflict-of-interest grounds on which to base a set of appeals, at the very least delaying any sentence. This of course would also delay the Whitewater investigation, probably beyond the next Presidential election.

With the trend of belated recusals undermining confidence in the regulators and the administration of justice, what's needed here is neither indictments nor yesterday's White House statement instructing officials to "bend over backward" to avoid Whitewater conflicts. What's needed is some public accountability. If Ms. Casey needed to recuse herself in November, why not September? Whose idea was it to fire all U.S. Attorneys in the first place? Our suspicion is that in the middle of it you will find Webster Hubbell, who could bend over backward by resigning. Is there anyone in Congress responsible enough to get answers to these questions?

Editorial Feature

Bargaining in Little Rock

Following is an exchange of correspondence between Randy Coleman, attorney for David Hale, and Paula Casey, U.S. attorney in Little Rock, just prior to the September indictment of Mr. Hale for fraud concerning the Small Business Investment Corp. he managed.

One of Mr. Hale's loans was for $300,000 to a concern owned by Susan McDougal, a partner with her husband and Bill and Hillary Clinton in Whitewater Development Corp. Some $110,000 of this money reportedly ended up in the Whitewater account.

Ms. Casey, a longtime associate of the Clintons appointed to her post when the incoming administration fired all sitting U.S. attorneys, subsequently recused herself from the case because of her association with some of the individuals involved. Independent counsel Robert Fiske has obtained a superseding indictment, and is prosecuting Mr. Hale as his first court case.

* * *

Mr. Coleman to Ms. Casey, Sept. 15, 1993:

This letter is written as a follow up to our recent personal phone conversations. . . .

Fletcher Jackson of your office has previously told me that Mr. Hale will be indicted on one or more charges on the third Tuesday of September, being September 21, 1993. Since first becoming involved in this matter approximately five (5) weeks ago and being informed of this anticipated event, I have been attempting to reach some form of negotiated plea with your office without any success.

I cannot help but sense the reluctance in the U.S. Attorney's office to enter into plea negotiations in this case. I cannot help but believe that this reluctance is borne [sic] out of the potential political sensitivity and fallout regarding the information which Mr. Hale could provide to your office, but at the same time it is information which would be of substantial assistance in investigating the banking and borrowing practices of some individuals in the elite political circles of the State of Arkansas, past and present. I can certainly understand the reluctance of anyone locally to engage in these matters, political realities being what they are.

Would it not be appropriate at this point for your office to consider terminating participation in this investigation and to bring in an independent prosecutorial staff, who are not so involved with the history of the personalities and circumstances of this case? Such action might serve your office better. It would certainly serve Mr. Hale better because I feel that he is being prejudiced by not being afforded opportunities that other targets of a potential criminal prosecution are afforded in the process of plea negotiations. . . .

Ms. Casey to Mr. Coleman, Sept. 16:
. . . My recollection of our meeting on September 7 is that I told you that I would not consider granting immunity to your client nor would I consider filing only misdemeanor charges. You made it clear to me that one felony would be as disastrous to your client as multiple felonies. Therefore, our plea negotiations are at an impasse.

I did tell you that if Mr. Hale was willing to offer substantial assistance in the prosecution of other defendants, I would consult with my Litigation Committee about requesting a motion authorizing a reduction in sentence. The motion to reduce sentences comes only after a plea of guilty to felony charges. If your client is interested in cooperating in exchange for such a reduction, he must make himself available to federal agents for questioning so that we can determine whether his proffer merits such a motion. I will be pleased to arrange such an interview at your earliest convenience.

The fact that I am not willing to enter into any other agreement with Mr. Hale should not be construed as reluctance on my part to prosecute any individual when the situation merits prosecution.

Mr. Coleman to Ms. Casey, Sept. 20:

Apparently we are not going to achieve anything further on plea negotiations in this case at the present time. Time is becoming a precious commodity. While we do not feel that the Government should proceed with an indictment against Dave Hale, we would suggest that any return of the indictment be sealed to allow the sides further time to negotiate a difficult situation.

Michael Johnson, for Ms. Casey, to Mr. Coleman, Sept. 20:
Earlier today I phoned you and requested that you provide a proffer of any information your client wished to bring to our attention. You have responded by letter dated this date in which you indicated that you did not believe we will achieve anything further in plea negotiations. As you acknowledged, your letter was in response to our earlier phone conversation.

Our position is as we have stated to you before, that is, we are fully interested in all information your client has to offer. Because of his significant involvement in criminal activity, it is unacceptable to us to grant him immunity. We are willing to provide your client with a motion authorizing reduction of sentence for substantial assistance upon his plea of guilty to a felony charge of fraud and his providing the substantial assistance. Of course to date your client has offered no tangible information on which any such arrangement could yet be made. My understanding of your letter is that he chooses not to do so at this time.

We see no reason not to proceed with the presentation of our case to the grand jury and our other normal process of handling grand jury matters. Should the grand jury decide to indict your client, we will remain ready to listen to any proffer you or your client have to offer and go forward on the basis that we have outlined above.

Mr. Coleman to Mr. Johnson, dated Sept. 20:
Thank you for your letter of September 20, 1993. The procedures proposed therein are an eleventh hour attempt to do what could and should have been done several weeks ago given some proper inducement to Mr. Hale. I previously indicated to your office that we were willing to listen to reasonable proposals other than immunity for some time, but did not receive any concrete offers. Also, I have previously indicated to Fletcher [Jackson] some time ago very definitive areas in which Mr. Hale had knowledge and also reviewed a list of

names involved as well. I made it known that Mr. Hale was willing to participate in undercover operations to develop additional information regarding same. This is much like the operations in Kentucky conducted by federal authorities which I read about in the morning newspaper. That opportunity will now be lost. We remain interested in plea negotiations. I will be in touch with you later.

Ms. Casey to Mr. Coleman, dated Sept. 21:

This letter is in response to your letter dated today which you faxed to my office.

You comment that the letter you received yesterday from my office is an "eleventh hour" attempt to set forth a procedure acceptable to your client. You complain that you have not received any concrete offers. You also complain that, because it is "eleventh hour," it will be too late to go forward to pursue an undercover operation in which your client is willing to participate.

Your references are misplaced. Our letter dated September 20, 1993, merely recapitulated discussions between you and this office over the last several weeks. You have sought to delay our proceeding on the aspect of this matter currently scheduled for this session of the Grand Jury. On each occasion you have rejected any possibility that your client would consider a felony plea and you have insisted on either immunity or, at most, a misdemeanor. Moreover, you have claimed that your client can provide information and have set forth names allegedly involved. However, on each occasion that you have been requested to furnish specifics, including again yesterday, you have declined to do so. Instead, you have responded with another general assertion and self-serving contention about the lack of interest by this office.

Let me again be very clear: this office and the Department of Justice has [sic] been and remains interested and willing to obtain any and all information your client has available. However, he must provide specifics and be willing to follow through. General assertions that he knows significant information regarding "important" people serves [sic] no goal other than his understandable, but self-serving, desire to avoid the consequences of his own significant criminal conduct. As AUSA [Assistant U.S. Attorney] Jackson advised you, the charges presently being considered are only one facet of this case, and your client faces potential criminal exposure on a number of other items. It is as to those items that your client claims to have information.

Last, as to your contention that our intention to proceed with indictment of your client compromises the potential for an undercover operation, I was contacted by a reporter from the New York Times last Friday. The reporter indicated to me that he had been in contact with your client and had interviewed him extensively on Thursday regarding this "information." The reporter also showed me copies of our past correspondence which you had provided to him. I declined to comment. Your client's efforts to put this information into the public forum belies any serious willingness on his part to leave open an undercover type of operation.

In short, we remain willing to hear what your client has to offer at such time he decides that he is ready.

* * *

From a Nov. 9 press release by the Justice Department:

WASHINGTON—Acting Assistant Attorney General John C. Keeney today said the Justice Department's Criminal Division will take charge of the government's investigation into matters concerning former judge David Hale and Capital Management Services Inc., and the now defunct Madison Guaranty Savings and Loan.

The Criminal Division took over the investigation after the U.S. Attorney in Little Rock, Paula Casey, informed the Justice Department last week that she and her staff had recused themselves because of their familiarity with some of the parties and the need to ensure that there be no misperceptions about the impartiality of the investigation.

* * *

From court papers filed by independent counsel Robert Fiske. They are addressed to arguments raised by another defendant, Eugene Fitzhugh, who will now stand trial separately from Mr. Hale.

. . . his entire argument for dismissal of the Superseding Indictment rests on the flawed premise that if Ms. Casey recused herself from this case in November 1993, then her office could not properly have appeared before the grand jury with respect to this case in September 1993. This argument must fail for three principal reasons. First, it wholly ignores the fact that Ms. Casey's reason for seeking recusal was not based on any actual conflict, but instead a concern about appearances:

"I am confident that I and my staff are capable of investigating and prosecuting these matters competently and dispassionately. Whether my participation and the participation of my staff raises questions of *the appearance* of impropriety is a different question." [Emphasis added.] (McInerney Affidavit, Exhibit A)

Second, it does not even provide a generalized allegation regarding anything that anyone in Ms. Casey's office may have done in the grand jury that was improper. And third, it suggests absolutely no prejudice that defendant Fitzhugh may have suffered as a result of the participation of Ms. Casey's office in the grand jury process.

. . . The Independent Counsel, and attorneys working at his direction, have commenced an investigation into President and Mrs. Clinton's relationships with MGSL [Madison Guaranty Savings & Loan], Whitewater and CMS [Capital Management Services]. As set forth above, one of the central allegations to be investigated is defendant Hale's claim, as reported in the press, that then-Governor Clinton "pressured" him into causing CMS to extend the $300,000 loan to [Susan McDougal's] Masters Marketing.

In order to investigate this allegation fully, it is imperative that the Independent Counsel interview defendant Hale, or compel his testimony. This cannot be done until the present case has been resolved.

Editorial Feature

Scandal and the Presidency

By Elliot Abrams

There comes a moment in any major Washington scandal when the ordinary rules of the game are suspended, and new "scandal rules" begin to apply. This week that moment was reached in the Whitewater affair.

The ordinary rules of Washington political life are somewhat lax. Officials can give heads-ups briefings to the White House about matters of political interest and are thought of as "team players."

In congressional testimony officials can bob and weave, and this is considered to be normal partisan or inter-branch combat. Information is shared with political allies and withheld from enemies. Such behavior is viewed as normal, even laudable. Officials act this way not only because they seek recognition and reward from the president and his team but because they believe in what they're doing. They seek to help and protect the president, to advance his agenda, and to benefit their own careers — all at once.

This pattern of conduct is simply stopped when "scandal rules" come into effect. All of a sudden, every action is subject to potential review not under political, but under judicial, standards. The normal briefings given to White House lawyers or political operators are now dissected on page one of the newspapers. Political opponents talk of conspiracy and demand resignations.

Testimony, speeches and press conferences are judged not by the broad and familiar standards of political exchange, but by whether the official told the "truth, the whole truth, and nothing but the truth." Officials who delighted at seeing their names in the newspaper, who indeed schemed to reach that goal, now wince as they unwrap the paper or turn on CNN.

Charges of coverup are heard and are often unfair. The problem, all too often, is time lag: Officials who do not realize that scandal rules are in effect continue to act under the old rules, which allow a certain amount of concealment of mistakes. Some will pay with their jobs; others may pay an even higher price.

For an official even remotely connected to the events or the people under investigation, the moment of recognition — when it becomes clear that a major scandal has been declared by the press — is a sad one. Henceforth, the official must reconsider every action he or she takes in the context of the courtroom. The imaginary interlocutor is no longer the White House political aide demanding to know why some action was not taken, but the independent prosecutor demanding to know why it was.

Now the demands of political and personal loyalty must be given lower priority, those of self-preservation a higher one. The official must contemplate hiring a lawyer, and paying for one out of a family budget that all of a sudden seems to be falling apart. He or she must consider trying to avoid people who were being cultivated just a few days ago, and must wonder how this government service — once seen as a ticket to the stars — will affect future employment possibilities. The effect on morale is obvious.

This is how the "scandal rules" affect the individual official. For the administration as a whole, the consequences are equally grave. When this conglomeration of officials begins to see some among its small and cohesive group as doomed, and some as dangerous, cohesion frays. The ability to take risks to advance the president's agenda declines precipitously. The assumption of future cooperation and success disappears. This turns a president into a lame duck overnight.

The time available to plan and implement effective administration action, always in short supply, is cut back because so much effort is diverted to handling the scandal. And above all, it's impossible for the administration to recover a sense of sure-footedness and confidence in its overall conduct. The application of new "scandal rules" that are both unfamiliar and somewhat indeterminate makes the administration tentative where it once would have been decisive, and present-oriented where it once would have been planning for future battles — and triumphs.

Thus the invocation of "scandal rules" this week permanently marks the Clinton administration, and not until Independent Counsel Robert Fiske closes his doors, years hence, will things ever return to normal. When cocktail party conversations turn to which famous criminal lawyer is representing whom, and who has been before the grand jury, the spirit of politics with which the new team came to Washington — of fun and excitement, of doing good and doing well — is gone forever.

Mr. Abrams, assistant secretary of state for Inter-American affairs in the Reagan administration, was convicted of withholding information from Congress in the Iran-Contra affair. President Bush subsequently pardoned him.

REVIEW & OUTLOOK

C.O.B.'s

In the Clinton era it's been fashionable to be an FOB, or Friend of Bill. With the forced resignation of White House counsel Bernie Nussbaum we would like to suggest a new category — COB, or Casualty of Bill. There seem to be more COBs all the time.

This new designation seems especially apt because some in Washington are portraying Mr. Nussbaum as a unique case, a lawyer with a "political tin ear," the main source of White House missteps. But what strikes us is how Mr. Nussbaum is just the latest in a remarkable string of departures that suggest there's more going on here than the judgment of a single White House lawyer. Maybe the problem goes higher up the chain of command.

By now the COB list includes Phil Heymann, the former Deputy Attorney General who was well regarded by just about everyone but Clinton officials. Clifford Wharton was shoved out the door as Deputy Secretary of State last year, joined later by then-Secretary of Defense Aspin. This followed the Lani Guinier fiasco, and of course the "diversity" search for an Attorney General without a y-chromosome. Two accomplished women, Zoe Baird and Kimba Wood, found themselves in tatters before that search was over. Senior White House aides Howard Paster and Roy Neel left voluntarily after only one year, claiming to be burnt out. The briefest brush with the Clinton administration left Admiral Bobby Inman a COB, his previously sterling reputation now warped. All of this in less than 14 months. We would even add George Mitchell's surprise resignation to this casualty list.

Maybe the Senate Majority Leader did want to clear the decks for any Supreme Court opening, but it's hard to believe he would leave so powerful a post if the Clinton presidency were a great success. If he felt any special loyalty to this presidency, why would the very liberal Mr. Mitchell make himself a lame duck in its crucial second year, with government health care on the line?

Mr. Nussbaum is of course the first member of the Clinton inner circle to be pushed over the side. In an irony for the ages, he first met Hillary Rodham Clinton when he hired her to join the staff of the House committee investigating Watergate. Mrs. Clinton was widely viewed as Mr. Nussbaum's shield after the Travelgate blunders last year. And we can only assume that Mr. Nussbaum hasn't done anything that the First Lady and/or the president didn't want him to do.

In fact, Mr. Nussbaum's tart resignation letter described a view of the White House counsel's job as geared principally to representing the First Couple. He said he was leaving "as a result of controversy generated by those who do not understand, nor wish to understand, the role and obligations of a lawyer." But the Clintons already have a personal lawyer, David Kendall of Williams & Connolly. A White House counsel has to make hard calls, but he is still paid by the taxpayers, which means he has a broader duty to the public trust. Just ask John Dean.

The same goes for the other FOBs who met with Mr. Nussbaum to discuss the "independent" Whitewater investigations. If Mr. Nussbaum's mistakes warrant dismissal, what about Roger Altman, the Treasury regulator who provided what he himself called a "heads up" to Mr. Nussbaum? Jean Hanson, the Treasury general counsel, went so far as to betray the fact that the Resolution Trust Corp. had made a criminal referral to Justice. The ethical blind spots go beyond Mr. Nussbaum.

This suggests the problem won't be solved by appointing Gergen II. (We wouldn't be at all surprised to see David Gergen announce his own resignation soon, declaring that he'd done his patriotic duty by saving Nafta — which would be right.) The names of those subpoenaed by a grand jury include FOB Bruce Lindsey, deputy chief of staff and FOB Harold Ickes, and the First Lady's chief of staff, Margaret Williams. It's hard to believe that some white-shoe Beltway lawyer/potentate would be able to rein in this crowd.

That said, we don't much like the grand jury spectacle. The mistakes so far (Arkansas goings-on excepted) don't seem to deserve criminal investigation. The Clinton team is suffering, alas, from the new standard of criminalizing politics that Congressional Democrats established to punish Reaganites in the 1980s. We'd prefer to see Mr. Altman and the rest testify before Congress, where the public can find out what happened. But when the stonewall fell, Democrats so dreaded a public accounting that they hid behind a special counsel, who is now issuing the subpoenas.

The larger problem, in any event, isn't the ethics of Mr. Nussbaum but the ethical tone set from the top. The president and First Lady came of age in an Arkansas political culture in which conflict of interest was a way of life. They've brought that same standard with them to Washington, and it will continue to produce casualties until they abandon it. Perhaps a razorback, unlike a leopard, can change its spots.

REVIEW & OUTLOOK

The Fiske Coverup

Independent Counsel Robert Fiske is a distinguished member of the New York bar, and he is only doing what any good lawyer would do. But when this approach is applied to broad public policy concerns, as distinguished New York attorney Bernard Nussbaum found, it can produce preposterous results.

So in preparation for Mr. Fiske's meeting this morning to urge Senator D'Amato and the rest of Congress to shut up and get out of the way, we'd like to offer an update on *Dow Jones v. Department of Justice.* As most readers know, we've filed suit under the Freedom of Information Act for the release of reports on the death of Vincent Foster. The Justice Department's reply consists of a letter from Mr. Fiske saying the reports should not be released because it would compromise his investigation.

At the time Mr. Fiske was appointed, we'd

Robert Fiske

already been waiting for these reports for five months. We filed our original FOIA request back in August, because we thought that's what the Justice Department was asking us to do. "As soon as the FOIA section processes the report, it'll be available to you. That has already started before this meeting even took place," spokesman Carl Stern told the press. So we filed the request and let the process proceed.

As it proceeded, Mr. Foster's death was widely blamed on us, because prior to his death we were the only people suggesting there might be an issue concerning ethics among former members of the Rose Law Firm. Michael Kinsley cast the first stone, as is his wont, and the blame-laying reached a crescendo with the headline on Jonathan Alter's Newsweek column: "Journalism as a Blood Sport."

We never viewed this theme as an accident. John Hanchette, national correspondent for the Gannett News Service, recently confirmed our suspicions, telling Peter Bronson of the Cincinnati Inquirer, "Reporters got unsolicited calls from the White House saying that they were at fault, that the press was vultures picking over his bones." And of course, we were designated as chief vultures, on the basis of the note found six days after Mr. Foster's death, torn up at the bottom of his briefcase but supposedly missed in previous searches.

In one of the copious leaks from the report that Justice and Mr. Fiske say we can't have, we learn that a Park Police investigator says he had earlier watched Mr. Nussbaum examine the briefcase. This account appeared in the New York Times the week after our suit was filed. Most people, having learned about Whitewater files in and mysterious visits to Mr. Foster's office, no longer attach much credence to the theme of blaming the press.

Leaks from the reports we're suing for, however, continue to press the original White House theme. In its Feb. 11 report based on "secret police files reviewed yesterday," the New York Daily News reports that Mr. Foster's widow said he suffered from "humiliation." The paper's Karen Ball added, "Foster and the Rose firm were the targets of acerbic Wall Street Journal editorials." And New York magazine quotes this comment on our lawsuit, " 'They didn't even have the grace to say they're sorry,' says a White House official. 'And they've picked up right where they left off.' "

In replying to our suit, the Justice Department concedes nearly all of our FOIA contentions, but claims an exemption for information on investigations. Mr. Fiske's supporting letter says, "The public disclosure of all or any part of the Park Police or FBI report at this time would substantially prejudice the ability of the Office of the Independent Counsel to conduct its investigation. For example, if a witness has access to what another person has said about a particular fact or to conclusions reached in a report, that witness's testimony or statements in an interview could be tainted by that knowledge."

Sounds lawyerly. What in blazes is he talking about? His witnesses are the same people who'd been sitting on this report for five months before he took office. Which of the following hasn't had access to it: Mr. Nussbaum, Bruce Lindsey, Harold Ickes, Mark Gearan, Maggie Williams, Lisa Caputo? These people or those who work for or with them, we feel entitled to suspect, are also behind the spin on the secret report intended to blacken our name. They and compatriots like Webster Hubbell at Justice also understand that Mr. Fiske will do what every good lawyer would, and that this will continue their coverup beyond the Congressional election and with luck beyond the Presidential one.

There's more. When we filed suit we also filed a separate request for a photocopy of the Foster note. The text had been released, and a photocopy has been available for inspection in Mr. Stern's office. The Justice Department has replied to this request with a letter saying "the handwritten note will be treated as part of your earlier request," throwing it under Mr. Fiske's "all or any part" umbrella. In other words, the distinguished lawyer is arguing that his investigation will be jeopardized by release of a letter the text of which has already been printed in every newspaper in the land, and the copy of which has been available for those willing to visit Mr. Stern's office.

Perhaps some of the members of Congress would like to explore this logic in their meeting with Mr. Fiske this morning. It is a taste of what they can expect if they defer to what any good lawyer would do, and shirk their own responsibility to air important concerns in public. They should tell Mr. Fiske that they ultimately don't care whether someone goes to jail; for our own part we hope no one does. The more important responsibility is to give the public the facts it needs to judge the performance of its government; deciding whether to indict is less important than deciding whether to throw the rascals out.

Letters to the Editor

Don't Include Me In Your 'Suspicions'

"Mr. [Vincent] Foster's death was widely blamed on us . . .," you write in an editorial March 9. "Michael Kinsley cast the first stone, as is his wont. . . . We never viewed this theme as an accident." You go on to cite a news article that "confirmed our suspicions" by reporting "unsolicited calls from the White House" urging this theme.

For the record, my column about The Wall Street Journal and Vincent Foster was not occasioned by any calls from the White House, solicited or unsolicited. I had no discussion about it (before it appeared) with anyone in the White House or otherwise Clinton-connected.

Also for the record, the column specifically said—twice—that the Journal should not be blamed for Foster's suicide. My point was that the Journal's editorials about Foster and the Rose Law Firm were shoddy and dishonest. Your March 9 editorial confirms my suspicions.

MICHAEL KINSLEY
Senior Editor
The New Republic

Washington

Editorial Feature

The White House Counsel's Job

In his letter of resignation to President Clinton, Bernard Nussbaum blamed his decision to quit on the controversy created by those "who do not understand, nor wish to understand, the role and obligation of a lawyer, even one acting as White House counsel." Mr. Nussbaum was right, in complicated and ironic ways.

By all accounts, Mr. Nussbaum, who spent 27 years as a top corporate litigator in New York City, is an excellent lawyer. He probably would have been a fine White House counsel — sometime before the 1970s. Mr. Nussbaum proved unable to cope effectively with the culture of scandal that has emerged since the late '60s and especially Watergate.

Rule of Law

By Terry Eastland

As his friend Leonard Garment, who served as counsel to President Nixon in 1973-74, sympathetically puts it, he was "not very well versed in the ways of Washington."

Ironically, Mr. Nussbaum served (along with Hillary Rodham Clinton) on the House Judiciary Committee during its investigation of Watergate, and it is more his party than the GOP that over the past 20 years has harped on the importance of "ethics in government," especially by the president and the executive branch. The culture of scandal that embraces that idea is defined by the ethics laws and regulations (most put in place in the past 30 years) that govern the executive and that are enforced by Congress, government ethics officers and, in its own loud and visible way, the press. Central to this culture is the independent (or special) counsel, who is summoned to conduct criminal probes of executive officers even in contexts in which ordinary prosecutors would find no reasonable basis to proceed.

Also central to this culture is the notion that executive officers are supposed to avoid even the "appearance" of impropriety. Found in an executive order issued by President Lyndon Johnson in 1965, this standard is especially endorsed by the press, which tends to regard any appearance infraction as a possible first step on the slippery slope to another Watergate.

The White House has denied interfering with the criminal investigation of Whitewater, but the mere fact that Mr. Nussbaum met on three occasions with Treasury Department officials to discuss the case was universally judged a violation of the appearance standard. Mr. Nussbaum wasn't the only one guilty of this infraction, and sooner or later most of the others who participated will be made to pay, with their jobs and reputations. But Mr. Nussbaum was made to draw the first black bead because he, as the White House counsel and its designated agency ethics officer, should have known better.

Lloyd Cutler

In fact, Mr. Nussbaum should have known better, although the reason is not just to satisfy the modern appearance standard. Mr. Nussbaum conceived of his job as that of protecting his client, the president, and were he in the private sector his Whitewater-related actions would have caused no problems. But the White House counsel's job involves more than that. "You are also counsel to the presidential office," says Boyden Gray, who held Mr. Nussbaum's job under President Bush. "And it's your responsibility to leave the institution as strong as it was when you went in."

By that standard, the most important one, Mr. Nussbaum failed spectacularly. Actions, however unremarkable in a previous era, that today can provoke subpoenas of many high-ranking White House officials cannot be regarded as excellent public service. A Clinton-Nussbaum legacy is that it will be easier to subpoena top White House officials. More broadly, it will be harder for the president's lawyers to defend what Hamilton called "the constitutional rights of the executive."

Mr. Nussbaum's successor, Lloyd Cutler, will have to grapple with this legacy. This is the second time around for Mr. Cutler, who served as Jimmy Carter's White House counsel. He knows the basic work of the office — examining legislation sent to the president, vetting presidential nominations, judging pardon petitions, reviewing all the official remarks of the president, considering ethics questions, and so on. Unlike Mr. Nussbaum, he has a public record of engagement with constitutional issues — although note well that Mr. Cutler, a strong advocate of independent counsel legislation and a critic of the Constitution's separation of powers, has not been a strong proponent of executive power. Also unlike Mr. Nussbaum, he is well versed in the ways of Washington.

Still, he will find this job more difficult than the one he had under President Carter. For one thing, he will arrive not knowing whether the president or the first lady has violated any laws. This is a very dangerous spot to be in as a lawyer. Mr. Cutler will have to assume his client has done nothing wrong. But if he advises the president to do certain things and the president disagrees and Mr. Cutler doesn't know why he disagrees, Mr. Cutler could be drawn into a coverup.

For another, Mr. Cutler will discover people on the White House staff and elsewhere in the administration who seem to think themselves a step above other mortals involved in politics. They see themselves as inherently good people who are doing good things for the country, and they could not possibly do anything wrong. The bad people were those Republicans who gave us the "greed decade," Iran-Contra and, long ago, Watergate. Whether Mr. Cutler — no personal friend of Bill's or Hillary's — can change this attitude is obviously doubtful; leadership must come from the president, whose public pronouncements so far would not appear to have encouraged penitence on the part of arrogant subordinates.

Finally, Mr. Cutler's job may be complicated by the unprecedented phenomenon of a de facto plural presidency. Past first ladies have influenced the decisions of their husband presidents, but Mrs. Clinton's different influence is not merely of degree but of kind. No first lady has ever been in charge of the most important policy initiative of her husband's presidency, and no first lady has had a political constituency within and outside the administration. She has in effect wielded the president's constitutional appointment powers, as her allies hold high positions in Justice and other agencies. It is not unthinkable that Mrs. Clinton's interests might diverge from her husband's, in Whitewater if nowhere else.

Mr. Cutler says he will serve the presidency and not be Mr. Clinton's private attorney. But which part of the presidency will he serve? If part of Mr. Nussbaum's job was to serve Mrs. Clinton, the "role and obligations of a lawyer," especially one asked to serve in this White House as its counsel, are more demanding and much trickier than anyone — save Mr. Nussbaum himself — has yet to understand.

Mr. Eastland is editor of Forbes MediaCritic and a fellow at the Ethics and Public Policy Center in Washington.

REVIEW & OUTLOOK

Who Is Patsy Thomasson?

Despite subpoenas for six other White House aides and the departure of the counsel and the Fiske-D'Amato meeting, Patsy Thomasson made it back into the news yesterday. The New York Post's Christopher Ruddy reports that three anonymous White House sources put her at the middle of a "cats and dogs" scramble to find the combination to Vincent Foster's safe the night of his death.

Patsy Thomasson

Ms. Thomasson is director of the White House's Office of Administration, which handles personnel, payroll and computer matters – and, Mr. Ruddy reports, safe combinations. The officer in charge of security was out of town, but the safe was eventually opened in the wee hours of the morning, his sources say, and documents were removed and sent to the Clinton's personal lawyer, David Kendall of Williams & Connolly. Yesterday, White House Chief of Staff Mack McLarty told reporters that to the "best of his knowledge" there was no safe in Mr. Foster's office: "I don't think there was a safe, as I understand it." Experience with this administration forces us to inquire what Mr. McLarty understands as a safe; previous members of the counsel's office say it always used to have one. For that matter, even explicit White House denials look thin after one of them was directly contradicted by President Clinton's admission that he knew about White

House contacts with regulators over Whitewater matters.

Ms. Thomasson is best understood as the White House Waldo. It was previously understood that she, Bernard Nussbaum and Margaret Williams, Mrs. Clinton's chief of staff, did visit Mr. Foster's office the night of his death. Ms. Thomasson was also at the crucial six-hour meeting on May 15 with the FBI and Associate White House Counsel William Kennedy III that led to the firing of the White House travel office's staff four days later. In October, she appeared before a House Appropriations subcommittee to discuss a General Accounting Office report that criticized the White House for lax personnel policies, including retroactive pay raises, dual payments and the backdating of forms.

This hearing, in turn, led to an extended campaign by Rep. Frank Wolf, a Virginia Republican, over clearance procedures for White House passes, the coveted identification cards that allow wearers to roam the White House halls and receive top secret briefings and documents. He noticed that Ms. Thomasson still had only a temporary pass, and asked why.

She replied that she was about to get a permanent pass, but when a Wolf aide checked back near the end of January, she still had only a temporary pass. Ms. Thomasson said that her pass was ready and she would pick it up on January 31, the next Monday; but on February 4, Ms. Thomasson again said her pass "was supposed to have been issued today," but that she "didn't get down to pick it up." When Rep. Wolf's aide called again on March 2, Ms. Thomasson denied she'd ever said she had been approved for a pass. Ms. Thomasson, who didn't return a phone call, may indeed finally have received a permanent pass last Friday, when subpoenas started arriving. This would be after 14 months, vs. the FBI's 45-day target for new employees.

Rep. Wolf's extensive correspondence has been highly instructive. White House Chief of Staff Mack McLarty rebuffed his letters asking for information on White House security procedures and the proliferation of temporary passes in the hands of FOB. He wrote that the list of pass holders is confidential. One letter added that "during the Reagan Administration, the Office of the Legal Counsel of the Department of Justice opined that the White House has authority to accept the services of volunteers, and that these persons may be paid by outside sources." The Congressman's requests for a copy of this opinion went unanswered (we have some vague recollection of a flaplet about the funding of inaugural balls). Mr. Wolf did determine, however, that the ultimate decisions on White House passes rests in the office of the White House counsel. And that it is being handled there by Mr. Kennedy, the former Rose Law Firm partner reprimanded in the Travelgate affair. Mr. Wolf wrote, "I would like to take this opportunity to express my opinion that this is not the right man for this highly sensitive position."

Since Ms. Thomasson is an old Arkansas FOB, we doubt that the delay on her pass was due to Mr. Kennedy. We suspect that instead it had something or other to do with her past association with another Arkansas FOB, bond trader and drug convict Dan Lasater. She worked for Mr. Lasater when his business prospered from handling $664 million in Arkansas bond contracts, and ran his affairs for two years after his conviction on drug charges.

Rep. Wolf doesn't think his questions on security procedures have been answered, especially in the wake of the Aldrich Ames CIA spy scandal. He sits on a House Appropriations subcommittee where Ms. Thomasson is scheduled to testify on March 22. When that's over we expect that who she is will not be much of a mystery.

Editorial Feature

Whitewater, Watergate

President Clinton denied earlier this week that the Whitewater-Madison contretemps is beginning to resemble the scandal that toppled Richard Nixon in 1974. "No one has accused me of any abuse of authority in office," Mr. Clinton declared. "That's what Watergate was about." His imagemeister, David Gergen, who played a similar role for President Nixon, echoed that view: "Whitewater is not about coverups, it's about screw-ups." We asked a number of figures involved in the Watergate scandal to comment on resemblances, and differences, between the two "gates." Excerpts from their replies appear below.

'IT'S EARLY DAYS, MR. PRESIDENT'

The president insists the two situations have nothing in common. That goes too far, though there are differences. The flames of Watergate ultimately engulfed the Nixon presidency. So far there are no flames — there are only wisps of smoke and a crackling sound from the tinder under the Clinton presidency.

Well it's early days, Mr. President. At a comparable stage of the Watergate investigation, nobody had accused President Nixon of an abuse of power either. There never was evidence connecting Mr. Nixon directly with the Watergate break-in. The end came when the Oval Office tapes showed the president planning to use the CIA to deflect the FBI investigation. If it is true, as Mr. Clinton and his defenders insist, that they have attempted no concealment of evidence, it is also the case that they have certainly given a virtuoso imitation of a coverup. One could easily mistake it for the genuine article.

We may never know whether there is serious wrongdoing that the White House is trying to hide, but the sounds of document-shredding raise legitimate questions and may amount to an obstruction of justice. If Mr. Nixon had burned the tapes, he might conceivably have avoided removal from office, but his presidency would have been paralyzed. If persons close to the Clintons should be indicted for the removal or shredding of files, a similar paralysis may afflict this administration.

Robert Bork

There was not in Watergate anything similar to Vincent Foster's death, nor to the inexcusable way it was handled by the White House: giving the Park Police responsibility for the investigation; the secret removal of files from Mr. Foster's office; the lame statement that the so-called suicide note in Mr. Foster's briefcase had been overlooked earlier. The litany goes on. There is far more evidence of a coverup here than there ever was in Watergate until the tapes were played.

I came to the Nixon administration on June 26, 1973. The Watergate break-in was long past and there was no House impeachment committee, but the acrid smell of the wisps of smoke was unmistakable. As matters grew worse, trips to the White House grew more frequent and steadily more depressing. The building exuded a thick atmosphere of desperation. Then, as now, senior staff rushed from one damage control meeting to the next. Then, H.R. Haldeman and John Ehrlichman were jettisoned; now, it is Bernard Nussbaum, with surely more to follow. Then, as now, under pressure, the attorney general appointed a special counsel. The "firestorm" that followed the firing of Archibald Cox, which fell to me, probably means that Robert Fiske's tenure is secure — unless the Clintons are determined to repeat every stage of Watergate.

A common element in Watergate and Whitewater is the hatred that both Mr. Nixon and Mr. Clinton arouse, though from different ends of the political spectrum. That contributed to the bunker mentality in 1973, as it appears to be doing in 1994, and that mentality produces mistakes.

I think I know a little of how the Clinton group feels. It is a unique experience to be inside an administration that may, or may not, be collapsing: the frustration of not knowing the facts; the anguish of hoping that ultimately investigation will bring vindication; the pain of seeing the desperation of those at the center of power. In Watergate only a very few people, perhaps no more than two or three, knew. That is probably true today; the rest must be hoping against hope, as we were.

ROBERT H. BORK
Nixon Solicitor General,
Acting Attorney General
American Enterprise Institute fellow

'BUNKER MENTALITY'

There are similarities between the two events. There are allegations of a Whitewater coverup, possible destruction of evidence, the appearance of subordinates involved in some form of "modified, limited hangouts," to use a Watergate phrase.

But there are significant differences as well. It is unclear at this time whether civil violations of the law occurred rather than criminal transgressions. President Clinton has thus far encouraged openness and urged that the investigation go forward, although his subordinates have demonstrated a bunker mentality reminiscent of the Watergate era.

SEN. WILLIAM S. COHEN (R., Maine)
House Judiciary Committee
member during Nixon
impeachment procedures

'DON'T GIVE UP HILLARY'

The parallels are uncanny between John Dean's situation in Watergate and Bernard Nussbaum's situation today. Bernard Nussbaum was counsel to the president; John Dean was counsel to the president. Bernard Nussbaum removed evidence from Vincent Foster's White House office to impede the investigation; John Dean removed evidence from Howard Hunt's White House safe to impede the investigation. All that, however, does not mean that Bernie has to turn rat just because John Dean did.

Despite our political differences, Bernie, I offer this letter of encouragement and urge you to do the right thing. Your actions and mine were motivated by the same desire to keep our respective presidents in the White House. What is important is that you remain loyal, keep your mouth shut and don't give up Hillary!

The feds will be angry when you refuse to turn rat. They will threaten you with a long prison term. They sentenced me to 21 1/2 years. Don't let that scare you. Hell, I did only five. They'll let you out shortly after the Clintons are run out of town. Be strong, Bernie.

G. GORDON LIDDY
White House aide convicted in
Watergate
Washington radio talk-show host

'50,000 PULITZER-SEEKERS'

In Watergate, there were two guys trying to get the Pulitzer and in Whitewater there are roughly 50,000. Therefore, there has been an intensification by a very large factor of the pressure for disclosure, the creation of a mood of suspicion, and a generalized sense of outrage in Congress and the press at any attempts to withhold information.

I think the multiplication of pressures has created a situation of terminal confusion in which matters not yet proved are taken to be proved and rumors are flying around like birds going south — in great flocks. This has its own momentum that could produce very serious injury to the Clinton administration even if one were to assume there was no significant wrongdoing in Arkansas, about which I do not have any information.

LEONARD GARMENT
Acting Counsel to President Nixon
Washington attorney

'A CREATION OF THE MEDIA'

Out across the country — I'm on the lecture circuit a lot — I don't find people suggesting there was any major corruption in the Whitewater case or a major breakdown of the president's authority. I think it's largely a creation of the media in New York and Washington. I don't see it as a major issue across the country.

Now, I have to confess that in the early days of Watergate, this was also true. When I tried to raise it as an issue in the '72 presidential cam-

George McGovern

paign, I got nowhere with it. I couldn't convince even audiences that were favorable to me that there was much to the Watergate break-in. The only thing we really knew about it at that point was that somebody from the president's re-election committee had broken into our headquarters. I thought the most serious offenses occurred in the coverup.

But here I don't see any really serious wrongdoing originally. And I don't see any devious coverup or anything unethical done to prevent the public and press and Congress from knowing what's going on. They may have been ill-advised to have the White House counsel try to get a report on what was going on—I think that was out of line — but I don't think it was a crime or anything that compares to the Watergate scenario.

GEORGE MCGOVERN
1972 Democratic presidential
candidate
President, Middle East
Policy Council

'WORSE THAN WATERGATE'

It occurs to me that — minus the federally insured part of the problem, minus the death, minus the large-scale coverup — Whitewater resembles Spiro Agnew's situation more than President Nixon's: the sale of influence by a governor. This would be fairly routine stuff except for the looting of a federally insured S&L (far worse than anything Richard Nixon was ever credibly accused of doing); the federally organized coverup at so many levels; the first lady's frightening, Evita Peron-type involvement; and the still-unexplained violent death of Vincent Foster (no one died in Watergate, except Mrs. Howard Hunt, and that was a clear accident).

If any large number of these recent allegations is to be believed, Whitewater is worse than Watergate.

BENJAMIN STEIN
Speechwriter to President Nixon
Actor/writer in Malibu, Calif.

'MAN IS A SINNER'

The most astonishing thing about Whitewater is that we are astonished by it. Our reaction — the press's feeding-frenzy and politicians' posturing — reveals how deluded we are about the most pernicious myth of this century: that man is good, and that with technology and education we can achieve utopian societies. So we regard Watergate and Whitewater and all "gates" in between as dreadful aberrations. Our founders were not so naive. They understood the Judeo-Christian truth that man is a sinner.

We moderns have forgotten this foundational truth. Then we are shocked that a governor apparently made sweetheart deals, and White House aides overzealously protected their president. Not to minimize wrongdoing, only to understand it, one should recognize that, like it or not, governors do make cozy deals and White House aides are by nature — I know — overzealous.

Charles Colson

CHARLES W. COLSON
White House aide convicted in
Watergate
Chairman, Prison Fellowship
Ministries

'A DEBILITATING THING'

One thing that is spookily similar to Watergate is that no matter what's happening at the White House, all questions focus on the scandal. In the Nixon White House, we had a meeting at 7:30 a.m. every day to plan the day. We would spend an hour talking about what we could say about energy policy or the economy or some domestic thing. I would then brief the press and, of course, I would get no questions about these matters. The questions were all on Watergate.

I would imagine that's the way [Press Secretary]. Dee Dee Myers finds things happening now. No matter what important developments there are on health care or welfare reform, the questions will be about Whitewater. That's a debilitating thing and that's what hurts government.

Incidentally, one of the people who sat in on those 7:30 a.m. meetings was David Gergen. I'm sure if they ask him, he can give very good advice.

GERALD WARREN
Deputy Nixon Press Secretary
Editor, San Diego Union-Tribune

'US THE PEOPLE'

I've tried to understand why the American people became aroused about Watergate, why there was a firestorm precipitated by the resignations of [Deputy Attorney General] Bill Ruckelshaus and myself. And why, on the other hand, people in Europe couldn't understand the uproar. My answer is that in this country, the executive branch, indeed all branches of government, derive their powers from us the people. That was the unique and revolutionary thing about the creation of the government of the U.S. In those other countries the sovereign was assumed to have all the power. And while progressively power was limited by the evolution of democracy, the sovereign's power is nevertheless the underlying assumption.

So we have always looked to the president and Congress as holding office by delegation from us. And whenever they behave in a way that avoids accountability, we get really excited about it. That's the common denominator between Iran-Contra and Watergate. I don't see that thread in Whitewater. At most I see questionable dealings at a financial level between a local savings and loan and the governor's office and the law firm where the governor's wife worked. On the scale of impropriety, any outcome would not rise to the level of a deliberate effort to avoid accountability to the people of the U.S.

ELLIOT L. RICHARDSON
Attorney General under
President Nixon
Washington attorney

'GET YOUR TICKETS NOW'

During the Watergate era, I recall receiving telephone calls revealing information about the status of the investigation and what questions likely would be asked. The White House, then as now, keeps track of matters that affect the King. Have these types of things occurred in the Clinton White House? Yes. Was it improper? Yes.

On reflection, I am torn between a part of me wanting to see the [Whitewater] show, and another part feeling we should not get carried away. The last thing anybody wants is a repeat of the gridlock that kept Richard Nixon from running the country and achieving his foreign policy goals. I have no doubt that the dreadful outcome of Iran and Vietnam was a result of Watergate. Can we risk failure to address issues such as nuclear proliferation, unchecked immigration, continuing deficits, and health care distribution and affordability? The answer is that we are our own worst enemy. Get your tickets now, the show is in town.

DONALD SEGRETTI
White House aide convicted
in Watergate
Newport Beach, Calif., attorney

'NONSENSICAL TO COMPARE'

The only thing that Whitewater has in common with Watergate is "water."

Watergate involved a president, Richard Nixon, who committed serious crimes in office solely to advance his political ambitions. Perhaps at no other time has our constitutional democracy been more in danger.

It is really nonsensical to compare these crimes with the undefined allegations relating to Whitewater. Whatever Whitewater is – and at this time we do not know and there has been no evidence of credible charges of wrongdoing – it involved commercial transactions that may have been engaged in by Bill and Hillary Clinton years before he was elected president. The special

Sam Dash

counsel's investigation has just begun – and we should all patiently await its outcome before pointing fingers and making accusations.

SAMUEL DASH
Counsel, Senate Watergate
Committee
Georgetown University law
professor

Editorial Feature

Ethics Irony: Free the Whitewater Ten

Roger Altman, deputy Treasury secretary and charter Friend of Bill, testifies before a grand jury next week. This gives his college chum and boss, President Clinton, plenty of time to do the honorable thing and pardon him.

While he's at it, Mr. Clinton might also examine the others who make up the Whitewater 10. Lisa Caputo, press aide to Hillary Rodham Clinton, testified yesterday for the high crime of having taken a phone call from another government flack. Or take Mark Gearan, the earnest, idealistic 37-year-old White House communications director; he's had to hire an attorney though everyone agrees he's too nice to be nefarious.

Potomac Watch

By Paul A. Gigot

Then there's the first lady, the erstwhile "St. Hillary." A year ago only a few raised doubts about a dual presidency; we were suspected of Neanderthal tendencies. Now the same liberals who put her on a pedestal are discovering that a first lady can't be fired like a Bernie Nussbaum. Anna Quindlen hath no greater fury than for a feminist icon who screws up. It somehow doesn't seem right that Mr. Clinton would subject these loyal, perhaps over-loyal, colleagues to the tender mercies of a special prosecutor.

Mr. Altman's case may be the most poignant, and not just because his chance to become Treasury secretary is probably dashed. Under the criminal standard of ethics established here in the 1980s, Mr.

Altman really does have a legal problem. His controversial testimony to Congress, we are now learning, bears an eerie resemblance to that of Elliott Abrams during the Iran-Contra mess.

President Bush took his time but in the end stepped up and pardoned Mr. Abrams. Would Mr. Clinton do anything less for his old Georgetown pal?

Roger Altman

Mr. Abrams, remember, wasn't punished for telling Congress an untruth. He ran afoul of not telling all that he knew. As the point man on Contra policy, he was asked at a hearing if countries other than the U.S. had given money to the Contras. He said no, which was technically true. But Mr. Abrams knew that the sultan of Brunei had promised some, though the money hadn't come through.

Mr. Abrams corrected his testimony on Brunei a week later. For this conscientiousness, special persecutor Lawrence Walsh used a felony threat and the risk of bankruptcy to force Mr. Abrams to plead guilty to having withheld information from Congress. The New York Times, panting heavily, declared that "Elliott Abrams Is Guilty."

Under this standard, Mr. Altman ought to be petrified. The former Wall Street banker touched off a furor when he told the Senate Banking Committee that he had met with White House aides about a Resolution Trust Corp. inquiry into the Whitewater matter. (He was running the RTC at the time.) This looks like a blunder — "a piece of awful judgment," Mr. Altman now says — not a crime.

But the trouble is, that may not have been his only meeting. The New York Times, panting less heavily (the story appeared on page A20), reported yesterday that Mr. Altman failed to disclose "two contacts between him and the White House about the agency's investigation." The Times quotes White House officials as saying Mr. Altman now intends to disclose those additional contacts to Congress.

If this seems like a technicality, what about special counsel Robert Fiske? Is he now going to throw out Mr. Walsh's Abrams Standard after it was blessed by the New York Times, Rep. Barney Frank and other liberal ethicists? A Treasury spokesman says Mr. Altman didn't disclose the other conversations because he didn't think they were "substantive." But how will a grand jury define "substantive"?

If this all seems amusingly weird, it certainly didn't seem so to Mr.

Abrams and his family. And rest assured it doesn't to Mr. Altman, his family and his newly retained lawyer. But this is what happens when politicians try to criminalize political differences instead of debating them out in the open.

In essence, the standards of the '80s are coming back to haunt the children of the '60s who are governing in the '90s. No doubt the Clintonites never imagined this as they savored the woes of Mr. Abrams, Ted Olson, Ray Donovan and other Reaganites unjustly persecuted. But rules don't change just because the players do.

In a bitter irony, it's the same Democratic fear of normal politics that is causing such hell for the Whitewater 10. In the '80s, Democrats criminalized politics in order to win arguments they thought they'd lose to Ronald Reagan. Now Democrats are afraid that Whitewater hearings in Congress will prove a boon to Republicans. So Louisiana Sen. John Breaux avers that "we don't need more political hearings. We need more legal hearings." Tell that to Lisa Caputo.

George Mitchell, who wrote a book praising the Iran-Contra hearings, now says that calls for Whitewater hearings are "partisan politics." Well, sure. But the state of our polity would be healthier if we had more free-wheeling "politics" in Congress and fewer TV-camera stakeouts in front of grand juries. Which is why Mr. Clinton should pardon the Whitewater 10, then send them to Congress to explain what they did and why they did it.

Of course, I'm not holding my breath.

News Story

Unproven Report On Foster Death Helped Sink Marts

By PAULETTE THOMAS

Staff Reporter of THE WALL STREET JOURNAL

WASHINGTON—Financial consultants eager to influence the markets can sometimes succeed, even with the latest wild speculation.

David Smick proven that yesterday when his financial-gossip newsletter printed a report — unproven, he readily concedes — about the suicide of deputy White House counsel Vincent Foster, and helped send stocks and bonds tumbling.

Concern that the Whitewater mess would derail the Clinton legislative agenda certainly helped depress the markets, but the periodic newsletter published by Johnson Smick International was cited in particular. The two-page issue reported that staffers in the office of Sen. Daniel Moynihan, the New York Democrat, said that the body of Clinton aide Vincent Foster was moved from an administration apartment in Virginia to the park location where it was found. If true, such a claim would raise shocking questions about the Clinton administration's investigation of the death of Mr. Foster.

But Mr. Smick, a one-time aide to former Republican Congressman Jack Kemp, said he was surprised by the market reaction to his column casually passing along a rumor. He said he didn't know whether it was true.

The tone of the newsletter was far more sober and authoritative. "Again, we normally ignore Washington's regular stream of rumor mongering every time a President gets into trouble because the rumors are almost always untrue," it read. "In this case, however, the offices of Senate Finance Committee Chairman Moynihan are putting the word out that Foster in fact committed suicide in a private apartment in Virginia."

The White House and Sen. Moynihan's office vigorously denied the rumor.

Mr. Smick and his partner, Manuel Johnson, the former Federal Reserve vice chairman, characterize their business as practicing "information arbitrage." Mr. Johnson's former position gives them entree to financial movers and shakers, but even they don't pretend that their information is 100% reliable. "If you're 55% to 60% right, you're gold," Mr. Smick has said in the past.

He won't disclose the circulation of his newsletter or its price, but both he and his partner have prospered with the firm, which also holds conferences and gives advice.

Washington has been rife with Whitewater rumors, but once the Foster rumor was set in the type of the Johnson Smick newsletter, it was given a wide airing. Market news services widely reported the newsletter was affecting the credit and currency markets. And the conservative talk-show host Rush Limbaugh discussed it on his widely followed radio broadcast.

Said Thomas D. Gallagher, a political amalyst for Lehman Brothers Inc. in Washington: "We're in a situation where the scandal has taken on a life of its own and the markets are going to be susceptible to rumors."

Letters to the Editor

Our Role Distorted In Whitewater Rumors

Our firm was mentioned in recent articles in this and other newspapers about the effect of Whitewater developments — and their related rumors — on financial markets. In some cases, including in this newspaper, our firm's role was so distorted that a correction of the record is necessary.

On March 9, our firm, which concentrates largely on analyzing issues of interest to foreign-exchange markets, issued a private memorandum to about four dozen financial clients in response to questions from them concerning congressional reaction to Whitewater. Ironically, while the memorandum was reported to have caused a market reaction, it actually made rather modest observations, including a prediction that changing White House tactics on Whitewater could bring a return to business as usual. Buried in the middle of the report was a brief mention that for months rumors had circulated among Republicans on Capitol Hill regarding the location of the suicide death of Deputy White House Counsel Vincent Foster. The point of interest: The rumors were now bipartisan, having originated also from a staff aide to an important Democratic senator who is responsible for health-care reform and other important legislation. The obvious question: how Whitewater might affect the president's legislative agenda.

Only the most imaginative of minds would conclude after reading the memorandum that a small economics consulting firm had stumbled upon the largest scoop since Watergate and then buried it in the middle of a private memorandum. Any logical reading could not help but conclude that the political source was the issue.

The memorandum circulated to clients for 24 hours without incident until it was misappropriated and loosely interpreted by a popular conservative talk-show host, among others. It was at that point that the memorandum drew broad-based attention.

Your article March 11 was particularly troubling. It inaccurately gives the impression that an interview had been done by the reporter. Moreover, it could easily lead the reader to the conclusion that our firm gleefully mass-marketed erroneous information in order to disturb financial markets as a means of marketing a retail-subscription newsletter. That impression is contrary to the facts, as our firm has a legal track record in trying to protect the confidentiality of the proprietary nature of our product. We also do not sell a broad-based newsletter. While apparently it isn't irregular for byline reporters to get input from other staff members and other sources, the process by which this story was prepared leads to confusion.

When we informally discussed market developments with your Washington bureau chief on March 10, he didn't make us aware that a reporter was preparing an article on our firm, so we didn't have an adequate chance to present our case.

The article's use of the quotation "If you're 55% to 60% right, you're gold" was taken from a two-and-a-half-year-old Journal article on our firm, and its context has long been in dispute. The quotation was referring to the most successful traders and investors, not to the field of economic consulting.

MANUEL H. JOHNSON
DAVID M. SMICK
Senior Partners
Johnson Smick International Inc.

Washington

Editorial Feature

Whitewater, Derivatives and the Urge to Regulate

On the front pages of American newspapers, Whitewater Development finally is becoming a big story. On the financial pages, the global market in something called "derivatives" is getting scrutiny. These two stories might seem unrelated. In fact, they fit together like mortise and tenon.

Most everyone by now knows about Whitewater. Indeed, my colleague David Brooks was questioned about it by Flemish students at a seminar in Leuven, Belgium, the other night. They were up to speed on the central question: whether Bill and Hillary Clinton, through a company called Whitewater Development, helped loot Madison Guaranty Savings & Loan of Little Rock, Ark. More to the point, are the Clintons now engaged in efforts at political damage control that involve further legal and ethical non-niceties?

Global View
By George Melloan

With financial derivatives, the issue is more illusive and abstruse. There is little evidence that their users have violated any laws — or created any problems of any kind, for that matter. But Fortune, Barron's and other forums are carrying debates on whether their mere proliferation — to a notional value of some $4 trillion — threatens the world with some as-yet-unforeseen financial catastrophe.

Readers already will have guessed the underlying relationship between Whitewater and derivatives. The issue is regulation.

Madison Guaranty was, at least theoretically, a federally regulated institution. Many people think that trading in financial derivatives should be more heavily regulated as well. But if Madison Guaranty could not be supervised effectively, why does anyone think financial derivatives can be?

The world's bank regulators get their heads together in Basel, Switzerland, from time to time. They think that bank trading in derivatives and other instruments should be backed with required amounts of capital relative to risks involved. In short, the Basel group wants to expand to bank trading the risk-based minimum capital requirements they established for bank lending in 1988. They are not deterred by the fact that the Basel requirements put a global damper on commercial lending by banks for some years and indeed caused banks to turn to their now-controversial trading desks to try to restore their profits.

To be sure, financial derivatives are rather strange little animals. They carry funny names, such as swaptions, strips, collars, captions — names that the rocket scientists who create them as hedging instruments think are descriptive of what they do. The fact that the creators often are mathematicians or computer nerds good at handling complex equations contributes to the suspicions of politicians and regulators that there is something going on here that the average person isn't supposed to understand. At $4 trillion, the kids at their computers are playing with what looks like big money. Some critics think that a big shock to financial markets might start a derivative chain reaction that would cause a global financial meltdown.

In principle, however, derivatives are not as complicated as they sound. They are merely contracts that derive their value from some underlying asset, such as a bond. If, for example, one party wants to hedge against a future risk by acquiring the revenue stream from a variable-rate security, he might swap the revenue stream from a fixed-rate security to someone with a fixed-rate preference. The two don't trade the underlying asset; they just make a contract to trade places for a while. At relatively low cost traders can hedge, perhaps in several different ways, to protect themselves against future changes in underlying values.

Whether the counterparties are each good for the amount of the contract is of course of some importance, but that's true in any contractual arrangement. As to the possibility of a meltdown, anything is possible. But presumably at any given point in time the hedges on one side of a market roughly equal those on the other side — lending, in theory at least, a certain stability to the complex network of hedges.

It is true, of course, that the traders are pretty much on their own with nothing much to protect them except their own judgment. Yet, there probably would not be $4 trillion worth of contracts floating around the globe unless large banking institutions felt they had at least some grip on the risks. And indeed, separate studies by the Commodity Futures Trading Commission and a task force set up by a banking industry organization called the Group of 30 could see no need for further regulation of these instruments. The Group of 30 study was led by former Fed Chairman Paul Volcker, who few would regard as a soft touch where banks and markets are concerned.

One of the interesting characteristics of derivatives is that even if someone decided they should be regulated, it would not be easy to devise a method for doing so. Trading in financial instruments today is global and moves with the speed of light. The rocket scientists running hedging operations are dealing rapidly with difficult equations as they try to balance risk against risk to protect the customer's underlying position. Former Chicago Mercantile Exchange Chairman Leo Melamed wrote in Barron's last week that Congress will find it just as impossible to fully direct the development of financial engineering as has been the case with another advanced science, genetic engineering.

The underlying question in both cases of course is whether the public is somehow endangered. For the answer, it is useful to ask exactly how effective Congress has been in protecting the public in the past. The U.S. financial services industry is arguably the most heavily regulated in the world, with five or six different regulatory agencies at the federal level not counting the Securities and Exchange Commission and state banking authorities. And yet large numbers of institutions in the vast savings and loan industry collapsed at great cost to American taxpayers. They collapsed not because of too little political interest, but because of too much. The safety net for S&Ls eventually became so cushy, through almost unlimited federal deposit insurance, that it attracted large amounts of cash and a ravaging horde of fast buck exploiters.

The issue on the front pages of the American press is whether the president and his wife were among those exploiters. The issue on the business pages is whether a financial service is safer if it relies on the individual judgment of its deliverers or if it is subject to intense regulatory supervision. Maybe the answer is by now self-evident.

REVIEW & OUTLOOK

The Fiske Coverup II

Subpoenas notwithstanding, Independent Counsel Robert Fiske's investigation into Whitewater/Madison is beginning to look less like an effort to get the facts and more like a sophisticated exercise in political damage control. In a word, like a coverup.

Mr. Fiske may not intend this to be the case, but on his record so far we wonder if Americans are ever going to get the Whitewater accounting they deserve. For contrary to White House spin that there exists not "a shred of evidence" of wrongdoing, the charges and the facts known so far are serious.

Robert Fiske

There is the suspicion that the president of the United States benefited from illegal actions, perhaps by trading political favors for campaign contributions or for a sweetheart investment deal. There is at least one allegation, made by former Judge David Hale, that Mr. Clinton himself personally encouraged a fraudulent loan. And there is by now also a trail of suspicious actions and meetings that suggest that Clinton administration officials have tried to interfere with investigation into these charges. More broadly, the issue is character; how much can we trust this president and this administration?

The Clintonites who appointed Mr. Fiske to investigate themselves now assure us that he will finally clear away all doubt. But our own doubts have grown as we've watched Mr. Fiske get in the way of legitimate inquiries by the press and the Congress. One immediate concern is our own lawsuit, *Dow Jones v. Department of Justice*, to obtain reports about the death of Vincent Foster under the Freedom of Information Act. Mr. Fiske's response has been an across-the-board stonewall.

In his meeting last week with Republican Sen. Al D'Amato, Mr. Fiske explained that it is simply easier for him to deny all documents under a FOIA request than to figure out which ones would really interfere with his own probe. This is why he's even blocking release of a photocopy of the Foster suicide note whose text has already been reported on everywhere. But the FOIA statute requires what lawyers call redaction, vetting individual documents and even parts of them. So what Mr. Fiske is saying is that he feels entitled to ignore requirements of the law. This does not exactly build confidence.

It also seems odd that Mr. Fiske's first act has been to prosecute Judge Hale, the one person who says he has first-hand knowledge of President Clinton's encouragement of illegal acts. Why?

The next act of this unelected counsel has been to shout that no one else should ask questions about Whitewater/Madison, especially not an elected Congress. As Congressman Jim Leach's nearby letter argues, this is an amazing attempt to interfere with Congress's clear constitutional duties of oversight. No less a prosecutorial zealot than Iran-Contra's Lawrence Walsh has concluded that when Congress and prosecutors clash "the law is clear that it is Congress that must prevail."

In practical terms, Mr. Fiske's crusade against Congressional hearings has even become an all-purpose political shield for all the president's men. When the subject was raised at a House subcommittee hearing last week, Treasury Secretary Lloyd Bentsen replied, "On the advice of Mr. Fiske, the special counsel, I refuse to answer." So the same Robert Fiske who was appointed by the president to investigate himself is now serving as a kind of backstop Fifth Amendment for the people he is supposed to be investigating. Too bad Tricky Dick never thought of this one.

The latest White House gambit is to suggest that Mr. Fiske issue an "interim" report on the various improper White House and Treasury meetings. Since Senate Republicans have generously, and we think prematurely, decided to postpone their hearing demands until after Mr. Fiske finishes this part of his investigation, the White

House will then argue that there's no need for any such hearings because Mr. Fiske has already looked into it. And if Mr. Fiske comes down with a decision saying there's insufficient credible evidence of actual criminal violations, we can expect the White House to ask that the records be sealed, denying voters a record on which they might make judgment on character.

But as we've argued before, the main public interest here is not in putting the likes of Roger Altman in jail but in finding out what the Clinton/Little Rock/Rose presidency is all about. Especially since Mr. Leach has now discerned a potential Keating Five-type twist to the Whitewater/Madison deal. His letter to Mr. Fiske says he is "concerned" that officials from the Resolution Trust Corp. in Washington "gagged and possibly coerced" RTC officials in Kansas City who were looking into the deal. Yet House Banking Chairman Henry Gonzalez, who didn't shrink from probing the Keating Five, is now also citing Mr. Fiske to block any such questions from an upcoming RTC hearing.

In practice if not intent, all of this adds up to a coverup. It amounts to one political faction manipulating all of the levers of government — executive, legislative and prosecutorial — in order to prevent public scrutiny. In some countries they'd call that a coup.

Editorial Feature

'A Chilling Effect'

Following are excerpts from a letter House Banking Committee rank-ing minority member James A. Leach sent to independent counsel Robert Fiske last week. A related editorial appears nearby.

Dear Mr. Fiske:

I am writing to make clear to you that, as Ranking Member of the committee of jurisdiction over an issue which you are probing, I am fully prepared to recognize the legitimate concerns, as indicated below, of your office. I believe, however, that you have an equal obligation not to interfere with the legitimate oversight responsibilities of Congress . . . .

. . . I hereby request that the special counsel do nothing that will: 1) put a chilling effect on our Congressional investigation and oversight, particularly with regard to witnesses and strategy you may gather from the material we have supplied you; 2) intervene or tilt the checks and balances between the Legislative and Executive Branches; or 3) pursue a course that tilts towards choosing sides in what is a legitimate difference between America's two great political parties.

With regard to witnesses we wish to invite, you have been provided our prospective list. I am prepared to agree that a week or two delay in hearings could be considered if you suggest time is inadequate for you to interview all on our witness list. But I would stress the minority does not control the hearing process. Given the manner in which the major-ity party has failed for over four months to accede to a restrained request for a hearing, we have no choice but to latch on to the one modest power we have: an insistence, that however uncomfortable, the majority comply with the law and hold a statutorily required oversight hearing on the RTC, with a date specific in the next four weeks . . .

. . . I would bring to your attention the following passage from Mr. Walsh's recent report on the Iran-Contra probe:

When a conflict between the oversight and prosecutorial roles develops—as plainly occurred in the Iran/Contra affair— the law is clear that it is Congress that must prevail. This is no more than a recognition of the high political importance of Congress's responsibility. It also is the appropriate place to strike the balance, as a resolution of this conflict calls for the exercise of a seasoned political judgment that must take a broad view of the national interest.

It is in this context that I must confess to more than a little concern about your assertion that you have a "strong concern" about "any hearing" our committee might hold and your belief that Congressional inquiry "would pose a severe risk to the integrity of our investigation." I reiterate this concern in light of the historical irony that it was Senator Ervin's committee that revealed the existence of the Watergate tapes and that it was the recent Senate hearing that revealed improper contracts between Executive Branch agencies and the White House. Hearings almost always reveal knowledge and perspective that is helpful to prosecutors. The major recent exception involved the excessive zeal of the majority party to embarrass President Reagan that caused it to offer immunity to certain witnesses.

Given the circumstance, unlike most of the past several decades where the majority party in Congress was opposite that of the White House, I am concerned that your public lobbying of Congress has the effect of sending a chilling precedent for Congressional oversight and a fatuous pretext for the majority party which controls the machinery of Congress to delay, defer, or avoid its Constitutional responsibilities.

I would . . . bring to your attention the following exchange between Mr. Livingston of Louisiana and the Secretary of the Treasury before a House Appropriations Committee this afternoon. Mr. Livingston asked if Secretary Bentsen had been apprised in advance of Roger Altman's meeting at the White House on the failure of Madison Guaranty. The Secretary responded: "On advice of Mr. Fiske, the special counsel, I refuse to answer."

[It] should be stressed that not only does the Congress have constitutionally-mandated oversight responsibilities, but that traditionally in all Western democracies it is the responsibility of the party out of power to hold the party in power accountable for breaches of the public trust.

It may be standard operating procedure for all prosecutors to be doubtful of intervention by the Congress. But it is not standard operating procedure to bias or tilt in any way the American political process or to make premature public judgments about the White House being "very responsive and cooperative" to a probe when there are indications to the contrary. I am particularly concerned that officials of the Kansas City RTC office are being gagged and possibly coerced by the Washington RTC office. (See attached confidential memo.)

It is also unprecedented presumption for a counsel to suggest, as reported today in the Washington Post: "I would prefer that there be no hearings."

I have known very few issues where public accountability is more important. This is after all an issue of public ethics as well as public law. Accordingly, as you vigorously seek documents, I would stress again my apprehension that at the end of the process the White House can be expected to seek to seal the vast array of documents related to your inquiry. Here the constitutionally differentiated distinction between a Justice Department inquiry seeking criminal and civil accountability and Congressional oversight which often involves the question of public disclosure is substantial.

But the differentiated roles of Congress and a special counsel does not mean, as you have implied, that the two are incompatible. The two are generally complementary. Indeed, one could credibly suggest that any attempt by a prosecuting attorney to constrain Congress beyond the standards indicated above is counterproductive. Constraining a Congressional inquiry has the effect of reducing knowledge, thus reducing prosecutorial discretion.

One of the understandably important aspects of criminal investigations from the prosecutorial standpoint is confidentiality. One of the understandably important aspects of democracy is openness. Both must be respected to the maximum degree possible and neither should or has to jeopardize the other.

JAMES A. LEACH
Ranking Minority Member
House Banking Committee

Washington

Roiling Rapids

The spring of 1994 brought a flood of Whitewater revelations. Associate Attorney General Webster Hubbell resigned due to mounting pressure over his activities in Little Rock and Washington. Doubts were surfacing about Vincent Foster's death. A New Republic writer claimed to be the victim of a violent attack in Arkansas. The New York Times, in a team report written by Jeff Gerth, disclosed that Hillary Clinton had made nearly $100,000 trading in cattle futures in late 1978 and 1979. And in Congress, questions were being raised about White House official Patsy Thomasson, a former aide to Arkansas bond dealer and drug convict Dan Lasater.

"Just as Watergate became more than a third-rate burglary," wrote Wall Street Journal columnist Paul Gigot, "Whitewater has become more than a two-bit land deal. It's now a metaphor for this president's character."

REVIEW & OUTLOOK

Who Was Webster Hubbell?—I

Needless to say, we don't think Webster Hubbell's resignation closes the book on any aspect of this affair. An anonymous White House official tried to spin the story toward closure when news was dribbling out yesterday afternoon about a resignation by the presidential golfing partner/Rose Law Firm partner/ Associate Attorney General. It's a private individual's problems that arose prior to his government service, problems with his prior law firm," said the official. That won't wash.

It was just over a year ago that we first raised a flag in an editorial titled "Who Is Webster Hubbell?" (March 2, 1993). The Clinton Administration was less than two months old. It

Webster Hubbell

had no Attorney General of its own, no Deputy Attorney General and few quality people in top positions. Instead it stuffed the White House with cronies from Little Rock, notably putting two of Hillary's Rose Law Firm partners in the general counsel's office and sending a third Rose partner named Webster Hubbell to be their "liaison" at the Justice Department.

The issue then was Webster Hubbell's interventions into Justice Department policy toward the federal legal troubles of Rep. Harold Ford, a prominent member of the Black Caucus. We wrote at the time: "We seem to have the spectacle of Hillary Clinton's former law partner fixing meetings between Justice officials and demand-waving pols, with the pols getting Justice to do their bidding." And concluded, "We are left to wonder what kind of Justice Department this will be, and what kind of administration."

We have pursued this initial question for 12 months now. So we were not shocked when it came out that the Treasury and White House counsel's office were holding "heads up" meetings over Bill and Hillary's potential problems with Resolution Trust investigations, the parties to which are now subject to special subpoenas.

Nominally, Mr. Hubbell's resignation has to do with allegedly unethical billing practices while back at the Rose firm. But we draw your attention to the nearby article [See Editor's Note], published last summer by the Des Moines Register. It's a fascinating tale of transactions involving a string of Iowa nursing homes, an effort that was brokered by then-Rose partner William Kennedy III, who is now Associate White House Counsel. Two Iowa court rulings refused to allow what the district judge called the deal's "excess profits," though the Rose firm's efforts kept its clients skating along the defensible side of the law. Once in the White House, William Kennedy's name surfaced for playing fast and loose with the FBI and IRS over Travelgate.

Janet Reno, announcing the Hubbell resignation yesterday, said: "He has been a tireless crusader for doing justice, for doing the right thing." Incredibly, she then added: "Webb was directly responsible for changes in the Justice Department's information policy, which had made the Justice Department and government more open and accountable."

This is Orwellian doublespeak, or perhaps Ms. Reno has just been out of the loop. After Ms. Reno loosened the rules governing requests under the Freedom of Information Act last October, Mr. Hubbell tightened the rules the following month for White House-related requests. Most pointedly, his order expanded the act's coverage to include the activities of the First Lady, specifically her top-secret health-care task force.

Ms. Reno's euphoria over Webster Hubbell leaving a legacy of "more open and accountable" government is so much blather. With interest in Whitewater now running at full tide, we have a public information blackout that has turned into an unbridgeable moat around the Clinton presidency. As we editorialized yesterday, our own FOIA request for the Park Police report on the suicide of former Rose partner Vincent Foster has now hit the ultimate contraction with Special Counsel Robert Fiske's blanket suppression of all documents and information relating to Whitewater/Madison.

Rose Partner No. 1, Hillary Clinton, is now appearing in newsmagazine interviews to announce that Whitewater has been blown out of proportion. That script may still play in various journalistic backwaters, but the more likely scenario is that there will be growing pressure to expose Arkansas mores to more public scrutiny.

Moreover, someone should put out a protective order for the Justice Department. After former deputy Philip Heymann threw in the towel, the White House nominated as his replacement Defense Department General Counsel Jamie Gorelick, a Beltway criminal lawyer whose client list included BCCI celebrities Clark Clifford and Robert A. Altman. Indiana basketball coach Bobby Knight drew boos for benching his first-string for a whole half this year, but Bill and Hillary Clinton seem intent on keeping their party's best people on the bench for the entire presidency. Why are they doing this?

With Webster Hubbell's resignation, this Administration has lost its Bert Lance, the Jimmy Carter confidant who at least brought animal survival skills to a floundering administration. There's an important difference, though. Jimmy Carter and Bert Lance were on different planets. The Little Rock crowd travels in a fixed orbit around the same Sun. Webster Hubbell's saying he quits doesn't change that. We still want to know who these people are.

Editor's Note: The Des Moines Register denied Dow Jones permission to reprint this article here.

Letters to the Editor

A Straight Shooter: Give Her a Chance

In regard to your March 15 editorial "Who Was Webster Hubbell—I?": As a former member of the Bush/Quayle '92 national campaign staff, I have no special brief for the Clintons or their administration, but still I think you have unfairly disparaged Jamie Gorelick, current general counsel of the Defense Department and deputy attorney general-designate, by suggesting that she's not a first-string player.

Ms. Gorelick, former president of the D.C. bar, is far more than some hack criminal lawyer. Her former firm is one of the premier appellate firms in the U.S.; she handled successfully many knotty civil matters as well as criminal, and she herself is a straight shooter, honest and candid. If confirmed, she'll make a good deputy attorney general and will serve the president and the country well. Give her a chance, will ya?

WEAVER H. GAINES

Gainesville, Fla.

REVIEW & OUTLOOK

The White House Passes

Herein, we offer a case history of why this White House routinely stumbles into trouble. It mainly has to do with what now appears to be some lemminglike instinct never to give straight answers to even legitimate questions about its behavior. By default, the world is left to speculate about what exactly is going on in there.

Last week, Press Secretary Dee Dee Myers acknowledged that she and more than 100 other White House staffers have failed to obtain permanent White House passes. Rep. Frank Wolf, a Virginia Republican who has been trying unsuccessfully for nine months to get a straight answer on security procedures out of the White House, asks: "What is going on over there? This is like no other White House I've ever heard of."

Mack McLarty

Why does this matter? Ever since Lyndon Johnson tightened White House security procedures, the Secret Service has screened presidential employees for security concerns as well as any "embarrassment or lack of suitability" they might pose for an administration. All staffers must fill out a Form 86 background questionnaire. This is then used by the FBI to conduct a 45- to 90-day background check, which then goes to the Secret Service.

The Service cannot decide who gets White House passes, but it would be unprecedented for its suggested turndowns to be overridden by the White House counsel's office, whose responsibility it is to rule on who gets a permanent pass. Such a pass is a prerequisite for a separate determination on who gets a security clearance. And yes, security still matters around the White House of the United States.

Ms. Myers says the problem is merely "procrastination." She says only a few senior officials lack permanent passes, but among them are herself and Ricki Seidman, who runs the president's scheduling office. Ms. Myers currently has routine access to classified material, even though she hasn't finished an FBI clearance. "I have no excuse," she says of her failure to provide the proper background data, saying she put it off because the process was so laborious.

William Kennedy III

We talked about this with Phil Larsen, who has worked for five presidents on budget and accounting issues. He was Jimmy Carter's White House administrative officer. Under President Bush he ran the White House personnel management office. "This administration's problems with people lacking permanent passes and security clearances has never happened before, to my knowledge," he told us. "Others had a problem case or two, but not dozens of people."

Despite Ms. Myers's assurances, several Members of Congress are concerned the security bottlenecks may be due in part to what the FBI discovered. The Washington Times cites intelligence sources who say that some of the current background checks have turned up the "use of illegal drugs, convictions of drug offenses, alcoholism and failure to pay federal or state income taxes." Ms. Myers told reporters last Friday that she "wouldn't know" about any details involving individual cases, and says she doesn't know if any passes have been pulled by the Secret Service but then reinstated on orders from the White House counsel's office.

Compounding the problem, a former Clinton White House aide told us that several three- or six-month temporary White House passes that are issued in lieu of a permanent pass have been extended with no questions asked. Paperwork is said to be piling up on the desk of Associate White House Counsel William Kennedy III, the former Rose Law Firm partner and the decision-maker on White House passes and clearances.

Congressman Wolf says he has received zero cooperation from the White House in finding out how many temporary passes exist and how many are held by "visiting" FOBs. Last October, Chief of Staff Mack McLarty wrote him to say that "identities of holders of passes to the White House are confidential." Last month, Mr. McLarty wrote Rep. Wolf again to assure him that "security clearances are being handled in a timely manner and in accordance with the procedures of previous administrations."

But Mr. Larsen and other former White House staffers say that previous administrations would not have stonewalled Members of Congress over who holds a White House pass. John Schmitz was deputy White House counsel during the Bush Administration, which was a fierce defender of presidential authority. "If a Member of Congress on an oversight committee wanted that information, we would have given a personal oral briefing to preserve confidentiality," he told us.

Rep. Wolf speculates that the White House may be stonewalling him because it's unwilling to rein in the many FOBs who don't work for the government yet have free access to the White House.

On Monday, Mr. Wolf wrote to Lloyd Cutler, the interim White House counsel, asking for his help on the matter. This was after the White House pass issue was raised with Mr. Cutler on "Meet the Press" the day before. "The first time I heard about this, I felt very strongly that there's no justification," he said. "Now that I've started to fill out my own form, I can see their problem. But, yes, that will be taken care of."

Rep. Wolf deserved some sort of credible answer to his questions. But providing something that's always short of that seems to be standard operating procedure, whether the questions are about White House passes or Whitewater. Then they complain that the press is engaging in speculation.

Editorial Feature

Whitewater and the Battle of Stalingrad

Whitewater is taking on the elements of the Battle of Stalingrad: Both sides sometimes deserve to lose.

The congressional Democrats resist hearings out of deference to the special counsel. It's hard to recall such procedural politeness surrounding the Iran-Contra scandal or the failed Silverado Savings & Loan involving President Bush's son.

The pious pronouncement that the Iran-Contra congressional hearings killed successful prosecutions doesn't wash. The hearings did allow Oliver North and John Poindexter to escape deserved prison sentences. But it was better to inform the public on this ignoble affair than to wait five years for a report, by which time it was all a distant memory.

Politics & People

By Albert R. Hunt

It's not clear that Whitewater will be nearly as sordid, but the same principles apply. Privately, Capitol Hill Democrats are petrified that Republicans will force a vote on hearings. Democratic leaders ought to immediately schedule hearings to start by early May. (The March 24 House Banking Committee oversight hearings will feature fireworks. But Republicans will complain, legitimately, that the scope is too proscribed.)

At the White House, Hillary Clinton has to stop the appearance of stonewalling. Analogies to Watergate are far-fetched, but, in a favorite phrase of that era, the first lady's short interviews with the news magazines typified the "modified limited hangout route."

Instead Ms. Clinton needs to brush aside the lawyers and do a

Ferraro — a full-fledged, lengthy, no-limitations press conference or credible interview. Geraldine Ferraro did exactly that on her financial problems and supposed family mob ties in 1984. The Mondale-Ferraro ticket won only one state that year, but the press conference ended that issue.

The next day you can bet that the Bob Doles will complain about unanswered questions, but the public will see that as piling on. One caveat: This is a nonstarter if Ms. Clinton stays as testy as she was in Colorado on Monday. But, with the help of some outsiders, she's easily up to a no-holds-barred encounter.

Roger Altman

The Democrats' efforts to whitewash Whitewater by impugning the critics won't work. Yet, just as the Republicans legitimately questioned Ted Kennedy criticizing Clarence Thomas for sexual harassment or Sen. Don Riegle of Keating Five fame railing against Silverado, so too are the character and motivations of the Whitewater critics legitimate fodder. (The Democrats' worst fear is the GOP effort will be spearheaded by Rep. Jim Leach and Sen. Bill Cohen, both credible and respected.)

Leading the GOP charge has been Sen. Alfonse D'Amato, who calls various Clinton associates "political hacks" and demands that all information be released and the statute of limitations on criminal prosecutions be extended.

Let's, as the Fons might say, look at the record. In 1991 the Senate Ethics Committee typically went easy on the New York Republican but still found that he acted "in an improper and inappropriate manner," permitting his brother, Armand, to use the Senate office for defense lobbying; his brother now is in the federal penitentiary for those offenses. The Senate Committee also found grounds that Sen. D'Amato used his office to "financially enrich contributors, cronies and relatives."

Alfonse D'Amato

The committee won't release the full record of these proceedings without Sen. D'Amato's consent. He won't give it. In a separate case earlier, three law school deans strongly suggested that Mr. D'Amato committed perjury when he said he was unaware of kickbacks, but the statute of limitations ran out on that offense. If the press wants to do its job fairly, every time Sen. D'Amato demands more information on Whitewater he should be pressed on when he's going to come clean and release the information on his ethical misdeeds, and asked if he supports extending the statute of limitations on perjury allegations against him.

Senate Minority Leader Bob Dole is a much-higher-class hit man, representative of the breed that after a 12-year hiatus has discovered ethics. Sen. Dole careens from alleging that the most important issue is the Clintons' actions in Arkansas a decade ago, to the alleged coverup today, to Vince Foster's suicide last July. Everything Bob Dole does is with an eye on 1996, not much different from some Democrats during the Reagan and Bush years.

But he's getting a free ride from the press. Take, for instance, his insistence that Roger Altman be fired. As the deputy Treasury secretary and acting Resolution Trust Corp. head, Mr. Altman gave top White House aides a Feb. 2 briefing on the procedures the RTC was following in a possible civil case against Madison Guaranty, owned by the Clintons' Whitewater partner James McDougal. That was, as Mr. Altman subsequently acknowledged, a dumb act, creating an awful appearance.

But what Bob Dole and others neglect to note is that a) that meeting was cleared with the Treasury's ethics officer – Dennis Foreman, a George Bush appointee – and b) a similar procedural briefing was given a week earlier to Sen. D'Amato's staff. Some Republican critics say it strains credulity that more wasn't discussed. But Mr. Altman has a reputation for integrity, and there has been absolutely no evidence to the contrary.

Moreover, this was a civil case, and prosecutorial experts, asked about the situation, suggest it's very hard to conjure up a legal case against Mr. Altman here. By contrast, the Treasury counsel's briefing of White House counsel Bernie Nussbaum earlier on a possible criminal referral against Madison is potentially more serious, though there's no evidence this affected the case. But Sen. Dole isn't interested in what's serious; all he wants is to put a political coonskin on the wall.

White House counsel Nussbaum performed miserably and had to

go, and the resignation this week of Deputy Attorney General Webb Hubbell was inevitable given separate ethical charges leveled against him. But if the president acquiesces to McCarthyite cries to dump innocent people, it'll be a far more serious long-term setback for his leadership than the continual sniping by critics.

Whatever he does, it's going to get uglier. There are Republicans who think this is merely payback time. But already some Democrats talk about delving into the ethics and past personal lives of GOP leaders like Newt Gingrich, and others eagerly await the 1996 candidacy of Bob Dole — "the senator from Archer Daniels Midland." Like Stalingrad, this battle will last a long time, and there are likely to be lots of casualties on both sides.

Correction

Armand D'Amato, brother of Sen. Alfonse D'Amato, is not in a federal penitentiary. Armand D'Amato has been convicted of mail fraud and sentenced to five months in jail. He is free on bond pending appeal.

REVIEW & OUTLOOK

In Defense of Arkansas

It's time to come to the defense of Arkansas, recently maligned with an image of a close-knit political circle of mutual back-scratching. In this department, Little Rock has nothing on Washington, D.C. With Webb Hubbell leaving the Justice Department, Jamie Gorelick is about to arrive.

Ms. Gorelick's nomination as Deputy Attorney General may be voted on in the Judiciary Committee today, with Senators anxious to rush some help to Attorney General Janet Reno. Ms. Gorelick seasoned her administrative experience the past year or so as general counsel of the Defense Department, but prior to that was a partner in Miller, Cassidy, Larroca & Lewin. This firm may not be familiar in Little Rock, but among Beltway bigwigs its phone number is posted right next to 911.

Jamie Gorelick

Miller Cassidy is totally nonpartisan, having helped Richard Nixon on his pardon. And "according to quiet rumors," as the National Law Journal put it, the firm advised Ronald Reagan on Iran-Contra. Good GOP clients also included Edwin Meese, Michael Deaver and former Attorney General Richard Kleindienst.

Ms. Gorelick has been active in intra-bar politics, rising to president of the D.C. Bar Association. But she has found time for her share of high-profile cases, most recently on behalf of Clark Clifford and

Robert Altman. Her part of their litigation has been trying to get reimbursement for their legal fees from First American Bank, where they worked when it was secretly owned by the Bank of Credit & Commerce International, or BCCI.

In a January 1993 letter to a lawyer for First American Bankshares, she wrote that her clients had "certified that they acted at all times in good faith with respect to First American, in a manner consistent with the best interests of the corporation, and neither of them had any reasonable cause to believe that his conduct was unlawful. Their proper stewardship of First American has been confirmed repeatedly by federal and state regulators, extensive company audits and testimony of bank officials."

Ms. Gorelick argued the bank should pay their legal fees. They have, she related, "been billed in excess of $8 million for legal fees and expenses by the law firms of Skadden, Arps, Slate, Meagher & Flom ('Skadden, Arps') and Davis Polk & Wardwell ('Davis Polk')." That is to say, the ultimate beneficiaries of Ms. Gorelick's letter prominently included Robert Fiske, independent counsel for Whitewater, who also led the Clifford-Altman defense at Davis Polk.

By the way, Ms. Gorelick also represented Senator Joseph Biden, chairman of the committee voting on her nomination, in the investigation of Anita Hill leaks. And Orrin Hatch, ranking minority member, hired one of her partners at Miller Cassidy in the Senate Ethics Committee investigation of allegations that some illicit influence was at work in his 1990 floor speech defending BCCI.

Now, we do not see in any of this reason to doubt Ms. Gorelick's personal abilities or integrity. We'd be happy to see her in some other government job at some other time. If we're in hot water, we'd be more than happy to have her on our side. Mr. Altman was acquitted in trial, we should also mention, though he and Mr. Clifford remain defendants in a civil suit by First American's trustee. And the Ethics Committee ruled that Senator Hatch was kosher. With all that said, Ms. Gorelick's experience and pedigree seem to us precisely the opposite of what we need entering the Justice Department at this particular time.

We also suggest Chairman Biden and Senator Hatch set up a phone call with Paula Casey, Friend of Bill and U.S. Attorney in Little Rock. After turning down plea bargain attempts from and launching the prosecution of David Hale, the fellow who said Bill Clinton urged him to make a fraudulent loan, Ms. Casey admitted she had a conflict in

handling Whitewater matters. Before the Senators cast their committee votes, maybe she can advise them on whether they should recuse
themselves.

Editorial Feature

Sans 'Telescope,' Will Janet Reno Find Her Way?

Janet Reno, the ostensible attorney general, has had the most dramatic political fall since King Lear. In less than a year she's gone from a Time magazine heroine to Webster Hubbell's de facto deputy. But with President Clinton's golfing partner now departing, Ms. Reno has a chance to rebuild the reputation she had as a Florida prosecutor.

The root of her problems in Washington isn't even her fault, after all. In hiring her though they'd never met, Mr. Clinton broke a cardinal rule of the presidency: Name someone to the sensitive attorney generalship whom you trust implicitly. JFK had brother Bobby, Jimmy Carter chose Griffin Bell, while Ronald Reagan named William French Smith and Ed Meese.

Potomac Watch

By Paul A. Gigot

Instead Mr. Clinton wanted a woman in the job to satisfy his pledge of "diversity." Yet he still needed a Justice Department he could trust, so he installed his pal, Mr. Hubbell, in the number three job as his eyes and ears. That undercut both Ms. Reno's authority inside Justice and her credibility outside it.

But with Whitewater seeping into the ship of state, Ms. Reno suddenly has a chance to reclaim her clout. Let's look at three ways she could now send a signal that she's become more than a nominal attorney general:

— No more Clincest. Ms. Reno's authority has suffered because Justice has been overstuffed with Friends of Bill. One joke has it that the department has joined MCI's Friends and Family plan, since everyone's so close.

Anne Bingaman, the antitrust chief, is married to New Mexico Sen. Jeff Bingaman and is part of Hillary Rodham Clinton's legal network. Eleanor Acheson, head of policy, was the first lady's Wellesley classmate. Al Gore's brother-in-law, Frank Hunger, runs the civil section. And Sheila Foster Anthony, the lead liaison with Congress, is the sister of the late Vincent Foster and is married to former Arkansas Rep. Beryl Anthony. No wonder Phil Heymann, an outsider, didn't feel he could make a difference as deputy attorney general and quit.

Janet Reno

In selecting a replacement for Mr. Hubbell, Ms. Reno would reassure everyone if she chose someone from beyond the Beltway and Little Rock. Jamie Gorelick, soon-to-be deputy attorney general, is a referral from elsewhere in the administration and won't fill that bill. Ms. Reno needs her own "Lloyd Cutler-type," as they like to say in the White House.

— Nominate Gary Gaertner. Mr. Clinton says he's open to judges of all political views. But when Rep. Dick Gephardt recommended the conservative St. Louis judge for the federal bench, liberal interests commenced a local Borking. His nomination now lies in limbo, as the White House ducks the pressure. Is Ms. Reno out of the judge-picking loop?

— Stand up to John Dingell. When Webb Hubbell was accused of overbilling his expenses by partners in the Rose Law Firm, Ms. Reno jumped to his defense. But when career prosecutors at Justice came under assault by Democrats on Capitol Hill, she dove for the tall grass.

Mr. Dingell is on one of his periodic jihads, this time against prosecutors in the environmental crimes section. He thinks they should be throwing more Americans in jail. General Reno turned the dispute over to Mr. Hubbell, who was only too happy to oblige a Congressional baron (especially one vital to passing a health care bill) by letting the Dingell staff interrogate career prosecutors about their cases.

I haven't yet found a lawyer who doesn't think this is an outrage. The Founders separated the power to prosecute from the power to legislate precisely to avoid political prosecutions. If career prosecutors know they'll be publicly keelhauled by John Dingell for refusing to indict, they'll indict in every close call. "Prosecutorial discretion," which is at the heart of any Justice Department, goes out the window.

John Dingell

Yet sources inside Justice say the department has now decided to cave on a new Dingell subpoena to turn over all internal memoranda — even those discussing how to respond to the Dingell inquiries. One lawyer in the office calls it a "complete breach of trust" with career attorneys who wrote the memos in confidence.

Ms. Reno will also have to decide whether to make a sacrifice of Neil Cartusciello, the ranking career lawyer in the environmental section. Mr. Dingell wants his head, even though a report by four career attorneys at Justice exonerated him this week. The Dingell accusations "stand as examples of how misleading or incomplete testimony" can "wrongly impugn the professional judgment and conduct" of prosecutors, the report said.

This dispute isn't about ideology, because Mr. Cartusciello is no Reaganite. He pioneered the use of the RICO statutes in financial cases during the 1980s, notably the Princeton-Newport case. So why won't Ms. Reno defend an able, nonpartisan career prosecutor?

At her confirmation last year, Ms. Reno snapped at one questioner, saying, "I keep politics out of what I do, Senator." Freed from the interference of the White House Hubbell Telescope, she now has a chance to prove it.

REVIEW & OUTLOOK

O Tempora! O Mores!

I was raised to believe the American dream was built on rewarding hard work. But we have seen the folks in Washington turn the American ethic on its head. For too long, those who play by the rules and keep the faith have gotten the shaft. And those who cut corners and cut deals have been rewarded.

> — Bill Clinton, in his acceptance speech at the Democratic National Convention, August 16, 1992.

Oh the times! The mores!

> — Cicero, First Century B.C.

The latest round of Whitewater news reports shows two things that anyone trying to comprehend this story has to understand. First, it wasn't only Whitewater; the Clintons were involved in at least one other fast-buck deal with other corporate interests heavily dependent on regulation. Second, it wasn't only Arkansas. The confusing, long-ago arcana from Arkansas's political backwaters are relevant because there are now signs that the same practices and same interests — the same mores — are spreading through the Washington bureaucracy.

* * *

Hillary Clinton, it turns out, pocketed $100,000 playing commodity futures between October 1978 and October 1979, with James B. Blair, the powerhouse attorney for food giant Tyson Foods Inc., looking over her shoulder. In a New York Times team report written by Jeff Gerth, Mr. Blair said Mrs. Clinton decided the size of the trade and "We discussed whether she ought to be long or short."

Mrs. Clinton's attorney says it was her own money at risk, and some of her administration defenders said that in playing commodities she studied up on financial data, including reading The Wall Street Journal. Thanks for the endorsement, but we wouldn't advise it to other commodities amateurs. Financial cynics would like to know more about the trades, and the market prices at the time, and about the accounts, both hers and Mr. Blair's. Their principal broker went bankrupt, but says that Mr. Blair "left happy."

We would also be curious about whatever other money Mrs. Clinton made in 1978 and 1979, years for which the Clinton tax returns have never been released. Correspondents for the Knight-Ridder newspapers asked the President about this in a March 12 interview, and provoked a tirade against the press. "Mr. Clinton's face reddened in anger," they reported, and he "abruptly ended the interview, strode past his visitors without shaking hands and stood behind his Oval Office desk until they were escorted out."

* * *

Tyson also figures in a new SEC investigation, reported Friday by the Journal's Bruce Ingersoll and Michael K. Frisby. The agency is looking into suspicious 1992 trading in the stock of Arctic Alaska Fisheries Corp. just before the announcement that it was being acquired by Tyson. Several Arkansas investors are under study, including Phoenix Group Inc.; the president of Phoenix was Patsy Thomasson, now director of the White House Office of Administration, former associate of drug convict Dan Lasater in a company that preceded Phoenix, visitor to Vincent Foster's office the night of his death and point-person in the controversy over White House passes and security clearances. She issued a statement saying she had nothing to do with trades in Arctic. A similar denial was issued by Associate White House Counsel William Kennedy III, who has a relative under investigation in the Arctic deal.

* * *

Mrs. Clinton's commodity streak started just before Bill Clinton's election as Governor of Arkansas, and just as he completed his term as Attorney General. The Times story recounts a series of regulatory decisions that favored the Tyson operations, as well as the appointment of Tyson executives to state posts, plus some allegations of Tyson benefits under the Clinton Presidency. A Tyson spokesman says it only took advantage of normal state industrial development programs, and "There is absolutely no evidence that Jim Blair's relationship with Bill or Hillary Clinton had any impact on our treatment."

Mr. Blair and his wife, our Mr. Ingersoll reported last week, slept at the White House the night of the Clinton inaugural. He also reported on a controversy about sanitary requirements. The Department of Agriculture has imposed on meatpackers a "zero tolerance" policy on fecal matter, and was considering a similar requirement for poultry. This initiative was stopped by Agriculture Secretary Mike Espy, whose brother had received Tyson contributions in an unsuccessful Congressional race in Mississippi. The AP followed this story, reporting a quote from Wilson S. Horne, who recently retired after being in charge of USDA's meat and poultry inspectors for six years: "The message was very, very loud and clear that we were to stop the process."

* * *

Since we've been known to express doubts on the merits of environmental and sanitary regulations, let us detail another matter only briefly touched on in the Times stories. The Pacific Fishery Management Council, a federal commission, issued an order last spring divvying up the $100-million-a-year whiting catch off Oregon, Washington and California. The big argument is always over how much can be taken by large factory-trawler operations and how much by mom-and-pop shore-based fishermen.

The spring ruling gave 63% of the catch to the on-shore operations. The council's decisions must be ratified by the Commerce Department but normally that's just a formality. On those rare occasions when Commerce has disagreed with a local decision, it has sent the issue back for reconsideration by the fishing council. Not this time. When the Federal Register appeared on April 15, 1993, fishermen were shocked to discover that factory trawlers had been allocated 70% of the whiting catch.

The largest operator of factory trawlers is Arctic Alaska Fisheries Corp., owned by Tyson (see above).

There have been the usual denials. Douglas Hall, head of the National Marine Fisheries Service, says the trawler take was in line with historical norms, and says that the decision was made in his office, not by Commerce Secretary Ron Brown. Rep. Elizabeth Furse, an Oregon Democrat, called for hearings on the issue, but was rebuffed by the Congressional leadership.

* * *

Tyson's legal work has long been handled, predictably, by the Rose Law Firm, which brings us to the final citation in the new crop, the current New Republic cover, "The Poisoned Rose." L.J. Davis's superlative account is must reading, above all for those who are confused by all the excitement about a two-bit land deal in the Ozarks. What Mr. Davis understands is that the Rose Law Firm, for all its color, is fundamentally an appendage of the Stephens interests, which use Arkansas as home base for a world-spanning financial empire. It financed Tyson and other successful Arkansas businesses, in addition to handling the brokerage when front men for BCCI bought into First American Bank and installed Clark Clifford to run it.

Arkansas, Mr. Davis writes, "bears a close resemblance to a Third World country, with a ruling oligarchy, a small and relatively powerless middle class and a disfranchised, leaderless populace." This kind of civic culture, we see in many actual Third World countries, is likely to produce a spoils-to-the-victor, above-the-law approach to government. That is to say, the kind of careless arrogance we have seen in the handling of Whitewater, in the White House passes, in Webb Hubbell's law firm billings, in Travelgate, in intervention into an ongoing corruption trial, in the handling of Mr. Foster's death and in the handling of various individuals including Zoe Baird, Kimba Wood, Lani Guinier, Bobby Inman and Chris Emery, a White House usher dismissed over phone conversations with Barbara Bush with no warning and less than a week's notice.

* * *

Whitewater is not merely about a land deal, it is about all of these things, and about the place they are bidding to assume in Washington, which God knows is guilty of enough sins of its own. Above all it is about hypocrisy. Say that one after another the explanations are innocent. Hillary was lucky in commodities and unlucky in land speculation. Jim Blair and Patsy Thomasson are just friends; James and Susan McDougal and David Hale and Dan Lasater are just former friends. Lay aside all suspicions and accept every cover story. We are now supposed to believe Bill Clinton was elected President to reform the sins of the high-flying 1980s?

Editorial Feature

Tabs Tangle Over Foster Death

By Erich Eichman

The producers of "The Paper" couldn't have timed it better. Just as their movie about a scrappy big-city tabloid was opening last week, two rival tabs in New York City went to war. The subject? The mysterious circumstances surrounding the death last July of Deputy White House Counsel Vincent Foster. "Doubts Raised Over Foster's Suicide," the New York Post had proclaimed in its opening salvo two months ago, inaugurating a series of incisive reports. "Case Closed," countered the Daily News last week.

Who's right? We may never know. But we certainly won't be able to grapple with certain crucial facts until the Justice Department deigns to release the police report of his death, something this newspaper has been calling for since last summer, when we filed our first Freedom of Information Act request. In the meantime, the war of the tabs proves that the old-fashioned art of enterprise journalism isn't dead.

As in the early stages of the Whitewater scandal — a matter that touches on Mr. Foster — the tabloids, unlike most of the establishment press, have shown a willingness to push hard on troublesome questions and odd details. By asking tough and important questions about Mr. Foster's apparent suicide, they may eventually force out the truth.

For the benefit of readers outside New York, here's what the two papers have been reporting:

Christopher Ruddy of the Post led the way, showing the enterprise to interview the emergency personnel who viewed Mr. Foster's body.

In late January, Mr. Ruddy was told by paramedic George Gonzalez that there was something "strange" about the Foster death scene. Mr. Foster's body was neatly laid out, with gun in hand, and there was surprisingly little blood ("a thin trickle" near his mouth). One expert told Mr. Ruddy that in 30 years he had "never seen someone shoot themselves in the mouth and still hold the gun perfectly at his side." According to Mr. Gonzalez and a law-enforcement official, the gun showed no traces of blood.

The park maintenance worker who found Mr. Foster's body had described a heavy-set man in a van who had pulled over and alerted him to the "dead body" in the park. Mr. Ruddy wondered, understandably, "Who was the man in the white utility van?"

All this prompted him to ask why the FBI had been kept out of the investigation. He was told by former FBI head William Sessions (who admittedly has his own ax to grind with the Clinton White House) that a "power struggle" with Justice had left the investigation in the hands of the less experienced Park Police.

Who handled (or bungled) the investigation became important when Mr. Ruddy discovered, the day after his first article appeared, that the Park Police had ruled the Foster death a suicide without running a ballistics test on the gun. The police asked the federal Bureau of Alcohol, Tobacco and Firearms to do a test only two days after the official police ruling was handed down, on Aug. 10.

But nothing was yet conclusive: Even the Park Police had questions, as it turned out. A Feb. 4 Washington Post report — perhaps inspired by Mr. Ruddy's hard-hitting articles the week before — confirmed the ballistics-test delay, and revealed that the ATF had been asked by the Park Police to look for powder residue on Mr. Foster's clothes as well, and to comment on the possible position of the gun at the time it was fired.

As it turned out, the ATF's conclusions were consistent with suicide, but the procedural confusion left Mr. Ruddy wondering about the integrity of the entire investigation. He was not alone in such musings. Special Counsel Robert Fiske has announced his intention to re-examine the entire Foster episode. In short: What else was there to know? And why has the official report — including photographs, autopsy results, and pieces of a suicide note — not been made public, to clear up the mystery and end the speculation?

The answer to that question is still incomplete, and the legal complexity surrounding Mr. Fiske's efforts may even add to the delay. But in last Monday's Daily News, Mike McAlary managed to push the story further toward openness.

Mr. McAlary got a chance to "review" the Park Police report "once" (it was made available, we may presume, to counter the Post's stories), and talked to unnamed investigators. His conclusion: Vincent Foster's death was "a simple story from a police blotter" — decidedly not something that would confirm the "ranting of some conspiracy theorist," whoever that might be.

The chief forensic investigator at the death scene found little blood on the front of Mr. Foster's body, but there was plenty in the back, where the bullet had exited his skull. Mr. Foster's right thumb was stuck in the trigger guard, Mr. McAlary reported, accounting for the gun's still resting in his hand when the body was discovered. Powder burns were found on Mr. Foster's palate and tongue, and on his right hand. The lack of disturbance to the dead man's "blood pools" suggested, as one investigator said, that Mr. Foster "died right on the hill where he was sitting."

All in all, Mr. McAlary concluded, there was no mystery left to this part of the story. Even the man in the white van turned out to lead nowhere: He was the invention of the park worker, who apparently embroidered his account to cover up a midday respite. Mr. McAlary triumphantly announced that Mr. Fiske and his chief Foster investigator had "accepted" the conclusions of the Park Police about Vincent Foster's death.

The Post fired back on Wednesday in an article by Thomas Ferraro. He cited mistakes that Mr. McAlary had made: the date of the suicide and the first name of Mr. Fiske's deputy, Roderick Lankler. More important, Mr. Lankler denied to the Post that he or Mr. Fiske had reached any conclusions about the Foster death. "Foster Suicide Probe Still Wide Open" the Post trumpeted. That lasted 24 hours — until the News's next salvo. "The Real News on Post Mortem," quipped the paper's headline writers on Thursday. On page two, they dropped the news that the Park Police confirmed that "the case is closed."

But it isn't, really. Despite Mr. McAlary's heroic effort to refute Mr. Ruddy, and despite the persuasiveness of his account, too much remains hidden about the entire Foster affair. After all, the Park Police report is still locked away — as are the Foster office papers.

Mr. McAlary presents a vivid account of the scene in Mr. Foster's office the day after the suicide. Furious FBI agents and Park Police officials were forced by Mr. Nussbaum to sit 15 feet away from Mr. Foster's desk as he rummaged through papers, saying repeatedly "We can't show you this, this is personal."

That scene, of course, suggests the possibility that secret, politically sensitive, truths lie behind Mr. Foster's actions. Such a suggestion also emanates — rightly or wrongly — from the "overlooked" suicide note that a White House aide found in Mr. Foster's briefcase five days after the Park Police had not seen it there. Mr. McAlary interestingly reports that, because Mr. Foster called the FBI liars in his note, the Park Police had one of their own sergeants do the handwriting analysis.

Obviously, until everything is made public and properly explained, a cloud of doubt will hover over the Foster affair. In the meantime, we owe a debt of gratitude to the aggressive and consequential fact-finding missions of tough tabloid reporters.

Mr. Eichman is an assistant features editor on the Journal's editorial page.

LEISURE & THE ARTS

TV: Whitewater Boils, Floods Media

It's been obvious for some time now, as the Whitewater saga rolls on, that the seizures of moral indignation that periodically afflict various quarters of the media are becoming more frequent.

These episodes, which have all the earmarks of an obsessive disorder — and which are characterized by repeated hand-wringing about "excessive coverage" and the like — can by now be predicted well in advance. That is, their pattern of recurrence shows that these fits almost invariably strike whenever the nation's press is onto a significant and substantial

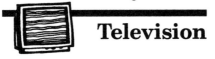

Television

By Dorothy Rabinowitz

story eminently worth the attention it is getting, such as violent crime — such as Whitewater.

We are just now beginning to hear the first rumblings of agitation and accusation that television news is devoting too much time to reporting violent crime. This plaint was triggered by a new study from the Center for Media and Public Affairs, which holds that the statistics don't bear out the picture of a crime-ridden society seen so often on the evening news. Neither these statistics nor the journalists gathered recently on CNN to bemoan excessive crime coverage are likely to impress citizens living in the real world.

As to Whitewater, it began to be clear a week or so ago (as the Whitewater coverage hit the screen full stride) that feverish charges of "feeding frenzy" and "excess coverage" were on the rise. That Sunday, on CNN's "Informed Sources" — where journalists gathered to discuss this grave issue — media critic Ellen Hume delivered an impassioned assault on the Whitewater coverage. Such was her excitation that Ms. Hume, whom the fevers seemed to have carried off altogether, plumb near bounced off her chair while decrying the lack of restraint shown by fellow journalists. Still, none of the hair-tearing about media overkill could stop the surge of Whitewater reportage and debate.

This is not to say that coverage didn't have its lighter moments. On NBC's "Meet the Press," the same Sunday, former New Yorker Washington columnist Elizabeth Drew succeeded in publicizing one of the sharper political rejoinders of the week — uttered by New York Sen. Alfonse D'Amato. The senator had been moved to respond (on the Senate floor) to President Clinton's ringing defense of the first lady ("I have never known anyone with a stronger sense of right and wrong than Hillary Clinton"). "That," retorted Sen. D'Amato, "would seem to be the problem."

"What had he meant by that?" asked the sly Ms. Drew, who knew exactly what he had meant. Mr. D'Amato proceeded, as expected, to recite a list, by no means complete, of some of the tawdrier characters with whom the Clintons have had dealings one way or another.

Meanwhile, administration spokesmen were busy making appearances of their own, and occasionally showing some strain. The new presidential counsel, Lloyd Cutler, lost his temper on "This Week" and proceeded to lecture David Brinkley on journalistic ethics. Presidential counselor David Gergen showed up at a Los Angeles Times editorial breakfast (carried on C-Span), where, looking a trifle dazed, as is only natural for one recently emerged from hiding, he spoke of fire walls and judgment calls and generally labored diligently to answer questions on Whitewater and the Clintons.

Other supporters of the first couple took to the airwaves as well, New York Times columnist Anna Quindlen among them. On the syndicated radio show "Imus in the Morning," Ms. Quindlen, only one among many journalistic sages who have taken to giving the Clinton's media advice, said she didn't think the first lady should hold any press conferences. She did, however, make the high-minded suggestion that Mrs. Clinton find some TV show where she could answer viewers' questions. This strategy, the columnist earnestly explained, would help the first lady create "the illusion" that people were partaking in the questioning.

Both the first lady and the President indeed had some need of advice last week, as talk of White House-related scandals reached their peak with the resignation of Webster Hubbell. On all three networks, this was the story that led the evening news. "Good evening," began the NBC news with Tom Brokaw. "This must be one of those days when the Clintons wonder whether it's all worth it. . . . Whitewater washed all over them and their carefully arranged new jobs agenda." On CBS, Dan Rather began with word that "Another high-ranking member of the Clinton administration was pulled down today in the spreading undertow of Whitewater." Stranded in Detroit, where the big story was supposed to be jobs, Peter Jennings instead found himself anchoring an extended lead item about Mr. Hubbell and the Rose Law Firm, all against a wonderfully irrelevant background of cars rolling off an assembly line.

"World News Tonight" nonetheless remains the first network news show to have provided a lengthy overview of Whitewater (reported by James Wooten), which served notice that reportage on this affair wasn't going to go away any time soon. Another report, by ABC's Cynthia McFadden, provided one of the more eloquent testaments to the current condition of the once-proud Rose Law Firm. The setting was a large charity benefit in Little Rock — where the cameras caught the Rose table entirely surrounded by empty chairs. For sheer toughness and color, though, no Whitewater reporting exceeded that of NBC's Lisa Myers. The high point of her two-part series, aired last week, had James McDougal (the Clintons' former business partner) holding forth in his softly menacing voice and looking for all the world as though he had stepped out of "Citizen Kane."

The watchdogs of journalism howl, but the Whitewater caravan rolls on.

* * *

Awards time has come round again, this time with the Rabbi Baruch Korff Citation for Meritorious Service. This award, presented to journalists who have distinguished themselves by zealous and unflagging devotion to a sitting president, is named for the Providence, R.I., rabbi who became Richard Nixon's most ardent champion, even unto the final hours of his presidency.

It can come as no surprise to her many fans that the hands-down winner of the Korff award this year — and probably next year — is Eleanor Clift of "The McLaughlin Group" and Newsweek, the most tireless of the first couple's cheerleaders. We could cite, in particular, the heartwarming Newsweek interview with the first lady, wherein journalist Clift assured Mrs. Clinton, in effect, that inquiries into her Whitewater dealings all came from people who wanted to launch careers, who wanted to burn witches, who didn't share Ms. Clift's own theory that the first lady resisted making her records public because "you have a thing about privacy."

Congratulations, Eleanor. Nobody could be more deserving.

REVIEW & OUTLOOK

Censored in Arkansas

Earlier in the week we commended L.J. Davis's New Republic cover story on Whitewater and the culture of Arkansas. But Mr. Davis modestly omitted a fascinating part of the tale, namely his personal misfortunes in reporting his article.

The omission reflects a curious dichotomy in Whitewater press coverage. A lot of the news has been broken by publications willing to report what they learn even at the risk that now and then some of it may be overtaken by other facts — The Washington Times, the New York tabloids, the American Spectator and the British press. The mainstream American press has come in for some derision overseas; the Economist likened Whitewater to the 1936 episode in which the American press was reporting and the British press covering up the romance leading to the abdication of Edward VIII.

This is not quite fair. Since the story came back to life in December, the American press has mostly done a commendable job of plumbing the finances of Arkansas and the Clintons and kibitzing every move in Washington's procedural chess. For better or worse, however, the respectable press has shown little-to-no appetite for publishing anything about sex and violence. Stories on these subjects of course circulate constantly among reporters, and shape understanding of events within the press corps, if not among its readers.

Somehow we think that readers ought to know the following account from Mr. Davis, a contributing editor to Harper's magazine since 1978: He was returning to his room at Little Rock's Legacy Hotel about 6:30 after an interview on the evening of Feb. 13. The last thing he remembers is putting his key in the door, and the next thing he remembers is waking up face down on the floor, with his arm twisted under his body and a big lump on his head above his left ear. The room door was shut and locked. Nothing was missing except four "significant" pages of his notebook that included a list of his sources in Little Rock. He didn't file a police report, saying he wanted to get out of town and wasn't sure what had happened to him.

"I thought I was walking on a trampoline for three days," he told us, and then consulted his physician. Mr. Davis says his doctor found his injury inconsistent with a fall, and that he'd been "struck a massive blow above the left ear with a blunt object." He suffered both a concussion and an "amnesiac episode" from the blow. With Mr. Davis's permission, Dr. Richard Wagman has confirmed this diagnosis to us.

Along similar lines, throughout the world except in the United States, Sally Perdue is a household name. She's a former Miss Arkansas and TV reporter who went on one talk show, "Sally Jessy Raphael," during the 1992 campaign to say she had an affair with Bill Clinton in 1983. This was only briefly noted, though the Washington Post did report that Jack Palladino, a San Francisco private investigator hired by the Clinton campaign to squelch "bimbo eruptions," called estranged relatives for damaging comments about Ms. Perdue. Like all the other bimbo eruptions, this one has been "spiked," subjected to a universal news blackout in the U.S. But the Sally Perdue story took a different turn.

Last January, Ms. Perdue told Ambrose Evans-Pritchard of the Sunday Telegraph that she'd been threatened with violence if she continued to talk. She named a name, Ron Tucker, who she said claimed to represent the Democratic Party. She says Mr. Tucker first offered her a federal job in exchange for silence, and added, "if I didn't take the offer, then they knew that I went jogging by myself and he couldn't guarantee what would happen to my pretty little legs."

Afterward, Ms. Perdue says she received threatening phone calls and letters, one of which she made available to the Telegraph. She says she found an unspent shotgun shell on the seat of her jeep, and that later the back window was shattered. She reported this to the FBI, which told the Telegraph there was an ongoing investigation. Mr. Tucker's employer at the time, John Newcomb of Marion Mining, added the confirmation that Mr. Tucker told him he had been asked "to get to this woman and get her to shut up." In an interview with us this week, Mr. Tucker responded, "Sally Perdue is a flake, stirring up a hornet's nest. I only met with her for 10 to 15 minutes once. I'm not a political animal," and then degenerated into a series of threats and obscenities.

Editors and reporters have to grapple with a flood of stories, charges and rumors of violence and even deaths in Arkansas. The state seems to be a congenitally violent place, and full of colorful characters with stories to tell, axes to grind and secrets of their own to protect. We believe Mr. Davis. The Telegraph story included a lot of corroboration, though of course no evidence that anyone ordered Mr. Tucker to say what Ms. Perdue charges he said. Yet as the story develops, we're increasingly coming to the conclusion that the respectable press is spending too much time adjudicating what the reader has a right to know, and too little time with the old spirit of "stop the presses."

REVIEW & OUTLOOK

Patsy Takes the Fiske

White House notoriety Patsy Thomasson actually showed up to testify to Congress Tuesday, and proved herself charming. She did little

Patsy Thomasson

to still concerns about the Administration's security procedures, however, and on the matter of her nocturnal visit to Vincent Foster's office in the wake of his death she pleaded the Fiske.

Ms. Thomasson "would like nothing better," she said, than to tell the subcommittee "what I did that night in that office." But due to Special Counsel Robert Fiske's probe into Mr. Foster's death, she couldn't possibly comment on that. Ms. Thomasson, in case you've spent the last month as an orbiting astronaut, is the FOB from Arkansas who was once the top aide of FOB bond dealer and drug convict Dan Lasater, and who has risen in life to be director of the Office of Administration at the White House, where she oversees personnel, computers and some security operations.

These responsibilities seem to weigh heavily in this Administration. The White House Counsel's office is responsible for security passes, the immediate responsibility of Associate Counsel William Kennedy III, the former Rose Law Firm partner now tottering on the brink of resignation (maybe by tonight's 7:30 press conference?) over a nanny-tax issue. Last night, the White House said Mr. Kennedy would no longer handle passes.

The security situation is so dire that Congressmen Dan Glickman and Larry Combest, Chairman and ranking minority member of the House Intelligence Committee, have written the Director of Central Intelligence more or less suggesting that he cut the White House off from classified information.

More specifically, they asked CIA Director James Woolsey what steps he had taken to ensure that White House staffers without clearances hadn't had access to classified material. The two Members said they were troubled, and that "The urgency of this matter has been highlighted by the arrest of Aldrich Ames" (for astronauts, the recently apprehended KGB mole in the CIA).

When Ms. Thomasson responded to similar concerns expressed this week by House subcommittee chair Steny Hoyer, a Maryland Democrat, she was hardly reassuring. "We don't think we have any Aldrich Ameses at the White House," Ms. Thomasson responded. "But we certainly could." Ms. Thomasson admits that she lacked a permanent White House pass or security clearance until earlier this month; despite that, she has had 24-hour access to the West Wing. At one point in her testimony, she also said she had "no need" to have the combinations to any safes in the White House; they are in the possession of Charles Easley, a security officer who works for her.

She also revealed that while Mr. Kennedy was handling clearances for White House passes, his own background check was finished in March 1993, but he didn't receive his own permanent pass until December. GOP Rep. Frank Wolf, who first agitated these issues on the House subcommittee that oversees the White House budget, told us that White House Chief of Staff McLarty's background check was completed on January 22, 1993—two days after the inauguration. He didn't get his permanent pass until just this past March 5, the day Mr. Fiske's first subpoenas arrived at the White House. House Members wanted to know what was going on.

Ms. Thomasson, however, persisted in telling Rep. Wolf on Tuesday not to worry. She said there was no reason for concern that senior White House aides lacked permanent passes because they nonetheless had gotten "requisite security" approval. She holds that Mr. McLarty's case was "fully adjudicated," which apparently means the background check was complete and accepted by Mr. Kennedy, who just hadn't gotten around to forwarding the Chief of Staff's papers to the Secret Service.

This is "malarkey," says Phil Larsen, who was administrative officer in Jimmy Carter's White House and ran personnel management under President Bush. The Secret Service must clear a final financial check, and is part of an adjudication. "None of this makes any sense," he told us; it would be "astonishing" if security clearances were issued before passes were. "The two always—and should—go together." After sleeping overnight on Patsy's testimony, Rep. Wolf and Rep. Bill Clinger, ranking Republican on the Government Operations Committee, called for a GAO investigation of the White House pass problem.

At 8:15 p.m. last night, AP reported Press Secretary Dee Dee Myers had suddenly issued a "fact sheet" indicating that more than 100 White House staffers lack security clearances and one-third of the 1,044 employees don't have permanent passes.

Editorial Feature

George Mitchell: Still in Control

George Mitchell doesn't talk like a lame duck, he doesn't act like a lame duck and, contrary to some expectations, he's not a lame duck as the Senate majority leader.

When the Maine Democrat stunned the political world earlier this month by announcing he wouldn't seek a certain re-election in the fall, it was widely assumed his considerable clout would wane. Yet today Sen. Mitchell remains a central player in the major battles occupying Washington: health care legislation, the China trade dispute and the Clintons' Whitewater woes.

Politics & People

By Albert R. Hunt

That's attributable to the special brand of Mitchell leadership. When Lyndon Johnson ran the Senate more than three decades ago he could a) reward and punish his Democratic senators by controlling committee assignments, b) decide whether there'd be a roll call vote on most amendments and c) parcel out campaign dough to supportive senators in the pre-election-reform era. The majority leader today has none of those perquisites of power; unlike most of his fellow Democratic and GOP congressional leaders, Mr. Mitchell doesn't even have his own political action committee to curry favor.

He has few carrots and almost no sticks. "I was asked if senators would no longer be afraid of me," he recalls in an interview this week. "The answer is no senator has ever been afraid of me."

But the 60-year-old majority leader possesses unusual skill and infinite patience. He can be fiercely partisan, single-handedly defeating

George Mitchell

President Bush's proposed capital-gains tax cut and giving the Democrats the tax fairness issue for the 1992 campaign. He also is exceptionally thoughtful and persuasive. Operating with archaic rules in a body of giant-sized egos, he commands extraordinary respect and credibility. Many colleagues realize he not only makes the place work as well as possible, but not infrequently protects senators from themselves.

That prowess is little affected by lame duck status. "I haven't detected the slightest diminution on my influence with colleagues," Sen. Mitchell says of the three weeks since he bowed out. "Maybe it has even been enhanced on issues like health care."

That is an issue that he knows thoroughly and cares about passionately. He expects that separate Senate Finance Committee and Labor Committee bills will reach the Senate floor in June or July — assuming earlier House passage — and he then will lead the tricky task of trying to stitch it all together.

Any successful bill will need some Republican support. Sen. Mitchell has served on the Finance Committee health subcommittee for 14 years with GOP Sens. John Chafee and David Durenberger, who are the type of Republicans more interested in accomplishing something than in making an issue or placating interests. "Not a single thing occurred on that subcommittee in 1987 and 1988 [when Mr. Mitchell was chairman] that would not have occurred" under Sens. Chafee or Durenberger, he pointedly noted at this week's Finance Committee health care retreat.

The sine qua non of successful health care legislation is universal coverage, and Sen. Mitchell knows that's possible only with mandates. Thus he sees no compromises with a GOP faction that opposes any mandates, but he's clearly flexible on how any requirements should be fashioned. Senate Finance Committee Chairman Pat Moynihan has worries about Republicans' threats to filibuster a health care bill they don't like. George Mitchell's astute political antenna tells him this is a bluff: "A number of Republicans have told me they would be very concerned about" any filibuster, he says.

"Politically, it'd be a dynamite issue."

He's no less involved in the highly sensitive issue of whether to deny China most-favored-nation trade status if significant progress isn't made on human rights by early June. George Mitchell was the chief Senate advocate of linking MFN to China's human rights record when President Bush vacillated after Tiananmen Square.

Sen. Mitchell says that unless China clearly improves its human rights performance in the next 10 weeks, President Clinton will have no choice but to revoke its trading status. He acknowledges this is a "blunt instrument," but adamantly insists: "It is very important not to capitulate to the pleas of businessmen who want it [MFN] renewed at any cost."

Yet, behind the scenes, he's encouraging efforts by a bipartisan group of senators, led by Democrat John Kerry of Massachusetts and Republican John McCain of Arizona, to try to shape a new approach that would get by the June deadline without capitulating on human rights or returning to the laissez-faire human rights policies of George Bush; the hope then would be to find levers other than trade to pressure China on basic human rights. He's engaged in similar high-level private consultations with the administration; without the active support of George Mitchell, these efforts are doomed.

On the touchy Whitewater scandal the Maine Democrat already rescued congressional Democrats and the White House from a steady drumbeat of stonewall allegations when he engineered a unanimous Senate vote to hold hearings at some unspecified future date. By then a lot more will be known about progress of the outside counsel's investigation.

The Senate Republican leadership now is demanding a special investigatory panel; Senate GOP leader Bob Dole doesn't want the lead on Whitewater to be taken by the Banking Committee, where the ranking Republicans would be New York's Alfonse D'Amato, an ethical embarrassment, and Texas's Phil Gramm, a likely 1996 Dole rival for the GOP presidential nomination. Sen. Mitchell suggests he's very unlikely to accommodate his friend and adversary Bob Dole.

George Mitchell, assured his place in history as one of the more effective Senate leaders of this century, privately is mentioned for every prominent position imaginable, ranging from secretary of state to baseball commissioner. With his background as a judge and leader of an egocentric legislative body, he's ideally suited for the Supreme

Court, especially to be the next chief justice. But as a man of principle, it would be a travesty if he worked for the likes of George Steinbrenner.

When he decided to retire, Mr. Mitchell went to the White House to inform the president privately. After meeting for over an hour in the family quarters, Bill Clinton took the Senate majority leader down to the Oval Office to try to talk him out of it. A few hours later he telephoned Sen. Mitchell once more, again to no avail.

Aides say the president is deeply saddened that Mr. Mitchell is leaving, fearing this will leave a huge void. He's right, but the good news for the White House is that the void won't open for six months.

Editorial Feature

School for Scandal

By MARK HELPRIN

Now that the bloom is off the rose, the White House oracles are thumping their naked tails in unison to protest that Whitewater is political. Surely they deserve the Nobel Prize for the discovery that political scandals have a political component, and if they continue their researches perhaps they will also learn that the measure of a scandal is not the material of scandal itself but the political dynamic of which the unfolding scenario is but an expression.

Though liberals hallucinate much about Watergate, Richard Nixon was forced to resign because he was the first American president to lose a war. The rest was merely the instrument of the underlying forces, a shadow play. By the same token, Iran-Contra was a result of the complete isolation of Republican political fortunes in the executive, an island in a tide of Democratic power that threatened to wash over it.

The corruptions of Whitewater are like the fruit of a richly bearing tree, and it seems that every day a new dead hand rises from a misty Arkansas lake, but they are not the true measure of Whitewater. Whitewater flourishes only because the Clinton administration is condemned to rest in a politically short-sheeted bed of its own making.

What a bad idea to begin a messianic presidency with only 43% of the popular vote: less than polled by Willkie, Dewey, Stevenson, Nixon, Ford and Dukakis when they lost. And of that 43% many were unaware of Hillary hiding in the bushes to the left of the candidate, like the 900-pound boyfriend of a voluptuous girl hitchhiker. As soon as Hillary got into the car, she bumped out all but the president's core constituency, the 25% to 30% who will be with him to the end.

You would think that with such a narrow base the White House "Hillarys" (highly inexperienced left-liberal academic righteous yuppies) would have trodden carefully. But they did not, for their abiding faith in the power of their own intelligence to manage the unmanageable amounts to nothing more than abject stupidity, and they acted accordingly. No president in living memory has exulted in his victory with the same immodesty, the immediate punishment for this being that the early Clinton administration came to resemble a science fiction character who ages 50 years in less than a minute.

They were blinded to their limitations by the slavish obedience of a press that, tempting the fates, portrayed the Clintons as saviors, saints, and divine beings, literally with angels' wings. And though flackery is just a rubber band — the more you stretch it out, the harder it snaps back — it did the impossible. It quintupled the arrogance of the most arrogant people in America, a triumphalist coterie of graduate students who accord to the hard left the same uneasy respect that most people reserve for the clergy, and grow teary-eyed over bats, squirrels and caribou as with barely concealable pleasure they sacrifice whole regions of rednecks.

This is not merely the arrogance of victory and of youth, but of lawyers. Lawyers, like undertakers, meddle decisively in everyone's business, but only after it fails. Most are redeemed by understanding that their power comes from this peculiar circumstance, but Clintillians seem to think it comes from a Christ-like glow within themselves. Is it surprising that they believe their first task is to heal the sick? And that to do so they need only redesign the country after they have given it "meaning," banished its greed, and put it on the information superhighway to laptop heaven? They are the missionaries, and we are the Hottentots.

Not everyone in this group is as callow as the president's media director, who told the Journal last year of his plans for "'BC-TV,' Bill Clinton, on TV, 24 hours a day." And not everyone is a networked crony or a token Zoe or a chicken tycoon, all put in place (if not yet confirmed) in the most incompetent explosion of patronage since Caligula appointed his horse.

For at least half a dozen grown-ups have agreed to help Bill Clinton, mostly eminent retreads who in their days of glory were

Carter's Little Liver Pills, and who, even now, after all these years, still move about on little marshmallow feet — Les Aspin, impotent even at his own specialty of gutting the military; Warren Christopher, breaking into every foreign garden and running away when the dog barks; David Gergen, hand welded to the ejection lever; Donna Shalala, praying that at the next state dinner she won't be seated next to George Hamilton; Lloyd Cutler, happy but worried, as if Neil Diamond had been asked to conduct the Berlin Philharmonic.

Even the grown-ups cannot save Bill Clinton from himself, if only because they cannot have any idea of how to carry the quicksilver from the flames. Granted, in questions of sincerity the president is perpetually condemned to be upstaged by his vice president, though for the country's sake let us hope that Al Gore is not as sincere as he appears to be, for with sincerity like his, who needs fraud? Fraud is what Whitewater, and the administration, are all about: fraud — pious, tawdry, financial, sexual, political, plain, simple and habitual.

Fraud. Somewhere between the core of the left and the 43% plurality that made Bill Clinton commander in chief are the American voters who thought they were supporting a "New Democrat" and wound up instead with a slightly more buttoned-up version of the Village People. Boris Yeltsin, who ought to know whereof he speaks, calls Bill Clinton a "socialist," and General Jaruzelski, the former military dictator of Poland, looking more than ever like one of the three blind mice, says that he still retains the values of the left and that, "Actually, in Clinton's program I see elements I like a lot."

Fraud. Thomas Mann of the Brookings Institution states that "We would be condemning him if he didn't pull back [from his campaign promises], because he would be an irresponsible president." That is, the president had to lie to you for your own good. The president lies responsibly. Not only does he remain morally superior when he lies, his lying actually makes him morally superior. This goes beyond the normal corruptions of American politics onto the airless and unfamiliar plains of totalitarianism.

Fraud. In a wonderful reversal of Boss Tweed's immense public outlays for "Brooms, etc.," the president tells the New York Times that he does not want a congressional inquiry into Whitewater because "it would not be worth the money it would cost." He doesn't want a congressional inquiry into Whitewater, because he wants to save money. Does the president think he leads a nation of idiots? The answer is yes, but he is just cautious enough to speak indirectly, when, of his wife, he says: "If the rest of the people in this country — if everybody in this country had a character as strong as hers, we wouldn't have half the problems we've got today."

These are not the words of Louis XVI, Juan Peron, or Nicolae Ceausescu, but of the president of the United States defending his overbearing wife by insulting the rest of the country. Had a Republican president said this, he would have been put in the ice cream case within minutes. Nor has any president of sound mind and body ever had the temerity to install the first lady in a virtual co-presidency in which she stalks about the country giving speeches, appears before Congress, supervises at least one cabinet department, and is the chief of his (her?) administration's most ambitious initiative. Though in Whitewater mode it is to the Clintons' advantage to dismiss this with offended innocence, they and their supporters have been trumpeting it for more than a year.

The president has reinvented government, and the United States of America now has not one chief executive, but one and a half. This rather profound change is not the result of a constitutional amendment or even informed debate. It just happened. It has embarrassed Congress and escaped the condemnation of an anesthetized press. It is the solid and identifiable core of an otherwise mercurial cloud of hubris, arrogance and petty corruption. It is the ultimate expression of the nature of this presidency, in which the rules exist only for everyone else, because the work of the elect in remaking the world is too important to fetter with laws and truth.

Were it not for the fact that the president's own party dominates Congress, the press, the universities, public education, Hollywood, publishing, local and state government, the unions, and bureaucracies everywhere, the assumption by Hillary Rodham Clinton of the powers of an office to which she did not accede would be a constitutional crisis. It should be a constitutional crisis. But it is not. It is, instead, sublimated in scandal. It is, instead, the driving force in the conflict of which Whitewater is but the instrument, the mere expression, and the shadow play.

Mr. Helprin, a novelist, is a contributing editor of the Journal.

Letters to the Editor

It's Just Scandalous

In response to Mark Helprin's March 25 editorial-page article "School for Scandal": Where was the national media 18 months ago? There are people in this country who almost seem surprised that the president they elected does not appear to be trustworthy. Even then there were allegations about his marital infidelity, the Whitewater land deal and his association with Dan Lasater, but the liberal media almost seemed to overlook all that in favor of reporting on bus tours and the proper spelling of "potato."

It is true that the economy was not in good shape, but what should we expect after eight years of staggering growth? One of the first things any student in any economy class learns is that it is normal for an economy to go from recession (1981) to recovery (1982) to prosperity (1983-9) to decline (1990). The Reagan-Bush years comprised the largest peacetime expansion the world had ever seen, yet the press chose to characterize that period as the decade of greed. If only we could repeat that awful time.

Now that the election is over, the press can no longer ignore the allegations; little by little it is all coming out. My questions remain: Where was the press when the Arkansas beauty queen was saying that she had had an affair with Gov. Clinton? Why didn't the press investigate Whitewater when it was first heard of? Why didn't the press discuss Dan Lasater? The only answers I can come up with are that either they were too busy taking aim at President Bush or that they so badly wanted one of their own in the White House.

KEVIN SHAUGHNESSY

New York

Mr. Helprin's essay was a wonderful read. I had my head stuck in bar-exam studies in the early '70s and was unaware that the Watergate break-in and coverup never happened: "Richard Nixon was forced to resign because he was the first American president to lose a war." I had never understood that this was why Spiro Agnew resigned and Attorney General John Mitchell went to jail. I have to read this guy's novels.

JOHN K. FORD

Washington

Mr. Helprin faults President Clinton for "insulting the rest of the country" when he said that this country would have fewer problems if more people had stronger character. Would Mr. Helprin also criticize Ronald Reagan, who frequently made such assertions? When George Bush and Pat Buchanan urged us to adopt their family values, was Mr. Helprin insulted and incensed?

Seeking to cremate Democrats for their arrogance, Mr. Helprin goes on to claim that the American people are blinded to scandal and bamboozled into acquiescence by the Democratic monopolization of not only the presidency, but also "Congress, the press, the universities, public education, Hollywood, publishing, local and state government, the unions, and bureaucracies everywhere." Of course: Those poor American people don't know enough to read, learn and then vote Republican; but Mr. Helprin would be glad to disabuse them of their piteous ignorance with his divine wisdom. Did the Clintons stuff the ballot boxes? I think not, Mr. Helprin: get over it; your team lost.

ANDREW C. COOPER

Washington

Mr. Helprin is too kind. The Clintons and their coterie are the most recent and blatant example of leaders who possess what F.A. Hayek called "the fatal conceit." Enamored by their own intelligence and good intentions, they feel destined to improve society by benevolently reshaping it from on high.

This top-down bias is as ineffective in public policy as it is in managing a business — or the White House, for that matter. It leads to a paternalism we see in the administration's health care reforms, industrial policy, the plan to ban public smoking, and the naive intent to "grow the economy." It is seen in a disdain for the rules ordinary mortals have to follow, such as tax laws, FOIA requests, security clearances and criminal-investigation procedures.

While top-down may work in theory, it fails in reality because people, markets, and events are far too complicated for even really smart FOBs to micromanage. The fraud Mr. Helprin overlooked is how this top-down administration continues to portray itself as egalitarian while casting its free-market, limited-government foes as elitist and greedy. Whitewater, if nothing else, is washing away this populist rhetoric, exposing the conceit that underpins the left's policies and character.

MARK HAMMITT

San Francisco

* * *

What an unexpected delight to find the staid editorial page enlivened with the hilarious musings of novelist Mark Helprin. His use of the mock-serious political commentary tone was brilliant, producing such howlers as the "real" explanation for Watergate (Nixon being punished for losing a war) and Bill Clinton as a stand-in for Nicolae Ceausescu and the Village People. Great stuff!

Equally sidesplitting was Mr. Helprin's pseudo-operatic bemoaning of fraud and scandal in the White House while citing no specific evidence of either.

I can't wait until he aims his rapier wit at Al D'Amato and Bob Dole. He will, won't he?

CHARLES PAIKERT

South Orange, N.J.

Editorial Feature

Even Dems Wonder Who We Elected

Breaux said . . . Mrs. Clinton will be as popular as ever, "when they find out what really happened, if nothing happened."

— SEN. JOHN BREAUX (D., La.) on Whitewater
Quoted recently by the AP

Mr. Breaux, keep in mind, was trying to defend President and Mrs. Clinton on Whitewater. Yet even he couldn't resist adding a caveat, just in case.

That about sums up what Whitewater has done to the Democratic mood, which ranges from terror to mere anxiety. Republicans are hogging the microphones in public, but what's more revealing is what Democrats are whispering in private. They're as jumpy as defendants before a mercurial judge.

Potomac Watch

By Paul A. Gigot

What'll happen next? What line will they have to defend? Press conferences notwithstanding (this column was written before last night's), it says something about this president's character when even Democrats aren't sure how much to believe him.

A vanishing species here is a Democrat who will flat-out defend the Clintons. Sure, every Democrat will repeat the by-now-cliched irony about Al D'Amato as GOP ethics czar, or rip the bloodthirsty press. But one prominent Democrat claims to be the 25th called by a TV network to talk about Whitewater, everyone else having declined.

Friends of Bill, once treated as celebrities on Capitol Hill, are now getting the treatment. When Patsy Thomasson, charter FOB, testified  about the many White House aides without security clearances, no Democrats came to her defense. Two weeks ago the party line was no Whitewater hearings; this week the House agreed to them after one of its grown-ups, Indiana's Lee Hamilton, said they were a good idea. Hill Democrats hate the idea of hearings, but they fear the GOP taunt of "coverup Congress" even more.

Ted Van Dyk, another Democratic grown-up, says that "people like me who care about the party are beside ourselves, because you can't have a failed presidency in the middle of the second year." He worries this will be the outcome without full disclosure by the White House.

Bill Clinton

That fear may be overdrawn, but it does illustrate how little residual trust this president can now count on. When Ronald Reagan stumbled over Iran-Contra, he had his political base to cushion the fall. Mr. Clinton is instead "a high-wire act," says a Democrat who worked on his campaign. "There is no safety net." If he slips over Whitewater, he'll hit the bottom of the pool.

One explanation for this, says iconoclast Rep. Tim Penny (D., Minn.), is "the old adage: He's neither fish nor fowl." Neither party liberals nor moderates, as writer Joe Klein has also observed, feel he is completely theirs. "He seems to express solid and admirable principles," says Mr. Penny, adding that he sees no evidence that Whitewater will amount to much. "But there are so many contradictions, and as a consequence it isn't easy for Democratic legislators to stick their necks out for him."

Congressional Democrats have also learned that the real powers in the Clinton world are the longtime FOBs — "the Arkansans and Oxford-Yale crowd," says one Clinton adviser. Leading Democrats are consulted, but they aren't confidants. And GOP Rep. Jim Lightfoot, an Iowan of moderate bent, says he doesn't know even a single Republican in Congress whom Mr. Clinton "is friendly with." The result is what another Democrat calls "a marriage of convenience" between Mr. Clinton and Capitol Hill, "not of passion."

But the deepest cause for unease is the mystery of this president's Achilles' heel, his character. Who is this fellow we elected, anyway? In 1992 we discovered the policy wonk, the gifted pol, and, even his friends now concede, the philanderer. But the multitude of stories we now call Whitewater is revealing another side — the favorite son of an Arkansas business-political oligarchy, the pal of such unsavory types as drug convict Dan Lasater.

Even more so in the case of Hillary Rodham Clinton, who we now know was doing more in the 1980s than raising money for the Children's Defense Fund. Whitewater has shown she is also a power politician, a lawyer who overlooks conflicts of interest, and even a high-flier in cattle futures (maybe her $100,000 profit is what Mr. Clinton meant when he called Whitewater charges "bull").

Perhaps none of this would matter if the Clintons had left it all behind in Little Rock. Harry Truman managed to shed the baggage of the St. Louis Pendergast machine as president, after all. But far from shedding the Arkansas political culture, the Clintons have brought it with them, complete with cronies, a mind-set for cutting ethical corners and the arrogance that often comes from governing a one-party state.

Just as Watergate became more than a third-rate burglary, Whitewater has become more than a two-bit land deal. It's now a metaphor for this president's character. And far from being overzealous, the media (me included) that fell too easily for Whitewater stonewalling in 1992 have a duty not to be fooled again. Even many Democrats seem to understand that Whitewater is about discovering who we really elected.

Letters to the Editor

Pendergast and Truman

In regard to Paul Gigot's March 25 Potomac Watch, penultimate paragraph: "Perhaps none of that would matter if the Clintons had left it all behind in Little Rock. Harry Truman managed to shed the baggage of the St. Louis Pendergast machine as president, after all. . . ."

President Truman hailed from Kansas City, not St. Louis. The Pendergast machine operated in Jackson County, which is, of course, Kansas City.

By the way, where was your editorial staff's moral indignation during the Silverado/Neil Bush scandal? Your editorial page is always fun to read; makes up for not having comics.

WOLFGANG G. ROESELER, PH.D.
Bryan, Texas

Letters to the Editor

It's Unfair to Compare Silverado, Whitewater

Wolfgang G. Roeseler (Letters to the Editor, March 31) questions why the Journal editorial writers did not reach the same level of indignation relative to the "Silverado/Neil Bush scandal" that they did relative to the Clintons' financial dealings.

From the perspective of someone who follows banks for a living (and occasionally sells them), I say the cases are very different. Neil Bush never ran for office, and there have been few accusations that he enriched himself at the expense of the taxpayers. He was guilty of poor judgment and technical violations, and he was sanctioned for it. Except for his parentage, his "sins" would not have rated a page 15 story in any newspaper.

The Clintons, on the other hand, are accused of benefiting directly and personally from abuses of power by Mr. Clinton when he was governor of Arkansas. Further, as Mr. Clinton does hold the most powerful elective office in the world, his actions are news, particularly when there are additional accusations of both past and current incidents that are equally questionable. To say that these two cases rate the same level of indignation is ludicrous.

Frankly, I am wondering when the rest of the media will summon up the same level of indignation and outrage at the Clintons as was heaped on Neil Bush. Should not a man who has run successfully for the highest office in the land be held to at least as high a standard as a man whose only "claim to fame" is being the son of a man who was elected president?

PETER H. BEHR JR.

San Francisco

Hillary

By the end of March, Hillary Clinton's $100,000 cattle futures profit had turned into another crisis for the White House. Wall Street Journal reporters conducted an in-depth examination of the trades.

As the crisis unfolded, a backlash against the Whitewater story was growing. "Republicans," charged Arthur Schlesinger on the Journal's editorial page, "are using Whitewater in an attempt to derail a reform program that was just beginning to gather steam and to discredit a presidential wife whose views they are reluctant to attack directly."

Five weeks after the trading story broke, Mrs. Clinton held a televised press conference to explain the extraordinary profits. It was, the Journal noted, "a stylistic triumph," but left viewers hungering "to know more."

MARCH 30, 1994

News Story

First Lady Turned $1,000 Investment Into a $98,000 Profit, Records Show

By MICHAEL K. FRISBY and BRUCE INGERSOLL

Staff Reporters of THE WALL STREET JOURNAL

WASHINGTON—The White House said Hillary Rodham Clinton turned a $1,000 investment into a $98,000 profit on the commodities market in less than a year. But when she became pregnant, she abruptly stopped trading because it was "too nerve-racking." Providing its most detailed account of Mrs. Clinton's commodities-trading activities, the White House released trading records showing that she made her profit in a Refco Inc. account between October 1978 and July 1979.

Separately, government investigators fear that Madison Guaranty Savings & Loan records may have been destroyed or discarded after the failed Arkansas thrift was acquired by a major Clinton political fund-raiser and other Arkansas

Hillary Clinton

investors. In a briefing on Mrs. Clinton's investments, aides acknowledged that she got advice from James Blair, then the outside counsel of Tyson Foods Inc., and that his counseling was "important," although she also talked with others and did her own research.

Lisa Caputo, the press secretary for the first lady, and John Podesta, the White House staff secretary, issued a statement saying, "Mrs. Clinton put up her own money, invested it in her own accounts, and assumed the full risk of loss."

Aides also said that Mrs. Clinton wasn't aware that her main broker, Robert L. "Red" Bone, of Refco's office in Springdale, Ark., had been disciplined by regulators for his trading practices, including allocating trades among investors in his branch office after he had determined whether the trades were winners or losers.

Mrs. Clinton's trades have generated attention because she was so successful in a such a short amount of time, even though 75% of the people who invest in the commodities market lose money. A month after Mrs. Clinton opened the Refco account in 1978, her husband was elected governor. Her profit has raised questions of whether outsiders helped the couple make money, at a time when they had gained in prominence but were far from wealthy.

According to Mr. Podesta, Mrs. Clinton opened a margin account with Refco in October 1978 with her $1,000 investment. Her first trade resulted in a profit of $5,300, and she reinvested her earnings in several transactions. For the rest of 1978, her trades resulted in $49,069 in profits, which were offset by losses of $22,548, leaving a net gain for the year of $26,541.

In the first seven months of 1979, her trading profits reached $109,600, while she sustained $36,600 in losses, leaving a net gain of $72,996. It was at that point, aides say, that Mrs. Clinton stopped trading because she had just become pregnant.

Later that year, however, her stockbroker, Stephens Inc. of Little Rock — which trades through ACLI International, Peavey Co. and Clayton Brokerage — opened a commodities account in her name with a $5,000 investment. At one point, her account reached a $26,894 profit, but by the time she closed it in early 1980, just after her daughter, Chelsea, was born, it had a net loss of $1,000.

Jack Sandner, chairman of the Chicago Mercantile Exchange, said Mrs. Clinton traded "in the biggest bull market in the history of cattle." He said that from the beginning of 1978 to the first quarter of 1979, the price doubled to 80 cents a pound. "If someone caught that trend and traded it well, they could make an extraordinary amount of money, a lot more than $100,000 on a small investment," he said.

But one expert was skeptical of Mrs. Clinton's success. "The idea that Mrs. Clinton could turn $1,000 into $100,000 trading a cross-section of markets such as cattle, soybeans, sugar, hogs, copper and lumber just isn't believable," said Bruce Babcock, editor of

Commodity Traders Consumer Report, a Sacramento, Calif., newsletter. Mr. Babcock, the author of several books including "The Dow Jones Irwin Guide on Trading Systems," said: "To make 100 times your money is possible, but it's difficult to understand how a newcomer could do it. I don't care who is advising her. It just isn't very likely."

White House aides said the majority of Mrs. Clinton's trades were "long-term" transactions rather than so-called day trades, which take place in a single day and where abuse is more prevalent. Aides did say that a few of Mrs. Clinton's transactions were day trades. In addition to cattle, Mrs. Clinton also traded in soybeans, sugar, hogs, copper and lumber.

Aides emphasized that these were Mrs. Clinton's transactions and that her husband wasn't involved, but they acknowledged that they hadn't asked her if Mr. Clinton was aware of the trading.

The White House decision to release the records comes as part of their new strategy to be more open about the questions regarding their personal finances. It seems to be working. Mr. Clinton's popularity has risen in public opinion polls after his prime time news conference Thursday, in which he answered a series of questions about their investment in Whitewater Development Co.

Some commodity traders seemed to be puzzled by the condition of the commodity trading records released to reporters. A number of the records indicate specific numbers of contracts traded but some records merely list a cash balance without backup information describing the commodity and the number of contracts.

The possibility of missing Madison Guaranty records was raised by a chronology of a criminal investigation by the Resolution Trust Corp. An RTC investigator discovered in May 1993 that several boxes of Madison files were missing from a Little Rock warehouse used by the successor institution, Central Bank & Trust, according to the chronology, which was released last week by Rep. James Leach (R., Iowa). The RTC has been looking into the failure of Madison, once owned by the Clintons' Whitewater partner, James McDougal.

(In Little Rock yesterday, Mr. McDougal filed to enter a three-way Democratic primary election for the U.S. House of Representatives. He ran for Congress unsuccessfully in 1982.)

Central Bank was headed until April 1993 by Leonard Dunn, finance chairman for Mr. Clinton's 1990 gubernatorial campaign and a Clinton appointee to the Arkansas Industrial Development Commission. In an interview yesterday, Mr. Dunn said he doesn't know what became of the Madison files.

"I didn't shred or dump any records" and didn't order anybody to do so, he asserted. "What motive would I have to dump records?"

Rep. Spencer Bachus, an Alabama Republican, asked Whitewater Special Counsel Robert Fiske Monday to investigate the matter. "It already has been widely reported that documents were shredded at the Rose Law Firm," said Mr. Bachus, a member of the House Banking Committee. "The destruction of the warehoused documents could be part of a larger effort to protect the Clintons and to obstruct justice."

In March 1992, two investigators for the RTC, the savings-and-loan cleanup agency, visited the warehouse and reported finding boxes of Madison records in serious disarray. One of the investigators, Jean Lewis, returned 14 months later and discovered that the records had been organized and "a number of boxes had been cleared out," according to the RTC chronology. Afterward, Ms. Lewis learned that some records had been moved to a back room at the bank.

The warehouse also was used by the law firm Mitchell, Selig, Jackson, Tucker & White, which handled much of Madison's legal work until government regulators took over in 1989, according to the chronology.

Earl C.Gottschalk Jr. in Los Angeles contributed to this article.

REVIEW & OUTLOOK

Hillary in the Pits

The 1980s ushered in a Gilded Age of greed and selfishness, of irresponsibility and excess and of neglect.

— BILL CLINTON
announcement speech for president
October 1991.

The 1980s were about acquiring — acquiring wealth, power, privilege.

— HILLARY CLINTON
in the Washington Post
May 6, 1993.

Whitewater Etc. has many unsolved mysteries, but few more curious than Hillary Clinton's cattle-futures trading in the late 1970s. It's been a wonder this Wellesley-cum-Yale legal activist for children would make a brief but apparently sensational venture into the commodity pits.

The mystery, raised by a New York Times revelation of nearly $100,000 in trading profits, took a few days to grow into yet another crisis on the White House doorstep. This delay was probably a measure of how removed the commodities business is from the Beltway consciousness.

Yesterday the spinmeisters at 1600 Pennsylvania were scrambling to knock down a Newsweek story suggesting Hillary had put no money into the deals, piggybacking instead on the trading success of an attorney for one of Arkansas's biggest companies. Yesterday afternoon the White House released some previously unavailable records to substantiate her commodities position.

No doubt the folks who do this business for a living are going to be  heard from in coming days as to what questions these records do answer and what they don't. But our initial look at these documents reveals that she made an instant splash, apparently walking away with $5,300 a day after depositing $1,000 in a margin account. From there it was up and down — mostly up — over a nine-month span in one account and subsequently five months in another. She later branched out from cattle to trade a half-dozen commodities, including hogs, soybeans, lumber and copper. Come again on the '80s?

Hillary Clinton

The White House has now added documentary support to the contention that Mrs. Clinton incurred her own risk in accounts that led to more than $26,000 in reported profits in 1978 and nearly $73,000 in 1979. But the handling of her main account is still something to wonder about.

The broker for that account, Robert L. (Red) Bone of Springdale, Ark., has a record that is checkered even by commodity-industry standards. The most pertinent to this matter may be a December 1979 disciplining by the Chicago Mercantile Exchange (which handles cattle futures) for "serious and repeated violations of record-keeping functions, order-entry procedures, margin requirements and hedge procedures." Whether Mrs. Clinton knew the sort of man she was dealing with, we don't know. But Jim Blair, the Tyson Foods lawyer who got her into commodities, was Mr. Bone's lawyer, too.

Mr. Bone in 1972 was an official of Tyson Foods when he, Don Tyson, the company and half a dozen other parties were accused of manipulating the egg futures market. They ultimately settled the case in 1977 with the Commodity Futures Trading Commission, not admitting or denying guilt.

Mr. Bone was suspended from trading for a year as a result of that. Meanwhile, in 1975, as the case was in limbo, he had become a broker and joined Chicago-based Refco Inc. to run its Springdale branch, according to Securities Week. This was a fateful match. Refco was as rough and tumble as they come in the commodities world. But, under the chairmanship of Thomas Dittmer, a cattle trader extraordinaire, it would enjoy a historic bullish play in that particular futures market during 1978-79. The remarkable story of Refco's rise in commodities under Mr. Dittmer was described in a long March 13, 1984, profile in the Journal. Hillary Clinton and Jim Blair were along for the ride. Their gains may, in that context, be perfectly explainable, though their exit timing had to have been good as well.

Apparently Red Bone was so gung-ho with Refco that he couldn't wait out the year's suspension he'd been given in 1977. In a case filed in 1980, he was accused of having traded (quite profitably) through an associate, Roy Woods, during the 1977-78 period, just prior to his business with Mrs. Clinton. For this he was fined $100,000 in 1981, a severe sanction, and barred again from trading. Reportedly he was bankrupted around that time, as the market turned against him, and his license expired in 1984. (Mr. Bone couldn't be reached. We did catch up with Mr. Woods, who was also sanctioned in 1981. He said he'd been in the trucking business for 12 years, didn't remember much of anything about trades, and had to hang up because his dinner was getting cold.) We dwell on Mr. Bone because as Mrs. Clinton's broker he is crucial to any resolution of the remaining murk around this deal. And for that matter, the record of Mr. Blair's own trades with his broker.

But even if Mrs. Clinton's records tell the full story and all was square in the Springdale office of Refco, this dated tale has a connection to American politics in 1994. If commodity speculation, where there's a loser for every winner, was the basis for the Clintons' rise to affluence, what has all the moralizing about the Decade of Greed been about? In any event, the '80s weren't even born when Hillary was cleaning up in cattle.

For several months this past fall and winter, the Clinton Administration enjoyed a streak of seeming successes that was beginning to rival Hillary's commodities cornucopia for its audacious improbability. Now, in both policy substance and personal image, this White House appears to have topped out. As fast as fortunes can change in these times, the First Couple might begin to weigh how much political capital they have to meet a margin call.

Editorial Feature

What Mr. Fiske Can't Do
With the Facts

As I have stated in its Introduction, this public report to the Congress is incomplete because, as you know, Federal Rule of Criminal Procedure 6(e) forbids disclosure of matters occurring before the grand jury, and this was very largely a grand jury investigation. Moreover, there are other legal and ethical considerations governing my release of any matters of a testimonial nature.

My report to the Attorney General, on the other hand, is complete and summarizes fully all that has been done and found in this investigation. Should the Congress in its wisdom decide that the public interest in favor of disclosure of that full report outweighs in this case the policy reasons underlying existing requirements of secrecy, Congress undoubtedly may act to release the full report.

So read the cover letter to Congress the last time the business affairs of the president of the United States were under investigation by a special counsel appointed on the same terms as Robert Fiske. In 1979 Paul J. Curran, a Republican former prosecutor, was called in to investigate President Carter's peanut business, which had received a swirl of loans from the National Bank of Georgia, owned by Mr. Carter's friend and budget director Bert Lance. The suspicion was that the loans were illegally diverted to finance Mr. Carter's presidential campaign.

Rule of Law

By Robert L. Bartley

That is to say that the Carter peanut investigation looked a lot like Whitewater. Or at least like a little Whitewater; Mr. Lance and Mr. Carter never actually entered into a partnership, and so far as is known Rosalynn Carter made no killings in the commodities market. But the cases are similar enough to shed light on what we can expect, and not expect, from Mr. Fiske's investigation. In particular, the testimony he is gathering before a grand jury will also be subject to rule 6(e).

In the peanut case, Mr. Curran and a staff of lawyers investigated for six months, reviewed 80,000 subpoenaed documents, heard 64 witnesses before a federal grand jury in Atlanta, conducted 34 additional witness interviews, complemented by 21 further interviews by the FBI. They also conducted a four-hour deposition of President Carter, under oath in the White House. In October 1979, Mr. Curran issued his report.

"There is no evidence to establish that President Jimmy Carter committed any crimes," he said. "Every nickel and every peanut have been tracked into and out of the warehouse, and no funds were unlawfully diverted."

While none of the loans were diverted into the presidential campaign, they did have their problems. The warehouse had expanded with equipment loans and took the usual commodity loans secured by its peanut inventory. But at one point there was no collateral when it owed Mr. Lance's bank over a million dollars. Overdrafts in the warehouse account at the NBG "appeared very frequently," with the peak being $369,415. The bank often held loan repayment checks until funds were available. Ultimately President Carter and Carter Farms, in which he held 91% interest, bailed the warehouse out of its financial difficulties with a loan of $440,000.

The tale did not concern a conspiracy to finance Mr. Carter's campaign, that is, but a failure of business management. Most of the loans were granted when the peanut business was run by the president's brother Billy. Mr. Lance's bank was surely forbearing, but its loans were ultimately redeemed by the presidential loan. Mr. Curran decided that none of this crossed the line of criminality — probably for lack of *mens rea*, criminal intent — and that "based on all the evidence and the applicable law, no indictment can or should be brought against anyone. None will be filed."

At the time, Mr. Lance was already under indictment for his banking practices on matters not related to the Carter loans; he was later acquitted on fraud charges and the judge dismissed lesser charges on which a jury deadlocked. By then, he'd resigned as budget director and sold his interest in NBG to BCCI figure Ghaith Pharaon.

At the end of the peanut investigation, Mr. Curran faced the issue of what he should do with all of the information he'd gathered. As a special counsel, he was bound by the rules that apply to criminal prosecutions, in particular rule 6(e) prohibiting the release of grand jury evidence. Since he had decided against indictment and trials, in an ordinary case this would have been the end of the matter. But stony silence scarcely seemed appropriate, especially since the attorney general asked for a public report.

So Mr. Curran prepared two reports, a 179-page public document and a 239-page report sent only to the attorney general. In the public version, he said, "I stress right here at the beginning, this public document cannot and does not purport to set forth the totality of the investigation."

President Carter could also have chosen to release his own deposition, as a New York Times editorial urged, speculating on the president's "continuing knowledge of the family business and its financial and legal difficulties." But the president never released the transcript, and Congress never asked for the full report.

In the peanut case this may have been a tolerable outcome, but Whitewater is a far more sweeping matter. Say that Mr. Fiske concludes that indictments are precluded by the statute of limitations; rule 6(e) would then prevent him from releasing the evidence he'd taken before his grand jury. Similarly, if he concludes it's a stretch to see George Stephanopoulos' phone calls to the Treasury as an obstruction of justice, the testimony on them would be kept from public view.

"Bob Fiske will get all the facts," Mr. Curran says in reflecting on the prospects for the Whitewater probe, but "Bob Fiske will never be able to get 'all the facts out.' If he did, he would be acting illegally and, in any event, it is not his right or his duty to do so." The claims of some Democrats and the expectations of the public will be frustrated by rule 6(e). He says, "Prosecutors are not investigating commissions."

Between the Curran and Fiske investigations, Congress tried to combine prosecutors with investigating commissions through the Ethics in Government Act. Under this act a judge might release some

grand jury testimony after lengthy arguments among the parties —
Lawrence Walsh's final report added little to the congressional hearings six years earlier. It would be better to face up to the fact that the
roles do not mix. Plain and special prosecutors decide whether to
indict. And let investigating commissions be run the old-fashioned
way, in public and under congressional authority.

———————

Mr. Bartley is editor of the Journal.

Review & Outlook

Sleazy Trades?

The Clintons have provided some commodity-brokerage printouts, thank you. But they are not, as widely believed, trading records. After spending two days with these incomplete numbers, we find that they answer fewer questions than they raise.

That is, the printouts don't put to rest the suspicion that someone cut a lot of corners to steer Bill and Hillary nearly $100,000 in commodities gains. These suspicions lurk because amateur commodities players simply don't make such money, because of what the whole Whitewater affair tells us about the way business and government mixed in Arkansas, because a powerful friend of Bill and Hillary loomed in the background, and because the trades were handled by a broker who was repeatedly sanctioned. The White House will have to go a lot further to demonstrate that Mrs. Clinton did indeed trade commodities as she says she did and not with undue assistance from Tyson Foods lawyer Jim Blair and/or his (and her) broker Robert Lee (Red) Bone.

What the Clintons released Tuesday were two types of monthly statements for the first eight months of activity. One showed the gains or losses being posted to her account as positions were closed; they don't reveal the types, the durations or the prices of the deals. The other statement showed open futures contracts at the end of each month. Except on the open positions, we can't tell a cattle trade from one in soybeans, for instance. Presumably these records were obtained from the Refco brokerage house or from the family files.

Either way, people in the business tell us, we should expect a third type of statement to be part of the package: a record of daily trade confirmations, with amounts and prices.

Once upon a time there would have been time-stamped trading slips that would allow checking the trades against exchange records of prices, but these are typically discarded after a few years. But confirmation slips would tell us what exactly she was trading, what her price in and out was, and where there were intra-day or adjusted trades — both of which would flag attention to possible misallocations by the broker.

The issue of intra-day trades is particularly relevant because of Mr. Bone's history. One of his disciplinary proceedings, according to sources quoted by Securities Week, "largely related to trade allocations, whereby customers of Bone's choosing would be given the good, i.e. profitable, trades at the close of the trading day and other accounts would get the bad trades." Allocations are easy on intra-day trades, and very difficult to do on longer trades without raising "as of" red flags. Mr. Bone was found to be playing with margin requirements, which also reflects on the Hillary matter.

To appreciate the essence of this, you don't have to go beyond the two first days of Mrs. Clinton's monthly statements. On Oct. 11, 1978, she made a cash deposit of $1,000. This is a curious figure for a prospective cattle trader, since the margin requirement for a single cattle contract was $1,200. The next day she closed out positions netting a profit of $5,300. Margins apply to overnight accounts, and since Hillary didn't meet the margin for a single contract, until we see the actual records, we have to presume her Oct. 12 profits came from day trades.

We and others have been asking around for explanations of how one makes 530% in one day, given the fact that, by exchange limits, the most a cattle contract (40,000 pounds) could move during that day was 1.5 cents up or down per pound. As best we can determine, the actual movement of the most volatile cattle contract on Oct. 12 was 0.8 cents. In other words, to make $5,300, one would have needed to own about 17 contracts.

A contract was worth about $22,000. Even if not all of them were held at once, if broker Bone were carrying off a string of amazing buys and sells as the day proceeded (with Hillary at his side, of course), we're talking about a position at any one time that dwarfed the worth of a couple who had a $42,000 income the previous year and didn't even own a home. The exposure to simply one day's swing would be many times the $1,000 Mrs. Clinton had put down. At the least, any broker actually making these trades had to assume there was a lot more behind the Clintons than what they showed on paper.

Or maybe they weren't her trades at all. That day's gains in Mrs. Clinton's account, says John Damgard, president of the Futures Industry Association, "very well may apply to trades that were on for some time and were liquidated that day." Indeed, the Washington Post quoted a White House official to the effect that Hillary believed her gains accumulated over several days. But if so, according to the records, they had to belong to somebody else, somebody who was willingly or unwillingly giving up his gain to her.

If Mrs. Clinton's account was cleared that first day, she survived the heavy exposure to loss. But if the records released so far are accurate, on that first day she was able to show profitable intra-day trades that seem wholly out of line with her financial resources. This raises a question about the rest of her trades, since the released records are ambiguous on which were day trades. Some trades, those held over the end of the month, are clearly of longer duration. But with the bulk of trades, and the bulk of the profits, the positions were closed within the month, and perhaps within the day.

It is true that Mrs. Clinton sustained losses, sometimes sizable ones, such as $17,400 on Nov. 22, but each time the debit was made up with gains on what may have been more of those easily manipulable day trades. It looks as if the intermonth positions were net losers and the intramonth trades net winners. Confirmation records would address what the intramonth deals were.

And, of course, if the balance of the trades were indeed overnight, it again raises the issue of margins. "Significant undermargining" at the outset, Mr. Damgard says, "raises the question of whether some-one was arranging her trades." Trader Morris Markovitz, quoted yesterday in USA Today, calculated that at one point her account was $90,000 short of margin, and commented, "I defy you to find any other account in the country where such a tiny amount of cash was allowed to risk such massive amounts of money."

While true trading records would tell much of the story, it would also be helpful to hear soon from Mr. Bone under oath. Especially so since he has told the New York Times, more than once, that he did not confer with Hillary over her trades, as the White House says he did, and in fact doesn't even recall doing them. Perhaps others in the Refco operation, past and present, could shed some light on whether it was standard procedure for a broker to permit an amateur with $1,000 to control perhaps 400,000 pounds of cattle. Refco itself was disciplined by the Merc in 1979 and fined $250,000 for record-keeping negligence. Any such testimony would require congressional hearings, not yet set for Whitewater. Robert Fiske's inquiry into possible crimes would appear to be irrelevant here, since the statute of limitations has long since lapsed.

When confronted with the messy circumstances of deals by which Mr. and Mrs. Clinton sought to "get theirs" earlier in life, this Administration's habit is first to brush off the questions as an impertinence, then to dribble out documents that purport to put matters to rest but (slyly?) don't, and finally to act victimized when the inquiries don't cease.

The President and his wife are not the first to have suspicions about their personal finances follow them into the White House. We remember a guy whose California "slush fund" hung over him for 20 years, until he clumsily gave the press something really to write home about. We're not suggesting this episode is pointed toward another Watergate, and for the sake of an unstable world and shaky markets we surely trust not. But at the very least, we have to note that the cover-up of the Clintons' 1978 and 1979 tax returns got them past not only the statute of limitations but some important political deadlines. If the commodities trading had come out during the 1992 campaign, for instance, or 1993 tax debate, the Clintons' effective rhetoric about greed in the 1980s would have been exposed as the hypocritical blather that it was.

Now, we're drawing conclusions from two days with incomplete records, and while our inquiries at the White House yesterday were unavailing, further explanations may dispel our suspicions. But by now the administration has welcomed to Washington nearly every Arkansas ally this side of Red Bone and Jim McDougal. So with the record so suggestive of sleazy trading, surely it is time for the Clintons to start doing some real explaining.

REVIEW & OUTLOOK

Greed and Hypocrisy

Hillary Clinton's magical mystery tour through the commodity trading pits in the late '70s is now being deconstructed by her defenders. Ellen Goodman, Anthony Lewis and even Nina Totenberg have now taken up cudgels in favor of capitalism and honest profit, or as their type once called it, greed.

The press is excited over Whitewater, Mr. Lewis philosophizes in the New York Times, because the Clintons weren't "holy creatures devoted to good government. They wanted to make some money, too." Ms. Totenberg, who won fame with Anita Hill's charges, opined on "Inside Washington" on standards of evidence for Mrs. Clinton's $1,000 into nearly $100,000 ploy. It would be worth covering if "she got something she didn't deserve and there was quid pro quo." No story merely "because of some airy-fairy, oh, they're hypocritical."

Ms. Goodman, writing in the Boston Globe, attempted an important distinction: "If the Clintons made money on beef 15 years ago, it wasn't a character flaw. Making a profit doesn't make a hypocrite. The trouble with the '80s wasn't that a Michael Milken made a fortune, but that he did so while wrecking other lives."

Ms. Goodman's theme is worth exploring. It occurs to us that "making money on beef" — in a cynical sense, literally "taking advantage" of the market — is the sort of brush with capitalism that would appeal to those members of a generation whose interests run toward more socially "responsible" financial transactions — for example, grants by foundations that have stock-fattened endowments. Mrs. Clinton's defenders have recently offered an apologia for whatever was going on between her and her husband and such economic pilot fish as Jim McDougal and Red Bone. They argue that most of her best working effort was reserved for the likes of education reform or the Children's Defense Fund.

This fits neatly with the '60s view of the moral universe. A foundation, for example, might derive its sustaining income from a previous economic activity seen as having no serious moral content, such as making Ford automobiles, but the better people are now taking what used to be merely corporate profits and redistributing them to grant seekers representing the "public interest."

This, in sum, is the holier-than-thou ethos that Bill and Hillary Clinton bragged about in the 1992 campaign and brought with them into the White House. The America for the 1990s would break with its unredeemable recent past.

Forget even Whitewater for a moment. Recall early last year when the President and Mrs. Clinton decided that the way to popularize their desire to expand childhood vaccination programs was to excoriate the profits of a heartless pharmaceutical industry. This was an act of demagogic scapegoating so breathtaking that the industry's most respected member, Merck chairman Roy Vagelos, took out newspaper ads to refute it. But then later, Hillary's preferred strategy for popularizing her health plan was to shout speeches about a profiteering insurance industry. When the industry defended itself with the Harry and Louise ads, the White House professed moral superiority in the face of corporate "lying."

The Clintons' current problems really are about much more than the details of a tax loss in the Arkansas outback. Bill and Hillary Clinton, and their supporters, like to remind people that they spent the '80s, like they spent the '60s, in a pose of opposition. They blithely wave away the entire economic history of the U.S. in the 1980s as "greed." They, we are given to believe, weren't party to that.

But now with Hillary's commodities revelations, the supporters of the '80s, we included, are accused of somehow reciprocating their hypocrisy. As Ms. Goodman puts it, "The Wall Street Journal, which has criticized her as a closet socialist, now gleefully trashes her as a closet capitalist."

Let us make ourselves clear. It wouldn't occur to us for a moment that Bill and Hillary's financial life, as now being unearthed by a competitive press, has much of anything in common with the economic life of the '80s. Not with the world of Route 128, the Genentechs, Silicon Valley, the growth of edge cities, the revival of Ford Motor Co. Nor with, for that matter, MCI Communications, McCaw Cellular, TLC Beatrice, Turner Broadcasting and all the other entrepreneurial companies that grew during the 1980s with the help of financing from Michael Milken. To give due credit, Mrs. Clinton sat on the board of Wal-Mart Stores, Arkansas's big contribution to the 1980s boom.

Yet it's laughable to think that any of this is related to the world of Red Bone, Jim and Susan McDougal, Dan Lasater or the famous four Rose partners of Little Rock. The financial life of Bill and Hillary Clinton reads more like the milieu of a David Mamet play, in which glib five-and-dimers swim along the edges of the real economy, living on fancy talk, cutting corners and hoping that one of the big boys will offer them a piece of the $100 sure thing.

The defenders keep saying that the Clintons' business history, compared with their current, large responsibilities, is so much "petty financial juggling." They're right. On the evidence so far, it is all very penny-ante. And there seems to be so much of it.

Editorial Feature

In Praise of Presidential Prerogatives

Two months ago when the State Department announced that it would focus on the treatment of women in its yearly report on human rights conditions, the New York Times reported that officials "denied" that the White House played any role in this new emphasis.

About the same time, the Justice Department, in a reversal from earlier positions, sided with the state of California and against Barclays Bank in a pending Supreme Court case on how states tax foreign-based companies. This prompted suggestions that the White House was interfering with the independence of Justice's solicitor general.

Politics & People

By Albert R. Hunt

Two weeks ago White House press secretary Dee Dee Myers was bombarded with questions at a press briefing on the propriety of the White House intervening in a Justice Department review of a clemency request for Jonathan Pollard, the former naval officer convicted of spying for the Israelis.

These three very diverse episodes share a common thread: the insane implication that the president of the United States is not supposed to set the policy of his own administration. This absurd notion has accelerated in recent weeks in the frenzy of the Whitewater scandal.

The president should not get involved in individual regulatory matters; that's why independent agencies — with members appointed by the president — were created. But certainly the president is supposed to direct the policy of his own administration. These recent anecdotes are illustrative.

Let's hope that the White House played a role in deciding whether to emphasize the treatment of women in U.S. human rights policies. That's not a decision that should be left to the striped-pants set.

The Barclays Bank taxation case is too arcane for my feeble mind, so it's an open question to me whether the administration is correct. But in 1992 Bill Clinton campaigned in California on precisely this position. Right or wrong, he got a lot more votes than any bureaucrats in the solicitor general's office.

As for complaints about any White House involvement in the Pollard clemency case, critics ought to read a simple document: Article 2 of the Constitution. It states the president "shall have power to grant reprieves and pardons." That responsibility rests exclusively with the office of president.

In the current climate, one top White House assistant says, "We hear footsteps every time we get involved in anything controversial."

The presidency, for all the desirable checks and balances, shouldn't function with such inhibitions. "The president ought to be actively involved in governmental decisions," says Terry Eastland, a conservative former Republican Justice Department official and author of an acclaimed book on the power and prerogatives of the executive branch. "That's why we elect a president. That's what the Constitution says he's supposed to do."

To be sure, some of the problems were initiated by liberals in the 1980s, especially in the judicial area, in an effort to stem the conservative Reagan tide. But today some conservatives, sensing weakness in an activist Democratic president, are seizing the moment to try to hamstring executive prerogatives. This sort of situational positioning is dangerously shortsighted.

The most dramatic catalyst was the story revealing that top White House aides George Stephanopoulos and Harold Ickes had expressed displeasure to two top Treasury Department officials over the appointment of Jay Stephens, a former Republican prosecutor, to handle some of the civil matters of the Whitewater-tainted Madison Guaranty. Yet a careful look at the particulars and the broader question on whether the administration has sought to manipulate the Resolution Trust Corp. to protect the president suggests there is little basis for such overreaction.

Jay Stephens is a former U.S. attorney of unbridled political ambitions who was fired by President Clinton a year ago and then blasted the president. Since then, he's been an actively partisan Republican whose conduct concerning the investigation of Rep. Dan Rostenkowski was so outrageous that his Republican predecessor as U.S. attorney called his actions "unprofessional."

It would have been unthinkable for any White House aide not to complain about this appointment; imagine John Sununu or Ed Meese timidly accepting the appointment of a ferociously partisan liberal Democrat to investigate matters involving President Reagan or Bush. But the most important point is that, private sniping aside, there's no evidence that anything was done to remove Mr. Stephens. If intemperate phone calls become a felony, we'll have to double the national debt to build enough new prisons.

And while it was clearly a bad idea to make Deputy Treasury Secretary Roger Altman the acting head of the RTC, it doesn't appear that this agency has been compromised by Clinton political appointees. Indeed, the administration nominated a prominent Republican, Stanley Tate, to head the agency last year; the selection won praise from such diverse editorial pages as the liberal Miami Herald and conservative Wall Street Journal. Mr. Tate dropped out late last year when Senate Banking Committee Chairman Don Riegle refused to move the nomination.

Republican Rep. Jim Leach, the most serious and level-headed Republican Whitewater critic, has alleged there has been political pressure on RTC investigators. But last week the two top RTC career officials, John Ryan and Ellen Kulka, wrote a letter to Mr. Leach flatly asserting that "no pressure has been exerted" by the Clinton administration on the Madison Guaranty and Whitewater investigations.

The bottom line is that an active Republican was nominated to head the RTC, a vehemently partisan Republican has been tapped to probe part of the Madison Guaranty scandal, and there is no documentation of any pressure or action by Clinton appointees to impede any investigation. On Whitewater, there remain some serious unanswered questions about dealings in Arkansas a decade or more ago. Not only is the special counsel in order but Congress ought to swiftly pass the independent counsel law and Robert Fiske ought to be reappointed as a truly independent counsel. Congressional hearings are absolutely essential.

But to leap from that to suggestions that this administration has engaged in systematic abuses of power and that the authority of this executive ought to be curbed is nonsense. Political opponents would like to use this as an effort to paralyze President Clinton. But they would do well to remember that's a weapon that not only can, but invariably will, be turned on them once one of their own returns to the Oval Office.

Editorial Feature

The Mystery of Hillary's Trades

By DAVID L. BRANDON

As former head of the IRS chief counsel's Commodities Industry Specialization Team in the mid-1980s, I have followed with great interest the media stories on Hillary Clinton's excellent adventures in the commodities markets. As a proud capitalist and free market proponent (and an avid beef eater), I would be the first in line to salute this woman's success with cattle futures. But based on my years of experience with these markets, her story just doesn't add up. In fact, the chances of someone making almost $100,000 in the futures markets on her first try are about as great as walking into a casino in Las Vegas, hitting the million-dollar jackpot on your first try at the slots, then walking out never to play again. It just doesn't happen that way.

For those unfamiliar with the details of Mrs. Clinton's remarkable venture into the commodities markets, she allegedly made more than $99,000 in cattle futures (and other commodities) in late 1978 and 1979, withdrawing from trading just before the markets went bust. No explanation has been offered of how Mrs. Clinton managed to satisfy state laws that require futures investors to demonstrate a minimum net income and net worth, nor how a novice could have such uncanny timing.

There is, in fact, a much more probable explanation for Mrs. Clinton's good fortune. The media have already suggested that trades may have been moved to Mrs. Clinton's account after gains had been realized. However, the stories thus far have not clearly focused on a common trading strategy called a "straddle" that was very much in vogue at the time.

Straddles have the unique ability to produce exactly equal and offsetting gains and losses that can be transferred or used by the straddle trader for a variety of purposes. During the late 1970s and early 1980s, straddles were used for all kinds of illegal activities, ranging from tax evasion to money-laundering and bribes. In fact, this activity prompted a number of legal and regulatory changes by the Reagan administration to curb the abuses. Although it sounds somewhat esoteric, a commodities straddle is a relatively simple trading device. A commodities futures contract is nothing more than an agreement between two parties to buy or sell a certain type of commodity (in Mrs. Clinton's case, cattle) for a stated price on some date in the future. If the price of the commodity goes up before the contract delivery date, the individual who agreed to buy the commodity will realize a gain equal to the difference between the current price and the contract price. The individual who agreed to sell will realize a loss in an equal amount. Conversely, if the price goes down, the buyer will lose and the seller will gain.

A straddle is created when an investor enters into contracts to both buy and sell the same commodity. In this case, any gain on one contract will be exactly offset by a loss on the opposite contract. While straddle trading today is used in a variety of legitimate ways, these transactions lend themselves to all sorts of abuses as well. Before regulatory changes in the 1980s, it was common to enter into straddles to wipe out large capital gains for tax purposes. For example, an investor who realized a $100,000 capital gain in the stock market might enter into a large straddle in the commodities market. When the commodity price moved, the investor would close the loss leg of the straddle and realize a $100,000 loss, which offset his gain in the stock market. The investor was not required to report the unrealized $100,000 gain in the opposite leg of the straddle until that leg was closed in the following year. Typically, the investor entered into another straddle in the following year, thereby indefinitely rolling over the capital gain into subsequent years.

Another ploy common during that time required the assistance of a friendly broker. An investor could create a straddle using two separate investment accounts with his broker. After the straddle had moved, so that a gain and an offsetting loss had been created, the friendly broker simply wrote in the name of the investor's tax-exempt retirement fund on the account that held the gain leg of the straddle. The result was that a loss was realized that was reported on the investor's tax return, while the gain went unreported in the tax-exempt retirement account.

In the late 1970s and early 1980s, the IRS began noticing large numbers of individual tax returns that curiously showed commodities losses just big enough to wipe out unrelated capital gains; no corresponding commodities gains, which would suggest a straddle, ever appeared on subsequent returns. Even more curiously, the profile of these investors always had one thing in common, which was limited experience or no prior experience in commodities trading. In the early 1980s, an IRS agent in Chicago thought to look into one taxpayer's retirement fund and, of course, found the hidden gain leg of the straddle.

After that experience, the IRS redoubled its efforts to seek out thousands of missing straddle gains. It found them in retirement accounts, in London, in the Cayman Islands—almost anywhere a taxpayer thought he might hide them from the IRS. With respect to these thousands of mysterious, isolated commodities transactions that showed up on tax returns, the IRS uncovered some form of questionable trading in virtually 100% of the cases it investigated. Well before the close of the 1980s, the IRS had assessed more than $7 billion in delinquent taxes and penalties attributable to these transactions and eventually settled these cases out of court for approximately $3.5 billion.

While most of the IRS's efforts were directed at finding hidden gains of the ubiquitous straddle, the trading device could just as easily be used to openly transfer gains while hiding the offsetting loss. If someone desired to make an illicit payment to another party, a straddle could be used to accomplish this purpose with no incriminating or suspicious-looking bank withdrawals or deposits. In fact, the IRS found numerous incidents of straddles being used for money-laundering purposes.

Does Mrs. Clinton's trading activity fit the profile of the illegitimate straddle trader? She was a novice in the commodities markets who, against all odds, realized large gains. Although she intermittently realized losses, it does not appear that she ever had to risk her own capital beyond her initial $1,000 deposit, which itself may have been insufficient to cover even her first transaction (which netted her $5,300). According to the trading records released by the White House, most of Mrs.

Clinton's gains were recorded as intra-month transactions. This means that these records include no information regarding key elements of the trade, such as the type and quantity of the contracts, acquisition dates, acquisition prices, etc. Such information is needed to determine whether trades were part of a prearranged straddle.

It also appears that Mrs. Clinton's broker, Robert L. "Red" Bone, was no stranger to the spicier practices of commodities trading, according to The Wall Street Journal's front-page article last Friday.

It seems more than coincidental that Mr. Bone was a former employee of Tyson Foods and that Mrs. Clinton's investment adviser, James Blair, was the company's legal counsel. Tyson, the poultry concern, is one of the largest employers in the state of Arkansas. The fact that the Clintons withheld disclosing only those tax returns that included their commodities gains until the transactions were reported by the New York Times in February also appears quite suspicious. From my standpoint as a former government staff attorney with extensive experience in these matters, Mrs. Clinton's windfall in the late 1970s has all the trappings of pre-arranged trades.

How would a straddle have been used in Mrs. Clinton's case? The Journal has already reported that gains theoretically could have been transferred to Mrs. Clinton's account, while "others" may have absorbed losses. Such a transaction could be accomplished with a straddle.

A party desiring to transfer cash to another's personal account for legal or illegal purposes could enter into a straddle in a particularly volatile commodity, such as cattle futures in the late 1970s. After gains and losses were generated in the opposite sides of the straddle, the gain side would be marked to the beneficiary's account, while the loss side would remain in the account of the contributor. The contributor might even be entitled to use the loss to offset other gains. Such a transaction would be not only well-hidden from government authorities but potentially tax-deductible.

No direct evidence of wrongdoing has been produced in the case of Mrs. Clinton's trading activity. In fact, no conclusive evidence of anything has been produced. In order to settle the legitimate questions surrounding her trades, a satisfactory explanation is needed for her apparently low initial margin deposit and whether the requirements relating to an investor's minimum net income and net worth were satisfied. In addition, the details of her numerous intra-month trades should be provided, as well as the details of the trades of persons who may have had a special interest in how well she did. If it is discovered that certain interested parties happened to realize losses in cattle futures at the same time, and they were comparable in size to the gains reported by Mrs. Clinton, this would amount to a "smoking gun."

This is not a matter of partisan politics. Even if the public had never heard of Hillary Rodham Clinton, the circumstances surrounding her unusual good fortune would still appear suspicious to anyone awake to abuses of the commodities markets. In this writer's experience, the normal trading world just doesn't work that way.

Mr. Brandon was a career attorney in the Office of Chief Counsel of the Internal Revenue Service from 1983 to 1989. During that time he also served as head of that department's Commodity Industry Specialization Team, which was responsible for coordinating and developing the IRS's legal positions on tax issues arising in connection with commodities transactions.

REVIEW & OUTLOOK

Justice Mitchell on Whitewater

Isn't it just like the Clinton Administration to dangle a lifetime Supreme Court appointment before the Senate's leading player in the decision on Whitewater hearings? Majority Leader George Mitchell hasn't been nominated to the court yet, but we somehow doubt he can put his prospects out of his mind as he negotiates how and whether to redeem the promise of hearings.

Congress returns from Easter recess today, and before leaving town both the Senate and House voted to go ahead with hearings. The majority leader could always simply keep this promise; or, with the court appointment now so prominently dangling, he could demonstrate judicial temperament by recusing himself from the decision. On the other hand, Mr. Mitchell is a proven master of using the powers of his office to stall promises to death, as in 1989 he managed to defeat a capital gains tax cut proposed by the administration, passed by the House and favored by a majority of his own chamber. Will Whitewater hearings

George Mitchell

meet the same fate?

So we note that putative Justice Mitchell is suddenly preoccupied with the timing and scope of hearings. "We're going to do it at a time and under circumstances which do not undermine the special counsel's investigation," he said Sunday. In other words, he's for letting

Congress hide behind special counsel Robert Fiske's probe. He wants to delay hearings until Mr. Fiske is finished with the Washington portion of his probe and releases some preliminary report, perhaps telling us if laws were broken but little or nothing about what actually took place. This would give Mr. Mitchell a fig leaf to say hearings really aren't needed on these matters. And if Republicans pressed the Arkansas portion of Whitewater, Mr. Mitchell would say Congress must again wait until Mr. Fiske finishes that part of his probe. That would conveniently push hearings beyond November's election and Mr. Mitchell's own elevation to the bench. If only Richard Nixon had thought of this.

Mr. Mitchell's other objection is that Whitewater hearings would somehow "prevent us from doing crime, welfare reform, health care reform and other things." But why should it? If there's as little to Whitewater as the White House says, it's hard to see how it would swallow all of Congress.

This fretting about Congressional hearings never bothered Democrats in the past. A recent study by George Mangan for the Congressional Research Service found that Congress held no fewer than 25 hearings or investigations into ethical or legal issues from 1981 to 1992. In only one of the 12 Reagan and Bush years—1991, the Gulf War year—did Congress not hold such hearings. In presidential election years, it held three each.

These inquiries included such momentous "scandals" as whether an ambassador misused a gift fund, whether Ed Meese misfiled a 1985 personal disclosure form, and the "background and propriety of telephone contacts" between a Reagan budget official and the Economic Regulatory Administration. Nothing came of these, and in any event at least Ed Meese never made a killing in cattle futures.

At least four of these 25 probes of GOP presidents took place while Republicans controlled the Senate. These were Iran-Contra (Senate-House Select Committees in 1986-87), an examination of Charles Zwick for telephone recordings (Senate Foreign Relations in 1984), and even probes of the private business dealings of Reagan officials John Fedders (Senate Banking in 1983) and Bill Casey (Senate Intelligence in 1981) that took place before they had taken public office. In three cases Congress also looked into matters that were also being pursued by an independent counsel. Congress "undermined" the special counsel in only one case, Iran-Contra, and that was because it granted immunity, which won't happen in Whitewater.

Republican leader Bob Dole is now requesting a single special committee to be composed of Members from each of the several committees that might claim a piece of Whitewater. That would at least eliminate the circus of several committee hearings, even as it ensured oversight of all the various parts of the story that now travel under the name of Whitewater (including, we hope, Hillary Rodham Clinton's cattle miracle). The House would still do its thing, of course, once Speaker Foley loses his mortal fear of Republican Jim Leach.

We hope Republicans are serious. The duty of a Congressional opposition is to scrutinize the executive branch, especially when the party in power won't investigate itself. Republicans are already holding up the nomination of bank regulator and friend-of-Hillary, Ricki Tigert; but they blinked Clark Clifford lawyer Jamie Gorelick into the Justice Department on a voice vote. The Justice Mitchell talk can cut both ways; Republicans have it in their power to make sure he doesn't get the expected smooth confirmation unless they get real Whitewater hearings.

Editorial Feature

Enough Is Enough on Whitewater

By ARTHUR SCHLESINGER JR.

"One great blemish in the popular mind of America, and the pro-
lific parent of an innumerable brood of evils," the English visitor tells
us, "is Universal Distrust. . . . You no sooner set up an idol firmly
than you are sure to pull it down and dash it into fragments. . . . Any
man who attains a high place among you, from the President down-
wards, may date his downfall from that moment; for any printed lie
that any notorious villain pens, although it militate directly against
the character and conduct of a life, appeals at once to your distrust,
and is believed."

The English visitor was Charles Dickens, and he was telling
Americans these things in 1842. A century and a half later, Universal

Board of Contributors

Distrust has clearly
not vanished from
the American psy-
che. Nor is a measure of distrust a bad thing for a democracy. It is
proper and necessary that presidents be held rigorously responsible
for everything they order or approve as president. The president, said
Andrew Jackson, must be "accountable at the bar of public opinion
for every act of his Administration."

But the current Whitewater hullabaloo introduces a startling and
unprecedented doctrine: that a president should be investigated not
for things he has done as president, but for things he might or might
not have been involved in a dozen years before he became president.

Has there been a previous instance in American history when congressional committees and special prosecutors were mobilized to investigate a president's pre-presidential career? I can think of none.

The traditional assumption has been that a candidate's pre-presidential career is an entirely legitimate election issue but that, once the election is over and the new president has been anointed by the voters, the slate is wiped clean, and the president is thereafter judged on his presidency. This is where comparisons with Watergate or Iran-Contra fail. In those cases, presidents were pursued not because of exhumations from the past but because of illegal projects undertaken in the presidential present.

The Whitewater doctrine, in short, is an astonishing historical innovation. If it had been applied to previous presidents — to Lyndon Johnson, for example — think what a field day congressional committees and special prosecutors would have had digging up political and financial dirt in Texas!

A rejoinder is that Mr. Clinton is being pursued not for what happened in Arkansas long before his presidency, but for a presumed coverup perpetrated by his presidency. It is true enough that Mr. Clinton has been ill-served by his White House staff. He has surrounded himself with people with limited government experience. His staffers have not known how little they know. The consequent succession of White House resignations and subpoenas feeds the suspicion that there must be something rotten in the inner circle. Reorganization of the White House staff and recruitment of people of experience and stature should be one of the president's top priorities. Bringing in Lloyd Cutler is an excellent, but apparently, by Mr. Cutler's choice, only a temporary, fix.

But the real issue is not Mr. Clinton's White House staff. It is whether anything happened in Arkansas a dozen years ago to justify this extraordinary detour from present urgencies of government. If all that is involved in Whitewater is Southern courthouse politics of a familiar sort, what does that have to do with the Clinton presidency a decade later? Did Harry Truman's association with the Pendergast machine disqualify him from the presidency? And if the press and the Republicans do come up with some major offense committed years ago, what do they have in mind as their next step? Do they really think that this would provide grounds for impeachment?

Obviously the Whitewater stalkers have other motivations than disinterested concern for the general welfare and for the historical record. Republicans are using Whitewater in an attempt to derail a reform program that was just beginning to gather steam and to discredit a presidential wife whose views they are reluctant to attack directly.

As for the press, some reporters, one fears, are engaged in a quest for Pulitzer prizes and Woodward-Bernstein notoriety. Others feel that they were deceived by the incomplete and inaccurate explanations the Clinton people gave them during the campaign (again the staff problem) and are determined not to be taken in again. And the dynamics of competition sometimes drive their sense of proportion in pursuit of a juicy story.

Little could be more ridiculous than the recent Time cover story hinting darkly that George Stephanopoulos might be obstructing justice because he queried the hiring of a former Republican prosecutor by a Democratic Treasury Department to look into an aspect of the Whitewater affair. I do not know of any White House in history, Democratic or Republican, that would not have objected to the appointment of a rabid partisan from the opposition to a post that could do damage to the administration.

Even the august New York Times devotes lead editorials to Whitewater as if this were the most urgent issue facing the nation. It calls on news organizations to "put more resources, rather than fewer, into the Whitewater story," citing the failure of the press to follow up on the Iran-Contra and savings-and-loan scandals. But those scandals were the responsibility of an administration in power. They were not scandals of Mr. Reagan's pre-presidential past.

One expects The Wall Street Journal, a newspaper that tolerantly endures my periodic heresies, to denounce a reform administration engaged in ventures of which the Journal's editors disapprove. But what in the world is the Times driving at? Why do Times editors think that putting more resources into an investigation of ancient history in Arkansas is so vital for the future of the republic as to justify bringing down an administration that the Times generally supports, or at the very least blocking action on reforms that the Times generally approves? The Times's priorities seem a trifle askew. "Fanaticism," as Santayana said, "consists in redoubling your efforts when you have forgotten your aim."

Reading the Times's self-righteous editorials today, one can only reflect what grand opportunities earlier Times editors missed in not demanding special prosecutors and congressional investigations of LBJ's Texas past, Chester A. Arthur's administration of the New York customhouse, and James A. Garfield's connection with the Credit Mobilier and the wooden-block pavement scandals.

And in the longer run one wonders why the Times — or even the Journal — endorses a doctrine, hitherto unknown in our history, that throws open a president's past to aimless investigation at the expense of the business of the present: a doctrine guaranteed to produce governmental paralysis on an unprecedented scale. As a historian and biographer, I am in favor of historical inquiries for their own sake, and I trust that in due course Bill Clinton will find his Robert Caro. But I doubt that such inquiries have much relevance to the actions of administrations in office. If they do shed light, Congress and the press should focus on present actions, not on alleged antecedents.

Unless putting in more resources produces some stunning disclosure, more and more people will agree with Barry Goldwater: Get off the president's back, and let him get on with his job. In the end, Whitewater may damage the press and the political opposition as much as it damages the Clinton administration. The initial impact came from exploitation of the Universal Distrust that Dickens saw as a great blemish in the American popular mind. But, if distrust is universal, it may bring down newspaper editors and leaders of the opposition as well.

Mr. Schlesinger is Albert Schweitzer professor of the humanities at the City University of New York and a winner of Pulitzer Prizes in history and biography.

Letters to the Editor

We Haven't Had Enough Yet

Arthur Schlesinger Jr., in his April 12 editorial-page essay "Enough Is Enough on Whitewater," argues that, because the media abstained from a full discussion of Bill Clinton's transgressions prior to the election, those things are now irrelevant.

It is precisely because the liberal media bias precluded a searching coverage of the Clintons' pre-election record that disillusionment is surfacing only now. What we are seeing in the White House is quite different from what was advertised — and media forbearance and incompetence deserve most of the blame. Incredibly, according to Mr. Schlesinger, because congressional committees and special prosecutors did not dig up political and financial dirt on LBJ in Texas, the Clintons should likewise be exempt from scrutiny. Not even a Democrat historian can now credibly argue that the media's failure to sufficiently illuminate LBJ's character and pre-White House record served our national interest.

Is it really a shame, as Mr. Schlesinger implies, that some journalists might consider a Pulitzer to be more important than covering up the character flaws and sordid behavior of a sitting president? If the Pulitzer motivated Woodward and Bernstein — and if Mr. Schlesinger then thought their reporting inappropriate because of it — his objections are not a matter of public record.

Finally, to equate Harry Truman's Pendergast association with the Clinton Arkansas machinations is ludicrous. Mr. Truman's personal character and rectitude survived massive attack and innuendo by his political opponents and critics. Mr. Clinton is no Harry Truman, but he may well be the second LBJ.

JAMES W. BUTCHER
Professor Emeritus
Department of Zoology
Michigan State University
St. Augustine, Fla.

* * *

If a public servant's pre-office record is of no relevance once he is elected, then why should it even be a legitimate campaign issue? Why should Oliver North be queried on his involvement in Iran-Contra while campaigning for the Virginia Senate? These issues are relevant, and just because we didn't know about them before the election does not place them off limits.

JIM SCHWAB
Boston

* * *

Does Mr. Schlesinger seriously believe that when Richard Nixon was "anointed" by the voters and became president, his slate was "wiped clean" in the eyes of liberals and Democrats?

Does he think he can browbeat the press by calling New York Times editorials "self-righteous" and reducing reporters' motives to a mere "quest for Pulitzer prizes"?

Does he think that the elfin-rallying cry, "Get off the president's back, and let him get on with his job" will deter legitimate dismay over cattle-futures hypocrisy and socialistic health-care plans?

All his scratching and clucking has no merit. He should get off the opposition's back and let it get on with its job.

CARL YOUNGDAHL
Sioux Falls, S.D.

* * *

I find it especially ironic that Mr. Schlesinger wonders what would have happened if Lyndon Johnson's pre-presidency transgressions had been widely publicized and investigated by congressional committees and prosecutors after he became president. What, indeed! Would we have been spared the leviathan welfare state and its endless cycle of dependency? Would we have been spared a botched war that cost tens of thousands of lives and billions of dollars?

If the news media had reported on Johnson's true character as revealed by his pre-presidential activities, Barry Goldwater might have won in 1964. Unlike Johnson, Mr. Goldwater would either have withdrawn from Vietnam or fought the war to win. Unlike Johnson, Mr. Goldwater would have preserved capitalism, free enterprise and personal responsibility.

I do not know whether the Clintons did anything wrong, but I want to know and I have a right to know.

ERNST PAUL JANENSCH

Scottsdale, Ariz.

* * *

Mr. Schlesinger omits those acts of the Clinton team in invading Vincent Foster's office immediately after his death to secretly remove various papers and files and turn them over to Clinton's personal attorney. Have any of those files been destroyed, as were the Foster files at the Rose Law Firm? Unless there is a congressional hearing to try to clear up this mystery, the public will never know the circumstances (motives) that led to the removal of the Foster files.

When the New York Times, which Mr. Schlesinger takes to task for its efforts, raises questions about a liberal Democrat president, one can be reasonably certain that there is something more than smoke to the many questions surrounding Whitewater.

FRED G. BUTLER

Marco Island, Fla.

* * *

What is wrong with good, investigative journalism? Mr. Schlesinger claims that reporters are engaged in a "quest for Pulitzer prizes and Woodward-Bernstein notoriety."

This type of reporting should be appropriately rewarded and indiscriminately applied, especially to politics. I do not think that we have to worry that it "may damage the press and political opposition as much as the Clinton administration," as Mr. Schlesinger states.

He also claims that the Republicans are using Whitewater to slow down reform and "discredit a presidential wife whose views they are reluctant to attack directly." The reality of the situation is that, once carefully analyzed, Hillary Clinton's so-called health-care reform has come to a standstill on its own lack of merit.

WILLIAM D. GAY

Chesterfield, Mo.

* * *

Mr. Clinton may indeed be a reform-minded president, but his actions, from Oxford to Little Rock to Washington, are inconsistent with his words and policies. Until there is full disclosure of the serious allegations of obstruction of justice, insider trading and tax fraud against the Clintons, the New York Times is rightly serving its role as the guardian of the public from a well-intentioned but arrogant administration.

JEFFREY K. SWANSON

Joplin, Mo.

* * *

"Get off the president's back, and let him get on with his job," Mr. Schlesinger says. Sounds familiar.

What was it Nixonites used to say? Wasn't it something like, "Get off Watergate and let the president get on with the important business he was re-elected to do: ending the war"?

Following Mr. Schlesinger's injunction to overlook wrongs done before attaining high office would have made Spiro Agnew president in 1974.

PATRICK NESBITT

Cincinnati

* * *

Mr. Schlesinger is now decrying the evils of the blood sport of "Borking." If Borking is so evil, where was Mr. Schlesinger while Clarence Thomas was under attack? After all, the wrongdoing alleged by Anita Hill had occurred some 10 years before. Or, if an election is a vindication that wipes the slate clean, then where was Mr. Schlesinger to defend Sen. Kay Bailey Hutchison against a politically motivated prosecution? On the other hand, a timely Borking could have spared our country the fruits of Lyndon Johnson's Great Society and War on Poverty.

EUGENE P. PODRAZIK, M.D.

Houston

* * *

Mr. Schlesinger asks, "Has there been a previous instance in American history when congressional committees and special prosecutors were mobilized to investigate a president's pre-presidential career?" Mr. Schlesinger stated that he thought not.

I bring to his attention events in 1991 and 1992, when President George Bush was investigated by Congress to determine if he had met with the Iranians in October of 1980 to delay the releasing of American hostages. In 1980, Mr. Bush was a private citizen, not yet elected to any public office.

THOMAS A. MILLER

Tustin, Calif.

* * *

If the media did not delve into questionable actions by LBJ or any other past political figure, we should be thankful it is doing a better job these days.

It is also laughable to paint a picture of Mr. Clinton as being persecuted. Not only did Presidents Nixon, Carter, Reagan and Bush face intense media scrutiny over activities in their administration, so did many presidents since Thomas Jefferson. And let us not forget that much of the current attention has been brought on by this administration's own actions, including attempts to stonewall, hide relevant documents, and alter explanations day by day. While we all bemoan inaccurate reporting, I believe most Americans can distinguish facts from supposition.

WILLIAM KERR

Davis, Calif.

REVIEW & OUTLOOK

TNR, TRB and Us

The New Republic, ever a contentious lot, has been arguing with itself over whether it should have reported its own reporter getting mugged in Little Rock. In his TRB column, Michael Kinsley says yes, the TNR editors say no. Both sides, inevitably we suppose, attack us. Mr. Kinsley calls us "zany," while the editors complain that "right-wing journalists have seized on the incident for their own political agenda."

This is triply curious since we were put on to L.J. Davis's feature on the Rose Law Firm and Arkansas generally by New Republic Chairman and Editor-in-Chief Martin Peretz, who clearly doesn't dictate everything his subalterns do. We noted that in his April 4 article Mr. Davis wrote that with "the honorable, largely ignored exception being the Los Angeles Times," no one in the national press understood that nearly everything in Arkansas is in one way or another influenced by the Stephens enterprises and fortunes. Somehow we think that, whether or not from a "right-wing" agenda, the Stephens family has been amply covered in this space. We're highly confident the Stephens agree.

Ignoring the slight, we were glad to cooperate in plugging the New Republic story. But on one particular we agree with Mr. Kinsley -- that Mr. Davis's personal experiences in Little Rock were inescapably part of it. So we reported this part of his tale as well, taking the precaution of talking directly to Mr. Davis's physician, who confirmed that the injury had to have come from a hard blow. Mr.

Davis told us that while he was unconscious, pages were torn from his notebook; he told others and now says the pages were torn but not removed. And he now finds himself in an argument with the hotel's former bartender over whether he had too many martinis, and precisely when.

Many citizens of Arkansas are upset to see their state denigrated, as Blant Hurt describes alongside. Our guess is that as a result of the scrutiny Arkansas will in fact be liberated from the one-party business-political culture Mr. Hurt also describes. Those who doubt that this includes an undercurrent of violence should consult the latest book by writer Gene Lyons, who himself has joined the Arkansas outcry against Mr. Davis's article. The hotel manager says he finally had to speak out, if you choose to believe, to protect the reputation of his establishment. The Arkansas offensive challenged Mr. Davis on many points of substance as well, but while he made a few minor errors and overplayed the repeal of usury laws, in our judgment most of the other points are matters of interpretation. On his own misfortunes, we continue to believe he was certainly hit on the head, and also that he initially told us what we said he did about the circumstances.

Mr. Davis's article and the reaction to it do little to change our impression of Arkansas. But the whole episode certainly confirms our impression of The New Republic as a place full of precocious talent badly in need of adult supervision.

Editorial Feature

In Defense of Arkansas

By Blant Hurt

LITTLE ROCK, Ark. – In the age of Whitewater, it has become fashionable to bash Arkansas. These pages have flogged "Arkansas mores." L.J. Davis, writing in The New Republic recently, characterized Arkansas as "a Third World country . . . with a ruling oligarchy, a small and relatively powerless middle class and disenfranchised leaderless populace." Even the stolid New York Times recently opined: "The genius of the Federal system does not reside in importing to Washington the faults and idiosyncrasies of the state capitals."

Thus, Americans are led to believe that the down-home ethics of Arkansas are cultural oddities that now threaten more sophisticated ethical norms prevailing in places like Washington and New York. I wish it were so – but it isn't. The same ethical habits and customs that have infected Arkansas are visible from coast to coast. Everywhere the problem is the same: an insidious business-government partnership that dates back to Franklin D. Roosevelt's administration. It's true that Arkansas, like every state, has its cultural and political quirks. Notably a 158-year tradition of one-party dominance made possible, in part, by the almost total ideological bankruptcy of the state's Republican Party. In this vacuum, the Democratic Party's machine-style politics have been honed to arrogant efficiency. Arkansas's image as an ethical banana republic is reinforced by the near-comic proportions of Mrs. Clinton's "bull market" success.

Yet Arkansas's politicians (and their wives) are not the first to fall prey to the seductions of self-serving deals with business interests and, unless there is a radical change of philosophy throughout the country, they surely won't be the last.This all started under the New Deal, which, as author Justin Raimondo points out, transferred huge amounts of capital (and power) from the private sector to the government via payroll taxes, taxes on profits and capital gains, and government creations such as the Reconstruction Finance Corporation (which at one time controlled half of the world's gold). "This was an entirely new power," author (and Wall Street Journal reporter) Garet Garrett wrote in 1953. "As the government acquired it, so passed to the government the ultimate power of initiative. It passed from private capitalism to capitalistic government. The government became the great capitalist and enterpriser."

Today, capitalistic government is an institutionalized phenomenon in Washington, and in every state capital. All levels of government find subtle ways to partner up with business interests. So-called Arkansas mores are ubiquitous. Whitewater fascinates because it offers us rather trifling, yet revealing, examples of the sleaze that inevitably arises out of the business-government partnership.

In 1954 the Small Business Administration was created by an enterprise-minded Congress and a GOP president. Some 30 years later, David Hale, a Clinton-appointed municipal judge in Little Rock, procured $3.4 million in SBA funds aimed at "the disadvantaged." According to the General Accounting Office, Mr. Hale funneled taxpayer money to 13 businesses he secretly controlled. Portions of Mr. Hale's SBA funds also found their way into the business ventures of Arkansas Gov. Jim Guy Tucker and possibly, via a $300,000 loan to Susan McDougal's Master Marketing, into the Clintons' Whitewater Development Co.

James McDougal also exploited government programs designed to help business — in this case, banks. Without FDR's federal deposit insurance, Mr. McDougal's Madison Guaranty never could have taken taxpayers for $47 million. No one should be surprised that Mr. McDougal's political idol is FDR (or that one of Mrs. Clinton's inspirations is Eleanor Roosevelt). Now Mr. McDougal is even running for Congress in Arkansas as a New Deal Democrat.

The McDougal mind-set — exploit business-government links while ignoring the ethical implications — is rampant in the Clinton administration, even among folks who weren't reared on grits and greens.

Labor Secretary Robert Reich, a prophet of modern-day Rooseveltian activism, wrote in his 1983 book "The Next American Frontier": "For America's next stage of economic evolution, the government's role in industry must become not so much more extensive as more open, more explicit, and more strategic." Mr. Reich's star pupil throughout the 1980s, of course, was then-Gov. Bill Clinton.

One can only hope that Whitewater and its related rascality spur Americans to reflect on the roots of the unethical, if not illegal, behavior that pervades the interactions between our capitalistic government and business interests. The ethical stench has already undermined public confidence. The only structural answer is to rethink the old Roosevelt paradigm even as it sags under its own scandal-ridden weight.

Criticisms of the Clintons for their ideas and ethics are perfectly reasonable. But for the press to smear an entire state because the ethics of its most notable political family are the seedy byproduct of a six-decade-old American tradition of government-business partnership is sanctimonious hooey. Unfortunately, the rest of America is just as tainted by the moral hazards of capitalistic government as we are.

Mr. Hurt is a Little Rock businessman and columnist for Arkansas Business.

Letters to the Editor

Arkansas Corruption Is a Special Brand

Blant Hurt's April 13 editorial-page article "In Defense of Arkansas" argues persuasively that 60 years of extensive government regulation of economic activity have created "insidious" business-government partnerships nationwide. He correctly asserts that political corruption at all levels of government is the inevitable result of government becoming a not so silent partner in virtually all forms of business.

However, Mr. Hurt plays down the unique circumstances in Arkansas—a small state, absolute one-party control of the governor's office, legislature and judiciary, and a small but extraordinarily powerful group of family business enterprises—which according to news accounts have bred a particularly odious form of systematic political corruption and lax ethical standards.

In a state like New York, for instance, competitive statewide elections coupled with an active media prevent such extraordinary conflicts of interest and influence peddling as exhibited by the Clinton governorship in Arkansas.

Mr. Hurt's central thesis correctly points out that the disease of excessive government regulation and the resulting ethical implications is a nationwide dilemma; however, it is clear that "Arkansas mores" are a particularly virulent strain of that disease.

NICHOLAS KAMILLATOS

Darien, Conn.

Editorial Feature

Taxing Tale: The Facts Are Woebegone

Garrison Keillor, the president's wittiest Whitewater defender, exhorts us running dogs of the media to stick to "facts." I agree, which is why the history of President and Mrs. Clinton's 1978 and 1979 tax returns is so troubling.

This week the First Couple amended their 1980 tax return to cover a $6,498 profit in commodities trading unreported at the time. By itself this is small beer, even on April 15. But add it to their answers and non-answers going back to the 1992 campaign and the total impact is more revealing. It becomes a chronology of incredibility. What does it say about our leaders that it took years of prodding to learn even basic facts about their personal finances?

Potomac Watch

By Paul A. Gigot

The tax tale begins back in Arkansas in 1990 during the president's last campaign for governor. Under fire from his opponent, Mr. Clinton releases his tax returns for the previous 10 years. This draws the line at 1980, even though he'd been governor in 1978-79.

The issue goes national, sort of, amid the hurly-burly of the 1992 primaries. Jeff Gerth of the New York Times starts asking how the Clintons could afford a $60,000 down payment on a house in 1980 when they'd both been earning only peanuts. The Clinton campaign won't release the 1978-79 returns, but quotes Mrs. Clinton saying the money came from "savings and a gift from our parents."

Keep in mind that tax returns are the stuff of Political Disclosure 101. Most candidates release them for their years in public life, taking whatever political hit ensues. Dan Quayle was ridiculed for his trust fund, while Ronald Reagan was skewered for not giving as much of his income to charity as he'd advertised. Yet somehow we media pit bulls became schnauzers regarding the Clinton tax records in 1992.

Flash to early March 1994. The redoubtable Mr. Gerth now has the goods on Mrs. Clinton's $100,000 cattle killing, which occurred in 1978 and 1979. The White House claims she'd invested her own money but won't say how much. It does finally admit, now two years later, that the windfall helped finance that $60,000 down payment.

But when reporters for Knight-Ridder ask Mr. Clinton about his 1978-79 taxes, he grows angry, abruptly ends an interview and declines to shake hands. Spinmeister Paul Begala tells Larry King that "both Clintons, they just missed the 80s . . . these people are just not motivated by money."

Pressure nonetheless builds for more disclosure, and on March 25 the president's attorney, David Kendall, releases the 1978-79 returns in what he calls "a spirit of full cooperation and openness." The returns show Mrs. Clinton's windfall but include no supporting records. Newsweek then reports, erroneously, that Mrs. Clinton had invested none of her own money.

This prompts the White House, on March 29, to declare that she had invested all of $1,000. Her resulting 10,000% profit is due, say White House aides, to her having "read The Wall Street Journal" and listened to "friends," including Tyson Foods' lawyer James Blair. She placed the trades herself, the aides say, and stopped "soon after Chelsea was born. The account was closed in March 1980." The trading had been too "nerve-wracking" for a pregnant woman.

But this line doesn't hold either; David Letterman mocks Hillary's "Top 10 financial tips." Reporters (rudely looking for facts) interview experts, who say the records released by the White House are incomplete and could mask special treatment. Defending his wife, Mr. Clinton says on April 5 that "she showed" reporters all of her trading records "as soon as they asked about them."

A few days later the White House admits that Mr. Blair, not Mrs. Clinton, had placed most trade orders. A White House official also calls "no longer operative" an April 5 comment from Mr. Clinton that his wife had received a "margin call," which is a request to deposit more money to cover losses. On April 10, CBS's "60 Minutes" gives Lesley Stahl $5,000 and unleashes her on the cattle pits; the nation sees how hard it is for an amateur to make a killing.

The next day, this past Monday, the White House releases even more trading records. It also says Mrs. Clinton didn't close her last account in March 1980 after all, but ran into May. The new records show that March, close to the time of Chelsea's birth, was in fact one of her busiest trading months. One irony is that these latest records tend to rebut the worst suspicions that profits were somehow steered to Mrs. Clinton's account, although we can't be sure without also seeing Mr. Blair's records.

Now, these are all facts, perhaps even by Mr. Keillor's standards. They show a First Couple who have evaded, dissembled and stonewalled to avoid disclosing their financial past. Having tried to suppress many of these facts, they now quote defenders who say there are none. Having stonewalled in 1990, in 1992 and later, the Clintons now cry foul at a skeptical press.

Maybe they just wanted to avoid the embarrassment of being accused of hypocrisy. And maybe the disclosure of Mrs. Clinton's cattle killing would have hurt in the election, or at least in the tax fight of 1993. But their coverup then has only made it more essential for the press to get to the bottom of it all now.

The issue now is credibility, which is every president's essential capital. Without it he can't govern, can't rally the country if he really needs to (as he might yet in Bosnia or Korea). If Americans can't trust a president on the most basic facts of his personal finances, what can they trust him on?

Editorial Feature

On the Mena Trail

By EDWARD JAY EPSTEIN

CBS News recently focused two segments of its investigative "Eye on America" on alleged goings-on in a remote place in rural Arkansas: Mena (population 5,600). This forlorn town made it on to the big-time geo-media map because of the intersection of a number of mysteries.

First, back in the Reagan years, there was the CIA connection. Landing strips outside of Mena were used by the Reagan administration to stage the clandestine flights to Mexico and Central America that airdropped weapons to the Contras. This 1980s activity was supposedly supervised by then-Lt. Col. Oliver North, now running for the GOP Senate nomination in Virginia.

Second, there is the cocaine connection. On their return flights from Nicaragua and Mexico, pilots allegedly smuggled back into Mena more than 20 tons of cocaine. This led to the Mena complex being investigated in 1984 by the Arkansas State Police. One of the pilots implicated in this smuggling was an entrepreneur named Barry Seal, who was allowed to continue his drug importing activities as a government informant. He was gunned down by hit men reportedly hired by Colombian drug dealers.

Third, there is the money laundering connection. The cash generated by secret arms deliveries and drug sales — reportedly $9 million a week — led to a scheme in which local businesses and Arkansas banks were used to illegally convert the proceeds into what appeared to be ordinary business transactions. This, in turn, led to an Internal Revenue Service investigation of the companies involved.

Fourth, there is the coverup connection. Despite all the evidence developed by the state police and IRS of gun smuggling, drug smuggling and money laundering, the Reagan and Bush Justice Departments failed to bring a case — or even present it to a grand jury. These mysteries, as well as the 20 tons of cocaine, might have become just another footnote in the morass known as the Iran-Contra scandal, if not for the coincidence that the governor of Arkansas at the time was Bill Clinton.

The attempt to connect President Clinton to the "Mena Affair" emerges in the new book "Compromised: Clinton, Bush and the CIA" by Terry Reed and John Cummings. Mr. Reed claims to have first-hand knowledge of the conspiracy, both through his work in training Contra pilots at Mena and his association with Barry Seal; Mr. Cummings is a well-respected reporter at New York Newsday, whose previous specialty was the Mafia. Their book attempts to graft the 1980s Reagan-Contra conspiracy onto the financial and political activities of Mr. Clinton and his Arkansas associates and, in the hybrid, provide, as the cover promises, "The Bigger Story Behind Whitewater."

If true, it would indeed be a big story: Gov. Clinton, the quintessential anti-Cold Warrior, making a secret deal with the Reagan Cold Warriors to support the Contras. But the book offers no credible evidence of such an arrangement. Despite the provocative subtitle, the book provides no link between Mr. Clinton and Mr. Bush; Mr. Clinton and the CIA; nor, for that matter, Mr. Clinton and Mr. Reagan. Indeed, the only basis for believing Mr. Clinton even knew about Mena is Mr. Reed's unconfirmed claim to have sighted the governor at a meeting that included Ollie North and other prominent Iran-Contra figures — a claim that I do not believe is credible.

The authors also try to connect Mr. Clinton through his associates. The argument is that associates of his, or associates of these associates, were involved in drugs, arms and money laundering at Mena, and, therefore, Mr. Clinton himself must have been privy to it. For example, Mr. Clinton's half-brother, Roger, was employed by a financier who purchased cocaine from someone connected to Mena.

The problem with such guilt by association is that Arkansas is a small place, especially when it comes to law firms, investment firms and politicians; most Arkansans are separated by far fewer than six degrees of separation. It is not necessarily incriminating to know someone who knows someone.

To be sure, illicit things happened at Mena and the Justice Department took no action. If this was a deliberate misprision of a felony, it may have proceeded from the Justice Department's reluctance to bring a case against Contra-support activities that were approved by the president and the CIA director. After all, why should the Reagan administration have prosecuted itself when it could legitimately evade the issue by citing national security? National security considerations certainly are what damped a General Accounting Office effort at investigating Mena.

The possibility that the federal government would raise such a concern might also have reasonably discouraged Arkansas prosecutors. After the smuggler Seal was shot to death, it is not clear that there was anyone to bring a case against: So why waste resources? Whatever reason the case wasn't pursued, no one has said that Mr. Clinton used his gubernatorial powers to quash legal proceedings.

What the Mena connection boils down to is speculation that the money trail from Mena, if it is not a dead end, could lead somewhere in the uncharted wilderness of Whitewater. Unfortunately, the present expose furnishes no reliable compass.

Mr. Epstein is the author of "Deception: The Invisible War Between the KGB and the CIA" and other books on espionage.

Letters to the Editor

Still a Strong Scent On the Mena Trail

We are glad that Edward Jay Epstein saw the CBS News report on Mena, Ark., which he discussed in his April 20 editorial-page piece, "On the Mena Trail." Our story, like others on Mena, raised questions. They won't be answered until reporters follow the money — millions of dollars generated out of the operations at Mena. That could either put it to rest, or lead to a story at least as important as Whitewater.

The original report on Whitewater by Jeff Gerth of the New York Times was ignored for many months. The Mena story probably will suffer the same fate unless other journalists pick up the trail. That might not happen if readers conclude, as Mr. Epstein seems to, that the only place Mena could lead is to Whitewater. What if Mena has nothing to do with Whitewater?

Our sources agree with Mr. Epstein on a number of things: There was most likely a CIA-sponsored Contra operation run out of Mena, as well as a huge parallel cocaine-smuggling operation, money laundering and a Justtice Department coverup. Much of this happened on Mr. Clinton's watch as governor.

But Mr. Epstein says that after smuggler Barry Seal was killed there was really no one else to go after. Investigators never targeted Mr. Seal. They knew he was working for the federal government and was therefore untouchable. Instead, they targeted Seal's associates — the bankers and businessmen who allegedly laundered his drug profits and illegally modified his planes so he could smuggle tons of cocaine into the U.S. They were never prosecuted by either the federal government or the state of Arkansas.

Mr. Epstein says that no one is claiming that Mr. Clinton blocked legal proceedings in this matter. But as the CBS News story revealed, Mr. Clinton was asked by a state prosecutor for help to pursue the case against Seal's associates. Help was promised but never arrived.

Arkansas Rep. Bill Alexander tried to save and then re-start an investigation of Mena. Mr. Clinton did not seize on this issue and offer support, despite the fact that a Republican administration was apparently sponsoring a Contra aid operation in his state and protecting a smuggling ring that flew tons of cocaine through Arkansas.

Mr. Epstein suggests there is no reason to believe Mr. Clinton knew about Mena. But the governor's own state police began investigating at Mena in 1984. Isn't it reasonable to assume that he was made aware of the investigation? Mr. Clinton did acknowledge learning about Mena as early as April 1988; Ross Perot, who had done his own investigation of Mena, was concerned enough about the drugs-for-guns operation to call Mr. Clinton. And former Clinton staff people have told CBS News that the governor was aware of what was going on there.

Mena is a perplexing and difficult story. There is a trail — tens of millions of dollars in cocaine profits, and we don't know where it leads. It is a trail that has been blocked by the National Security Council.

The FAA, FBI, Customs, CIA, Justice, DEA and the IRS were all involved in Mena. They won't say how they were involved, but they will tell you there is nothing there.

BILL PLANTE
CBS News Correspondent
MICHAEL SINGER
Producer, CBS News

New York

Letters to the Editor

Secret Meetings in Arkansas

On your April 20 editorial page, Edward J. Epstein gave his opinions of "Compromised: Clinton, Bush and the CIA," a new book by Terry Reed and John Cummings. I am Mr. Reed's attorney in a civil rights suit pending in federal court in Little Rock against Raymond Young, Bill Clinton's chief of security when Mr. Clinton was governor, and Tommy Baker, a former Arkansas state trooper. The facts of the case are intimately entwined with the material in "Compromised" and, based on hard evidence I have seen, I find the book compelling and credible. I wish Mr. Epstein's opinions of the book had been supported by some evidence (or any evidence) to rebut Mr. Reed's experiences as a CIA contract agent, training Contra pilots at Mena, Ark., while Bill Clinton was governor.

"To be sure," wrote Mr. Epstein, "illicit things happened at Mena . . ." He cites recent CBS Evening News segments that uncovered evidence of drug smuggling, gun running and money laundering. In the first segment that aired March 25, Mr. Reed was interviewed while flying in airspace over Mena familiar to him from 15 months of teaching Nicaraguan Contras how to fly in combat.

Yet Mr. Epstein opines that "the only basis for believing Mr. Clinton even knew about Mena is Mr. Reed's unconfirmed claim to have sighted the governor at a meeting that included Ollie North . . . a claim that I do not believe is credible." Mr. Epstein rests his argument there, content to gainsay what is a central event in "Compromised."

What Mr. Epstein characterizes as Mr. Reed's "sighting" of Bill Clinton was made during a secret meeting at Camp Robinson, Ark., attended by Mr. Reed, Gov. Clinton, Lt. Col. North, future Attorney General William Barr, and several resident CIA personnel. What, then, was Mr. Clinton's purpose in visiting this remote army camp one evening in spring 1986? It wasn't a social call. The meeting gave Gov. Clinton an opportunity to take the agency to task for its abrupt withdrawal from his state due to compromised security following the drug bust of Roger Clinton. It was also an opportunity to discuss the containment of potential "long-term liabilities" to the ambitious politician. The entire meeting is fully described in three chapters of the book—somewhat more than a "sighting."

"Arkansas is a small place," admits Mr. Epstein, and he argues that close relations among lawyers, businessmen and politicians are insufficient to extend guilt by association. We won't argue here that a competent governor of a small state ought to know what's going on.

Lastly, Mr. Epstein states: "No one has said that Mr. Clinton used his gubernatorial powers to quash legal proceedings." Mr. Epstein, if he found "Compromised" too long a read for its meticulous documentation, surely should have watched all of the CBS "Eye on America" segments to which he, himself, refers. On it, Arkansas Deputy Prosecutor Charles Black states that he never received the $25,000 Mr. Clinton promised to fund a grand jury investigation—a sum, he told a correspondent from Time magazine, "tantamount to trying to extinguish a raging forest fire by spitting on it."

The inference is clear. Mr. Reed is ready to go toe to toe with anyone named in the book willing to take a polygraph examination with him. If there are any takers, which I doubt, now is the time to step in the ring and take your best shot. "Compromised" remains a meticulously documented, intensely personal political document that has yet to be refuted.

ROBERT S. MELONI

New York

Editorial Feature

Agnew Card Bids To Finesse Whitewater Woes

By Robert L. Bartley

DES MOINES — "Nattering nabobs of negativism" Spiro Agnew called them — or, come to think of it, us. The now-defrocked vice president pioneered what is by now a standard political card: In a corner, blame your troubles on the press.

The alliteration leaps to mind because the Clinton administration is playing the Agnew card to finesse its Whitewater woes. The president lectures the American Society of Newspaper Editors that the press is detracting from more important issues with preoccupation over twists and turns of his finances. He then proceeds to drop a few bombs in Bosnia, hold lots of public meetings to deny that his health plan is price control, motor in his old Mustang and spend 90 minutes fielding teenage questions at an MTV youth forum. Meanwhile his subordinates complain about the "frenzy" of press coverage of Whitewater.

And here in an unseasonably summery Iowa, Clinton house philosopher James Carville bragged Tuesday that he's not running away from the Whitewater story, but traveled 1,500 miles to confront it with Rush Limbaugh and some bigfoot editors on Ted Koppel's ABC "Nightline." He then of course proceeded to run away from it with nearly every word, along the way spewing a lot of disinformation — for example retreating to the "inoperative" story that Mrs. Clinton had only one commodity trade after Chelsea's birth. The latest records disgorged by the White House list nine.

* * *

If there's recently been a frenzy in the press, much of it was caused by James Carville, simply because he's so good at what he's paid to do. It's true of course that in the last presidential campaign he played against the second team, the Bush presidency being unable to sustain the enthusiasm of the likes of Roger Ailes and Peggy Noonan. And that in New Jersey's gubernatorial race he blew a big lead even to Ed Rollins. Still, the "ragin' Cajun" spun the 1992 campaign masterfully, not least in suppressing scrutiny of his candidate and his background.

As a result, Mr. Clinton repeatedly got free rides. There was no big fuss, for example, about his claiming "privacy" in refusing to release his 1978 and 1979 tax returns, even though he was elected governor in 1978. There was no "frenzy" over Gennifer Flowers, the press deciding that if she took money from the sleazy Star she must be lying. And when Jeff Gerth of the New York Times raised Whitewater Development Corp., the story died with the Lyons report, supposedly a complete accounting.

Nothing quite makes a frenzy, we've learned since mid-December, like a whole flock of chickens coming home to roost. The Lyons report, under scrutiny by our Bruce Ingersoll and others, turned out to be a study in fragmentary disclosure. And it turned out the 1978-79 tax returns were withheld for good reason, which is to say bad reason. The privacy protected Mrs. Clinton's flaming cattle trades, which may not be criminal but certainly would have made hash of campaign rhetoric about 1980s greed and might very well have lost Mr. Clinton the election.

With curiosity reawakened, we've also learned that Whitewater papers were taken from Vincent Foster's office after his suicide. That Madison Guaranty Savings & Loan, owned by the Clintons' Whitewater partner James McDougal, was referred for possible criminal prosecution. That when the Justice Department fired all U.S. attorneys, a Clinton crony was put in charge in Little Rock, only belatedly recusing herself from Whitewater. We saw Webster Hubbell resign from Justice, and William Kennedy demoted at the counsel's office. White House officials admitted they talked to regulators about the Whitewater investigation. The only trouble here, the Clintonites have it, is heavy breathing by the press.

* * *

The mainstream American press remains uncommonly gentlemanly, indeed, about one strain of the story, namely sex. It was leery of the four Arkansas state troopers, even though their stories and Miss Flowers's corroborated one another. There has been no frenzy about Sally Perdue, who says she was threatened into silence about her affair with Gov. Clinton. Paula Jones, who says he subjected her to a gross sexual advance and offers affidavits from two other women she confided in at the time, is so invisible that conservative media policegroup Accuracy in Media has been taking out ads asking whatever happened to her.

There is a respectable argument that such anecdotes are not front-page news, of course. But it's hard to say they are being judged by the standards applied to the reporting about Anita Hill or Sen. Bob Packwood.

* * *

The Agnew card may be trump, but the Clinton camp has already drawn the suit twice. In the campaign, Mr. Carville frightened both the press and his opposition by waving the Willie Horton symbol; it's a dirty trick, the notion went, to publicize a candidate's faults, or even his record. The second press assault also succeeded, silencing questions about Vincent Foster's death. The third has produced a lull in Whitewater coverage.

If you can't draw the final trump, though, you can find yourself doubled and vulnerable. In Des Moines, Times Executive Editor Max Frankel described Whitewater as "unfinished business" from the 1992 campaign; we await Mr. Gerth's next story. For my part, I can testify that getting tagged with blame for the Foster suicide powerfully focused my own attention on Whitewater. This third time around, I doubt that the press will be cowed for long.

Recent history suggests, indeed, that press-bashing is a sign of desperation. In the end, after all, Spiro Agnew went out with a plea of nolo contendere.

Mr. Bartley is editor of the Journal.

REVIEW & OUTLOOK

In the Pink?

The news conference intended to put an end to the Hillary Clinton commodity story was a stylistic triumph, all agreed. In its staging and her expressed innocence, the production was a direct hit on the intended target, the casual audience of Americans who want their leaders to succeed, free of harassment, and aren't much interested in the fine points of futures trading or what happened 15 years ago. But more curious minds will read what Mrs. Clinton actually said, comparing it with what actually was done by her or for her at a go-go Springdale, Ark., brokerage. They'll find that the basic questions in the case of Hillary's Hundred-to-One linger: How and why did it happen? The answers bear on her honesty as a policy maker today and on the Clintons' political standing to decry the "greed" of the 1980s.

Hillary Clinton

The White House helped considerably by earlier releasing many of the documents we wanted to see when last we visited this issue on Good Friday. These showed nearly all of her trades were over the course of more than one day, which vastly reduces the room for manipulation inside the brokerage. Mrs. Clinton's account sported a string of exceedingly good, clean trades. Her "win" rate, at more than 80%, was phenomenal for any trader, and it was achieved with short as well as long positions in a basically rising market.

According to some versions, this stunning fortune was enjoyed by other friends of the cattle crowd at the Refco trading stable in Springdale and elsewhere. It was a looser, wilder era, and some people got taken along for a hell of a ride. Hillary at least had the prudence to bail out with a nice stake in life. Why can't we leave it at that and get on with the affairs of the nation?

* * *

Well, it might have been easy to accept an explanation like that, but that isn't what we got from the White House. Instead, after a series of shifts we're left with this story: A Watergate Committee attorney out of Yale Law is introduced, ingenue-like, to the exciting world of commodities where, with only $1,000 "to start with" but a skilled mentor named Jim Blair to guide her, she picked her spots ably and stayed on her game until the birth of her child caused her to lose heart. Friendship's bounty, but no favoritism. It was there for anybody to get with pin money.

Not quite. There was a smart loser for every smart winner in this market, which any bright entrant would realize. The fact is that Mrs. Clinton made her killing through the most heavily disciplined broker at the most controversial institution in the financial community's most speculative market. Access to good advice wouldn't be enough to entice most yuppies in, but Hillary was different. And no soft pink suit and oblique-angle chatter in the White House State Room on a late Friday afternoon is going to change that. The basis for doubt remains.

For one thing, even the latest serving of records has one conspicuous omission: There is no confirmation slip elaborating the initially reported first trade, when Mrs. Clinton walked away with a $5,300 profit a day after putting down her $1,000. It now develops that the Chicago Mercantile Exchange has further records, presumably gathered in the investigation leading to the discipline of Red Bone and Refco, that would shed further light on this matter. It told Senator D'Amato it would release these records only under subpoena.

If the Democratic majority will agree to an investigation subpoenaing these records, it's likely they would also shed light on the trading by Jim Blair, the Tyson Foods attorney and friend of Hillary and Bill. Theories about how Mr. Blair's larger positions related to Mrs. Clinton's are conjectural and conflicting, and could be tested only by a look at his trading records. Such grist might add some substance to last week's gloss.

Even with the records already released, there is the matter of margin requirements. Six weeks after her account was opened, a short position in cattle was closed out with a $17,400 loss that brought her balance to $1,401. (She had cashed out $5,000 a month before.) Such a setback might have spooked the ordinary dabbler, even one who thought she was privy to inside knowledge. But that same day, Nov. 22, Mrs. Clinton was back in the hunt, going long on five cattle contracts and adding 60 more on Dec. 11. Under the rules, that meant she needed $78,000 behind her position, yet on that date she had $6,171 in her account. (She sold all 65 the next day, for a $4,000 profit after commissions.)

Hillary Clinton had at least two margin calls, according to her records, and probably others, based on what we can tell of her exposures. We know about the two because they were in force at the end of a month and were recorded on regular statements. Her memory of these events—searing for most amateur traders—is rather, well, marginal. When her account dipped below the threshold, "I would either close out my position or use the equity that I had. . . . Nobody ever called and asked me for anything. They just, I guess, took the money that I had in the account and closed out the position." She was a small customer "and I don't think [Refco] paid any attention to my particular situation."

Like all brokerages, Refco had flexibility in covering for people, though it was on the hook to a clearing house for client positions and did answer to the Merc. But let's look at her account. The first margin call, for approximately $6,000 only two weeks after she opened, apparently went unanswered for seven days, even though normal practice is to deal with such a problem almost immediately. This episode presumably ended with the closing out of 10 cattle contracts on Nov. 2. But on Nov. 8, Mrs. Clinton was right back into a similar 10-car short position, with no capital infusion into her account! Maybe that meant nothing to the boys in Springdale, but most brokers get a little edgy when you try it.

At the end of April 1979, Mrs. Clinton was under margin again, and apparently was indulged until May 4, when her 15 short cattle contracts were covered for a $12,900 gain. See, Mr. Broker, a little patience can pay off.

The most captivating period in the Clinton account was the flurry of trading in July 1979, the last bout of activity at Refco. With 65 live-cattle and feeder contracts outstanding (plus 50 in an intraday trade), Mrs. Clinton again appears to have been under margin. And she was getting hammered: The price movements on live cattle alone had more than erased (on paper) her $36,000 account balance by July 11; she closed out the feeders for a $27,000 loss on July 17. Much more slippage on the cattle and the $39,000 in profits she'd already pulled out (for other uses) would be wiped out and the Clintons would be down to their salaries.

But she stayed a few extra days, the market moved dramatically in her favor and she walked away a $100,000 winner overall. Mrs. Clinton left Refco behind for some comparatively minor speculating through affiliates of the Stephens empire in Little Rock. The cattle craze soon crashed down on the Springdale crowd.

* * *

Most people in the business stress the seriousness of a margin call, particularly when the customer is of modest means and experience. Mrs. Clinton's defenders, including the commissioner Leo Melamed of Chicago Mercantile Exchange fame, stress that Refco of 1978-79 was a case unto itself, ultimately drawing an unprecedented fine for its lack of restraint. It carried margins of "$200,000 or more for hundreds of customers," Mr. Melamed says. She "on occasion" had much less of a gap; so what? Hillary, he infers, played with her winnings in July and mostly let go after that—smart. Whatever was irregular in her streak you could ascribe to the Refco of that era. She received no "favoritism" because Mr. Bone was playing fast and loose with all of his accounts, whether or not they were held by the governor's wife.

But the point must be, if this was such a rogue outfit, how could a Yale-Watergate staff lawyer believe that in doing business there she was playing by the rules? Indeed, how could she think that even now, since she herself was co-counsel on one of the lawsuits against Refco after the cattle crash?

As to the First Lady's overall spin on the family's finances, similarly, let's put it this way: Hillary Rodham was in Washington once before, as it prepared to impeach a President. One would think she might have learned firsthand about its nosy expectations. Now, however, she says she's resignedly "trying to find my way through" an off-the-wall ethical inquiry of her own co-presidency. When the klieg lights went out in the stately White House dining room, that acquired ingenuousness was just one more reason why some of us hungered to know more.

Arkansas Tales

Whitewater was drawing the media back to Arkansas, a state awash in stories about its long-serving governor. While continuing to press for Congressional hearings, the Journal examined Bill Clinton's allies and enemies, the swirl of accusations surrounding the President, and a mysterious airport at the western edge of the state.

On May 6, former Little Rock resident Paula Corbin Jones filed a suit against the President, charging that he had sexually harassed her while governor.

On June 30, Special Counsel Fiske issued a report concluding that Mr. Foster's death was a suicide, and that there had been no obstruction of justice in the contacts between the Treasury Department and the White House regarding the Resolution Trust Corp.'s probe of Madison Guaranty. The way was clear for Congressional hearings limited to the two subjects.

Editorial Feature

Another Arkansas Tale

By MICAH MORRISON

Former Arkansas Attorney General Steve Clark faces a new trial later this year in Little Rock on charges that he owes the state more than $18,000. In 1990, Mr. Clark was convicted of "felony theft by deception" for putting nonbusiness entertainment charges on his state credit card; he was driven out of politics and disgraced. Four years after his conviction, the state of Arkansas has decided it wants another piece of him.

Mr. Clark's downfall opens a window on the incestuous political culture out of which President Clinton's current Whitewater troubles emerge. The story begins in late 1989, when Mr. Clark staked out his opposition to then-Gov. Bill Clinton and the Stephens Inc. financial empire in a dramatic speech to the board of the Arkansas Development Finance Authority (ADFA). The board was meeting to consider a bond issue to finance the sale of Arkansas nursing homes to Texas financier Bruce Whitehead. A similar deal in Iowa, involving Mr. Whitehead and the Rose Law Firm, would soon be raising concerns of profiteering.

Specifically, the ADFA board was considering a $75 million bond issue for the sale of 32 Arkansas nursing homes, owned by the Stephens-controlled Beverly Enterprises health care giant, to Mr. Whitehead. Mr. Clark, readying a bid to challenge Gov. Clinton for the Democrat gubernatorial nomination, told the board he had been offered a $100,000 bribe by a "Beverly-Stephens representative" to withdraw his criticism of the deal. In a blistering speech, Mr. Clark condemned Stephens Inc. for "arrogance of wealth" and Gov. Clinton for "arrogance of power."

"In one speech," wrote Arkansas Gazette columnist John Brummett, "Clark broke every rule of good-ol'-boy, inside-the-family politics, the kind that runs Arkansas." But by breaking the rules, Mr. Clark "may have killed a growingly odorous bond deal . . . which has been kept alive by Gov. Bill Clinton's vacillation and his appointees on the ADFA board."

Burdened with debt and reeling from cuts in Medicaid reimburse-

Messrs. Clark and Clinton jogging

ment, Beverly was seeking to sell off its nursing homes in a number of states, including Iowa and Arkansas. This was of more than passing interest at Stephens Inc. headquarters in Little Rock. Beverly was in trouble and Stephens, which controlled the company through ownership of a preferred stock issue and dominance of Beverly's board, could sustain heavy losses. Stephens tapped the Rose Law Firm to find a buyer for the nursing homes, turning the matter over to Rose partner Vincent Foster Jr. Mr. Foster passed the deal to William Kennedy III, now White House associate counsel.

Mr. Kennedy found a buyer for the Iowa and Arkansas homes in Mr. Whitehead, a high-rolling Texas financier. Mr. Kennedy and Mr. Whitehead quickly put together a deal for the Iowa homes that later would be sharply criticized. In a two-step transaction, Mr. Whitehead's for-profit Ventana Investments bought 41 nursing homes for $57 million. The homes were then immediately purchased by a Whitehead-controlled nonprofit corporation, Mercy Health Initiatives, for $63 million, with money borrowed from the state under an $86 million bond issue.

The deal netted Mr. Whitehead and the bond underwriters up-front profits of more than $15 million and gave Beverly a cash infusion of about $10 million, according to the Des Moines Register. The Rose firm made "hundreds of thousands of dollars," estimates Little Rock financial adviser Roy Drew. Unfortunately, the deal also saddled Mercy Health with millions in debt — Mr. Whitehead soon fled the organization — and raised the cost of patient care by 14%, according to a study by Iowa authorities.

Iowa Judge Gene Needles later ruled that Mercy was a "shell non-profit corporation" used "to make millions of dollars of excessive profits." He called the deal "unconscionable." An Iowa lawyer hired by the state to investigate the deal, Frank Pachacek, told the Washington Times that it was "the worst case of profiteering" he had seen in 20 years.

Mr. Whitehead and Mr. Kennedy hoped to pull off a virtually identical transaction in Arkansas, where Stephens exerted powerful influence. Stephens executives had good reason for confidence that the publicly funded deal would come together without a ripple. Two ADFA board members were employed by Stephens-controlled organizations. The politically hyper-connected Rose firm, which counted Stephens among its major clients, was shepherding the arrangement. And Gov. Clinton himself retained final authority over all ADFA bond issues.

(It wasn't until years later that the Arkansas public learned that Rose was handling the bond deal, the fiction being advanced at the time that former Rose managing partner Joseph Giroir was representing Beverly. But documents show that Rose was stage-managing a transaction that could have brought them $500,000 in fees. In a May 9, 1989, letter to Mr. Whitehead regarding "the sale of facilities in Iowa and Arkansas," William Kennedy III wrote that he was "awaiting instructions from the appropriate Beverly personnel.")

The bond issue sailed through an initial ADFA board meeting, then started to come undone when the underwriters withdrew and the Arkansas Democrat newspaper, prompted by longtime Stephens critic Roy Drew, began a tough series investigating the financing of the deal. At a second meeting, under growing public pressure, the ADFA board decided to delay final approval. An angry Bruce Whitehead then challenged the ADFA board president to a fistfight. At the third and final meeting, on Dec. 20, 1989, Steve Clark's bombshell announcement of a bribe attempt and attack on Gov. Clinton and Stephens Inc. killed the deal. It was, wrote columnist Brummett, "either the bravest or stupidest move of his political life."

According to Mr. Brummett, it probably was the bravest — "though it may be plenty stupid to make the kind of enemies he made" with the speech. Within 24 hours, the alleged briber, Earl Jones, a lobbyist for the nursing-home interests, came forward to deny that the $100,000 figure was a bribe. Mr. Jones told the Gazette that he had indeed called Mr. Clark, asking him to get off his car phone and on to a "secure line." They discussed the bond deal, and toward the end of the conversation Mr. Jones told Mr. Clark that "down the road" he probably could raise $100,000 for Mr. Clark's gubernatorial campaign.

Mr. Brummett noted that around the same time that Mr. Clark heard from Mr. Jones, he also received a phone call from Stephens Inc. chairman and Arkansas kingmaker Witt Stephens, "to suddenly tell him that he was his 'boy for governor.'" What a coincidence. "I bet Clark is not Mr. Witt's 'boy for governor' anymore," Mr. Brummett wrote.

Soon, Mr. Clark would not be anybody's boy for anything. Officially entering the gubernatorial race a month after the Beverly debacle, Mr. Clark was considered Bill Clinton's most formidable opponent. Within weeks, however, he would be ruined — a victim it seems of both his political enemies and his own extravagance.

Within days of his announcement of a challenge to Gov. Clinton, Arkansas newspapers ran a story detailing the travel and dining expenses of state officers. Attorney General Clark led the way, with over $60,000 in expenses. Some of Mr. Clark's expenses were legitimate. The attorney general's salary was only $26,000, with a $15,000 public-relations supplement.

But what appeared to be a middleweight political embarrassment turned into a disaster when Mr. Clark's alleged dining partners started phoning the Arkansas Gazette to deny their having dined with him. The first person to contact the Gazette was a major Clinton fundraiser, Marilynn Porter. The first person called by the Gazette was Judge Richard Arnold, an FOB currently on the short list for the Supreme Court. Both denied having dinner with Mr. Clark. Ms. Porter would later testify that she had been called by Bruce Lindsey, then Mr. Clinton's campaign treasurer and now a senior White House aide, who drew her attention to the article. When she asked what she should do, Mr. Lindsey suggested she contact her lawyer, Rose partner and FOB Webb Hubbell.

Despite apologies and payments to the state of more than $4,000, Mr. Clark was finished, the object of suspicion and ridicule. A few months later, he was indicted on felony theft charges, accused of stealing more than $8,000 in state money by putting personal charges on his state credit card. He was convicted and ordered to pay a $10,000 fine, plus court costs.

Lobbyist Earl Jones, meanwhile, was cleared of the bribery charge, in a trial that focused on Mr. Clark's lack of credibility. Mr. Jones's attorney successfully argued that the lobbyist was operating in a two-track role as agent for the companies involved in the Beverly buyout and campaign fund-raiser.

Mr. Clark left the state, perhaps seeking to fade into obscurity but courting notoriety again when he was photographed jogging with President Clinton on the Mall in Washington in August 1993. According to Arkansas Assistant Attorney General Angela Jegley, the photograph reignited interest in Mr. Clark. Investigations completed after Mr. Clark's criminal trial, Ms. Jegley said, had determined that Mr. Clark "had not paid in full." Ms. Jegley, who held a Clinton-appointed post as a chancery judge prior to joining the attorney general's staff, contacted the ubiquitous Mr. Brummett, who tracked down Mr. Clark, whereupon the state filed civil charges.

Through a spokesman, Mr. Clark pointedly declined to comment on how it was he came to be jogging with his former rival, or why. As attorney general for most of Gov. Clinton's tenure, Mr. Clark was privy to much sensitive information, sources in Little Rock say. The two men certainly had a long and complicated relationship. His spokesman said, declining to elaborate, that Mr. Clark believes the new trial "is politically motivated," and added: "Steve Clark just wants to put Arkansas behind him and get on with his life." Apparently when you've done political business in Bill Clinton's Arkansas, that's not always easy.

Mr. Morrison is an editorial page writer.

Letters to the Editor

A Long Paper Trail Led To Clinton Foe's Fall

Micah Morrison makes a leaping assumption about Arkansas cronyism in his May 2 editorial-page article "Another Arkansas Tale" when he deduces that the downfall of Steve Clark, Arkansas's former attorney general, was the doing of then-governor Bill Clinton and the Stephens Inc. investment firm.

As the reporter for the Arkansas Gazette who exposed Mr. Clark's use of his state-issued credit card for personal entertainment, I know that Mr. Clark withdrew his gubernatorial bid against Mr. Clinton, was convicted for theft and ultimately resigned because of his own failings and not because of political sabotage.

Mr. Morrison was right when he portrayed Mr. Clark as a pugnacious challenger to the controlling financial and political forces in Arkansas. And I don't doubt that Mr. Clinton eventually would have found a way to undermine a formidable opponent. But Mr. Morrison incorrectly insinuates that political operatives went to work on Mr. Clark with the help of the Arkansas Gazette.

The Gazette over six months chronicled how Mr. Clark during successive years spent tens of thousands of dollars in state money on expensive meals, luxurious hotel rooms and $80 shots of cognac for friends and dates. We didn't need the Clinton campaign staff or FOBs as sources for the stories—Mr. Clark left a paper trail a mile long.

Although not required by state laws, Mr. Clark documented each expenditure on his expense account and listed "phantom" guests whom he claimed he was entertaining for state business. Hundreds of guests listed by Mr. Clark were contacted, some who were well-connected to Mr. Clinton, but the interviews were limited to verifying whether or not they had eaten with Mr. Clark.

Mr. Morrison's version would have made a good story if it were correct. What he neglected to report was Mr. Clinton was merely the timely beneficiary of aggressive independent journalism and Mr. Clark's own criminal acts.

ANNE FARRIS

Little Rock, Ark.

REVIEW & OUTLOOK

Judicious Precedent

We woke up Monday to find ourselves, and even our editor, being called names in an Anthony Lewis column entitled "The Politics of Hate." The crucial sentence read, "Scandal sheets print charges about President Clinton's sex life, and they are taken up by television networks and some serious newspapers." Also, "There is a difference between the heat of policy criticism and personal vilification."

Now, those who read these columns know that we have turned with great alacrity to covering Mrs. Clinton's commodity trades, as befits our interests and audience. We fear that some of Mr. Lewis's readers may think our preoccupation lies elsewhere, based on his denouncing the sexual charges and then calling us the "most important voice" of the "extreme right" (which under Ronald Reagan won as much as 59% of the popular vote). But never mind, the New York Times has been both good on Whitewater and elsewhere recently generous to us.

More to the point, we understand that in Mr. Lewis's column we're only a proxy. His real but unmentioned subject is Paula Jones, who has gone public with charges of sexual harassment against Mr. Clinton and hired a lawyer in Little Rock. The statute of limitations on the incident runs out this Sunday, so this is sex week on the press rumor circuit. The White House has let her lawyer know he'll be going up against Bob Bennett, one of Clark Clifford's defense team, and Mr. Lewis is chipping in to tell the rest of the press not to cover her charges.

We do not know what either Ms. Jones or the rest of the press may do, but we do remember the Anita Hill case. Just for the record, here is a digest coverage of those sexual harassment charges by Anthony Lewis:

Oct. 11, 1991: "Then came the Senate Judiciary Committee's disaster: its failure to inquire properly into Professor Hill's charge that Mr. Thomas, when she worked for him starting 10 years ago, asked her to go out with him and told her in graphic detail about pornographic movies he had seen."

Oct. 14, 1991: "Judge Thomas was a fervently effective witness. He was, at least, until he carried his outrage to a point of self-pity that is not in order, saying that he had not had 'a single day of joy' since he was nominated to the Supreme Court last July."

Oct. 18, 1991: "When Prof. Anita Hill testified in convincing detail that she had been sexually harassed by Clarence Thomas, the defense was to attack: Destroy Anita Hill. Attack the committee. Charge racism."

Feb. 27, 1992: "[W]hat could be a more important issue than the one these reporters were covering, the fitness of a nominee for a lifetime position on the Supreme Court. . . . The serious question is why the Judiciary Committee — in particular its chairman, Senator Joseph Biden — tried to sweep the Hill charge under the rug. The possibility that a Supreme Court nominee who had had the job of preventing sex discrimination in fact practiced it demanded airing. Only the leak prevented its suppression."

REVIEW & OUTLOOK

No Standards

Can a President be sued? Does it count legally as sexual harassment if the accused wasn't in a direct supervisory role? Should a president's legal-defense fund take contributions from private citizens who may have future claims before the government? Do motives matter?

Welcome to America, 1994.

The short answer to all of the above questions is: The answer is irrelevant.

If what Paula Jones alleges is true, it certainly bears on the President's character. We noticed that even Eleanor Clift said on television over the weekend that if the charges had been made during the campaign he'd never have been elected. In a lawsuit, however, the law deserves some attention. Mrs. Jones's charges would clearly make a sexual harassment case, but the statute of limitations on that has expired. So she has brought other more problematical charges, and Beltway superlawyer Robert Bennett will be arguing for dismissal.

Yet even it he wins his legal point it may not matter. We are living in an age of sexual abuse filings against the likes of Cardinal Bernardin, class action lawsuits against manufacturers of silicone breast implants and, yes, this is the age of Anita Hill. The prevailing legal strategy in this era is to publicly torture your opponents until they "settle." Some do, some don't. But most come away largely ruined, financially or emotionally.

Conservative and liberal activists are currently tangling over whether Paula Jones's lawsuit against President Clinton poses tough double-standard issues for Anita Hill's supporters. That misses the point. We should be so lucky to have actual standards; the problem is that where matters of sexual harassment and American law are concerned, there are no standards.

If, fairly or not, Mr. Clinton is in trouble this week over the Jones charges, the wild, no-standards milieu in which he and his defense team must now operate is really one of his friends' making.

The originators of sexual harassment theory, such as the famous Catharine MacKinnon, argued and implemented the concept in a way that always—and from the outset—stacks the deck in favor of the accuser. After years of books, TV movies, talk-show appearances, Take-Back-the-Night marches, campus date-rape codes, court decisions and federal rule-making, there is now a generalized presumption that if a woman files claims of sexual harassment, there must be "something to it." That is, the proponents have won; they should be pleased with the status quo. Too bad if it caught a promising liberal President.

The American legal system, in its current anything-goes incarnation, is a perfect adjunct to this political movement. The movement's most effective strategy has been to generate waves of highly publicized moral outrage, which washed away the former standards of relevancy that were posed by law or politics. Politicized lawyers originated moral trumping as a weapon; lawyers in it just for contingency fees perfected it. How ironic that among this liberal President's biggest campaign supporters was the Association of Trial Lawyers of America.

Plaintiffs lawyers, abetted by willing judges, have spent years waving every imaginable, sobbing victim into America's courtrooms—from Love Canal to exploding fuel tanks to the recovered-memory industry that made "abuse" a household word. Endless discovery proceedings, the black hole that Mr. Clinton's lawyers are striving to avoid, unearth "damaging" evidence, which finds its way to the front pages or into prime-time exposes (the plaintiffs laywers' role in the story is almost never made explicit). The details keep dripping until the defendant screams for a settlement.

If President Clinton wants a shoulder to cry on, we recommend all the corporate defendants who've had to set aside their own agendas to sit through depositions, the professors whose careers have been tainted by campus kangaroo courts, or day-care workers such as

Kelly Michaels hounded across the years on child-abuse charges.

But he shouldn't go looking for help from his old allies. Anita Hill was advised by a team of high-powered authorities on sexual harassment, who did it for love. They won't be coming forward on the President's behalf. Mr. Clinton is now being ably represented by Mr. Bennett, who's doing it for money.

Our current environment of no-threshold litigation and low-threshold sexual harassment claims is too financially or politically lucrative for its creators to reform merely because it devours a liberal President along with sundry Bob Packwoods. But if the President's former liberal supporters won't recognize the necessity of some useful reforms, we will.

Let's start by enacting a federal fund to pay legal expenses for accused executive branch officials, starting with President Clinton. We have already seen a world of special prosecutors whose threshold for creation can be as low as that for an Elliott Abrams or Ted Olson, and this is now opening the way for private suits by the plaintiffs' bar. We'd better think about appropriating public defense-fund money, because the legal costs for normal people are impossible.

The private defense fund now being discussed for Mr. Clinton's skyrocketing legal expenses is obviously fraught with conflict problems. But whether the target is Bill Clinton or his press secretary Mark Gearan or Reagan Administration officials, this legal-fee problem deserves attention.

For a more thorough reform, let's adopt the "English rule," or loser pays. As proposed by Vice President Dan Quayle, and opposed and hooted at by the American Bar Association, plaintiffs who lose would pay some or all of their opponent's legal fees. That way, you have to win in court with serious legal arguments, not out of court with public relations. Speculative suits wouldn't be filed.

This rule, standard in other serious countries, would protect Mr. Clinton and future presidents from being hounded to death by publicity-driven lawsuits. And it would protect thousands of private Americans similarly situated.

Editorial Feature

What to Expect From Plaintiff Jones and Defendant Clinton

Despite the impression left by the media coverage, the suit filed Friday by Paula Corbin Jones in U.S. District Court in Arkansas is not a sexual harassment action. Her suit does not seek damages based on federal or state sexual harassment statutes. For those claims, the statute of limitations has already run out.

Rather, the complaint contains four charges: intentional infliction of emotional distress ("outrage" under Arkansas law); civil rights (Title VII) violations; constitutional (equal protection) violations; and defamation. That said, the success or failure of each of the claims will ultimately rest on the same factual basis: the events on the afternoon of May 8, 1991, at the Excelsior Hotel in Little Rock. And it will rest on the same legal question: Does the defendant's conduct constitute sexual harassment?

Rule of Law

By Kellyanne Fitzpatrick

Given the context of Mrs. Jones's charges, it is useful to review where the still-evolving law on sexual harassment now stands. Sexually harassing conduct was actionable under the law long before Anita Hill and Clarence Thomas had us glued to our television sets in the fall of 1991. The rationale for allowing individuals to sue supervisors and employers for such behavior has been reaffirmed by the courts since the early '80s.

The most common misperception about sexual harassment is that it need be sexual. It need not. Rather, plaintiffs may prevail if they can prove that conduct directed at them because of their gender created an "abusive" or "hostile" work environment that impaired their ability to perform on the job. This is called "environmental sexual harassment." Quid pro quo harassment is the other most commonly

Paula Jones

recognized form of sexual harassment under the law. The quid pro quo theory posits that an employer or colleague has used his or her authority to curry sexual favors from another in exchange for that person's ability to secure, retain or improve employment-related benefits.

In *Jones v. Clinton,* the complaint suggests both types of sexual harassment. Mrs. Jones charges sexually explicit conduct on the part of Mr. Clinton, who as governor of Arkansas was ultimately responsible for her job with the Arkansas Industrial Development Commission.

The complaint states that at the time of the alleged incident, "Clinton, by his comments about [AIDC director David] Harrington to Jones, affirmed that he had control over Jones' employment, and that he was willing to use that power." Mrs. Jones further alleges that following this encounter "enjoyment of her work was severely diminished" and "she was treated in a hostile and rude manner by certain superiors in AIDC."

To win, Mrs. Jones must prove her allegations in court. Before that, however, the president has until the end of the month to file an answer to her complaint. He is almost certain to ask to have the case dismissed. After Mr. Clinton's answer is filed, the next step is discovery, which the court may allow to continue even while it considers the motions to dismiss.

If the case goes to trial, Mrs. Jones will be helped by her apparent ability to produce corroboration, the linchpin in such he-said-she-said cases. Through the testimony of those who observed her and those to whom she described the alleged incident shortly after it occurred, Mrs. Jones must prove that she was "visibly shaken and upset," as she claims in her complaint.

This is one distinctive legal difference between Bill & Paula and Clarence & Anita; lack of corroboration was Ms. Hill's shortcoming. Moreover, as will be seen if *Jones* goes to trial, the judicial system does not allow for a free-for-all question-and-answer session. Rather, the form and substance of questions must conform to rigid sets of rules, rules that would have disallowed most of what transpired before the Senate Judiciary Committee.

In sexual harassment cases, courts have invoked both an objective and a subjective standard in deciding whether harassment took place. In applying the objective standard, the jury must consider whether a reasonable person placed in the same circumstances (in the Excelsior Hotel room before the person ultimately responsible for her employment) would have felt the same way (sexually harassed and emotionally distressed), given the same conduct (touching, attempted kissing, the request for oral sex).

But this "objective, reasonable person" will not steal the show. If her case goes to trial, Mrs. Jones will have an opportunity to testify under oath and tell the jury how she felt. The jury will be obliged to weigh this as well.

The question of a subjective standard was addressed in November by the Supreme Court in *Harris v. Forklift Systems Inc.* Writing for the majority, Justice Sandra Day O'Connor said that harassing conduct need not lead "to a nervous breakdown" before a victim can bring suit. As Justice O'Connor wrote: "A discriminatorily abusive work environment, even one that does not seriously affect employees' psychological well-being, can and often will detract from employees' job performance, discourage employees from remaining on the job, or keep them from advancing in their careers." Justice Ruth Bader Ginsburg, the lone Clinton appointee to the court, concurred.

Another question Mrs. Jones will likely face in court is why she waited "so long" before filing her lawsuit. This, too, is covered by the law. Regardless of why she waited until the statute of limitations was in its final countdown, the fact remains that her complaint was filed within the prescribed three years; that's all that matters under the law.

The purpose of such a rule operates to the benefit of defendants, in that it allows would-be defendants a sense of legal repose—a cutoff date after which they no longer face the possibility of being sued. Of course, it also offers a would-be plaintiff ample time to confer with counsel as to the viability of the claims, with family and friends about the practicality of bringing suit, and with oneself, in a struggle to decide whether the potential "human toll" of litigation is worth the possible gain.

In the past week, we've heard a lot about Paula the Gold Digger,

Paula the Tramp, and even Paula the Poor Girl Victimized by Gov. Clinton. The judicial process, however, will focus only on Paula the Plaintiff. The eventual result of this latest celebrity sex scandal will not be decided by the media, the electorate or top advisers in the White House. Rather, if the case is not dismissed, a dozen of Mrs. Jones's peers will have the final say as to whether infamy has been cast upon her, or whether she has pursued it at the expense of the president of the United States.

Ms. Fitzpatrick is counsel for Luntz Research Companies, a Washington polling and consulting firm, and adjunct professor of law at George Washington University.

Editorial Feature

Bill and Me

By Bob Packwood

In 1991 the Clarence Thomas/Anita Hill hearings awakened the collective American conscience to the issue of sexual harassment. These hearings sparked a national dialogue about exactly where the line is between actionable misconduct and mere boorishness. Three years later, we still do not have an answer.

Now that President Clinton faces similar allegations, we are about to embark on the next installment of this debate. This time, the question of just how far back we go has moved into the spotlight. Without serious examination of this question we may face an epidemic of old complaints dredged up against public officials who have recently won election or re-election.

Sexual harassment is a serious issue for men and women. It has a specific legal definition, and there are established guidelines as to what is actionable and what is not. There is a statute of limitations on the filing of grievances.

Paula Jones

By contrast, public officials may face amorphous "sexual misconduct" and "unwanted advance" allegations that rely on the public mood of the day for definition and have no statute of limitations.

What is "sexual misconduct"? Standards may change—and rightly so—but exactly what is the current standard? Have we come to the point where any conduct is actionable?

There are 22 allegations filed against me. Most were not made by current or former employees. Seventeen are 10 or more years old; five of those are a quarter-century old. In the past 10 years, there are five allegations against me. Of them, one was by an intern who claims that five years ago I told her a joke she now says she found offensive. Today, however, she cannot even remember the joke. Another complaint is from a woman who was not an employee; she says that I complimented her on her outfit and put my arm around her "as one would a close friend or relative" at a reception in front of scores of people. A third accuser is a woman, again not an employee, who says I looked at her in a way she didn't like.

Certainly a person has a right to not like the way another treats him or her. But are these the kinds of events that rise to the level of "sexual misconduct"? Are these the kinds of allegations that should spur someone to call for my resignation?

Fifteen or 20 or 25 years ago if a man made a pass at a woman and she accepted, it was OK. If a man made a pass, was rebuffed and that was the end of it, he may have been accused of boorish behavior, but he was not accused of "sexual misconduct." Attitudes change. Labels change.

Will it now be the standard that any person can bring any complaint against any public official over whatever span of time that person has served in office? If so, will it be the standard that any alleged conduct be judged by today's standards?

Driving while intoxicated was a modest offense 30 years ago with minor penalties. Today it is recognized everywhere as a gravely serious crime for which one may lose the privilege of driving and serve time in jail. If in 1994 a person comes forward and says he saw politician X driving drunk in 1969, should the politician be clapped in prison and stripped of his license?

President Clinton says that he does not remember his accuser, Paula Jones. I can understand that. Governors and members of Congress and senators meet thousands and thousands of men and women every year. I am pilloried for not remembering people I met only once 20 to 25 years ago at social events that were attended by dozens or hundreds of people.

Just how far back do we go to dig up complaints? As the years slip by, memories fade, potential witnesses move around and cannot be found, and, as in my case, some die. That is why we have a statute of limitations on legal cases.

Isn't it reasonable to ask that a person bring a complaint at the time of the alleged incident? The person bringing a complaint today under the law must bring it in a timely fashion—usually within six months and at most two years. None of my accusers complained to me at the time of the alleged events. They did not complain to any supervisor at the time. They did not complain publicly at the time.

The press called hundreds of women who had worked for me and aggressively sought complaints about me. Other accusers didn't come forward until a telephone hotline was set up to solicit complaints about me. Some didn't come forward until the Ethics Committee sent out two registered letters to every woman (but, interestingly, not to the men) who had ever worked for me, and in many cases followed up with a phone call, seeking complaints.

Another question is: Do we consider these types of allegations from the past to the exclusion of a public record of accomplishments? Regardless of the allegations against me, I stand firmly behind my record on women's issues during my time in the Senate. I offered the first national legislation to legalize a woman's right to choose in 1970, three years before *Roe v. Wade*. At the time, I could not get a single member of the House or Senate to co-sponsor it. Since then, I have stood alone many, many times—often against my own party and president—to protect that right to choose.

In my office, women make on average $10,000 more a year than men. The managers of my past four campaigns have been women. My chief of staff is a woman. The manager of my Oregon office is a woman. My chief legislative aide is a woman. Twelve of the women in my office have been with me for a decade or more. In my office a person rises to his or her level based on the excellence of his or her work—not based on gender. There is no glass ceiling in my office.

The media, of course, play a significant role in this debate. Media are largely responsible for the way these allegations are character-ized, no matter who is being accused. I hope that the differences in media portrayal between my case and President Clinton's are based on the fact that the media approach to this kind of story has evolved over the past 18 months.

Many of the issues raised to cast doubt on Paula Jones's credibili-ty could have been raised in my case, but they were not. The

Washington Post suggests partisan motives by saying of Ms. Jones's lawyer, "Gilbert Davis, a Fairfax lawyer who has been active in Republican Party politics. . . ." The Post and others in the press are diligently pursuing that angle in the Paula Jones case, but not in mine.

My most vocal detractor, a woman who has no allegation or other connection to the case, is a woman whom I handily defeated in the 1974 Senate election. Several of the accusers are Democratic Party insiders. Some contributed to my 1992 opponent's campaign. Most are Democrats.

This is a watershed moment. I hope that through this latest dialogue we can move forward to a time when public officials know what standards they are held to, and that we achieve balance between public official accountability and the responsibility for timeliness in bringing complaints. Otherwise we risk entering a season of unprecedented and unbridled divisiveness.

Mr. Packwood, a Republican, is the junior senator from Oregon.

REVIEW & OUTLOOK

The Congressional Coverup

In *U.S. v. Nixon,* the landmark Watergate case, a unanimous Supreme Court ruled that the President does not have blanket power to withhold pertinent information from the courts and Congress. Brushing aside the argument that this was purely a political dispute, Chief Justice Burger cited *Marbury v. Madison* in writing, "We therefore reaffirm that it is 'emphatically the province and the duty' of this court 'to say what the law is' with respect to the claim of privilege presented in this case."

Henry Gonzalez

The courts will have another opportunity to revisit the coverup issue in *Leach v. RTC,* now before Judge Charles Richey in Federal District Court in Washington. Rep. Jim Leach, ranking minority member of the House Banking Committee, has sued the Resolution Trust Corp. and Office of Thrift Supervision for release of documents on the handling of Madison Guaranty, the Whitewater S&L. Regulators at those agencies have denied him these documents, at the behest, presumably among others, of House Banking Chairman Henry Gonzalez.

To get some idea of what the thrift regulators and the Clinton Administration have to hide, study the accompanying documents, first released back in the midst of the torrent of publicity over Rep. Leach's pre-recess floor speech and President Clinton's press conference. The handling of the Madison referral has political fingerprints all over it; the only question is precisely whose. The documents constitute a prima facie case demanding a serious Congressional inquiry into such questions as:

(1) Was Charles Banks, U.S. Attorney in Little Rock under the Bush Administration, correct in referring Case No. C0004 to main Justice in Washington?

(2) Who reviewed the case there?

(3) Is it accurate, as Justice's Donna Henneman told the RTC's Jean Lewis, that all referrals with "political ramifications" go to the Attorney General? What kind of justice is this?

(4) Is Paula Casey, current U.S. Attorney in Little Rock, correct in suggesting that someone else made the decision to decline the referral? If so, who takes responsibility for the decision?

George Mitchell

(5) Since Ms. Casey, a longtime Clinton friend, ultimately recused herself from Whitewater matters, why didn't she do so initially before she participated in refusing the referral?

(6) Who in Justice made the unprecedented decision to fire all sitting U.S. Attorneys, which facilitated Ms. Casey's appointment, and why?

(7) Why was Ms. Lewis removed from the case 10 days after her letter to Ms. Casey? Who made this decision?

(8) What instructions was FDIC attorney April Breslaw given before her Feb. 2 interview with Ms. Lewis, and by whom? How was Ms. Breslaw chosen for this task?

(9) Is it true that Ms. Breslaw was instrumental in hiring the Rose Law Firm for the Madison case in 1989, despite objections by other government attorneys, and how does she presently regard that decision?

(10) Ms. Breslaw has "categorically denied" she said anyone in Washington favored any particular findings, and dismissed Ms. Lewis's account as a "complete fabrication." Rep. Leach says Ms. Lewis's account is supported by tape recordings. What is the truth?

(11) What instructions were given to RTC Kansas City investigators about interviews with Robert Fiske's investigators? What are the implications of Ms. Lewis seeking the protections of whistleblower status?

With all this on the table, the RTC stonewall can only be described as outrageous. Requests for similar documents by the Congressional minority were honored in the investigations of Columbia Savings &

Loan, Lincoln Savings & Loan, Silverado Savings & Loan and Centrust Savings & Loan. Criminal investigations proceeded concurrently in all these cases. A presidential directive instructs departments and agencies to provide information to Congress upon request unless the President himself invokes executive privilege, which in Whitewater would be a burlesque. Yet in the Madison case the regulators plead the need for privacy and trade secrets.

And of course, Congress is not fighting the coverup but leading it. The point man is Chairman Gonzalez. He canceled the Whitewater hearings he once promised. He's also canceled oversight hearings on RTC reports, which are required by law. And he has written the RTC and the OTS explicitly instructing these executive branch agencies not to cooperate with other members of Congress.

Coverup Henry is aided and abetted on the Senate side by Majority Leader George Mitchell. Two months ago, the Senate piously voted 98-0 to hold hearings on Whitewater, but none have been scheduled. Sen. Mitchell is the master of stalling tactics, and negotiations for a hearings mechanism have bogged down. In particular, he has insisted that any inquiry focus narrowly on Banking Committee matters, though the list above shows that the most serious questions concern the Department of Justice.

The issue here is whether the Congressional majority can simply disenfranchise the minority. If the majority fails to raise pertinent questions about an administration led by its own party, can the minority be prevented from raising them in an informed and effective way? It will also be the issue before Judge Richey and eventually, we assume, appellate judges. They will have to decide about whether to intervene, as the Burger Court did in Watergate, or simply say the minority's redress is with the voters.

Rep. Leach himself said after return from recess that Whitewater deserves a respite. And Republicans have been largely silent as the news columns were filled with Paula Jones and $100,000 commodity trading profits from 1979. The commodity trades deserve their own investigation, since unexamined records still exist at the Chicago Merc. But the Madison referral is not about sexual titillation or decades-old records; it is about the administration of justice by the Clinton Presidency in the here and now. It is entirely appropriate that Rep. Leach asks for the help of the courts in the responsibilities he was elected to discharge.

At least as important, though, the time is rapidly coming when the Republicans have a responsibility to make Madison and Whitewater an election issue, asking whether the voters want to return a majority that has had complicity in a coverup. Senator Malcolm Wallop took to the floor Tuesday to issue the first complaint, quoting New York Times Executive Editor Max Frankel about "a massive blockade" of the facts.

Rep. Gonzalez and Senator Mitchell are making themselves part of the Whitewater scandal by promoting a Congressional coverup. This is the same Congress that huffed and puffed over other failed thrifts, not to mention the fiction of the "October Surprise." The Democratic administration, its appointees at the RTC and its Congressional allies are circling the wagons to prevent embarrassing disclosures. Now that the Congressional Democrats have a Democratic President, they don't want oversight, they want a stonewall.

Editorial Feature

Case #C0004:
Nothing to Investigate

In an editorial nearby, we discuss the lawsuit by Rep. Jim Leach (R., Iowa) to obtain documents from regulators on Madison Guaranty, the Arkansas savings and loan with connections to the Clinton Whitewater affair.

The following are documentary materials released by Rep. Leach on March 24, in conjunction with his speech on the House floor. Under Chairman Henry Gonzalez, the House Banking Committee has refused to investigate the matter; Chairman Gonzalez has also written the regulators advising them to deny Rep. Leach the information and further documents he has requested.

According to the chronology prepared by investigators in the Kansas City office of the Resolution Trust Corp., Criminal Referral Number C0004, concerning Madison Guaranty Savings & Loan, was forwarded to Charles A. Banks, U.S. attorney in Little Rock, and Steve Irons, head of the local FBI office, on Sept. 2, 1992.

No acknowledgment had been received by November of that year, so RTC Kansas City investigators began a series of verbal inquiries. On Jan. 4, 1993, a letter from Don K. Pettus of the FBI said the referral had been received, and directed inquiries to Assistant U.S. Attorney Floyd Mac Dodson. On May 4, investigators sent a letter to Acting U.S. Attorney Richard Pence, who responded that the referral had been sent in September to the Office of Legal Counsel at Justice in Washington.

* * *

An RTC e-mail message by L. Jean Lewis, senior criminal investiga-

tor in the RTC Kansas City office, May 19, 1993:

In following up on the suggestion that Mr. Daniel Koffsky, Acting Assistant Attorney General, be sent a copy of Madison referral No.C0004, I contacted the Office of Legal Counsel to verify the correct address. In speaking with Dyone Mitchell of that office, I reiterated the address provided by US Atty Richard Pence which reads:

Office of Legal Counsel
Executive Office for the U.S. Attorneys
U.S. Justice Department
Washington, D.C. 20530
The letter provided the phone number (202) 514-2041.

Ms. Mitchell advised that the Office of Legal Counsel and the Executive Office for the U.S. Attorney's were two separate sections, and that the referral may have been forwarded to the Executive Office instead of Legal Counsel. She then connected me with the operator, who put me through to the Executive Office where I spoke with Stephanie Kennedy. I explained to Ms. Kennedy what I was looking for, and she said she would get back to me this afternoon.

She called me back at 3:30, and advised that she had forwarded the matter on to Donna Henneman in "Legal Counsel", who would check it out and call me back tomorrow. I then contacted Ms. Henneman to offer background information on what I was looking for. When I explained that it was a referral out of Madison Guaranty, forwarded to that office by Chuck Banks, she had immediate knowledge, stating "oh, the one involving the President and his wife." She then stated that the referral had been sent to that office (exactly which office is still unclear to me) as a special report for the attention of the Attorney General, and not as a referral for prosecution. She then stated that "anytime a referral comes in that would make the department look bad, or has political ramifications, it goes to the Attorney General." She further added that the referral had been submitted to that office "because of the political ramifications and political motivations", and then told me that referrals were not prosecuted out of that office. She then stated that the referral had been declined. I advised her that the referral had not been declined, and read her the letter sent to this office by U.S. Attorney Richard Pence. She acknowledged that she was confused, and told me she would speak with her supervisor, Deborah Westbrook, and have her call me back tomorrow. I then asked for Ms. Henneman's title, and she informed me that she was the Ethics Program Manager. I thanked her and ended the conversation.

I'll keep you posted if and when I hear from Ms. Westbrook.

* * *

A letter from Paula J. Casey, U.S. Attorney in Little Rock, to Ms. Lewis, Oct. 27, 1993:

Re: No.7236 Madison Guaranty Savings and Loan

Criminal Referral Number C0004

Dear Ms. Lewis:

I am writing at the request of the Office of Legal Counsel, Executive Office for U.S. Attorneys of the U.S. Department of Justice to let you know the status of this referral.

As you know, this referral was reviewed by the Criminal Division of the U.S. Department of Justice at the request of the previous United States Attorney for the Eastern District of Arkansas. The matter was concluded before I began working in this office, and I was unaware that you had not been told until I was contacted by the Office of Legal Counsel. After receiving the call from Legal Counsel I reviewed the referral, and I concur with the opinion of the Department attorneys that there is insufficient information in the referral to sustain many of the allegations made by the investigators or to warrant the initiation of a criminal investigation.

Although I am declining to take further substantive action on this referral, my decision does not foreclose future prosecutions about the matters covered by the referral or related matters in the event that my office and the FBI are given access to records or information indicating that prosecutable cases can be made.

Sincerely,

PAULA J. CASEY

United States Attorney

cc: Debra [sic] Westbrook, Office of Legal Counsel

* * *

A letter from Ms. Lewis to Ms. Casey, Nov. 1, 1993:

I have received your October 27, 1993 letter regarding the above captioned thrift and referral. On the basis of comments contained within your letter, I am interpreting that correspondence as a formal declination to prosecute referral No.C0004. You stipulated in your letter that this matter was concluded prior to the beginning of your tenure as the United States Attorney for the Eastern District of

Arkansas. Prior to the receipt of your letter, RTC Investigations was not advised that the matter had been formally concluded.

Between September 1, 1992 and today's date, this office has received a total of three letters with regard to the aforementioned referral, including your letter of declination. The other two letters were from FBI/SAC Don Pettus, 12/15/92, Richard Pence, 5/10/93, advising this office that he was unaware of the referral status as it had been forwarded to the Executive Office for United States Attorney's by former United States Attorney Chuck Banks.

If there were other documents produced that are relative to the conclusion of this matter, I would appreciate receiving the appropriate copies. . . .

Very truly yours,
L. JEAN LEWIS
Senior Criminal Investigator
cc: Debra Westbrook /Office of Legal Counsel
L. Richard Iorio /Field Investigations Officer/KCO
Lee Ausen /Supervisory Investigator/KCO

* * *

An RTC e-mail message by Ms. Lewis, Nov. 10, 1993:

Hey you! Just a heads up to let you know that Mike Caron, Senior Criminal Investigator, is now the lead investigator on Madison . . . so anymore faxes you send should come to Mike's attention, and any further communication about Madison should go to him, too. The Powers That Be have decided that I'm better off out of the line of fire (and I ain't arguing), but please let me assure you, that we are leaving you in very capable hands! Got any questions beyond that, ask Lee or Richard. . . .

* * *

A Nov. 15, 1993, RTC e-mail message by L. Richard Iorio of Kansas City investigations:

On Thursday, November 11, 1993, there was an article that appeared in the Washington Post concerning declination of prosecution on the first Madison referral that was transmitted to the Department of Justice (DOJ) on August 31, 1992.

Contained in the article was information that the referral had been reviewed by DOJ and that a decision had been made early on to decline on this referral and that when Paula Casey US Attorney, Little Rock, Arkansas, in fact issued the declination in October 1993, she was simply bringing this matter to a close.

The document attached clearly refutes this train of thought. In fact, it appears that no thorough review of the document had been conducted as late as June 23, 1993, some ten months after the referral had been initially transmitted. It was not until September 29, 1993 that this office was advised that the referral would be reviewed.

The whole issue might not be important, however, for purposes of credibility with regard to the RTC's efforts in this area, this memo and attachment are submitted for factual clarity.

[The attachment is a chronology of the RTC investigation and contacts with Justice, partially summarized above. It also summarizes the documents printed above and concludes:]

On November 11, 1993, RTC Investigations learned through an article in the Washington Post that Paula Casey had recused herself and her staff from any further dealing with the Madison referrals.

* * *

Notes by Ms. Lewis on her conversation with FDIC attorney April Breslaw, Feb. 2, 1994:

• April stated that "the people at the top" keep getting asked about Whitewater, which seems to have become a catch all phrase for Madison and it's [sic] related investigations. She said that eventually "this group" is going to have to make a statement about whether or not Whitewater caused a loss to Madison, but the fact that Whitewater had no loan at Madison provided less potential for a loss. April stated very clearly that Ryan and Kulka [Jack Ryan, deputy chief executive of the RTC and head of the agency on this matter following the recusal of Roger Altman; and Ellen Kulka, the agency's general counsel], the "head people", would like to be able to say that Whitewater did not cause a loss at Madison, but the problem is that so far no one has been able to say that to them. She felt like they wanted to be able to provide an "honest answer", but that there were certain answers that they would be "happier about, because it would get them off the hook."

• April felt that it would have been difficult to determine exactly what happened with the Whitewater account, because so many checks had gone in and out of the account, and made a reference to the end resulting [sic] netting itself out. She asked about Greg Young's work papers on the Maple Creek Farms reserve for development analysis, and how it didn't seem to have any apparent tie to

Whitewater. I concurred that it didn't have any legitimately defined tie, which is precisely why it was included in the referral.

• She inquired about the $30,000 check to Jim McDougal from Whitewater in 5/85, and about the disposition of the funds, I explained the transaction as I know it: the $30,000 had been converted to a MGS&L cashier's check, which was subsequently endorsed by [blacked out in document] and deposited to Riggs National Bank. I explained that when the check was force paid, the Whitewater account was overdrawn by over $28,000 which was then subsequently covered by the payment of a $30,000 bonus from MFC to Jim McDougal, deposited directly to Whitewater on McDougal's orders.

• She asked how we could get to a clear cut answer as to whether or not Whitewater caused a loss to Madison. I stated that, as far as I am concerned, there is a clear cut loss. I also stated that any attempt to extract Whitewater as one entity from the rest of the McDougal controlled entities involved in the alleged check kite will distort the entire picture. I further pointed out that I would produce the answers that were available, but that I would not facilitate providing "the people at the top" with the "politically correct answers just to get them off the hook".

• She asked questions about the specifics of the checks going through the Whitewater account. I stated that it appeared that the majority of the checks written out of the Whitewater account during the window time frame were going to other financial institutions to make loan payments. I also said that the referral focused only on a short time frame, but that if that same research were conducted for a two year period, it was my belief that the losses to Madison from the Whitewater account alone would easily exceed $100,000, given that $70,000 had gone out of the account during the six month window time frame. I further added that the end loss result from the entire scam, using all 12 companies/entities, would be hundreds of thousands of dollars in what were essentially unauthorized loans.

• I stated that if she wanted me to tell her, unequivocally, that Whitewater didn't cause a loss, I could not do that. I could only reiterate the allegations contained in the referral, which are based on fact, and that it is my opinion and belief that Whitewater did, in fact, cause a loss to Madison because of the amount of the unauthorized loans that McDougal made, through the check kite, to entities in which he was a primary party and beneficiary. I also pointed out that this ultimately benefited his business partners — the same business partners that knew they had real estate ventures that were not cash flowing, but that also knew their mortgages and/or notes were somehow being paid. I pointed out that these business partners are intelligent individuals, the majority of them being attorneys, who must have concluded that McDougal was making the payments for their benefit. I posed the question to her, if you know that your mortgages are being paid, but you aren't putting money into the venture, and you also know the venture isn't cash flowing, wouldn't you question the source of the funds being used to your benefit? Would you just assume that your partner was making these multi-thousand dollar payments out of the goodness of his heart? Wouldn't you wonder even more if you knew that your business partner's main source of income, an s&l, was in serious financial difficulty, which by 1985 was fairly common knowledge?

We discussed the initiation of the MGSL investigation, and how evidence of the check kite came to light. I explained that after reviewing a series of checks, all of which noted "loan" in the memo field, I discerned a pattern that looked like a check kite, and proceeded to trace funds through the various accounts, which is a standard investigations procedures [sic]. The end result was the referral alleging a massive check kite. I also advised April that I had been told by both the U.S. Attorney's office (Mac Dodson) and the FBI (Steve Irons) that this was a highly prosecutable case of check kiting. I also told her that I disputed the declination of that referral on the basis of "insufficient information". She commented that "that's what Grand Juries are for", and I pointed out that it generally seemed to be the policy of the U.S. Attorney to agree to open a case before they would start Grand Jury proceedings. I also noted that I found the treatment of that particular referral by the Justice Department to be highly unusual. This concluded our discussion.

REVIEW & OUTLOOK

Ira's Little Lie

What with Whitewater, cattle future trades, Paula Jones's lawsuit and David Watkins's helicopter trip, most Clinton-watchers probably have forgotten the legal tiff over the First Lady's health care task force. Yet the case not only drags on, but is worth a special look as Republicans ponder a "compromise" to resuscitate the health care bill. With an increasingly frustrated and angry judge about to order oral arguments on whether health czar Ira Magaziner should be held in contempt of court, it's a reminder of how the health proposal was conceived and propagated.

Ira Magaziner

The administration celebrated last June when the D.C. Circuit Court of Appeals ruled that the First Lady is the "functional equivalent" of a government employee in this case, *Association of American Physicians and Surgeons et al. v. Hillary Rodham Clinton, et al*. In commenting, we ourselves wrote of "Vincent Foster's Victory," since the late White House Deputy Counsel fashioned the argument that the Health Care Task Force was beyond the reach of the Federal Advisory Committee Act (FACA, or "focka" to aficionados). Because its members were all government employees, the group could meet in secret, without all of the requirements for notices and minutes that Congress has decided apply to Presidential advisory groups including private citizens.

In a concurring opinion, Judge James Buckley thought the "functional equivalent" argument a stretch, but declared that FACA should simply be declared unconstitutional as an intrusion on a President's right to take advice his own way. (Stephen D. Potts, director of the Office of Government Ethics, also agrees that Mrs. Clinton is not a government employee, arguing that this status absolves her of short sales in pharmaceutical companies while her speeches drove down their stock.)

Judge Buckley looks pretty wise to us, especially given the ongoing result of the Circuit Court's caveat: Mrs. Clinton is kosher, it said, but it couldn't tell about all the members of subgroups. It remarked that "the working groups, on the whole, seem more like a horde than a committee," but wanted to know more. So it remanded the case to Judge Royce Lamberth of the District Court, and granted the plaintiffs expedited discovery.

The record since then has been government stalling and foot-dragging. Last November, an enraged Judge Lamberth complained that the government "submitted meritless relevancy objections in almost all instances," and labeled the government's responses "incomplete and inadequate" and in one instance "preposterous." This kick in the pants finally produced some documents, and since the government hadn't done a person-by-person list of members, the plaintiffs did their own, submitting 37 pounds of evidence finding, among other things:

• The working groups contained more than 1,000 participants, not 511, as claimed by the Task Force. Nearly half of the members were private citizens.

• Large numbers worked for managed-care interests, most notably the Robert Wood Johnson Foundation and the Henry J. Kaiser Family Foundation. Both foundations have supported managed-care reform in several states. In addition, six members the White House passed off as Congressional staffers turned out to be Robert Wood Johnson fellows assigned to the staffs of four Democratic Senators; all were on the foundation's payroll.

• Dozens of other private interests were represented in the working groups — Aetna, Prudential, Kaiser-Permanente, Mr. Magaziner's former consulting company Telesis, to name a few. Conspicuously absent were physicians in private practice.

• The Task Force spent at least $4 million and possibly as much as $16 million on expenses, salaries and consulting fees. In the charter it filed with the GSA in March 1993, the Task Force said expenses would total $100,000.

The government says that all of this is irrelevant. It maintains that the working groups were too amorphous to be subject to FACA. The government now argues that the Task Force's myriad working groups were really just an informal bunch of folks interested in health care who got together to chat — often in living rooms and over computer terminals. There was no formal structure, no agenda, no advice to the President. Just a lot of schmoozing. Task Force? What Task Force? Only a horde.

Even if that argument succeeds, which a reading of the Circuit Court opinion leaves plenty of room to question, there is the little matter of Mr. Magaziner's initial sworn declaration. He said in March 1993 that "only federal government employees served as members of the interdepartmental working group." He did add some caveats about "special employees" and "consultants," but the plaintiffs argue that he submitted a deliberate falsehood that prolonged and complicated the case, and should thus be held in contempt. (Perjury charges are unlikely, since the government's rather hot reply brief is signed by U.S. Attorney Eric Holder.) The final briefs have been filed, and it's up to Judge Lamberth to schedule oral argument.

Whatever the ultimate decision on the contempt allegations, the record of the case is strewn with bad faith on the part of the government. From the first, the First Lady's task force was a cheap and duplicitous publicity stunt, which needed to be defended by evasions and distortions. Rather than trying to patch up a bill misbegotten in this same process, Congress and especially Republicans should call for a fresh start after a new election.

Editorial Feature

No Immunity for Clinton

Before Paula Jones's lawsuit against Bill Clinton proceeds in the Eastern District of Arkansas, an unprecedented constitutional matter regarding presidential immunity will have to be settled. This issue will be joined soon—probably by July 15, when the lawyer for defendant Clinton is to respond to Ms. Jones's complaint. Probably in the fall of 1995, the Supreme Court will hear arguments in *Jones v. Clinton,* and by the summer of (campaign year) 1996, the court likely will have ruled. If the court follows the Constitution, Ms. Jones finally will have her day in court, although perhaps not until after the 1996 election.

Rule of Law

By Terry Eastland

Defining discussion over whether Mr. Clinton might enjoy immunity from Ms. Jones's suit is a 1982 Supreme Court case, *Nixon v. Fitzgerald.* After testifying in Congress that cost overruns on the C-5A transport plane could reach $2 billion, Ernest Fitzgerald lost his job as an Air Force management analyst. Denying that his dismissal, for which President Nixon publicly took responsibility, was an act of retaliation, the government explained it in terms of a departmental reorganization and reduction in force. Eight years later Mr. Fitzgerald sued the former president, seeking civil damages.

Mr. Fitzgerald lost, with the court holding that a president is entitled to "absolute immunity from damages liability predicated on his official acts." The four justices who dissented (Brennan, Marshall,

White and Blackmun) presumably would have been even less impressed with the claim to be litigated in *Jones v. Clinton*—namely, that a president enjoys immunity from lawsuits involving acts occurring before he took office. (Mr. Clinton must hope that the passage of years has increased the wisdom of his vice president. Then a

Paula Jones

Tennessee congressman, Al Gore joined a congressional amicus brief in *Fitzgerald* on behalf of the plaintiff. The brief argued that "incumbency does not relieve the President of the routine legal obligations that confine all citizens.")

While the court's opinion in *Fitzgerald* made references to the Constitution, it relied heavily on "public policy" considerations. The basic argument was that private lawsuits might divert a president from the duties of governing and that if the litigation door were not closed, more lawsuits would follow. *Fitzgerald* was not the first case in which the court has argued from public policy, but that does not mean it was properly reasoned. The correct argument is rooted in the Constitution.

In a 1983 article in the University of Pennsylvania Law Review, Stephen Carter, the Yale law professor, showed that the *Fitzgerald* decision could have been well anchored in constitutional history and structure. Mr. Carter's bottom line is that "the Constitution vests in the political system. . .the decision whether to punish the President of the United States" for misconduct while in office. "The political system" established by the Constitution includes Congress, which can impeach, and the public, which can vote.

This poses a problem for Mr. Clinton's private lawyer, Robert Bennett, and for the lawyers at the Justice Department, which, given its responsibility to the presidency as an institution, can enter the case as an amicus. The constitutional argument that supports *Fitzgerald* does not also immunize a president from civil lawsuits for acts that took place before he became president. By definition, what is pre-presidential is not presidential; it is not political in a constitutional sense and cannot be remedied through the political system in the same way that an act by a president pursuant to his official duties can be. The Constitution does not protect a president from what he did in his former life. So far as that life goes, he cannot escape those routine legal obligations confining all citizens.

Not surprisingly, the public remarks by Mr. Bennett and White House Counsel Lloyd Cutler argue not the Constitution but *Fitzgerald*-like public policy concerns. Mr. Cutler asks, "If you value the presidency, do you really want the president putting his time on this kind of an exhibition?" Mr. Bennett says that if Ms. Jones's lawsuit is allowed to go forward, others will be emboldened to sue over pre-presidential acts. He speaks of "thousands of lawsuits" and of the president being tied up in depositions "365 days a year."

This is an exaggeration. *Jones v. Clinton* is, after all, a civil case. The president would not have to be present in court. His deposition would require an hour or so of his time, and he could be deposed through written questions that he could answer via satellite from the White House. A judge sensitive to the demands of the presidential office could and should manage the case in a way that would least burden him.

That said, Mr. Clinton's best hope in *Jones v. Clinton* lies in the demonstrated susceptibility of federal judges to the public policy argument. To make a judgment for the president more attractive to the courts, some lawyers filing on his behalf likely will narrow the argument so that the courts are not asked to immunize a president from all civil suits; they will concede the viability of suits for which "immediate relief" is required—such as in a divorce or child-custody case (Mr. Cutler's examples). The *Jones* case, they will say, is different, because Ms. Jones waited three years, and the relief she is seeking is, in the scale of things, rather small.

Robert Bennett

Some lawyers will even contend that the courts should balance competing public policy considerations in all civil suits involving pre-presidential acts, deciding on a case-by-case basis. In this case, of course, they will say the court should decide in favor of Mr. Clinton.

It is appropriate for Congress to weigh public policy considerations; that is its job. It is not, however, the job of the judiciary. In regard to immunity for suits involving pre-presidential acts, Congress could enact legislation that identifies the kind of lawsuits that should go forward and those that should not. If the administration is worried about a litigation explosion that could engulf this and future presidents in civil suits over pre-presidential acts, Mr. Clinton can recommend suitable legislation; don't forget that both houses of Congress are controlled by his own party.

Ultimately, Ms. Jones's case should proceed. Whatever one might think of Paula Jones, to have her case dismissed or postponed for public policy reasons until Mr. Clinton leaves office would effectively amend the Constitution.

Mr. Eastland is editor of Forbes MediaCritic and a fellow at the Ethics and Public Policy Center in Washington, D.C.

REVIEW & OUTLOOK

Don't Go Near the Whitewater

Mother, may I go out to swim?
Yes, my darling daughter:
Hang your clothes on a hickory limb
But don't go near the water.
ANON (BARTLETT)

So the World's Greatest Deliberative Body decided this week, as a memorial to the retirement of George Mitchell. We take Senator Mitchell's announced retirement as testimony to his status as a decent human being, and his disposition of Whitewater hearings as testimony to the single-minded partisanship that has marked his tenure as Majority Leader.

On a straight party-line vote of 56-43, the Senate adopted the Mitchell version of how to redeem its promise, by a 98-0 vote on March 17, to hold hearings on "all matters related to Madison Guaranty Savings & Loan Association, Whitewater Development Corp., and Capital Management Services Inc." In the Mitchell version, "all matters" are confined to Vincent Foster's suicide, the handling of his papers and contacts between the White House and Treasury on the criminal referrals of Madison. In other words, little on Madison, nothing on Capital Management and nothing on Whitewater.

In perpetrating this coverup attempt, Senator Mitchell predictably accuses the Republicans of wanting a "partisan circus." This is the same World's Greatest that under a Republican majority held hearings on the conduct of a Republican Administration in the Iran-Contra affair, not to mention the business dealings of William Casey in private life prior to his appointment as head of the CIA. While the Whitewater debate never became big news among the 6,500 members of the Capitol Press gallery the first three days it stopped the Senate, after the vote the New York Times' David Rosenbaum observed that "Mr. Mitchell was left to carry the defense of Mr. Clinton almost alone, with an occasional assist from the Democratic Senators from Arkansas, David Pryor and Dale Bumpers."

Mr. Rosenbaum added that Maine Republican William Cohen, "one of the least partisan of Republican lawmakers," argued that it was a "terrible precedent" for the Senate to defer to prosecutors such as Robert Fiske. When Republicans held the White House, the Senate held repeated hearings into matters under criminal investigation. But now, the World's Greatest cannot deliberate without a "mother, may I" to Mr. Fiske, the former Clark Clifford lawyer appointed special counsel for Whitewater during Webb Hubbell's tenure at Justice.

Whether this coverup will in fact succeed is in some doubt. On the Senate floor yesterday, soon-to-be-famous freshman Senator Lauch Faircloth gave a preview of his coming performance in hearings by the Banking Committee. Detailing connections between Governor Clinton and drug convict Dan Lasater, he demanded, "The United States Senate should have Dan Lasater's cocaine list — now."

When the North Carolina hog farmer offers this demand on national television, the script runs, he will be ruled out of order by Banking Chairman Don Riegle (D., Mich., Keating Five, retiring). Chairman Riegle will then explain how Mr. Lasater is irrelevant to his chief of staff Patsy Thomasson, who is irrelevant to the Foster papers though she was in his office the night of his death. Mr. Keating's Senator will also explain why the incomplete Presidential blind trust and Whitewater documents were irrelevant to Mr. Foster's death. And that Paula Casey's appointment as U.S. attorney after summary dismissal of all U.S. attorneys, and her torpedoing of the Madison referral before her recusal from the Madison referral, is irrelevant to the Madison referral.

Whether this spectacle will serve Senator's Mitchell's partisan purpose is not exactly beyond doubt. Likely it will only invite real hearings by the next Senate, bound to be far different and conceivably even controlled by Republicans. But by then the Majority Leader, having gone down with his President's Whitewater defense as Senator Moynihan went down with his President's health plan, will be safely out of the line of fire.

REVIEW & OUTLOOK

The D'Amato Opportunity

George Mitchell's Senate Democrats voted for the 11th time this week to block full hearings into Whitewater, but paradoxically this gives Republicans a huge political opening. They can now take the offensive by cleaning out their own stables in a way that Democrats won't. The contrast would be instructive come November.

Alfonse D'Amato

Republicans merely have to show the fortitude to discipline their own Members who have run into ethical trouble, from Senators Al D'Amato and Orrin Hatch to Congressman Joe McDade. Democrats have shown they won't do it to their own, which is one reason the country believes the Beltway doesn't play by the same rules as everybody else.

So Don Riegle can still run the Senate Banking Committee despite the Keating Five, while Tom Foley remains House Speaker despite his believe-it-or-not 40 for 42 winning streak in initial public stock offerings (IPOs). Republicans now have a chance to prove they'd be different if they ran the asylum, though on present evidence they may likely blow it.

They could start with Sen. D'Amato, who is the ranking Republican on Banking and thus a GOP point man on Whitewater. Roll Call, the Capitol Hill newspaper, has just disclosed that Mr. D'Amato made a $37,000 profit in one day on an IPO, based on advice from a broker who is the son-in-law of one of the senator's best friends.

Now, this is not illegal and deserves some perspective. Unlike Speaker Foley, Mr. D'Amato's deal wasn't part of a pattern that suggests a regular padding of income. Unlike Hillary Clinton, Mr. D'Amato has never denounced others for "greed." And while liberals accuse him of "sleaze," their evidence is that he pushes too hard for constituents, who keep re-electing him. This image will be further diluted when Mr. D'Amato's brother's conviction for mail fraud is overturned, as it probably deserves to be. Law professor Richard Painter has argued persuasively on these pages that Armand D'Amato did only what most lawyers do while billing clients.

That said, the IPO was on its face an attempt to buy political influence, and Mr. D'Amato should have rejected it. This doesn't mean he should be exiled from the Senate, but it does mean he isn't the best leader on Whitewater. We suspect Senator Mitchell wants hearings confined to the Banking Committee precisely so Democrats can divert attention away from Whitewater toward Mr. D'Amato. If the New Yorker would volunteer for a reassignment, he'd help both his party and the cause of exploring Whitewater.

More, it would increase his stature. It isn't yet widely understood what he has pulled off inside New York's Republican Party. Just as Sen. D'Amato methodically found his way to George Pataki as the GOP's opponent for Mario Cuomo, he should compose a list of characteristics of the person most likely to succeed taking on Whitewater. We suspect he wouldn't be at the top of the list now.

More broadly, Republicans also have to face up to Members confronted by other ethical questions. In the House, Joe McDade, the ranking Republican on Appropriations, has been indicted for racketeering, conspiracy and accepting $100,000 in illegal gratuities. Mr. McDade deserves the presumption of innocence, but even Dan Rostenkowski has had to give up his committee chair while under indictment. Mr. McDade, a legendary pork-barreler, is no symbol of reform.

Nor is Senator Hatch, who in our view still sits under a cloud from his entanglement with the corrupt banking empire of Bank of Credit and Commerce International (BCCI). Mr. Hatch once delivered a speech on the Senate floor defending BCCI; government investigators later learned the speech was written by Robert Altman, who was president of a bank illegally controlled by BCCI.

As the ranking Republican at Judiciary, Mr. Hatch has since

helped whoop through the nomination of Jamie Gorelick as deputy attorney general on an expedited voice vote. Ms. Gorelick had represented Mr. Altman while in private practice, and Mr. Hatch had employed one of Ms. Gorelick's law partners to represent him in the BCCI matter. So you have one BCCI player confirming another to a Justice post with responsibility for looking into BCCI. While the Senate ethics committee cleared Mr. Hatch "of a violation of any law" or "rule of the Senate," its four-paragraph statement doesn't deal with these cozy conflicts of interest.

A large public complaint against the Beltway is that its denizens write laws for everyone else even as they are exempt from normal ethical constraints. Republicans who want voters to give them a chance to govern have to show they can police their own.

Editorial Feature

Mysterious Mena

By Micah Morrison

MENA, Ark. — Reporters now trolling Arkansas are pulling up many stories that may have only fleeting relation to Whitewater or the Clintons, but are worth telling simply for their baroque charm. And none is more baroque than the tale of the Mena Intermountain Regional Airport, a site connected with aircraft renovation, apparent CIA operations and a self-confessed drug runner.

There is even one public plea that Special Counsel Robert Fiske should investigate possible links between Mena and the savings-and-loan association involved in Whitewater. The plea was sounded by the Arkansas Committee, a left-leaning group of former University of Arkansas students who have carefully tracked the Mena affair for years.

While a Whitewater connection is purely speculative, Mena certainly does seem a fruitful opportunity for thorough investigation, by Mr. Fiske or any other competent authority. It's clear that at Mena Airport unusual things took place.

What the Arkansas Committee calls the "complex of events" surrounding Mena is the stuff of spy novels and thrillers, potentially including smuggling, CIA and Drug Enforcement Agency covert operations, money laundering and murder. There is no reliable evidence linking any of these events to Bill Clinton, except that he was governor of Arkansas when state and federal investigations of Mena were frustrated.

Mena is a good setting for a mystery. The pine and hardwood

forests of the Ouachita Mountains surrounding it have long been an outlaw's paradise, home to generations of moonshiners and red-dirt marijuana farmers. In 1981, cocaine smuggler Adler Berriman ("Barry") Seal arrived on the scene, establishing a base of operations at Mena Airport. Mr. Seal's record is well-known to law-enforcement officials; he often claimed to have made more than $50 million from his illegal activities.

Working out of a hangar at Rich Mountain Aviation, one of the local businesses that was turning Mena into a center for aircraft refurbishment, Mr. Seal imported as much as 1,000 pounds of cocaine a month from Colombia in the early 1980s, according to Arkansas State Police Investigator Russell Welch, who pursued the Seal case for over a decade. In 1984, Mr. Seal "rolled over" for the DEA, becoming one of its most important informants. He flew to  Colombia and gathered information about leaders of the Medellin cartel, including drug kingpin Carlos Lehder, and testified in other high-profile cases.

He also flew at least two drug runs to Nicaragua, one of them entangling him in the Reagan administration's anti-Sandinista effort. On a mission in mid-1984, Mr. Seal later testified, the CIA rigged a hidden camera in his C-123K cargo plane, enabling him to snap photos of several men loading cocaine aboard the aircraft — one of them allegedly an aide to Sandinista Interior Minister Tomas Borge.

Back at Mena, meanwhile, Mr. Seal's business associate, Fred Hampton, the owner of Rich Mountain Aviation, purchased a land tract near the tiny backwoods community of Nella, 10 miles north of Mena, and cut a runway into it. Local law enforcement officials believe the land was purchased at the behest of Mr. Seal.

By 1984, reports were filtering in about odd military-type activity around Nella. "We had numerous reports of automatic weapons fire, men of Latin American appearance in the area, people in camouflage moving quietly through streams with automatic weapons, aircraft drops, twin-engine airplane traffic, things like that," says former Internal Revenue Service Investigator William Duncan, who began investigating Mena in 1983. Residents of the countryside around Nella confirm reports of planes dropping loads in the mid-1980s. "But people don't talk much about that around here," said one local resident. "If you do, you might wake up one morning to find a bunch of your cattle dead."

Mr. Duncan and Mr. Welch, the Arkansas State Police investigator, pressed forward with their probes of Mr. Seal and Rich Mountain Aviation. They suspected that Mr. Seal, despite his deal with the DEA, was continuing to import drugs and launder the money through local businesses and banks, possibly using the Nella airstrip as a base for drug drops.

In 1986, Mr. Seal's wild ride came to an end. Three Colombian hitmen armed with machine guns caught up with him as he sat behind the wheel of his white Cadillac in Baton Rouge, La., and blasted him to his eternal reward. Eight months after the murder, Mr. Seal's cargo plane was shot down over Nicaragua. Aboard was a load of ammunition and supplies for the Contras. One crew member, Eugene Hasenfus, survived. With the crash, and the Iran-Contra affair surfacing, investigators started looking at the Nella airstrip in a new light. Maybe Barry Seal was not just flying drugs into the U.S. Maybe he also was flying newly trained Contras and weapons out.

But if Mr. Seal's odyssey was over, the long and frustrating journey for Mena investigators was just beginning. Messrs. Duncan and Welch believed they had pieced together information on a significant drug smuggling operation, perhaps cloaked in the guise of a covert CIA operation, or perhaps in some way connected to the intelligence community. Yet repeated attempts to bring the Mena affair before grand juries in Arkansas, Gov. Bill Clinton, and federal authorities all failed, meeting a wall of obfuscation and obstruction.

The "CBS Evening News," one of the few national news organizations to take a serious and discriminating look at Mena, recently broadcast an interview with Charles Black, a prosecutor for Polk County, in which Mena is located. He said he met with Gov. Clinton in 1988 and requested assistance for a state probe. "His response," Mr. Black said, "was that he would get a man on it and get back to me. I never heard back."

Asked for comment, White House spokesman John Podesta cites a state government offer of $25,000 to aid a Polk County investigation, an offer long under dispute in Arkansas. "The governor took whatever action was available to him," Mr. Podesta says. "The failing in this case rests with the Republican Justice Department."

Following pressure from then-Arkansas Rep. Bill Alexander, the General Accounting Office opened a probe in April 1988; within four months, the inquiry was shut down by the National Security Council. Several congressional subcommittee inquiries sputtered into dead ends.

In 1991, Arkansas Attorney General Winston Bryant presented Iran-Contra prosecutor Lawrence Walsh with what Mr. Bryant called "credible evidence of gunrunning, illegal drug smuggling, money laundering and the governmental coverup and possibly a criminal conspiracy in connection with the Mena Airport." Seventeen months later, Mr. Walsh sent Mr. Bryant a letter saying without explanation that he had closed his investigation.

Mr. Duncan resigned from the IRS after repeatedly clashing with his superiors over the Mena affair. Mr. Welch was given a number of strong hints that he should devote his energies elsewhere. "I believe there was a coverup of events at Mena," Mr. Duncan says. "We don't really know what happened out there. Every time I tried to follow the money trail into central Arkansas, I ran into roadblocks."

But what, if anything, does Mena have to do with Whitewater? A small conspiracy-theory industry has grown up around the mysteries of Mena. In a new book, "Compromised: Clinton, Bush and the CIA," authors Terry Reed and John Cummings claim that Gov. Clinton and his inner circle, along with Lt. Col. Oliver North and the CIA, were involved in a conspiracy that included training Contras at Nella, sending weapons to Central America, smuggling cocaine into the U.S. and laundering funds through Arkansas banks. Little hard evidence is presented to back up these startling claims, yet the book should not be dismissed out of hand. Certainly, something was going on at Mena and Nella. And the authors raise the interesting question: What happened to all of Barry Seal's cocaine money?

In an intriguing coincidence, while running Barry Seal as an agent, the DEA also was conducting an investigation into the drug-related activities of Little Rock bond dealer and Clinton supporter Dan Lasater. In October 1986, as Mr. Lasater was being charged in Little Rock with conspiracy to distribute cocaine, the DEA confirmed that he was the target of a drug-trafficking probe involving his private plane and a small airfield at the New Mexico ski resort Angel Fire, which Mr. Lasater purchased in 1984.

Mr. Lasater's bond shop also executed a mysterious series of trades on behalf of Kentucky resident Dennis Patrick, who says he had no knowledge of the millions in trades reflected in his account in 1985 and 1986. It's unclear what these trades represent, since Mr. Patrick's confirmation slips show only paper transactions, with little money in or out. Yet it's interesting to note that the hectic activity in the account came to an abrupt halt in February 1986 — the month Barry Seal was killed.

Of course, it all may be just a coincidence, and perhaps Gov. Clinton did not even know that drug smugglers, the CIA and the DEA were operating in his backyard. Perhaps he did not want to know. After all, as we have come to learn, Bill Clinton's Arkansas was a very strange place.

———————

Mr. Morrison is a Wall Street Journal editorial page writer.

Letters to the Editor

Why Big Barry Seal Died in the Big Easy

It is surprising to see Oliver North ever play second fiddle to anyone in your pages. But in Micah Morrison's account of strange doings in rural Mena, Ark., during the 1980s ("Mysterious Mena," editorial page, June 29), Ollie was justifiably dwarfed by the near-mythic Barry Seal. Mr. Seal, a 300-pound mountain of a man, who at age 26 was flying 747s for TWA, was indeed a commanding figure in the sinister world of guns and drugs. Mr. Morrison, however, should have included an account of the time when Ollie did a little one-sided *mano a mano* with Seal, because the incident reveals a lot about the aspiring junior senator from Virginia.

Mr. Morrison correctly reports that Seal was killed by a Colombian hit squad in New Orleans in 1986—but he doesn't explain why the hit went down. As Elaine Shannon details in her book "Desperados," DEA agents in 1984 became furious at Col. North because they believed that he, in a fit of pique, had blown Seal's cover while Seal was working as a DEA informant inside the Medellin cartel. Ollie, the agents told Ms. Shannon, was angry at DEA because the agency wouldn't denounce the Nicaraguan Sandinistas as drug traffickers. With Seal defrocked as an informant, the angry Colombians took their efficient and predictable revenge.

GARRY EMMONS

Cambridge, Mass.

REVIEW & OUTLOOK

Sweetheart Justice

While the release of Robert Fiske's first Whitewater report starts to clear the obstacles to a public accounting of these events, the most significant legal news yesterday concerned the Bank of Credit and Commerce International. It seems the Justice Department has cooked up a sweetheart deal for the biggest BCCI crook it's been able to lay hands on.

Apparently our legal eagles would rather not know what happened to $9 billion in world-wide loot. Worse, they don't want to know how a band of Arabs illegally took control of the biggest bank in Washington, D.C. Swaleh Naqvi, BCCI's number two man finally extradited from Abu Dhabi in May, has not been forthcoming to investigators. But Justice has struck a deal with him anyway, to be presented on July 9 to Judge Joyce Hens Green, over the certain objection of Manhattan District Attorney Robert Morgenthau.

The plea bargain, as detailed by Sharon Walsh in the Washington Post, would provide a sentence of nominally nine to 11 years for Mr. Naqvi. However, he would receive credit for three years of "house arrest" in Abu Dhabi, whose ruler was BCCI's majority shareholder. With the possibility of parole, he will escape with only a short sentence for $9 billion in larceny, instead of the 35-year maximum cited on his arraignment.

Now, this deal was reached by the same Justice Department where Webster Hubbell recently held sway, brokering meetings that reversed the Department's position in a corruption trial. The same

Justice Department that fired all sitting U.S. attorneys and appointed a Friend of Bill to squelch the criminal referral of Whitewater before recusing herself from the case.

The dominant figure at Justice, now that Mr. Hubbell has resigned, is Deputy Attorney General Jamie Gorelick, who as a private attorney was involved in BCCI affairs in representing Clark Clifford and Robert Altman, who ran Washington's First American Bank when it was illegally owned by BCCI. Her confirmation, despite such problems as no experience in law enforcement, was whisked through the Senate Judiciary Committee by Senator Orrin Hatch, who had been represented by one of her partners when he was cleared by the Senate Ethics Committee of impropriety in a Senate speech defending a previous BCCI settlement now understood as a wrist-slap.

Jamie Gorelick

Ms. Gorelick's part in the BCCI legal festivities was to try to get First American's trustee to pay legal bills for Mr. Clifford and Mr. Altman. That is, to collect money for Mr. Fiske and for present presidential lawyer Robert Bennett, both of whom also represented Mr. Clifford and Mr. Altman. One of Mr. Bennett's law partners, John Schmidt, was also recently appointed Associate Attorney General, the number three post at Justice. The BCCI case is directly handled by Gerald Stern, special counsel for financial institution fraud, who admittedly has no BCCI connection; his private experience was as general counsel to Armand Hammer's Occidental Petroleum.

While attorneys are entitled to have clients, the Clifford imprint on Justice is surely remarkable. For that matter, the White House press briefing of December 7 has an intriguing exchange about Mr. Clifford and Mr. Altman entering the West Wing, and briefer Dee Dee Myers promising to inquire who they were visiting but saying they were not scheduled to meet with the President. Perhaps Mr. Clifford has resumed his role as eminence grise. And why not, since he did not stand trial for his First American role, and Mr. Altman was acquitted on charges of misleading regulators about ownership of the bank?

But if Mr. Clifford and Mr. Altman did not hoodwink regulators, what did happen? We do after all have laws about who can own an American bank, and clearly they were violated when the capital's biggest institution was taken over by front men for a criminal enterprise. What precisely was the regulatory failure? What do we need to do to keep it from happening again?

This is a pressing question because all signs suggest we're entering a new phase of international criminality. FBI director Louis Freeh is even now touring Eastern Europe seeking ways to combat the large and sophisticated criminal enterprises that have grown in the vacuum created by the collapse of the Soviet empire. As the CIA and for that matter Russian President Boris Yeltsin have also warned, it will be a growing international problem. And since the big international drug trade depends on money laundering, the regulation of financial institutions is central to both the problem and solution.

We've also learned that when drugs and money laundering arrive, political corruption cannot be far behind. If we had an explanation of how BCCI got away with its illegal purchase of First American, we could afford to dismiss such ambiguous connections as lawyer-client relationships. But we have no such answer, and are left to speculate why, in the Naqvi plea-bargain, the Justice Department does not seem to be pressing for one.

Editorial Feature

Why a President Shouldn't Have To Go Begging

Now that President and Mrs. Clinton have established their Legal Expense Trust, I'm thinking about writing a check for $500. Since Mr. Clinton will be informed of my gift, maybe I'll get that interview he's somehow always resisted. Come to think of it, if I double my gift to $1,000, maybe I'll get Hillary too.

I'm only dreaming, of course, but I wonder how many donors to the first presidential defense fund in history will in fact be making such quid-pro-quo calculations. That's just one of the many reasons Americans might worry about the spectacle of the U.S. head of state panhandling for dollars.

Potomac Watch

By Paul A. Gigot

Another reason is Ronald Olson, one of the new fund's trustees. Be not misled by Theodore Hesburgh and Barbara Jordan, two upstanding Democrats who are also trustees; they're the ethical showhorses. Mr. Olson is the cash cow. As a trial lawyer in the Los Angeles firm of Munger Tolles & Olson, Mr. Olson stands at the confluence of two mighty rivers of money—the trial bar and Hollywood.

In 1980, Mr. Olson served as Southern California finance chairman for then-Sen. Alan Cranston, who later became a campaign-finance legend as one of the Keating Five. Federal records show Mr. Olson is a generous donor to many Democrats, especially those like Sen. Ernest Hollings who vote to protect the interests of the plaintiff's bar.

So here we are in late 20th century America: A president who is sued for harassment under the flimsy legal standards encouraged by the trial bar now has to go back to that same trial bar to raise money to defend himself. Is this a great country or what?

It's always possible Mr. Olson's motives are as patriotic as George Washington's. But how are we to know? Perhaps instead we are now establishing a new standard for political loyalty. Ambassadorships have always gone to big campaign givers. Will lawyers who want to be judges now feel they have to give to the legal defense fund?

The precedents being set here aren't reassuring. The trust agreement says that, after all legal expenses are paid, any remaining cash will go to Mr. and Mrs. Clinton. They say they'll turn it over to charity, but the trust agreement includes no such promise. There's nothing to

Bill Clinton

stop them from turning it into a retirement fund after they leave office.

The White House claims that by accepting no more than $1,000 from any individual the Clintons are behaving better than the Senate, whose members can accept $10,000. Leaving aside that Congress isn't exactly the gold standard for ethics, Bob Packwood has one vote. A president has the power to pardon, to appoint, to let contracts, to regulate, to veto and in general to influence all legislation that passes through Congress.

Indeed, that's why Congress passed a law (5 U.S. Code 7353) that says executive branch officials can't "solicit or accept" gifts from people whose interests they might affect. In view of this ban, I asked a senior White House official for the defense fund's legal rationale.

"We have no written opinions," he said, in a remarkable admission. Nothing from Justice's crack Office of Legal Counsel. Zip from White House Counsel Lloyd Cutler. "We have had consultations with some of the Office of Government Ethics people," this source said.

Stephen Potts, the Bush appointee who runs the ethics shop, confirms he wrote no legal opinion either and advised the White House only "in general terms." Mr. Potts nonetheless says he thinks the president and veep are exempt from this gift ban. But his judgment is based on a regulatory exception (5 C.F.R. 2635.201-204) that applies only to "considerations relating to the conduct of their offices, including those of protocol and etiquette." In other words, to Christmas turkeys, or Chinese vases and the like received from official visitors.

I doubt Congress meant this loophole to include $1,000 checks bundled together by trial lawyers. Yet the normally zealous Mr. Potts is suddenly a soft touch: "The rationale is that as long as it's made public, if the president receives gifts that are inappropriate, unlike a career civil servant he could be voted out of office." However consoling, that's still a legal leap. A.B. Culvahouse, White House counsel under Ronald Reagan, is more skeptical: "I'm surprised they could get comfortable with it."

All of this goes beyond law to the power and conduct of the presidency. By so blithely ignoring the law, the Clinton White House has again shown how easily it will cut ethical corners. And by begging for money, it undermines the president's credibility and demeans his office.

Which is why someone else should try to restore presidential dignity. First someone could sue to test the legality of the defense fund. Meanwhile, Bob Dole could take the high ground by introducing a bipartisan bill to pay Mr. Clinton's legal fees out of public funds while he's in office.

In return, a grateful Mr. Clinton could agree to advocate the English Rule that plaintiffs (such as Paula Corbin Jones) who lose lawsuits must pay the legal costs of the winner. Trial lawyer Ronald Olson might object, but Americans would be grateful their president is no longer panhandler-in-chief.

REVIEW & OUTLOOK

Beyond Fiske

After spending some time with Robert Fiske's first Whitewater report, we have two sets of reactions. Naturally we want to defend our own record against its critics, but more broadly we see the public policy point that Mr. Fiske's criminal investigation is no substitute for political accountability.

The bulk of the report is devoted to forensic evidence on the events surrounding Vincent Foster's death. Here the report is extensive and persuasive. Barring some unimaginable new disclosure, we find no reason to doubt that the former deputy White House counsel committed suicide in Fort Marcy Park, as first reported. This should end much mystery and speculation, and here Mr. Fiske has performed a public service.

* * *

Mr. Fiske's question-stilling probe, we'd note in our own behalf, is precisely what we suggested immediately after Mr. Foster's death. For this suggestion – since we'd also been the first to question the mores of the administration's Rose Law Firm transplants – we were pilloried by the White House and our critics in the press. Yet rumor and speculation were entirely predictable results of confused responsibility, leaps to conclusions and a profusion of loose ends. When Lloyd Cutler portrays the White House as a victim of rumor, he should remember that Mr. Fiske located the witness who found the body thanks to G. Gordon Liddy.

Even more to the point, we first learn from Mr. Fiske that before

Mr. Foster ever left Arkansas he'd experienced brief periods of depression and panic attacks marked by heavy sweating and a strained voice. And that in 1992 he'd confided to his physician that he

was feeling depressed and anxious. The account of his last weeks does indeed paint a picture of clinical depression; much mystery and confusion would have been avoided if the complete facts had been released promptly instead of nearly a year after the death.

Yet after stalling on its promises to release the original Park Service Police report, the Justice Department has in recent weeks hotly resisted our Freedom of Information suit concerning it; with Mr. Fiske's support, it has refused to submit the earlier report to a judge to

Robert Fiske

see what might be released without compromising investigation now completed and partly reported.

Mr. Fiske's report, too, provides a platform for shedding further blame on us, namely in interviews directed at dismissing the chance that Whitewater "triggered" Mr. Foster's depression. We are accustomed to controversy, but this obscures the central point that depression is a disease. It is not caused by travel office scandals, press criticism or the normal stress of public or private life. It is caused by biochemical changes in the brain, and while these are poorly understood they are treatable. When we wrote that if Mr. Foster's death had purely personal roots we would join the mourning, we had in mind that posthumously he might do for depression what Betty Ford did for alcoholism. But advancing such understanding, we suppose, is not an independent counsel's writ.

* * *

Which brings us to the issues of public policy.

Foremost among them is the need for the American public to know what Whitewater and its attendant events were all about. The tenor of the Fiske report should make it clear to a lot of people that the public's need to know and the charge of a special counsel are by no means the same thing.

Mr. Fiske may choose to pursue only indictable offenses. This is fine by us, but the implication is that whatever else he may discover would then be swept into a sealed bin called "insufficient" evidence, with Rule 6-e cited as forbidding him from ever revealing its contents. But it's also true that an election is coming, and it follows that the public should know what its government is up to. A criminal investigation cannot fill this need.

That is — or should be — the purview of Congressional oversight. That has been the function of such hearings stretching back throughout our history — until this. Teapot Dome, yes; the Pecora hearings, yes; the Kefauver hearings, yes; Watergate, yes; Iran-Contra, yes, even under a Republican Senate. But for Whitewater an increasingly desperate Democratic majority has erected a series of roadblocks and restrictions.

Under this strategy, Henry Gonzalez's House Banking hearings will call as their first witness Special Counsel Robert Fiske, who will once again describe all the things he doesn't want anyone to talk about for fear this information might mar his pursuit of an imprisonable felon somewhere. Thereupon, all relevant parties who follow him before the committee will read from the same script by taking the Fiske. Like the Fiske interviews, the Park Police report, the FBI report or anything else anyone actually would like to know about, their lips are sealed by the special counsel's needs.

Rep. Jim Leach, the committee's ranking minority member, has already submitted a list of witnesses he would like to call to open up the Whitewater history. It is a credible and relevant witness list. It most certainly will include inquiries into the White House-RTC contacts, which constituted the Fiske report's biggest surprise: There were 20, not just the three acknowledged by the White House. Clearly, whatever was going on there needs to be opened up, but just as clearly we're not going to get credible answers unless the minority party is somehow empowered to responsibly pursue the issue. Perhaps the most relevant legal proceeding is Rep. Leach's lawsuit to force agencies to comply with minority requests for relevant documents; a good precedent here would do more than any independent counsel law to open government.

If in the end the Democrats thwart any such public airing, voters should hold the majority party responsible in the fall elections. As to Mr. Fiske himself, we trust no one understands better than he that the office of independent counsel, which has just been reauthorized and signed into law, is no substitute for an open system that conveys to the American people an understanding of something that has vital relevance to their political interests. The Democrats, invoking the special counsel at every turn, are now trying to pretend that Mr. Fiske is a substitute for the political process. Unless he wants to advance the coverup, he should not let them get away with it.

REVIEW & OUTLOOK

Sweetheart Justice—II

O.J. Simpson has hired some big-name lawyers, but maybe what he really needs is a change of venue to Washington, D.C. If somehow the trial worked out badly in the nation's capital, there's always the possibility of cutting a sweetheart deal of the sort that Swaleh Naqvi just made with the U.S. Justice Department.

Naqvi is merely the biggest fish yet caught in the biggest bank robbery in history, the scam involving the Bank of Credit and Commerce International. For helping to steal $9 billion or so as BCCI's number two man, Naqvi has been handed a generous plea bargain that could get him out of jail within five years. It's too bad Court TV wasn't on hand last Friday to catch the argument for why this is supposed to be adequate punishment for 20 years of really grand larceny.

Judge Joyce Hens Green accepted the deal at Friday's hearing, which is not surprising since it's rare for a judge to overrule a plea bargain. But to do so she had to overlook the objections of Manhattan District Attorney Robert Morgenthau, who has been the most dogged pursuer of BCCI crooks. In a seven-page letter protesting the plea, Mr. Morgenthau noted that "Naqvi has not, in our view, supplied significant cooperation," so there's no reason he should be given a sweetheart deal.

Looking at the sentencing guidelines, Mr. Morgenthau calculated that Naqvi deserved at least 17 $^1/_2$ years to 21 years, and "probably" should get 27 to 33 $^3/_4$ years—at least as an incentive to cooperate with U.S. officials. "The bare number does not adequately describe the injury," Mr. Morgenthau wrote about the sentence. "The defendant's crime was a long-term, calculated crime of treachery."

Yet Justice officials spoke as if they'd been listening to a different Naqvi. They asserted that Naqvi had answered every question he's been asked so far, as if "no" and "I don't recall" are adequate measures of cooperation. In terms of specific evidence of cooperation, they offered none. Most troubling, they argued that the Naqvi plea "gives the full story of the violation of American laws" by BCCI.

Robert Morgenthau

But of course we still don't know very much at all about how BCCI managed to fool regulators in so many countries. Nor do we even know the story of how BCCI managed to illegally penetrate the U.S. banking system and gain control of the largest bank in Washington, D.C. Justice prosecutor Anthony Leffert's account of the plea bargain was long on generalizations about Naqvi's use of Arab "nominees" to disguise BCCI's control of the bank, but short on facts about who helped them in Washington. And if Naqvi is "destitute" and stole no money for himself, as Mr. Leffert also claimed, then who's paying for Naqvi's very pricey attorneys?

Mr. Leffert also acknowledged that he and other investigators haven't yet even compared Naqvi's "cooperation" with the thousands of documents turned over when Naqvi was finally extradited from Abu Dhabi in May. We hear Naqvi's memory sometimes returns when presented with these documents. It's hard to believe Naqvi will be any more helpful now that he has a get-out-of-jail-early card.

Our suspicions are further aroused, we admit, because of the relationships of senior Justice officials to the BCCI case. The most powerful person at Justice now is Jamie Gorelick, the deputy attorney general who in private life played a role in representing Clark Clifford and Robert Altman, the pair who ran Washington's First American Bank when it was illegally owned by BCCI.

Arguments will be offered that this is irrelevant to the Naqvi plea. Maybe, but Justice could reassure us if it doesn't now interfere with Mr. Morgenthau's prosecution of Naqvi under New York laws. Justice's plea doesn't bind Mr. Morgenthau, but the department could block Naqvi from cooperating because he is a federal witness, at least until Naqvi is formally sentenced on Oct. 19. Naqvi's attorney, Beltway operative Joseph diGenova, has indicated he will try to block New York from proceeding. Justice could further ease suspicion by allowing Messrs. Clifford and Altman to testify as part of the Federal Reserve's civil action in the BCCI case. Mr. Altman was acquitted and Mr. Clifford never tried for reasons of health in criminal proceedings in BCCI.

We'd expect that an administration keen on denouncing "greed" would be more zealous than it's been in pursuing BCCI. Yet Americans have discovered more about the rogue bank from the work of a single district attorney than from the Justice Department with all its many resources. If Naqvi now slips into oblivion without offering further cooperation, the suspicion will linger that maybe someone in Washington just didn't want to know.

Letters to the Editor

I've Kept Arm's Length From All BCCI Matters

Your editorials on BCCI suggest that, having represented Clark Clifford and Robert Altman while I was in private practice, I am now influencing the conduct of the Justice Department investigation into the BCCI matter ("Sweetheart Justice," July 1, and "Sweetheart Justice II," July 12). Were that suggestion true, it would constitute a violation of the Rules of Professional Conduct and the Justice Department rules on conflict of interest.

It is a matter of public record that I am recused from any matter in which I was involved in private practice, including this one. For the record, from the middle of 1992 until early 1993, I represented Messrs. Clifford and Altman with regard to their claims against First American Bank for indemnification from legal fees incurred in the BCCI matter. I was not involved in the criminal cases in any way and never dealt with the federal or state prosecutors. Contrary to a suggestion in one of your editorials, I have never even met or spoken with Robert Fiske. At the beginning of my tenure at the Justice Department, I recused myself from the entire BCCI matter, which is being handled by others within the department.

JAMIE GORELICK
Deputy Attorney General

Washington

REVIEW & OUTLOOK

The Falwell Tape

Had it not been for the efforts of partisan Democrats and their media allies to discredit the religious right as extremist, we might have missed Jerry Falwell's videotape "The Clinton Chronicles." But we had to order up a copy (1-800-828-2290) to check out the accusation that the Rev. Falwell was accusing President Clinton of murder.

As it turns out, the tape might better be described "The Larry Nichols Story." Mr. Nichols, former marketing director of the Arkansas Development Finance Authority and a devoted Clinton foe, puts the most tendentious possible face on a succession of controversies from the Clinton governorship. We're not sure this is extremism by contemporary standards ("Hey, hey, LBJ; how many kids did you kill today?"). But it surely doesn't produce a reliable account. While Mr. Nichols cites former IRS agent William Duncan on money laundering through ADFA, for example, Mr. Duncan tells us he can make no more sense of Mr. Nichols's account than we can.

And yet, the Falwell tape and the controversy around it get at something important about the swirl of Arkansas rumors and the dilemma it presents a press that tries to be responsible. The "murder" accusation, for example, is not made by Mr. Falwell or Mr. Nichols, but by Gary Parks, whose father was gunned down gangland style on a parkway near Little Rock last September. Luther "Jerry" Parks was head of a concern that provided local security for the Clinton presidential campaign in Little Rock. The younger Mr. Parks says his father had investigated Clinton indiscretions and that his files were stolen shortly before his killing.

This is old news to any of the journalists covering Arkansas scandals, but few of us have shared any of this knowledge with readers. We suspect Jerry Parks had plenty of reason to have enemies, and that his family may be overwrought. Finding no real evidence of a Clinton connection, and feeling the President of the United States is entitled to a presumption of innocence, we decline in the name of responsibility to print what we've heard. And then it is left to less responsible sources to publish the first reports, and the disclosure of basic facts adds credibility to their sensational interpretation, especially among those losing trust in the mainstream press.

Interestingly, the British press has had a different approach. A full account of the Parks incident was published last March, for example, by Ambrose Evans-Pritchard of the Sunday Telegraph. And now the Economist, surely not a sensationalist sheet, has published a violence scorecard under the headline: "Whitewater: Curiouser." Besides Mr. Parks, it mentions:

— Kathy Ferguson, former wife of Danny Ferguson, the Arkansas state trooper who is a codefendant in the sexual harassment suit against the President. Her May 11 death by gunshot was ruled a suicide.

— Bill Shelton, Mrs. Ferguson's boyfriend, found dead on her grave. His gunshot death was also ruled a suicide.

— Jon Walker, a Resolution Trust Corp. investigator interested in Whitewater Development Corp., leapt to his death from the Lincoln Towers building in Arlington last August.

— Gary Johnson, a lawyer who lived in the next apartment to Gennifer Flowers, who was beaten so badly he had to have a ruptured spleen removed.

— Dennis Patrick, whose account at Lasater & Co. recorded millions in mysterious transactions, who has survived three attempts on his life.

— Stanley Huggins, a Memphis lawyer who headed a 1987 examination of Madison Guaranty Savings & Loan, who died suddenly in June, apparently of viral pneumonia.

"All of this may be a pack of cards piled up by overeager conspiracy theorists and ideological opponents of the president," the Economist warns. For our own part, we cannot for a minute imagine Bill Clinton knowingly involved, even tangentially, in plots of violence. We believe some of the deaths are indeed coincidental suicides and that most of the violence has separate causes. Finally, we believe that some of the Arkansas tales, such as the 1987 murders of teenagers Kevin Ives and Don Henry, are the result not of political conspiracies but of drug smuggling. The Falwell tape makes much of the activities at Mena airport — painstakingly described by our Micah Morrison on this page on June 29. But it does not persuasively connect them to Governor Clinton; nor does it mention evidence that Mena was also the site of CIA operations in support of the Nicaraguan Contras.

Pondering the string of violent coincidences, we feel some duty to share with readers one factor that colors our own thinking about the Arkansas connections. In particular, with drugs does come violence, and also money laundering. And laying aside any thought of Presidential involvement, there is a story here worth our attention and yours.

REVIEW & OUTLOOK

The Meese Test

So the President of the United States asked the Comptroller of the Currency for "advice" on his personal problems with the banking laws. White House 130-day Counsel Lloyd Cutler dismisses the President's approach to Comptroller Eugene Ludwig as "an absolute nothing." Now *you* tell one.

We propose a simple test: What if it were Ed Meese? What if Attorney General Meese had been caught, say, whispering in the ear of his buddy Ed Gray about his own political and legal problems in Mr. Gray's bailiwick as chief thrift regulator? Why, both of them would have been on the next plane back to California. But of course, Mr. Meese wasn't caught leaning on Mr. Gray. Rather, Alan Cranston, Don Riegle and Dennis DeConcini were; they stuck it out inside the Beltway until they faced the prospect of elections.

What Mr. Ludwig's memo on the New Year's weekend conversation shows is that Mr. Clinton is perfectly capable of calling personally on the cronies he has so assiduously salted throughout the financial regulatory and law enforcement agencies. Mr. Ludwig, after all, is a certified friend of Bill from their days at Yale and Oxford together. A lawyer by profession, Mr. Ludwig was named to run the comptroller's office, which examines and regulates national banks.

The old friends have stayed close, as the American Banker described earlier this year in a report on a videotape taken at that annual Clintonian seance, Renaissance Weekend: "The tape featured Mr. Clinton. But it was hard to miss Mr. Ludwig in a bright blue sweater and white shorts. Almost every shot of the President showed the beaming comptroller at his shoulder." Now we learn that it was at this very same meeting that Mr. Clinton asked his "beaming" friend for advice.

We also know that a few weeks before his chat with the President, Mr. Ludwig had generously sent copies of Freedom of Information Act requests relating to Whitewater to the White House and Treasury. These FOIA requests had been made to the Federal Deposit Insurance Corp. (FDIC), which is supposed to be an independent agency. What are friends for?

Meanwhile, the Washington Post has just reported that another Clinton schoolmate/buddy, Deputy Treasury Secretary Roger Altman, told Treasury counsel Jean Hanson "to brief White House officials last fall on the Whitewater investigation." This is the same Roger Altman who described just a single "heads up" meeting with White House aides when asked about such contacts earlier this year under oath in Congress. Later it turned out that there had actually been several such contacts between Treasury and the White House, but both Mr. Altman and the White House insisted they had nothing to do with the substance of Whitewater. At the time, Mr. Altman was running the Resolution Trust Corp. (RTC), which was investigating Whitewater.

Asked about these contacts at a press conference in March, Mr. Clinton himself protested that, "I can tell you categorically I had no knowledge of this and was not involved in any way, shape or form." Perhaps Mr. Clinton wasn't outright lying, because Mr. Ludwig didn't technically supervise the RTC. But his answer, which responded to a direct question about his personal knowledge, sure sounds like an evasion. Sort of like "didn't inhale."

Disclosure of the Ludwig memo to Treasury has the feel of a calculated leak, putting the best possible spin on bad news bound to come out at the Whitewater hearings set to begin in Congress next week. Both Mr. Ludwig and the White House were well-prepared with explanations for the memo on Monday. Mr. Ludwig was quickly on the phone to reporters saying that, after consulting with Treasury and White House aides, he had decided in January that helping Mr. Clinton with Whitewater would have been inappropriate and that their conversations went no further. (The memo was dated March 11.)

Yet the bottom line here is that a President of the United States intervened with a bank regulator/crony whom he appointed in order to seek help on a matter of profound personal and political importance to him. This is the same President, moreover, who has tried to name another Renaissance Weekend buddy, Ricki Tigert, to run the FDIC. (Her nomination is being blocked by Republicans.) Who has done his best, if Bob Woodward's account is to be believed, to cozy up to the other major bank regulator, Federal Reserve Chairman Alan Greenspan. And who larded his Justice Department and White House counsel's office with cronies from Arkansas, including the now-resigned Webster Hubbell and a U.S. Attorney in Little Rock who poisoned the Madison referral before recusing herself from it.

Robert Fiske, the Whitewater special counsel, looked at these contacts between regulators and the White House and concluded that "the evidence is insufficient" to prove that anyone "acted with the intent to corruptly influence" an investigation into Whitewater. But this is a criminal standard, designed to weigh whether someone should be sent to jail. For holding the trust of high office, there is also a more important standard called political accountability. This gets to questions of character, of ethics, of openness and honesty with the public. As they approach November's ballot box, Americans deserve to know what Bill Clinton's buddy system is all about, and whether their Congress is trying to find the truth or trying to hide it.

REVIEW & OUTLOOK

Drug Unintelligence

The Clinton Administration's drug policies are a running sore. The President didn't inhale. The Surgeon General muses about legalization as her son is busted on a drug offense. A former associate of a drug convict runs White House administration, including drug testing for staff members. The biggest whopper of all: The Administration stops sharing radar surveillance of air flights in drug areas in the Andes because Colombia threatens to shoot down suspect planes.

This is because the Pentagon is worried about potential legal liability, they explain. Only in America. Various efforts, mostly clumsy, are under way toward resuming sharing intelligence, but it will take a long time to repair the damage already done to a painfully forged program of cooperation with Colombia and Peru. The spectacle is a telling one.

Now, the legal issues involved are real enough. In the wake of the Soviet downing of KAL 007, international aviation conventions adopted some sweeping prohibitions on attacks on civil aircraft, and these have been implemented in U.S. law. Even in the Bush Administration, Defense Department lawyers were arguing that this prohibited aiding and abetting drug interdiction in the Andes. This legal fanaticism was suppressed by the Bush foreign policy apparatus, but it burst out when the DoD summarily suspended its intelligence sharing on May 1. And in a Clinton Administration fillip, a coven of lawyers decided that the laws would subject individual government personnel to criminal penalties.

Deputy Attorney General Jamie Gorelick has taken most of the heat for these decisions, with some Republicans on Capitol Hill wondering about her representation of BCCI-scandal figures Clark Clifford and Robert Altman. It is certainly true that if some similarly bizarre policy came out of the Colombian or Peruvian governments, we would be scrutinizing their officials for suspect associations. But Ms. Gorelick's letter to the national security agencies saying that the suspension was "imperative" came after the policy was already in effect, and she has written relevant Congressmen to deny she addressed the issue in her previous post as Pentagon general counsel.

The initial impetus for the policy change, rather, seems to lie in the military's discomfort with anti-drug missions. This underlying impulse was no doubt aggravated by a long-running dispute over a 1992 incident in which Peruvian jets accidentally fired on a U.S. C-130, killing an Air Force sergeant. And by the accident in which American fighters shot down two U.S. helicopters in Iraq. While held in check during the previous Administration, in the current one these emotions forged ready alliances with notions about the transcendence of international law and doubts about "militarizing the drug war."

And legal opinions were allowed to overwhelm policy. If Colombia cannot shoot down planes it suspects of drug-running, are we to give drug-runners flying over our borders free rein to ignore attempts to force them to land? When the Justice Department hypothesizes about criminal penalties, is it actually threatening to bring such prosecutions against government officials rather than apply its discretion to cases where there was no criminal intent? And in the end, is it not an executive decision whether certain legal risks should be run?

Despite some hypothetical legal risk, after all, the circumstances would seem to offer a de minimis "business risk," as a private lawyer would call it. No lawsuits have been filed, nor, it seems, have any planes been shot down. The Colombians have discussed careful procedures about when they would or wouldn't shoot. Surely the intelligence cooperation could have been continued while any necessary legal changes were made; the abrupt rupture was flatly unwarranted.

What we are dealing with here is abject failure of leadership. It is up to a President to keep his generals in line, and his lawyers too. If generals don't respect their commander or his entourage they can call on well-honed bureaucratic skills concerning drug policy or shipboard bathrobes. If lawyers aren't given clear direction, they will take over any business. And if a leader communicates that he's not serious about some policy area, private agendas will take over.

Faced with Congressional outrage and political embarrassment, the Administration now backs a provision that says shooting down civil aircraft is OK under certain circumstances, and this has been adopted by the Senate. The House, by contrast, has approved an amendment simply saying that providing intelligence does not imply intent to break international law. But much damage has been done, and what's really needed is for Mr. Clinton and the Administration to show in word and deed that they're serious about drugs.

Hearings

Congressional hearings on Whitewater in the summer of 1994, narrowly limited to Vincent Foster's death and White House contacts over the Resolution Trust Corp.'s probe of Madison Guaranty, turned out to be surprisingly informative, despite sharply partisan limits placed on House hearings by Banking Committee Chairman Henry Gonzalez (D., Texas). The Senate, intent on preserving its prerogatives, forcefully pressed the inquiry, questioning top government officials for hours. Deputy Treasury Secretary Roger Altman and General Counsel Jean Hanson resigned.

Many new details emerged about White House contacts regarding Madison Guaranty and pressure exerted on the Kansas City RTC investigators who had initiated the Madison probe. In the Journal, questions were raised about the role of White House aides and the conduct of the U.S. Attorney in Little Rock, Paula Casey.

On August 1, the White House revealed that Whitewater files had been removed from Mr. Foster's office and held in the Clintons' personal residence for five days. Four days later, a three-judge federal panel, acting under the revived independent counsel law, removed Mr. Fiske and appointed Kenneth Starr as the new independent counsel.

REVIEW & OUTLOOK

The Fiske Hangout

We don't recall offhand whether it was H.R. Haldeman or John Erlichman who suggested dealing with Watergate by a "limited, modified hangout." But the wonderful phrase captures the essence of the Whitewater hearings about to begin today — an exercise intended to create the illusion of openness while revealing as little as possible.

Provided essential political cover by independent counsel Robert Fiske's grandiose view of his own prerogatives, Congressional Democrats have officially limited the hearings to preclude such interesting areas of inquiry as Bill Clinton's Arkansas slush fund for legislative initiatives, Hillary Clinton's commodity trades, Dan Lasater's drug convictions and whatever hap-

Robert Fiske

pened at Mena airport. Questions will be allowed only on matters Mr. Fiske has already certified as non-indictable. Rep. Jim Leach estimated this at 5% of Whitewater. He lowered the number to 2% to 3% when Mr. Fiske declined to bless Congressional nosiness about the handling of Vincent Foster's office papers after his suicide.

The sliver of the case remaining, to be sure, is pregnant with embarrassment for the Administration. It concerns Washington contacts on the regulation of Madison Guaranty Savings & Loan, and press leaks over the past week depict an Administration with a progressive case of mutual recrimination. Will Deputy Treasury

Secretary Roger Altman take the fall? Which of various high officials is lying? What did the President know and when did he know it? Amid the often contradictory denials by Washington officials, one thing should be kept in mind.

To wit, that investigators in the field clearly feel they were sat upon to suppress the Madison investigation. A proper investigation would start with RTC Kansas City attorney L. Jean Lewis, and work its way back up the chain of command. It would certainly include the handling of Madison by Paula Casey, the Friend-of-Bill implant as U.S. Attorney in Little Rock, and the circumstances of her appointment. Instead, the hearings will start with denials at the top and work down, maybe. As of yesterday, House Banking Chairman Henry Gonzalez had formally scheduled only one witness: White House 130-day counsel Lloyd Cutler.

Henry Gonzalez

To get a sense of the coverup being conducted, consider that Rep. Leach has felt it necessary to bring suit in federal court in an attempt to get documents on Madison from the Resolution Trust Corp. and Office of Thrift Supervision. Such documents were routinely provided to the minority banking staff in previous S&L scandals — Lincoln, Silverado, Centrust, Columbia and others. But when it comes to Arkansas, the supposedly independent regulatory agencies have gone into a protective crouch.

The ranking minority member of the House Banking Committee is entitled only, John E. Ryan of the RTC wrote Mr. Leach, to those documents "otherwise available to the public pursuant to the Freedom of Information Act." Mr. Ryan is the deputy in charge of the RTC after Mr. Altman recused himself. Jonathan Fiechter, longtime acting director of the OTS, took the same position. When Mr. Leach requested the documents for oversight hearings mandated by statute, Chairman Gonzalez wrote the regulators instructing them not to comply. Mr. Leach brought suit for the documents, and Judge Charles Richey is to decide whether the agencies can ignore the law if a chairman tells them to. Lawyers for the agencies now urge the court not to interfere in a dispute within the Congress.

What you have here, it could scarcely be clearer, is a Democratic Congressional majority protecting a scandal-ridden Democratic executive branch, and bending banking regulators to this purpose (assuming they need to be bent). The Congressional majority has a monopoly on Congress's right to learn the truth, lest the minority inform the voters. Judge Richey plainly understands the danger of this doctrine, but in oral arguments said he was troubled by an appellate precedent, even though "I thought it was dead wrong then. I'll go to my grave thinking it's dead wrong."

Judge Richey also, wrote Glenn Simpson in the July 18 issue of Roll Call, "denounced Whitewater independent counsel Robert Fiske for his efforts to limit the scope of the Whitewater hearings that will be held by the Banking Committee later this month, saying Fiske was infringing on constitutionally guaranteed Congressional rights and obligations." The Judge said directly, "I don't believe the independent counsel has the power to tell Congress what they have the power to look into, and when."

It is too much to hope, we suppose, that Judge Richey's view is held by the panel actually overseeing the independent prosecutor law — headed by Judge David B. Sentelle of the D.C. Circuit and including Senior Judges John D. Butzner Jr. of the Fourth Circuit and Joseph T. Sneed of the Ninth Circuit. Interestingly, however, they have not acted on Attorney General Reno's nomination of Mr. Fiske, forwarded July 1, a day after the signing of the new Independent Counsel Act.

That afternoon Senator Lauch Faircloth took the Senate floor to urge "a new, truly independent counsel," who might of course retain Mr. Fiske in some capacity. Senator Faircloth cited Mr. Fiske's involvement in defending Clark Clifford and Robert Altman in the BCCI case, in collaboration with Robert Bennett, the President's lawyer in the Paula Jones case. Also Mr. Fiske's firm's representation of International Paper Co., which had land dealings with Whitewater Development. And Mr. Fiske's role in the appointment of Louis Freeh as FBI chief and his private legal work with former White House counsel Bernard Nussbaum. This is not a trivial list; in our own view no one with any role in BCCI should be appointed to anything until we know the full story.

Yet Judge Sentelle's panel should think even harder about whether it agrees with Judge Richey on the balance between prosecutorial and Congressional prerogatives, or whether it wants to endorse Mr. Fiske's view by reappointing him. Does the Judicial Branch really want to take responsibility for the farce about to unfold in Congressional hearing rooms and on the nation's TV screens?

Editorial Feature

Whitewater, Watergate
— the Numbers

By J.T. YOUNG

Today is the first day of Whitewater hearings in the House. While many commentators have noted that the hearings are a lose-lose proposition for Democrats, just how much the governing party has at stake doesn't become apparent until you look at the poll numbers. By the numbers, Democrats are in many ways more vulnerable electorally than were Republicans heading into the Watergate hearings.

Richard Nixon

Watergate began on June 17, 1972, with the botched burglary of Democratic headquarters. In August, President Nixon insisted that the White House was not involved, but by January 1973 the burglars went on trial and the Senate voted to hold hearings. Senate hearings lasted from May to August 1973, followed by House impeachment hearings from May to July 1974. Mr. Nixon resigned on Aug. 9, 1974.

As would be expected, Mr. Nixon's approval/disapproval rating showed a steady decline throughout the ordeal. From his January 1973 inauguration to just prior to his resignation, it dropped from 67% approval/25% disapproval to 24% approval/63% disapproval in the Gallup poll.

Even more amazing than the effect in the polls was the effect at them. Mr. Nixon had crushed Democrat George McGovern by 520 to

17 in electoral votes in 1972. His popular vote advantage was 61% to 38%, or an incredible 17 million votes. He won every region with at least 57% of the vote and was below 55% in only five states (Wisconsin, South Dakota, Rhode Island, Minnesota and Massachusetts). In Congress, Republicans held 43 Senate seats and 192 House seats.

Not surprisingly, things changed in 1976. Republicans lost 8 million votes off their presidential total. Their ticket garnered just 49% of the popular vote and 240 electoral votes. The fallout extended well beyond the White House. In Congress the GOP fell to just 38 Senate and 143 House seats.

The contrast between pre-Watergate and pre-Whitewater couldn't be more striking. While Richard Nixon rolled to victory in 1972 in one of the greatest landslides in history, Bill Clinton eked out the narrowest of wins in 1992. While beating George Bush 370 to 168 in electoral votes, Mr. Clinton gained only 43% of the popular vote and beat George Bush by just 6 million votes. Even more telling, Mr. Clinton won 17 states by less than 92,000 votes each. Those 17 are worth 128 electoral votes – more than enough to tip the scales to the GOP.

In office, Mr. Clinton has done nothing to shore up his popularity. His approval/disapproval rating at inauguration was 58%/20%, lower than Mr. Nixon's. When Watergate hearings began in May 1973, Mr. Nixon's "approval/disapproval" had fallen to 44%/45%. Twenty years later, and months before Whitewater even appeared as a story, Mr. Clinton's "approval/disapproval" was just 41%/48% – three points lower. Even if the beginning of Whitewater as a major story in December 1993 is taken as a starting point, Mr. Clinton's 57%/37% approval/disapproval rating at that point was worse than Mr. Nixon's in January 1973.

Finally, despite a year's worth of strong economic news, Mr. Clinton's approval/disapproval rating stood at an abysmal 42%/47% on July 20, according to the CBS News/New York Times poll. These were the lowest figures in a year, and they came a week before the Whitewater hearings.

Heeding the history of Watergate, Mr. Clinton's numbers should be especially frightening to congressional Democrats. By 1976, Republicans had lost 10% of their Senate seats; a similar loss for the Democrats by 1996 would leave the Senate split 50/50. By 1976, the GOP had lost 26% of its House seats; similar losses for Democrats would leave them with 190 seats and minority status for the first time in a generation.

To all this gloomy extrapolating Democrats will be quick to reply: "But Whitewater is not Watergate." Admittedly. Yet it's important to remember that Watergate wasn't Watergate either . . . at first. It was hearings and public exposure that turned the name of a ritzy apartment complex into a byword for scandal. Recall the almost nonchalant admission by Alexander Butterfield that Mr. Nixon had taped conversations in the Oval Office? You can bet that prominent Democrats do.

The Whitewater hearings, even in their current limited form, are likely either to produce fresh evidence of wrongdoing — abuse of office, something-for-nothing deals, etc. — or to reinforce Mr. Clinton's old weaknesses: lack of veracity, character questions, etc. While Whitewater may be a complex press story, congressional Democrats know how simple hearings will make it. In the public glare, Whitewater will distill down to two questions: Was political influence used in an attempt to gain financial benefits, and was political influence used in an attempt to cover it up? The verdict could be "yes," if not in a court of law, then in the even more important court of public opinion. Given their already low poll standing, it's not a setback that Democrats can readily afford.

Mr. Young is legislative director for Rep. Lamar Smith (R., Texas).

REVIEW & OUTLOOK

A Tale of Two Nominees

With Whitewater explanations continuing to effloresce, we thought readers might want to ponder the ethical standards the Administration and the Congress have applied to two different nominees, John Dalton and Admiral Stanley Arthur.

Mr. Dalton is now Bill Clinton's Navy Secretary, but we've recently learned that in the 1980s (a.k.a. the decade of "greed") he ran a Texas savings-and-loan that tripled its assets in four years, but collapsed at a cost to taxpayers of some $100 million. It further turns out that federal regulators charged Mr. Dalton with "gross negligence" in running the thrift, and he and others settled the claims by having insurance pay $3.8 million.

John Dalton

Also that the Federal Home Loan Bank Board, which regulated thrifts in the 1980s, took the rare step of blocking Mr. Dalton, who ran the San Antonio office of Arkansas' Stephens Inc., from accepting a $750,000 finder's fee for brokering the sale of some Texas S&Ls. And that only last week—after the above facts were disclosed by Jeff Gerth in the New York Times—Mr. Dalton settled an old personal debt to the new S&L regulating agency, the Resolution Trust Corp., by repaying $17,900 for a loan on a condo he'd taken out in the 1980s.

None of this has proved the least hindrance to Mr. Dalton's nomination. Indeed, it seems that Roger Altman chewed out his RTC sub-ordinates for failing to get his permission to dun Mr. Dalton. And Sam Nunn's Senate Armed Services Committee waved through Mr. Dalton after considering the S&L matter only in secret session.

Admiral Arthur wasn't so lucky, despite a brilliant career that has

Stanley Arthur

included running the Allied naval force during the Gulf War. He flew more than 500 combat missions in Vietnam, earning a remarkable 11 Distinguished Flying Crosses. But after he was nominated to lead the Pacific Command, he ran afoul of charges that he may have mishandled a sexual harassment inquiry. In fact, all he did was sign off on a lower level report, but the Tailhook scandal has elevated every sexual harassment charge to holy writ.

In the case Admiral Arthur approved, the Navy found that the complaining woman officer had indeed been subject to sexual harassment, and disciplined a flight instructor. When she failed a later flight course, she charged that her grades had been marked down because of the first incident. The Navy said she failed on performance, and the inspectors general of both the Navy and Defense Department agreed.

Yet Admiral Arthur's nomination was held up by Senator David Durenberger, himself currently under indictment for cooking his expense accounts. And though we might have thought an Administration having to cope with Paula Corbin Jones would give the benefit of the doubt to anyone wrapped up in a harassment case, a politically intimidated Navy withdrew the promotion.

Meanwhile, the same Administration is doing all it can to save Mr. Dalton, a Clinton fund-raiser and a graduate of the Stephens financial empire. It now informs reporters that he did in fact report his chairmanship of Seguin Savings Association, though only on a form that isn't routinely released to the press. But his formal Navy biography mentions not Seguin but only its holding company, Freedom Capital Corp. As for the condo loan, Mr. Dalton says that he delayed repayment because he thought he was going to be able to repurchase the mortgage.

Mr. Dalton says he merely got caught like others in the oil and real estate bust of the mid-1980s. But the same Members of Congress who gave him a pass were never so forgiving to Neil Bush. Even if Mr. Dalton is telling the truth when he says that, "I raised this issue from day one" with Clinton officials, it's clear that Clinton officials and Sam Nunn didn't want to raise the issue with other Senators, much less the rest of America. Senator Nunn says that closed hearings were needed because the information was in an FBI background report, and that Mr. Dalton's settlement with regulators contained a clause saying that both parties were obligated to "not initiate the release of any information to the media regarding the Settlement Agreement." How convenient.

In the Whitewater hearings yesterday, the mores of both the Clinton Administration and the current Congressional leadership were painfully on display. Perhaps the glimpse will help the public understand how it can be that a naval hero finds his career detoured for innuendo, even while a well-connected S&L high-flier rises to run the same Navy.

REVIEW & OUTLOOK

Asides

The Coverup Hearings

You have to credit the Whitewater defense team with ingenuity. If you can get White House papers subpoenaed, then you can prevent their release. If you get a criminal investigation started, whenever anything sensitive comes up you can take the Fiske.

Now we learn how to conduct a coverup through public hearings. A Lloyd Cutler filibuster will put even the camera crew to sleep. While Mr. Cutler could talk indefinitely, today's less accomplished witnesses will get the benefit of the "five-minute rule." If they can keep their lips moving for five minutes, a Democratic Congressman will come on stage to bail them out.

The flaw (or saving grace, depending on how you look at it) is that Banking Committee Chairman Henry Gonzalez is innocent of any hidden partisanship. He keeps it right out front.

LEISURE & THE ARTS

Back Home With Slick Willie

By PHILIP TERZIAN

To those of us for whom Bill Clinton is a comic, rather than a malevolent or even an admirable, element in American political life,

 **Bookshelf**

"On the Make: The Rise of Bill Clinton" By Meredith L. Oakley

Meredith L. Oakley's "On the Make: The Rise of Bill Clinton" (Regnery, 592 pages, $24.95) may prove to be required reading. This thick volume is not so much about "the rise of Bill Clinton"—of which we know enough already—but about the whys and wherefores of his lifelong campaign for the presidency.

There is much that is amusing about this smart, profoundly instinctual, glad-handing politician and his friends, family and associates. But there is also much that is disconcerting, sometimes frightening.

Just as Bill Clinton is no Emperor Augustus, it must be said that Meredith L. Oakley is no Edward Gibbon. She is a longtime political reporter for the Arkansas Democrat-Gazette, not a stylish practitioner of English prose. Then again, she is neither a Friend of Bill nor an unrelenting critic of the governor-turned-president.

Mr. Clinton tends to have a polarizing, sometimes paralyzing, influence on most journalists; Ms. Oakley is an honorable exception. She does not embrace him with the nearly erotic fervor of some chat-show hosts, nor does she disdain the air he breathes. She is, instead, a solid, unpretentious chronicler of her subject, whom she first encountered at the dawn of his career. She recognizes strengths and weaknesses in equal measure, and lets her readers draw conclusions on their own.

Bill Clinton is, by the author's reckoning, an immensely skilled politician with a number of appealing, sometimes startling flaws. Chief among these is an inability to distinguish truth from fiction. Many presidents have possessed this charming trait—FDR loved to embroider his resume, Truman rewrote history to his liking—but few have been so compulsively deceptive, and self-deceptive, in executive life.

When Mr. Clinton told the nation's governors the other day that he was prepared to compromise on universal health care coverage, and then insisted the following morning that he hadn't said such things, he was merely persisting in a curious technique first honed in Arkansas. As Ms. Oakley observes, it is too early to discern whether Washington will tolerate such lapses as readily as Little Rock always did. But the signs, at this juncture, are not encouraging.

The other point the author tends to emphasize is the extent to which Bill Clinton, in office, is a creature of habit. All the mistakes that derailed his first term as governor, and led to his one and only statewide loss, have been repeated in his up-and-down, yes-but-no, roller-coaster presidency. His overconfidence, his contempt for opposition, his arrogance, his secretiveness, his immature subordinates, his weakness for betrayal—all these fascinating defects tend to put him in the sort of peril that delights Republicans and confounds his loyal allies.

His famous education-reform proposals, begun in his second gubernatorial term, are offered in evidence. They began with a series of heroic declarations, and public platforms for extended discussion, but were largely designed in private, under the watchful eye of Hillary Rodham Clinton. When they finally took legislative form, then-Gov. Clinton systematically responded to the various special interests that made up his constituency, betraying the reformers, subverting those supporters in the general assembly who had taken some risk by voting to raise taxes. The whole peculiar episode left Arkansas with a series of underfunded programs, accomplishing little for the schools, but giving Gov. Clinton a national reputation for brains, reform and innovation.

Does any of this sound familiar?

Indeed, the very characteristics that can make Bill Clinton so appealingly diverting on a national scale were always there in Arkansas, in shopping malls and diners instead of on MTV: his oily sincerity, self-pitying demeanor, aptitude for selling out his legislative patrons, fondness for state-federal partnerships and scams. Even Mrs. Clinton's periodic reinventions of her own image began a dozen years ago, and show no signs of stopping.

That is the professional Bill Clinton; the personal is more fun. As Ms. Oakley makes abundantly clear, the Clinton clan, from the musical Roger to the formidable Hillary, have given the nation its first Dogpatch presidency—an uncomfortable admission for an Arkansas reporter.

Forget Oxford: When the president talked wistfully of his AstroTurf-carpeted Chevrolet truck bed, he spoke from the heart. Those who wonder about the veracity of Gennifer Flowers or Paula Jones will profit from reading the biography of the president's father, or Ms. Oakley's rendition of the president's much-advertised academic career. And those of us who have emerged, drenched but still breathing, from the posthumous memoir by the president's mother will appreciate the author's corrective accounts of many famous anecdotes. From her skunk-style bouffant to her two-dollar wagers to her nursing career, which ended in a pair of patient deaths and lawsuits, Virginia Cassidy Blythe Clinton Dwire Kelly was clearly the formative influence on the nation's commander-in-chief.

Mr. Terzian writes a column from Washington for the Providence Journal.

Editorial Feature

Even These Non-Hearings Have Their Uses

Henry Gonzalez has always had a kind of odd charisma, and after watching the Texas Democrat conduct Whitewater hearings this week, I appreciate him even more. The man is without artifice. When Gonzo is going to stiff you, he tells you right to your face.

So Mr. Gonzalez is the perfect host for what may be the first non-hearings on a scandal in U.S. history. In a city of blue suits, the House Banking chairman dares to wear white. Among polished showmen, the Texan is all barbed wire. And while another Democrat might have played the TV smoothie and at least spoken about getting to the truth, Mr. Gonzalez is too honestly irascible for that.

Potomac Watch

By Paul A. Gigot

He simply declared at the start that doubts about Whitewater amount to no more than "outright lies, or distortions, or exaggerations." If you're going to hold non-hearings, you might as well have the chairman assert that there's nothing to hear.

In pursuing his strategy, Mr. Gonzalez has certainly been creative, if not subtle. On Tuesday the tactic was to let Lloyd Cutler, the White House replacement counsel, absolve everyone of everything while taking hours to do it. Most reporters naturally judged the hearings a bore, as Democrats hoped. Because Mr. Gonzalez imposed a five-minute rule on each member, stopping any good questioner in his tracks, the most memorable line of the week was,

"The time of the gentleman has expired."

Then yesterday Mr. Gonzalez pivoted neatly to employ a Tower of Babel play. This was to call all 10 White House witnesses, all at the same time, and all to be questioned by 51 committee members for five minutes each.

And to have them testify only after letting Bernard Nussbaum, the defrocked White House counsel and experienced trial lawyer, give another hours-long brief for the defense. Democrats had no real questions for Mr. Nussbaum but jabbered on anyway — no doubt hoping to keep questioning of the White House 10 off the evening news (and past a columnist's deadline).

Henry Gonzalez

Republicans haven't kept up with Gonzo's quick moves. Perhaps because as the minority they never get on TV, on Tuesday they made too many speeches. And of course, Republicans let themselves be hornswoggled from the beginning by agreeing to let special counsel Robert Fiske limit the scope of hearings.

Then yesterday Jim Leach, the cool and usually clear Republican, gave a long, convoluted opening statement that had something to do with Ptolemy and Copernicus, who haven't yet turned up in the Clinton White House.

Yet for all their evasion, even these non-hearings have so far been able to reveal some intriguing facts, and especially a list of Clinton administration contradictions. There's turmoil at the Treasury, for example, where Deputy Secretary Roger Altman and his boss, Lloyd Bentsen, don't recall what General Counsel Jean Hanson recalls. The betting here is that Ms. Hanson, the one without close ties to the White House, will be the first to lose her job.

There's also the news, broken merely in passing by Mr. Cutler, that Mr. Clinton himself was told of disputes over Mr. Altman's role, though in a March 7 press conference the president said he hadn't been.

We are even being asked to believe that, in Rush Limbaugh's phrase, some officials lied to their own diaries. According to Mr. Cutler, Mr. Altman now disavows his diary entries about Hillary Clinton's chief of staff, Maggie Williams. He had written that "on Whitewater, Maggie told me that HRC was 'paralyzed'" and that

"HRC doesn't want (the counsel) poking into 20 years of public life in Arkansas."

The Treasury chief of staff, Josh Steiner, will also reportedly deny his entries about Mr. Altman. Mr. Steiner had written that White House officials put "intense pressure" on Mr. Altman not to recuse himself from overseeing the regulators looking into Whitewater, lest Clinton aides have to cope with "people they didn't know." Maybe it's safe to keep a diary in Washington again if you can claim it's just your crack at the great American novel.

By taking the president's side so strenuously, congressional Democrats are gambling that Whitewater details are too obscure for Americans to care. But there's another possibility, which is that the public has already included Whitewater in its judgment about the Clinton presidency.

This would explain why he stands near 45% approval, despite a growing economy. Why voters dislike the Clinton health plan, even as they say they want reform. And why only 39% find Mr. Clinton "honest and trustworthy" in a USA Today-CNN poll — numbers usually accorded to used-car salesmen and journalists.

Perhaps voters outside Washington will see in these hearings a gaggle of politicians trying to defend an administration that inspires no confidence. British historian Paul Johnson writes in the new Commentary magazine about the sorry state of all Western leaders right now. Even America, he writes, is now led by a man "haunted by his disorderly past" and "increasingly entangled in the dishonest measures taken by himself and his staff to keep it buried."

Review & Outlook

Who Is Jack Ryan?

Among the Whitewater witnesses to come before Congress this week, potentially the most interesting is one of the most unheralded: John E. "Jack" Ryan, the career regulator left behind at the Resolution Trust Corp. when Friend of Bill Roger Altman departed. Mr. Ryan has been even more directly involved than Mr. Altman in some of the most curious aspects of the handling of Madison Guaranty, the Whitewater thrift.

Jack Ryan

Mr. Ryan might also be able to shed some light on the mystery of how the Bank of Credit & Commerce International won approval to buy First American Bank in Washington; he was head of Bank Supervision at the Federal Reserve when the purchase was approved. For that matter, during a brief sojourn in the private sector somehow not mentioned in recent biographies, he worked for a law firm connected to two other major financial scandals, the collapse of ESM securities in Florida and the related Ohio thrift debacle. Mr. Ryan came in as Mr. Altman's deputy at the RTC last January, along with RTC general counsel Ellen Kulka; White House counsel Bernard Nussbaum testified last week that both appointments were vetted by the White House.

"April stated very clearly that Ryan and Kulka, the 'head people,' would like to be able to say that Whitewater did not cause a loss to

Madison, but the problem is that so far no one has been able to say that to them," read notes of a conversation with RTC Washington attorney April Breslaw written by L. Jean Lewis, the senior criminal investigator in charge of the Madison Guaranty investigation in the RTC Kansas City office. Ms. Lewis responded that the Whitewater account alone might show losses exceeding $100,000.

Ms. Lewis was subsequently removed from the Madison case. Ms. Breslaw denied she had said the things recorded in Ms. Lewis's notes, but Rep. Jim Leach said Ms. Lewis's account was corroborated by a tape recording she had made and he had heard.

Under Mr. Ryan's tenure, the RTC also upheld Mr. Altman's unprecedented decision to deny Rep. Leach's requests for documents relating to Madison. Though the RTC had provided the minority staff of the banking committee with independent access to documents regarding other thrift scandals, Mr. Ryan wrote Rep. Leach that he was entitled only to documents "otherwise available to the public pursuant to the Freedom of Information Act."

We hope that when Mr. Ryan appears before the Senate Banking Committee this morning, the questioners will pause for a moment to complete his resume. When asked for a biography, the RTC supplies a release from the Office of Thrift Supervision, where Mr. Ryan served immediately before Mr. Altman chose him as a deputy. It says he joined the Fed in 1960 and served as Director of the Division of Banking Supervision and Regulation from 1977 to 1985. And that he joined the Federal Home Loan Bank of Boston in 1986, before moving to the OTS Atlanta office in 1989. Similar accounts appear in the Treasury news release announcing his RTC appointment and in an interview in the agency's own Resolution Trust News, entitled, "Getting to Know Acting CEO Jack Ryan."

In fact, according to news reports at the time, Mr. Ryan left the Fed in February of 1985 to become financial adviser to the Miami law firm of Arky, Freed, Stearns, Watson, Greer, Weaver & Harris, P.A. The next news report on his career comes in September 1986, with the announcement of his appointment to the Boston Home Loan Bank. Through an RTC spokesman, Mr. Ryan declined to be interviewed about his 18 months in the private sector.

Stephen Arky, head of the law firm that hired Mr. Ryan, committed suicide in July 1985, leaving a note declaring his innocence in the collapse of ESM Securities, and blaming his friend and client Ronnie

Ewton. Mr. Arky was also son-in-law and business partner of Marvin Warner, owner of the Home State Savings Bank and also ambassador to Switzerland during the Carter Administration, partly thanks to Bert Lance, a banking friend from Georgia. The ESM collapse jeopardized Home State and led to runs on other state-insured thrifts in the 1985 Ohio banking crisis. Mr. Warner and Mr. Ewton served jail sentences for securities and banking fraud.

Senators responsible for banking regulation might want to inquire about Mr. Ryan's impression of these events, which seem to have taken place during his tenure at Arky, Freed. They might also ask about the 1981 regulatory failure that allowed front men for BCCI illegally to buy an important U.S. bank. Robert Altman was acquitted of misleading regulators, and his partner Clark Clifford was excused from trial because of age and infirmity. So we have no good account of what the mistake was.

In their cross-examination of Mr. Ryan and other witnesses at trial, Robert Altman's lawyers repeatedly suggested that the Fed was not misled because it already knew what was taking place. Mr. Ryan's supporters say that the federal regulator suspected that BCCI was behind the takeover, but lacking hard proof, did not have the political weight to go up against the mighty Mr. Clifford, a Washington icon.

Whatever the full story, Mr. Ryan joins a cast of figures with BCCI connections who also figure in the Whitewater controversy. Attorneys for Mr. Clifford and Mr. Altman included independent counsel Robert Fiske and Deputy Attorney General Jamie Gorelick, as well as Robert Bennett, President Clinton's attorney in the Paula Corbin Jones case. And, of course, Arkansas investment banking giant Stephens Inc., which says all connections with the BCCI front men ended in 1978, does acknowledge it handled their initial brokerage for the purchase.

Indeed, in the early takeover maneuvers Financial General Bankshares, First American's predecessor company, brought a 1978 lawsuit naming "Bert Lance, Bank of Credit & Commerce International, Agha Hasan Abedi, Eugene J. Metzger, Jackson Stephens, Stephens Inc., Systematics Inc. and John Does numbers 1 through 25." The suit was ultimately settled, but intriguingly, briefs for Systematics, a Stephens property, were submitted by a trio of lawyers including C.J. Giroir and Webster L. Hubbell and signed by Hillary Rodham.

We've compiled this list of coincidences in our role as aficionados of financial scandal, and recite it here because we're not confident either readers or Senators have been watching as carefully. We hope the Senate Banking Committee could help us understand what it means, if anything, and Mr. Ryan's testimony looks like a good opportunity to start.

REVIEW & OUTLOOK

Elephant in the Corner

While Roger Altman may be the last to understand, everyone else sees he's the designated fall guy in Whitewater, the Friend of Bill thrown off the back of the sleigh to allay the pursuing wolves. So when he appears before the Senate Banking Committee today, both Republicans and Democrats will be swarming over the various discrepancies and inconsistencies in his statements and contacts on the Resolution Trust Corp.'s handling of the case against Madison Guaranty and Whitewater. But will anyone notice the elephant in the corner?

To wit, Mr. Altman, how did you ever end up running the RTC in the first place? It's supposed to be an independent regulatory agency, and you are a political appointee at the Treasury. An independent regulator inevitably will and probably should be sensitive to an incumbent administration, but his first loyalty

Roger Altman

is to the mission of his own agency. This will not mix with your first loyalty, to the success of the President and his policies. Your tenure at the RTC was a conflict of interest waiting to happen, as it did in spades.

The history of Mr. Altman's dual role is worth recounting. Indeed, it tells more about the subversion of the regulatory process than Senators are likely to divine in the bones of his diary.

When the Clinton entourage arrived in town, the RTC was in the very capable and highly independent hands of former airline executive Albert Casey. He had managed to unload huge hunks of assets  from seized S&Ls, to the great benefit of the economic recovery. He planned to close the agency by the end of 1993, folding any remaining problems into the FDIC; he branded as "obscene" the agency's 81,000 lawsuits seeking retribution for S&L losses from their directors, their accountants and their cousins and aunts. Others, starting with Banking Chairman Don Riegle and Rep. Bruce Vento, had different ideas. So there were some scandals about what the RTC paid Price Waterhouse in copying charges.

Don Riegle

Days before President Clinton's inauguration, Mr. Casey submitted a letter of resignation effective when his successor was confirmed by the Senate. The RTC took the position that the agency could not function without a Senate-confirmed chief executive. But when Mr. Casey found no support in the Administration and especially when Treasury Secretary Bentsen joined the copying-cost outcry, he resigned, remarking, "I feel that they want their own person in there."

When Mr. Casey departed in March, Deputy Treasury Secretary Altman stepped into the breach, temporarily, they said, until a new permanent chief executive could be found. In mid-July, the Administration announced the selection of Stanley Tate, a Republican real estate developer from Miami. Mr. Altman's role was extended pending the nominee's confirmation, but Mr. Tate quickly became an object of controversy. He attended a meeting prematurely, it was alleged. "Whistleblowers" appeared to charge the agency was mismanaged, and Chairman Riegle demanded a plan to deal with their concerns. The veteran of the Keating Five and chairman of the current investigation refused even to schedule confirmation hearings on the new nominee.

So at the end of November Mr. Tate withdrew. He said he'd compiled a 200-page book on what was wrong with the agency. But he said "very high-level" Treasury officials warned that he should issue only a brief withdrawal statement, or he "would be dragged through the mud." Mr. Altman's role continued. A Treasury spokeswoman said that it would take time to find a new nominee for the permanent slot: "We really weren't prepared with a backup list."

In December, interim CEO Altman brought in a new team at the RTC, John E. Ryan as deputy director and Ellen Kulka as chief counsel. In February, Mr. Altman said on television that a new nominee as permanent CEO would be put forth "shortly," but nothing happened. Someone determined that Mr. Altman could continue as interim CEO for 120 days following Mr. Tate's withdrawal, and this period expired on March 30, 1994. Mr. Ryan, already handling the agency's day-to-day affairs, took over completely with Mr. Altman's official departure.

Mr. Ryan, "who will carry the title 'acting' CEO, can serve in that position indefinitely," a Treasury Department spokesman said. No Senate confirmation is required, he said, adding Treasury has no timetable for nominating a permanent CEO, the Dow Jones Ticker reported. As we explained yesterday, Mr. Ryan is one of the most important regulators who approved BCCI, and later left to work for a law firm with suspicious connections. Now he runs the supposedly independent RTC without benefit of Senate confirmation.

All this while, of course, the RTC has been dealing with a criminal complaint listing the President of the United States and the First Lady as possible witnesses in a case against their former friend and business partner. Was there undue influence? Do we really need to deconstruct Mr. Altman's diary to decide that? Nothing in its details is likely to be as compelling as what we already see on the face of the matter.

Editorial Feature

Dear Diary,
I Hope You Don't Get Subpoenaed

By THOMAS MALLON

Among the more interesting denials in the Whitewater affair is one from Reid Weingarten. He is the attorney for Joshua Steiner, the chief of staff to Treasury Secretary Lloyd Bentsen who testified yesterday before the Senate Banking Committee. Mr. Steiner's diary

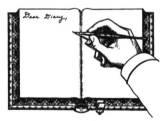

notes that Clinton advisers "told RA [Roger Altman] that it was unacceptable" for him to remove himself from the federal government's investigation of Whitewater — an awkwardly telltale entry that Mr. Weingarten explains by declaring: "It was never Josh's intention that the diary would be a complete and accurate recordation of historical events."

Mr. Weingarten's explanation may seem as curious as his diction, but that is only because of our relatively recent inclination to think of political diaries as forensic evidence. In the past two decades the term "private diary" has gone from being a redundancy to an oxymoron. Whenever a diary is now spied bobbing on the muck of scandal, a lunge is made for it.

It was, of course, the Nixon tapes, with their "smoking gun," that established the reflex. The tapes seemed like the ultimate diary, not so much a record of life as a replica of it, a mammoth auto-diary that served finally as an auto-da-fe. Since the 1970s, a politician's diary has been catnip to subpoenas. Some officeholders, like former Defense Secretary Richard Cheney, have refused to keep one; some, like Sen. Robert Packwood, may regret they did.

At yesterday's hearing, Mr. Steiner expressed the wish that his diary "was more accurate," but explained that the journal was "more than anything a way to reflect on events and draw lessons for my personal and professional experiences." Indeed, political diaries have never been notable for their accuracy. They are usually less full of facts than spin, with ample portions of anger, self-pity and puffed-up pride.

The recent best-selling, egoless "Haldeman Diaries" are extremely unusual in the absence of these things. Even in their printed (as opposed to CD-ROM) format, they come so close to uncommented-upon exactitude as to feel slightly cyber. "P" moves through them, unjudged, like the flashing cursor on a computer screen. Take this entry for Aug. 3, 1972: "The P had E [John Ehrlichman] in this morning to discuss the basic problem of domestic intelligence, the need for our moving on IRS and Justice to get some action on tax and other matters involving people supporting the opposition."

President Nixon's own diary — not the tapes, but the one he dictated — is far more typical, and exposing. Note his account of the same Aug. 3 meeting: "Haldeman said after the election we really could then take the steps to get loyalists in various positions that were sensitive. Of course, we should have long ago. Certainly we have been above reproach in this respect and have not used the enormous powers of the office — the Internal Revenue files, the Justice Department files. . . ." Here, with the accidental revelation of apologia, is the essential Nixon, reproaching himself for being above reproach. Mr. Haldeman gives you the facts, but Mr. Nixon, blind to it himself, provides the higher truth.

Perhaps the most useful political diaries — to the politician as well as posterity — are the ones in which the writer actually is, if only for a moment, onto himself. Mario Cuomo's journal of his 1982 campaign for the New York governorship, full of aggrieved piety and sentimental determination, sounds in most places like the answers he's doled out to interviewers a dozen times during the day now ending. Even an entry made at 4:30 a.m. on Oct. 22, 1982 — in which Mr. Cuomo tries to overcome momentary discouragement by recalling how his immigrant father re-rooted a big spruce tree that had been knocked over by a storm ("we gonna push 'im up, he's gonna grow again") —

sounds like the draft of a speech, missing only the Neil Diamond music to accompany it.

And yet, here and there are moments when writing the diary leaves Mr. Cuomo wiser for having faced a few facts: "Whether in tragedy or triumph, my psyche seems incapable of going all the way. There is a balance wheel that drives me back. . . ." If his decision not to run for president a decade later was personally a good one, he probably owes a debt to his diary-keeping for whatever self-knowledge went into making the choice.

British politicians still speak better on their feet than their American counterparts; they also write better sitting down. In recent decades, a number of absorbing parliamentary diaries have seen the published light of day. The latest of these to come along is Alan Clark's, due out in the U.S. next month under the title "Mrs. Thatcher's Minister."

The son of Baron Kenneth Clark ("Civilisation"), Alan Clark entered the government in 1983 as parliamentary undersecretary of state at the Department of Employment: "I just can't make up my mind if I want a job or not," he writes on June 5, before immediately coming clean with himself. "Fool, Clark, of course you do." But in the diary, he remains aware of the war between his political ambition and country-squire contentment: "I'm not a 'hungry fighter,' being too fond of my Baldwinesque leisure and hobbies."

It is this lack of single-mindedness — along with the uninterrupting ear of the diary — that allows him to make a hilariously candid account of all the busy-work, arse-licking and envy that go with being in service to a "shameless and brave" leader, "the Lady." Mr. Clark charts his own physical decline and restless libido, worrying about dismissal and staying on for all the wrong reasons: "I'd gladly chuck the whole thing . . . if it were not for the satisfaction this would give to others."

Like the greatest diarists, Mr. Clark has a self-fascination large enough to cherish even his most ridiculous moments. Outside his office, there "is a tiny *balcon,* a gutter really, with a very low parapet, below knee height. Certain death on the Victoria Street pavement eight floors below. Sometimes I get a wild urge to relieve my bladder over it, splattingly on the ant-like crowds. Would this get one the sack?"

He is a better man for having written such nonsense — and for being able to publish it at a moment of his own choosing. The self-deception that comes from being in a business requiring mass approval makes it important that the diary remain available to politicians, even functionaries like Mr. Steiner, as the one private place where they have an honest opportunity to shake hands with themselves.

Mr. Mallon, whose new novel is "Henry and Clara" (Ticknor & Fields), is the author of "A Book of One's Own: People and Their Diaries" (Penguin, 1986) and literary editor of GQ.

REVIEW & OUTLOOK

What Has Fiske Wrought?

The week of Whitewater hearings has been illuminating after all; indeed it will take time to plumb the significance of revelations such as the material reprinted nearby. But already two things are clear.

Henry Gonzalez is a disgrace, and Robert Fiske looks curiouser and curiouser.

By putting Chairman Gonzalez on the nation's TV screens, the House hearings gave a big boost to the movement for term limits. His colleagues have long understood him as a preposterous figure, of course, but the system nonetheless assigns him a post of high responsibility. Indeed, other Democrats on his committee sheepishly join him in turning an inquiry into a blatant cover-up, for which they should be held to account.

Robert Fiske

It need not be, as the Senate hearings demonstrated. Despite ethical clouds over both the chairman and the ranking minority member, the Senators did a quite creditable job of probing the sliver of territory special counsel Fiske deigned for them.

By the end of the week, Administration spokesmen had clearly established an image of people with something to hide. The nation is naturally curious about what it is, but Mr. Fiske won't tell, or even let anyone ask. The hearings were limited to two items: Vincent Foster's death, which Mr. Fiske had ruled a suicide, and moreover declared that there was no evidence linking his depression to Whitewater. And White House contacts regarding the Resolution Trust Corp. investigation into Madison Guaranty and Whitewater; Mr. Fiske had finished this investigation by deciding there was "insufficient evidence" that it was anyone's "intent" to derail the investigation. The likes of Whitewater itself in Arkansas, or the handling of Mr. Foster's papers after his death, were off limits because Mr. Fiske hadn't made up his mind about them.

A moment's reflection on the week's revelations, though, reveals that these distinctions are arbitrary if not ludicrous. How can you make any decisions about the Washington contacts without understanding what happened in Arkansas? You're not likely to find a memo to Roger Altman saying deep-six this Madison investigation or we're all going to jail. Power in Washington is exercised by, say, keeping a friend in a position to erect bureaucratic detours until the statute of limitations runs out. In deciding the "intent" of the "Washington phase," wouldn't you inquire about motive, which is to say, what folks now in Washington actually had to fear from the "Arkansas phase"?

Worse, Mr. Fiske's distinctions can only have the effect, intended or not, of erecting a fire-wall around high officials in Washington. Naturally they would like their winks and nods weighed as only that, without reference to their effect in the real world. Rep. Jim Leach now reports that one day after a White House meeting, the RTC headquarters started a legal review that tried to delay the criminal referral in *Madison*. L. Jean Lewis, the RTC Kansas City criminal investigator, clearly felt pressure to quench her probe of Madison. She was interviewed by Mr. Fiske's office, but so far as RTC press officials know, did not appear before the Washington grand jury that ruled on the intent of the White House contacts.

The same kind of artificiality appears in Mr. Fiske's attempts to acquit Whitewater in Mr. Foster's suicide. Of course he didn't fret aloud over Whitewater with his wife or friends; the whole reason for suspecting he might have worried about it is that his closest associates worried enough to want control of the Whitewater papers in his office. But Mr. Fiske can tell us Whitewater worries were not a factor in the suicide without telling us what he's learned about what happened to the papers. Some early reports raised suspicions they'd been tampered with the night of his death. Now the White House admits that before being turned over to a lawyer they were stored for five days in the family quarters of the White House.

We do not question Mr. Fiske's basic conclusion that the Foster death was a suicide due to depression. And we have a certain sympathy with his decision not to indict Washington officials. We hope we don't arrive at a point where it's illegal for the White House to inform itself of what the government's doing. We think the coerced plea bargain under which Elliott Abrams confessed to not fully informing Congress was a travesty we do not want to see repeated with Roger Altman or Jean Hanson. A good browbeating by a Senate committee and wrecked public careers may be quite sanction enough.

If, that is, there really was no intent to obstruct justice. But on this key point, the past week leaves us less persuaded than we were on reading Mr. Fiske's original report. With Lloyd Cutler playing Fiske games on redaction (see nearby), are we to believe anything of the rest? What was the ultimate source of the pressure felt in RTC Kansas City? What does it mean that President Clinton wants his face on TV this week, too, professing that he believes Mr. Altman's latest explanations even if no one else does?

The public and the political process will be in a state of perpetual confusion until Whitewater is resolved, and the immediate obstacle to any resolution is Robert Fiske. Or perhaps more charitably, the very notion of special counsels. The criminal process and open politics do not mix, and in nearly all cases the latter needs to take precedence. Mr. Fiske's elevation to a court-appointed independent counsel is still pending; the panel ought to at least tell him to stick to any indictments and stop providing an excuse for a cover-up.

More to the point, the Senate and House ought to go ahead with the remainder of their responsibilities. Fiske or no, they have an obligation to hold more hearings to tell us about the rest of Whitewater.

Editorial Feature

From the Whitewater Folder
Today we present some documents from this week's
Whitewater hearings. First, we print a statement delivered
Wednesday by Rep. James Leach (R., Iowa), the ranking
minority member on the House Banking Committee, which
includes a report of an RTC legal review starting one day after
a White House meeting, and discussion of Washington contacts
with RTC Kansas City investigators.

Mr. Leach also demands a review of all documents that
have been redacted, the process by which the White House
staff blacks out sections of documents it judges are not rele-
vant to the hearings. Second, we reprint materials on a
redacted document supplied in full under pressure from the
Senate Banking Committee.

Candor Was the Casualty...

As we return to this theater of the surreal, if not the absurd, with
its "shut-up" standard of comity, and its "shut-down" dismissal of
free inquiry into the causes of taxpayer losses associated with a failed
savings and loan in Arkansas, where are we in this probe?

The limited subject matter of these hearings — White House contacts
with the Treasury and Resolution Trust Corp. — is sandwiched between
two circumstances: a) conflicts of interest in Arkansas that led to a $67
million loss to the taxpayer; and b) efforts by one part of the RTC to
delay and object to criminal referrals developed by another part.

Here let me lay on the record the following new facts. While White
House witnesses denied any improprieties in their contacts with the
Treasury and RTC, and left the impression that no overt or subtle
hints for action were related to appointees in the regulatory agencies,

it is impressive that one day after the Sept. 29 meeting at the White House an unprecedented legal review of the referrals was commenced. On Sept. 30, the Professional Liability Section of the RTC attempted to negotiate a three-week delay before submission of the referrals to the Justice Department. One week was agreed to by the Kansas City criminal investigations unit. Subsequently a legal analysis was developed objecting to the criminal unit's conclusions primarily on statute of limitations and double jeopardy grounds.

According to testimony [that] Acting RTC General Counsel Glion Curtis gave the Treasury inspector general, [Treasury General Counsel] Jean Hanson appears to have been consulted on the development of the critical legal analysis on Oct. 4. On the 8th the analysis was provided [to] the criminal investigations unit, which held firm, refusing to capitulate to PLS objections. The referrals were then sent to the U.S. attorney in Little Rock. So apparently, in an unprecedented procedure, were the PLS objections.

It may be true that criminal referrals were not effectively blocked, but it is not true that an effort to do so was not made. There is, for instance, a Sept. 30 e-mail from RTC-PLS attorney Julie F. Yanda to L. Richard Iorio, head of the Kansas City criminal investigations unit, which establishes that Glion Curtis, who apparently at this time reported "de facto" to Ms. Jean Hanson, was in telephone contact with Kansas City about the referrals on that date.

In retrospect, the testimony of White House witnesses last week remind[s] me of the comments journalist I.F. Stone made of Pentagon body counts during the Vietnam War. Pentagon spokesmen weren't telling complete falsehoods, Stone argued, but they failed to reveal the full story. It would be, he suggested, like bumping into a man running out of a bank with a satchel full of money, waving a gun, and asking: What are you doing? If the man answered that he was waiting for a car, he would be telling the truth but not presenting a fair representation of the circumstances.

The "see no wrong, hear no wrong, do no wrong" assertions of the White House staff are premised on the notion that it is not wrong to provide insider notification to a public official of the details of a criminal investigation being commenced against him, despite the fact that the official could realistically expect that elements of the federal bureaucracy, especially his political appointees and private-sector friends, especially those also potentially touched by the investigation, might have reason to help him, either in stalling an investigation or frustrating a probe through evidence destruction.

Today candor and cronyism are on trial. On the one hand we have a witness [Treasury Deputy Secretary Roger Altman] who testified to one known agency contact with the White House, which now turns out to be 40. On the other, we have an independent institution, the RTC, run for a year by [Mr. Altman], who was a college buddy of the president but who was confirmed by the Senate not for an RTC job but for a Treasury post. Clearly, as evidenced in the president's reported anger at Mr. Altman's recusal almost a year after he ran the agency, the president wanted his man to be in charge of his investigation.

As for the Altman-directed briefings of the White House on the referrals, it should be clarified that they were not reviews of press inquiries. It appears that the press had gotten wind of the existence of the 1992 referral and an inkling of the possibility that a campaign referral was in the works, but the White House, as established by [White House attorney] Cliff Sloan's Sept. 30 notes, was apparently briefed on key points in all the referrals, including the possibility that [Arkansas] Gov. [Jim Guy] Tucker and [former] Sen. [J. William] Fulbright might be subjects, which wasn't known to the press for another six to nine months.

With regard to information passed on to the White House counsel's office, it should be pointed out that no precautions were taken to limit access to the information to nonsubjects of a criminal probe, and with respect to the information immediately shared with [presidential adviser Bruce] Lindsey (not a member of the counsel's office) no precautionary warnings were given to ensure that he did not mention such to the president and first lady, who at this early point in the investigation were witnesses and possible beneficiaries of alleged criminal acts.

The importance of the potential exposure of the Clintons [is] highlighted in the following two sentences from the previously redacted [White House Associate Counsel W. Neil.] Eggleston memo: "The RTC could also sue outsiders, including the President and Mrs. Clinton, if the RTC found that the outsiders worked with insiders illegally to divert assets of the savings and loan. For example, if the RTC believed that the Clinton campaign knowingly diverted Madison assets at the April 19 fundraiser or that the Clintons knowingly received other diverted Madison Guaranty assets through

Whitewater, it could bring suit." Given that prospect, how could the White House counsel's office not be mobilized?

Moreover, the repeated assertion that this information was being accepted in order to conduct official, press and other business is neither sensible nor consistent with the facts. It is not sensible because the White House could have avoided press inquiries easily by referring them to the RTC and the Justice Department. It is inconsistent with the facts because it is clear this information was not used for the very purpose it was supposedly needed [for] — that is, to keep the president from meeting with people or doing things which might reflect poorly on either him or his office. In that regard, [White House Counsel Bernard] Nussbaum, Messrs. Sloan, Eggleston and Lindsey were all aware prior to Oct. 6, 1994 that Gov. Tucker might be a subject of one of nine criminal referrals. Surely one of them should have advised the president about not attending that meeting. Moreover, Mr. Lindsey, besides briefing the president, followed up certain press inquiries by requesting Clinton '84 campaign documents at a time he was aware that they might possibly be the focus of an RTC criminal investigation.

With regard to the RTC, it appears that an extensively redacted memo about the status of the RTC's reinvestigation of Madison, the subject of which was leaked to the press, represented insider information given Treasury. Given the startling relevance of the memorandum to the first lady, the Senate demanded it be provided in full. I would renew my request that the White House allow majority and minority counsel to review all redacted material.

Finally, let me conclude by observing that the minority had hoped these hearings would be conducted very differently. A government of too little candor cannot be overseen by a legislative body with too much partisan control. The minority chafes at the scope of the hearings, at the majority's refusal to acknowledge and address the egregious conflicts of interest which precipitated the investigation of Whitewater in the first place, and at a process barren of comity and common sense.

Just as no president is entitled to insider notification of criminal proceedings, no Congress is entitled to stifle the public's right to know.

JAMES A. LEACH

...And Redaction
the Weapon of Choice

"We have not redacted anything relevant to the committee's inquiries, and I'd like to add that as a lawyer who has been in the business of producing documents to other lawyers for a good 50 years, this is the first time that any other lawyer has ever questioned whether the production of redacted documents under my supervision has been unethical."

— LLOYD CUTLER, special counsel to the president, before the House Banking Committee on July 26, 1994.

Friday July 29, 1994:

Joint statement by Chairman Donald W. Riegle Jr. and Ranking Minority Member Alfonse D'Amato, of the Committee on Banking, Housing and Urban Affairs. . . .

"Mr. Cutler has today at the Committee's request released the full contents of a March 1 memorandum previously provided to the Committee in redacted form. We are appreciative of the willingness of the White House to go beyond the Committee's earlier request and to provide this additional material. We commend the White House for its good faith and cooperation in this matter."

* * *

[In the following, the bold-face material had previously been redacted, presumably because Mr. Cutler's office judged it not relevant to the congressional inquiry as limited by the narrow guidelines established in agreement with Independent Counsel Robert Fiske:]

Memorandum

Confidential

To: The First Lady

From: Harold Ickes

Date: 1 March 1994

Re: Resolution Trust Corp.

Attached is a copy of W. Neil Eggleston's 28 February 1994 memorandum to me regarding certain issues involving the RTC and Rose Law Firm ("Rose"). . . .

It is my understanding that shortly after Roger Altman met with Bernie Nussbaum, me and others concerning the RTC statute of limitations, he received an opinion from an ethics officer of the Treasury Department that he, as the acting head of the RTC, did not have to recuse himself from matters involving Rose/Madison Guaranty. I will confirm this situation.

Please let me know if you want to discuss the attached.

[Attached was a 35-page memo, all of which had been previously redacted. Some highlights:]

Memorandum for Harold Ickes

Deputy Chief of Staff

From: W. Neil Eggleston

Associate Counsel to the President

Re: Whitewater — FDIC and RTC Rose Law Firm Issues

The recent release of the FDIC and RTC reports addressing the possible conflict of the Rose Law Firm in its representations of Madison Guaranty raises a number of issues. . . .

On the factual issue of whether the Rose law firm had disclosed to the FDIC its prior representation of Madison Guaranty, the FDIC concluded that the record was unclear. . . . On the issue of whether Mr. Hubbell had disclosed his relationship with his father-in-law, Seth Ward, who was then in litigation with Madison Guaranty, the FDIC stated that it was uncertain whether Mr. Hubbell had disclosed the relationship. Nevertheless, the relationship was plainly known to the FDIC within three months of retention. . . .

As noted above, it is not clear whether the FDIC or the RTC will review this matter under an actual conflict standard or as an appearance of conflict standard. . . . The most severe sanction that would likely flow from a finding that the Rose law firm had a duty to disclose its prior representation of Madison Guaranty and its relationship with Mr. Ward and that it breached that duty would be that the Rose law firm would be permanently barred from any further work for the RTC or the FDIC. . . .

Under the facts as we now understand them, it would seem quite unlikely that the RTC could bring a civil action against the Rose firm or any of its attorneys for failure to disclose the conflict. . . . Criminal liability for the Rose firm would seem even more remote. . . .

The RTC is investigating whether it has a civil tort action against anyone who caused a loss to Madison Guaranty. This would include insiders such as James and Susan McDougal and members of the Board of Madison. It also includes professionals who provided service to Madison Guaranty, such as the Rose law firm, other law firms, and accounting firms. The Frost & Co. suit is an example of a suit against a professional service provider that caused loss to Madison Guaranty through a negligent audit. The RTC could also sue outsiders, including the President and Mrs. Clinton, if the RTC found that outsiders worked with insiders illegally to divert assets of the savings and loan. For example, if the RTC believed that the Clinton campaign knowingly received diverted Madison assets at the April 1985 fundraiser or that the Clintons knowingly received other diverted Madison Guaranty assets through Whitewater, it could bring suit. The RTC commonly sues the recipient of a loan where it has information that the borrower knew that the loan was improper. . . .

Now that Mr. Altman as Acting CEO of the RTC has recused himself from further involvement in Madison Guaranty matters, who at the RTC will be the decision-maker on whether to bring a civil action arising out of the failure of Madison Guaranty?

The top official at the RTC who will be making these decisions on Madison Guaranty is Jack Ryan. Mr. Ryan was formerly with the Office of Thrift Supervision. He is a career official. His principal adviser will be Ellen Kulka, now General Counsel of the RTC, who also came from OTS. Ms. Kulka is also a career official. . . .

Editorial Feature

On Whitewater, Clinton Team Doesn't Inhale

In his Norman Vincent Peale-ish press conference this week, President Clinton tried the power of positive avoidance: "I've watched none of these hearings." That's a shame, because if he had tuned into the Whitewater proceedings, Mr. Clinton might better understand his credibility problem.

Last week's House farce mainly revealed Henry Gonzalez as a walking ad for term limits. But this week's Senate hearings revealed new information, exposed deceptions and altered reputations. It may not be O.J. and murder, but bearing false witness has its own drama. Donald Riegle, the Democratic banking chairman, has risen above his Keating Five past to conduct a fair, bipartisan probe.

Potomac Watch

By Paul A. Gigot

For viewers seeking a plot amid the blame-shifting and half-truths, here's one: How a White House, far more preoccupied with Whitewater than it ever admitted, worked to keep Friends of Bill in key jobs that could monitor any investigation and blunt political embarrassment. And then tried to conceal that intent.

Roger Altman, the conflicted deputy Treasury secretary, has been the main target, but he is also a victim. His mortal mistake was to play the too eager courtier.

His Treasury advisers, and probably his conscience, told him to recuse himself from running the Resolution Trust Corp., which was looking into Whitewater. He'd even decided to do it.

But under "intense pressure" from the White House, according to Treasury Chief of Staff Josh Steiner's now-famous diary, Mr. Altman changed his mind the next day (Feb. 3). Then three weeks later Mr. Altman "gracefully ducked" telling the Senate about this and other White House contacts.

That may not rank as a lie in Washington, but it also wasn't the truth. It's a lot like "didn't inhale," or the First Lady's making a commodities fortune just by reading The Wall Street Journal.

Mr. Altman may be the only person in America who thinks his recusal had nothing to do with Whitewater. His sincere evasions were too much even for nonpartisan New Mexico Republican, and Altman friend, Pete Domenici, who concluded that, "You were expected to stay there for some very special reason."

Mr. Clinton's defenders, trying to limit the damage, claim that "nothing happened" to the

Roger Altman

Whitewater probe because of this. But the point is that nothing had to happen. The White House knew that the statute of limitations on any Whitewater civil suit would expire on Feb. 28. If it could keep Mr. Altman in his chair through that date, he could ensure that nothing happened to extend the statute. (Under media pressure, Congress expanded it anyway.)

Besides, something may have happened that we don't yet know about. Rep. Jim Leach has released (see nearby) evidence that suggests that someone at the RTC did try to interfere with Whitewater criminal referrals to the Justice Department. Given how much we've learned that the White House once dismissed as fanciful, one safe conclusion is that there's more to learn.

White House worry over Mr. Altman's recusal also makes more sense when you consider the other FOBs named to run key agencies that might deal with Whitewater. At the Comptroller of the Currency's office, Mr. Clinton placed his old Oxford chum Eugene Ludwig. Thanks to these hearings, we know the president asked him for Whitewater "advice" last New Year's weekend.

To run the Federal Deposit Insurance Corp., Mr. Clinton tried to appoint Ricki Tigert, a friend of Hillary Clinton, before the Senate put her nomination on hold. On Feb. 1, Ms. Tigert told the Senate she wouldn't recuse herself from Whitewater matters; we now know that was the same week the White House leaned on Mr. Altman not to recuse.

Meanwhile, Webb Hubbell was well positioned to monitor criminal referrals at Justice, while Paula Casey, another Arkansas crony, was named U.S. attorney in Little Rock. If there's nothing to hide on Whitewater, why the all-star FOB lineup?

Even now bobs and weaves continue, even at the top. On Wednesday, Mr. Clinton was asked about Josh Steiner's diary entry noting that he'd been "furious" when Mr. Altman finally did decide to recuse himself from the RTC.

"The only thing that upset me was I did not want to see him stampeded into it," Mr. Clinton replied. But the only stampede was at the White House, and the horses were asking Mr. Altman to do just the opposite — to refuse to recuse.

Mr. Steiner now claims he lied to his diary. Maggie Williams, Hillary Clinton's chief of staff, doesn't recall saying what Mr. Altman's diary claims she said. So many people can't recall so much that one wag says the young Clinton aides must be suffering from attention deficit disorder.

So while these hearings haven't revealed crimes, they have revealed a political mindset of conceal and evade, a pattern of behavior that goes to the heart of public confidence. White House officials say they desperately want Americans to believe that the Clinton presidency is "productive." But they might have better luck making their case if they understood that Americans also care if their leaders lie.

REVIEW & OUTLOOK

Next, Empower the Minority

Kenneth Starr's appointment as independent counsel for Whitewater at least provides the opportunity for a new look, but in truth the problem with the post far transcends Robert Fiske. Whatever his name or views, an independent counsel has too heavy a load to carry. The answer to the Constitutional question of how to investigate political scandals is more likely to be found in Rep. James Leach's lawsuit to compel agencies to cooperate with investigations by the Congressional minority.

For an independent counsel we much prefer, as we have said from the first, someone who was never a lawyer to BCCI figures. And we devoutly hope that Mr. Starr will adopt the attitude toward Congress expressed by Lawrence Walsh and Judge Charles Richey, that an independent counsel should respect the Congressional prerogative to investigate. Congressional oversight is a powerful investigatory tool more likely to advance than impede criminal probes – even, as we've seen in the last week, when limited by Mr. Fiske's strictures.

Kenneth Starr

Still, we have now had two awful experiences with independent counsel. First Mr. Walsh's Ahab-like quest for the Iran-Contra whale, and now Mr. Fiske's damper on public accountability for the conduct of justice and banking regulation. This should warn everyone that something is wrong with the conception for the office, as we have in fact argued from the outset. A prosecutor is supposed to follow criminal procedure rule 6 (e), keeping grand jury testimony secret except in an indictment or trial. Yet we expect independent counsel also to inform the public about the scandals we hand them. While we admire Mr. Starr, even he cannot follow these two masters.

We would do better to stop searching for philosopher kings to deal with our scandals. Thankfully, our government does not depend on virtue but on checks and balances. The Founding Fathers may not have anticipated organized political parties, but they very well understood both the dangers and uses of factions. While partisanship is out of fashion in today's conventional wisdom, who but the minority is to scrutinize the majority?

Jim Leach

In Federalist No. 10 Madison observed that factions simply cannot be eliminated from government. He further warned, "It is in vain to say that enlightened statesmen will be able to adjust these clashing interests and render them all subservient to the public good. Enlightened statesmen will not always be at the helm." The alternative Madison elaborated in the Federalist No. 51:

"Ambition must be made to counteract ambition. The interests of the man must be connected with the constitutional rights of the place. It may be a reflection on human nature that such devices should be necessary to control the abuses of government. But what is government itself but the greatest of all reflections on human nature?" Madison concluded, "In framing a government which is to be administered by men over men, the great difficulty lies in this: you must first enable the government to control the governed, and in the next place oblige it to control itself."

Rep. Leach's lawsuit before Judge Richey goes to the heart of this great issue of checks and balances. As ranking member of the House Banking Committee, he seeks to compel the Resolution Trust Corp. and Office of Thrift Supervision to honor his request for Whitewater documents, over the objection of Chairman Henry Gonzalez. The issue, in short, is whether the Congressional majority can frustrate an investigation by the minority. The agencies take the position that Rep. Leach is only an individual Congressman, with no more rights than a private citizen.

Put in balder terms, John E. Ryan, the acting CEO of the RTC whose resume we detailed last week, declares that his obligation to Congress begins and ends with Chairman Gonzalez, whose performance at the hearings led the New York Times to brand him a "court jester." Jonathan Fiechter, acting director of the OTS also never subject to Senate confirmation, takes the same position. The facts of the case cry out for some recognition of Mr. Leach's position as "shadow chairman" of the committee overseeing these agencies.

Parliamentary governments have a "question hour," forcing incumbent administrations to respond to the minority. For that matter, the independent counsel act itself gives the minority a right to trigger an investigation, recognizing its special role in policing the majority. And if it is to fulfill this role, surely the minority needs access to information.

Align the interests of the man with the Constitutional rights of the place, Madison suggested. The public's interest in policing its government is parallel to the minority's interest in discovering its wrongdoing by the majority. We can let Mr. Starr or Mr. Fiske or Mr. Walsh clean up criminal cases, but we need not ask them to be philosopher kings and also inform the public. We can do the latter simply enough by empowering the minority with its own right to inquire and investigate.

REVIEW & OUTLOOK

Closing a Case

If nothing else ever comes of last week's Whitewater hearings, they did point toward one clear legislative reform. Congress needs to revisit 18 U.S. Code Sec. 1751, the President and Presidential Staff Assassination Statute.

This law requires that the FBI investigate the assault, kidnapping or homicide of a high government official. As Deputy White House Counsel, the late Vincent Foster would have been among the officials covered, but instead his death was investigated by the U.S. Park Police. The FBI did not take over because, rather than an assault, kidnapping or homicide, Mr. Foster's death was an apparent suicide. This early impression has of course since been confirmed, to our satisfaction and nearly everyone's, by Robert Fiske's workmanlike report, which drew a compelling picture of clinical depression.

Even so, the case shows that the law should be amended to include any sudden death among covered officials. Considering the stressful situation, the Park Police did about as well as anyone has a right to expect, but they were not the FBI.

Park Police investigator John Rolla testified that he and his colleague Cheryl Braun were "stonewalled" at the Foster home. Park Police Sergeant Braun said she had just begun an interview with Mr. Foster's sister when Associate Attorney General Webster Hubbell entered the home and pushed her aside; Ms. Braun says she is uncertain whether Mr. Hubbell's actions were "a function of grief" or an attempt "to prevent me, you know, from getting information." A few minutes later the President of the United States himself showed up, ending all investigation.

The next day, Park Police investigators were barred from Mr. Foster's White House office. When they returned the following day, they were made to wait in the hall while Counsel Bernard Nussbaum and his staff retrieved documents — including Whitewater material which, we learned last week, was delivered to the family quarters of the White House.

Mr. Foster's autopsy was performed by James Beyer, chief medical examiner for northern Virginia. No X-rays were taken; "We'd been having difficulty with our equipment and were not getting readable X-rays," Dr. Beyer explained. He declined to call a nearby hospital for a portable X-ray machine, saying the nature of the wound did not require it. Yet the autopsy report showed that X-rays had been taken; Dr. Beyer told the Senate panel that he had completed the first pages of his report before actually performing the autopsy. The initial autopsy also missed chemical traces in blood later found by the FBI lab.

Laying aside serious questions on the handling of papers, we find nothing sinister here. Dr. Beyer has performed numerous autopsies, and his judgment proved correct about what was needed to resolve this individual case. The President's actions and Mr. Hubbell's are entirely human, and early reports denying signs of clinical depression are also typical. In the wake of a suicide, complex emotions of grief and guilt batter surviving friends and associates. The gaps are probably not particularly unusual.

The Presidential assassination statute says, however, that in such cases there is a public interest in closing as many gaps as possible. White House officials deal in high-stakes policy, after all, and intelligence services, drug kings and Mafia dons have been known to disguise assassinations as suicides, accidental deaths or even illness. A President should not be put in the position of having to worry about what agency should investigate the death of a friend and colleague; cases of FBI jurisdiction should be immediate and automatic.

A few liberal commentators complained about Senator Lauch Faircloth and other Republicans asking any question about the suicide, but no part of the hearing had a clearer legislative purpose. An unambiguous law would have averted much doubt and uncertainty, not only for the country but for the Foster family. And amending the statute would provide a fitting closure to a tragic case.

REVIEW & OUTLOOK

Who Is Paula Casey?

Even in a hearing about White House contacts, Senator Lauch Faircloth found in the exchange reprinted nearby, White House contacts with Paula Casey were "out of the realm." Paula Casey is U.S. Attorney for the Eastern District of Arkansas, and was instrumental in the Whitewater cases until she recused herself from them last November.

Paula Casey

Ms. Casey is also a long-time Friend of Bill (and Hillary). She first met the future President when she was his student at the University of Arkansas School of Law, Fayetteville, in 1976. She went on to work as a volunteer in every one of Mr. Clinton's many gubernatorial campaigns, as well as his successful presidential quest. Her husband was appointed to a state agency by Governor Clinton and currently is counsel to the Arkansas Public Service Commission.

Ms. Casey's career prior to becoming a U.S. Attorney intersects with the Clintons at many other points, for example a stint on Governor Clinton's Commission on Juvenile Justice. It includes early membership in Arkansas Advocates for Children and Families, founded by Hillary Rodham.

Ms. Casey, in short, is a strand in the web of Arkansas cronyism that gave birth to Whitewater. Doubtless after 16 years of Clinton campaigns, Ms. Casey is acquainted with Mack McLarty and Bruce

Lindsey and Betsey Wright and Jim Blair and Webster Hubbell and David Watkins and Jim Guy Tucker and James McDougal and David Hale and the rest of the Whitewater cast.

On August 16, 1993, she took office as U.S. Attorney in Little Rock under temporary court appointment. The previous March, the Justice Department had asked all the 93 sitting U.S. Attorneys to resign. July 20, Vincent Foster committed suicide, the same day a search warrant was issued for the offices of David Hale of Capital Management Services, Inc.

On Sept. 7, according to their later correspondence, Ms. Casey held discussions with Randy Coleman, Mr. Hale's attorney. In a plea bargain, the correspondence said, Mr. Hale would offer information on "the banking and borrowing practices of some individuals in the elite political circles of the State of Arkansas." (The increasingly acrimonious letters were reprinted on this page on March 4, 1994.)

Ms. Casey refused the plea bargain, and Mr. Hale was indicted on Sept. 23. On the same day, Ms. Casey was one of a group of U.S. attorneys formally appointed by the President after Senate confirmation. Upon his indictment, Mr. Hale told the Arkansas press that Bill Clinton and Jim Guy Tucker had urged him to make some of his bad loans. As later detailed, this included a loan of $300,000 to a company controlled by Susan McDougal, a partner with the Clintons in the Whitewater land deals; about $110,000 of this money ended up in a Whitewater account.

Also in late September 1993, investigators in the Resolution Trust Corp.'s Kansas City office informed the Justice Department they had received no notification of the disposition of Case #C0004, concerning Madison Guaranty and originally referred in September 1992 to Charles A. Banks, then U.S. attorney in Little Rock. According to a chronology prepared by Kansas City RTC, they also informed Justice that new referrals were pending. On Oct. 8, 1993, nine new criminal referrals were sent to Ms. Casey's office. RTC officials told the Senate Whitewater hearings that the new referrals named the Clintons and Arkansas Governor Jim Guy Tucker, among others, as possible witnesses to, or beneficiaries of, criminal actions.

On Oct. 27, Ms. Casey wrote L. Jean Lewis of the Resolution Trust Corp. that Justice had declined to pursue the criminal referral of Case #C0004, concerning Madison Guaranty. The letter said that, "The matter was concluded before I began working in this office, and I was unaware you had not been told. . . ." On Nov. 1, Ms. Lewis responded, "You stipulated in your letter that this matter was concluded prior to your tenure. . . . If there are other documents produced that are relative to the conclusion of this matter, I would appreciate receiving the appropriate copies."

On Nov. 9, the Department of Justice issued a press release saying that the Criminal Division was taking over the case involving Mr. Hale, Capital Management and Madison Guaranty. It said that Ms. Casey "informed the government last week that she and her staff had recused themselves because of their familiarity with some of the parties. . . ."

On Nov. 10, Ms. Lewis announced to her RTC colleagues that she had been replaced as lead investigator in Madison: "The Powers That Be have decided that I'm better off out of the line of fire (and I ain't arguing)." (The correspondence involving Ms. Lewis was released by Congressman Jim Leach, and reprinted here May 19, 1994.)

In January 1994, Robert Fiske was appointed special counsel for Whitewater, and in March he accepted guilty pleas on two charges of financial fraud from Mr. Hale. Sentencing was delayed for at least 120 days to allow testimony on his allegations. In questioning Attorney General Janet Reno before the Senate Judiciary Committee, as noted by William Safire of the New York Times last week, Senator Arlen Specter suggested that Mr. Fiske was conducting a criminal investigation of a U.S. Attorney for obstruction of justice. Mr. Fiske has of course since been replaced by Kenneth Starr. Possible criminal investigations entirely aside, though, Senator Faircloth's question remains pertinent.

It would indeed be interesting to know whether anyone at the White House was in contact with Ms. Casey. It would be especially interesting, for that matter, to know who made the decision to take Ms. Lewis off the Madison case, and why. But as the Senator noted, there are a lot of remaining questions waiting to be answered.

Editorial Feature

Bred in a One-Party State

By John H. Fund

LITTLE ROCK, Ark.—The Clinton administration is partisan, almost to the point of self-destruction. It managed to squeak its 1993 budget through Congress solely with Democratic votes, but last week its one-party approach led to a crime bill that couldn't pass. Hillary Rodham Clinton still hopes to push a health bill through the Senate with 51 Democratic votes, but that highly partisan approach has put the whole reform effort in peril. The Clinton plan, which the administration hatched in secret with Democratic allies, has already been interred.

By contrast, it was a bipartisan coalition that produced the administration's shining success, the ratification of the North American Free Trade Agreement. It remains a mystery, therefore, why an administration elected with 43% of the vote should continue to behave in such a relentlessly partisan manner.

A key to that mystery may lie back here in Arkansas, where the Clintons' political instincts were formed. The Washington Monthly claims that national reporters portray Arkansas "as a podunk swamp filled with hillbillies and nitwits." They don't, and that stereotype isn't accurate. What is true—and unarguable—is that Arkansas is a one-party state. Michael Kelly, author of a pathbreaking New York Times article last month called "The President's Past," notes that Arkansas "is not really a democracy" and is largely ruled "by a thin upper crust of Democratic Party officials and Democratic legislative leaders and important landholders and businessmen."

Bill Clinton never experienced two-party politics back home, so it should not be surprising that he can't effectively appeal for Republican congressional support, or that he reacts with such hostility to opponents.

Only two Republicans have won statewide in Arkansas in the past quarter-century. Indeed, an ideologically bankrupt GOP has often provided voters no choice at all. In 1992, there were 135 races for the state Legislature, of which Republicans won 15. An astounding 102 races, or 75%, had only one candidate on the November ballot, the highest percentage of any state. This year, GOP prospects for defeating Gov. Jim Guy Tucker are poor in part because the party's candidate, Sheffield Nelson, headed an agency under Bill Clinton and doesn't strike many as a genuine reformer.

Gov. Clinton inherited a well-oiled political machine and became its undisputed boss. Julia Hughes Jones, the state's elected auditor, has known Bill Clinton for 20 years. She says he has always been obsessed with political power. "He governed out of a textbook: a book on Mayor Richard Daley called 'Boss' by Mike Royko," she recalls. "He urged his aides to read it."

Mr. Clinton's machine and the business interests that backed it held such a firm grip on power in part because of Arkansas's unique political traditions. Among them:

• Arkansas is the only state where the political parties, and not the state, operate and pay for primary elections. The costs are covered by steep filing fees that serve as the equivalent of a poll tax on candidates. A place on the U.S. Senate primary ballot costs $9,000, the highest in the nation. Filing fees for local judgeships (judicial races are partisan) often range from $2,500 to $5,000. Running is affordable for the politically connected but not for unwanted outsiders.

Six counties do pay for party primaries, but almost always only for Democrats. The GOP filed suit against this peculiar system, and in a February decision Judge Stephen Reasoner, a chief U.S. district court judge, noted that under current law "the burdens placed on the Republican Party and upon voters are heavy." Judge Reasoner concluded that the law is discriminatory and prevents the growth of a viable two-party system. However, the state's right to decide its own electoral rules is such that he wasn't convinced that the burdens were unconstitutional. Nonetheless, he concluded that in Arkansas today:

"Influence is distributed on the basis of wealth. . . . The Democratic Party is placed at a deliberate advantage in the competition for votes. . . . Potential candidates are often discouraged from associations with the Republican Party."

• Until this year, the Arkansas Democratic Party required every candidate in its primaries to sign a loyalty oath pledging "to vote for and actively support all the nominees of the Democratic Party." Gene Wirges, author of a book on Arkansas called "Conflict of Interests," says the loyalty oath had a corrosive effect on justice. "Everyone knew the judge on their case would be, more or less, part of the Democratic machine," he says. "Very few judges went against the machine." Publicity finally led Democrats to drop the oath, but it was in effect during Mr. Clinton's 12 years as governor.

• When Ed Rollins spun his fantastic tale of the GOP paying street money to black ministers in New Jersey last year, President Clinton was sharply critical. But such practices are routine in Arkansas. Meredith Oakley, an Arkansas Democrat-Gazette columnist and author of a new Clinton biography, says that in many counties "black preachers still deliver votes in return for financial considerations." In 1992, her paper reported that the Democratic Party paid out at least $89,000 in street money, much of it to black ministers and funeral-home owners. Payments were also made to two county election commissioners charged with overseeing elections.

• Richard Winger, the editor of Ballot Access News in San Francisco, says Arkansas hasn't accepted multiparty politics. "They are often simply lawless," he says. In 1987, Gov. Clinton signed a bill moving the deadline for a third party to qualify for the ballot from May to January of an election year. "Federal courts had ruled Arkansas couldn't require such an early deadline, but it imposed one anyway," he says.

• Independent voices are often muffled in Arkansas politics. This spring, Federal Judge Richard Arnold, a Clinton finalist for the U.S. Supreme Court, ruled that state-owned Arkansas Educational Television had violated the constitutional rights of Ralph Forbes, a 1992 independent congressional candidate, by refusing to include him in a debate it sponsored. The director of Arkansas public broadcasting stated in court that he was so opposed to Mr. Forbes's participation that he would not have broadcast the debate if Mr. Forbes had been included.

Ironically, some of the scrutiny that has fallen on Arkansas since the Clintons moved to Washington seems to have prompted something of a perestroika. Last year, the Democratic machine suffered a humiliating defeat when Republican Mike Huckabee was elected lieutenant governor. Three months later, Ms. Jones, the state auditor, became a Republican, and is now running for secretary of state.

Ms. Jones says the biggest reason for her switch to the GOP was the Democratic machine's hysterical opposition to the term-limits law approved by 60% of Arkansas voters in 1992. Then-Democratic Party Chairman George Jernigan said he would "find somebody" to sue and overturn the voters' decision. A suit was filed by the pliable League of Women Voters and Rep. Ray Thornton, a nephew of Little Rock banker Jackson Stephens. In July 1993, Little Rock Judge Chris Piazza declared term limits invalid. The Arkansas Democrat-Gazette noted that the judge's decision "was written out and ready to be distributed before he had heard the arguments." After a public outcry, the Arkansas Supreme Court voted five to two to uphold term limits on the state's Legislature. Since then their mere prospect has upended the Legislature. A record 27 out of 135 legislators are retiring this year.

Christine Brownley, a black GOP state legislator, says minority support for the machine is eroding. In 1992, Mr. Clinton won Arkansas with 54%, but exit polls found vast generational disparities. Voters 45 and older went for Mr. Clinton by 70% to 26%. However, those under 45 voted for George Bush, 43% to 41%. A popular Arkansas bumper sticker reads: "Unplug the Machine."

"Bill Clinton did Arkansas a favor by getting people to realize the machine's damaging influence," says Ms. Jones.

Such influence was sometimes wielded with real malevolence. Author Gene Wirges became a folk hero as a crusading Arkansas newspaper publisher in the 1960s and 1970s. After he printed evidence of ballot-box stuffing, he escaped nine attempts on his life. He was indicted a total of seven times on slander, conspiracy and perjury charges. Once sentenced to three years at hard labor, he was only exonerated after the main witness against him was found to have lied. Mr. Wirges says Arkansas politics still resemble those of Mexico: a one-party state where the police are sometimes used for political repression. "Bill Clinton presided over the machine and fine-tuned it," says Mr. Wirges. "Now he has transplanted to Washington its unusual pro-business policy—favor one business at a time, starting with your friends."

Mr. Wirges and others make a distinction between the values of the machine and the state's people. Arkansas itself, they say, isn't corrupt, but the ruling political class includes ruthless people who are. Indeed, the mores of that class can certainly be found in other states, and Bill Clinton isn't the first president with a machine past—Harry Truman got his start with Kansas City's infamous Pendergast machine. But Mr. Truman dropped that association when he went to Washington. Mr. Clinton is being forced to drop many of his Arkansas friends. But his administration retains the relentlessly partisan-style politics of his Arkansas past.

Mr. Fund is a Wall Street Journal editorial writer.

Editorial Feature

Troubles in a Two-Party Town

From the Senate Banking Committee hearings on Whitewater, Aug. 4, 1994. A related editorial appears today.

Sen. Lauch Faircloth (R., N.C.): Mr. McLarty, we have talked a lot here about the RTC criminal referrals that named the Clintons and about the so-called heads-up that was first given to the White House on September the 29th of last year. But that was not the first time a Clinton appointee knew about these criminal referrals. In fact, a Clinton appointee not only knew that those referrals existed; she knew what was in them. Early in the administration, President Clinton asked for the resignation of every U.S. attorney in America, even those in most cases he did not have a replacement for. But one place he was ready, and that was Little Rock. He immediately appointed Paula Casey. A campaign worker, former law student of Bill Clinton, became the U.S. attorney in Little Rock. She not only had the criminal referrals in Little Rock; she knew what was in them. . . . Do you know Paula Casey?

Thomas (Mack) McLarty, White House adviser: I'm acquainted with Paula Casey.

Sen. Faircloth: I do not, Mr. Chairman, plan to go—go outside the scope of these hearings, so I won't ask why Paula Casey failed to act on the criminal referrals that the special counsel now has, but I do want to ask some other questions. Did anyone in the White House have any communication of any kind with Paula Casey or any of her staff—

Sen. Christopher Dodd (D., Conn.): Mr. Chairman that's out of order. This is far beyond the scope. . . .

Chairman Donald Riegle (D., Mich): The problem with that area [is] it does cross . . . the line into the areas that we've been asked not to go into by the Senate and by the special prosecutor. . . .

Ranking Minority Member Al D'Amato (R., N.Y.): So I would ask my friend and my colleague to pursue another line.

Sen. Faircloth: Well, are you saying . . . Paula Casey is out of the realm?

Sen. D'Amato: As it relates to the criminal referrals at this time, yes. As it relates to any meetings that she may have had with the White House . . . I think that we have to be very careful. . . .

Sen. John Kerry (D., Mass.): But every time these questions are dropped, and then there is a sort of statement about well we can't go into these things, then the listening public says, "Well, what's going on? What's going on?" And I think it bears repeating in fairness that this committee is not trying to not go into something. . . . We are simply adhering to the standards established by the committee and the Senate to protect the investigation of the special prosecutor. There is going to be a second go-around. . . .

Sen. Riegle: It should further be said, every White House person is appearing here voluntarily, all the documents have been turned over voluntarily, we haven't subpoenaed anybody, haven't had to, and so everything that we can properly look at at this time that we've asked for we've been given. But the things that are outside what we can do now, we—we'll just have to wait for another time.

Sen. Kerry: But most importantly, the reason we are not pursuing them now is to protect the integrity of the process and not for any other reason. . . .

Sen. Pete Domenici (R., N.M.): I think the flip side's true also. I think it's important that the public know that there's a lot more to this than we're able to ask about. Because some of the things lead to some very logical follow-ups, and—

Sen. Kerry: Mr. Chairman, that's not true. . . . This is the . . . the Washington component. Anything that has to do with the president at this moment, with respect to contacts between Treasury and the RTC investigation.

Sen. D'Amato: Let me say, if I might, Mr. Chairman. . . . We are limited by the scope as it relates to that which was laid down and passed in the Senate . . . .

Sen. Riegle: We've discussed this now . . . and I want to finish with the questioning. . . . So, Senator Faircloth, I would ask you then to keep the questions within what we can properly cover now. . . .

Sen. Faircloth: All right. Mr. Chairman, I want to start out by saying I thank you for the fairness with which you've conducted the meeting and I respect your judgment in this. But, Senator Kerry, if you're concerned that the public is having questions in the audience about where we're headed and why we're headed there, and in what way, you're absolutely right, and we have probably opened up a lot more questions than we've answered, and they're going to expect us to be answering them.

Editorial Feature

Cutler's Lessons for Mikva

Testifying before the Senate Banking Committee two weeks ago, White House Counsel Lloyd Cutler reminded the lawmakers, "I didn't ask for this job." Last spring, wanting what he called "a Lloyd-Cutler type" to succeed Bernard Nussbaum, Bill Clinton resorted to asking Mr. Cutler himself, who held the same job in the Carter White House and, at 76, in the twilight of a distinguished legal career, was not exactly looking to enhance his resume. Mr. Cutler agreed to serve but on his own terms, as "a special government employee" with a term of no more than 130 days. Last week, Judge Abner Mikva was named to replace him.

Rule of Law
By Terry Eastland

As Mr. Cutler prepares to hand over to Judge Mikva, it's an appropriate moment to review his tenure as counsel—with particular reference to his main job of handling Whitewater.

The job of White House counsel is not an easy one at any time, but that's especially true in a time of political crisis. Mr. Nussbaum, a long-time friend of the Clintons, would still be White House counsel had he handled Whitewater differently. "I was not a friend of theirs," says Mr. Cutler in an interview, explaining why he decided to take the job, "but I liked the Clintons. And given the crisis they had, especially when the president asks you to do something and you believe in him, it's hard to say no."

In dealing with the Clintons' crisis, Mr. Cutler reviewed the White

House-Treasury Department contacts over the Resolution Trust Corporation's inquiries on Whitewater. In his testimony, he conceded only "mistakes in judgment" that produced too many contacts, 40 in all.

He specifically cited as one such "mistake" his predecessor urging Roger Altman, acting head of the RTC, not to recuse himself from the RTC's civil case involving the Clintons. Mr. Cutler likewise scored  Mr. Altman for discussing recusal with Mr. Nussbaum and other White House aides. Such discussions, he said, "should not have taken place." Mr. Cutler says he hopes that had he been counsel at the time, he would have declined to advise Mr. Altman against recusing himself.

Whatever else a White House counsel should do, he at least should defend the presidency as an institution, consistent with the demands of law and conscience. And on one key issue with implications for all presidents, Mr. Cutler is

Lloyd Cutler

right—though for a stronger reason than he offers—to disagree with Rep. Jim Leach (R., Iowa), the leading Republican investigator into Whitewater. It is Mr. Leach's position, oddly unremarked upon in the media, that a president may not know about an investigation that in any way involves him.

According to Mr. Cutler (and Mr. Nussbaum), the president is the center of press attention and needs to know about every investigation in order to be in a position to respond to media inquiries. This is a practical argument shaped by an understanding of the presidency in which public affairs considerations dominate and governing is an extension of campaigning.

But the better argument is the formal one evidently lost on Rep. Leach: The Constitution vests all of the executive power in the president. And because that power encompasses his law enforcement duty, the president may know about anything he wants to know about relating to that duty. Constitutionally speaking, it is not wrong for the president to know about an investigation that involves himself.

Of course, knowing something is not the same as doing something about it; through obstruction of justice lies the way of impeachment. A White House counsel thus will want to establish procedures that minimize the possibility that the president and his aides will act improperly on the basis of knowledge about an investigation involving the president. The best way to do that is to cut out of the information loop everyone but the lawyers.

Mr. Cutler is designing a system of this kind (though the channel will also include the press office). The system will, he says, cover criminal but not civil investigations. That would appear to leave open the possibility of unchanneled contacts between the White House and an agency with civil law enforcement authority. In any event, the question of whether what Mr. Cutler calls the "performance standard" of White House aides will improve will be answered over time, after he has left office.

Far from burying Whitewater, the congressional hearings highlighted it by raising the new question of whether certain Clinton appointees lied to Congress. Mr. Cutler dismisses the idea, arguing that "there are some differences in recollection that are natural enough."

As a general matter, Mr. Cutler says that "willful lying" to Congress by an executive official should be prosecuted. But Mr. Cutler, who told me that he's read Elliott Abrams's "Undue Process," which recounts Lawrence Walsh's zealous pursuit of a withholding-information-from-Congress charge against the author, says he's not enamored with the lying-to-Congress cases pursued in recent years against executive officials.

Mr. Cutler says it's "a terrible idea" to pursue a false-statement case against an executive official for unsworn remarks made to Congress. An independent counsel pursued such a case against former Reagan Assistant Attorney General Theodore Olson in 1985. Today, the rhetoric of some Republicans suggests that Mr. Altman's unsworn Feb. 24 testimony is indictable under the false-statement statute.

There is considerable irony in the idea that a Democratic presidency might have to endure indictments for lying to Congress. There is more irony in a Democratic presidency finding itself under constant suspicion. If one is to do a full accounting of the current culture of scandal, the Democratic Party is largely responsible for refining the instruments by which a president and his aides today may be tortured. Democrats far more than Republicans have supported the independent counsel law, and Democrats far more than Republicans endorsed independent counsel prosecutions for lying to Congress.

Like the president, Mr. Cutler despairs over what he calls "the growing cynicism in Washington about people who serve in government," a product of perhaps, he says, the growth of investigative journalism and the modern experience of big government. The idea that government officials are "presumptively crooked, dishonest liars," he says, will discourage young people from serving. As was true for Mr. Cutler, much of Judge Mikva's job will require grappling with the culture of scandal in which a Democratic White House now finds itself enmeshed.

———————

Mr. Eastland, editor of Forbes MediaCritic, is the author of "Energy in the Executive: The Case for the Strong Presidency" (Free Press, 1992).

News Story

Boatmen's Sets Acquisition Of Worthen

Pact, Valued at $583 Million, May Trim Fed Scrutiny Of Stephens Operations

By CARLEE R. SCOTT and ARTHUR BUCKLER

Staff Reporters of THE WALL STREET JOURNAL

Boatmen's Bancshares Inc. agreed to acquire Worthen Banking Corp., a Little Rock., Ark. bank-holding company partly owned by the controversial Stephens family, for Boatmen's stock valued at about $583 million.

Boatmen's, a St. Louis bank-holding concern, said its acquisition of Arkansas' largest bank—with 112 branches in that state and $3.5 billion in assets—will give it a "dominant" 20% share of the Arkansas banking market. The planned transaction also would boost Boatmen's presence in Texas, where Worthen has offices in the Austin area. Boatmen's has assets of $28 billion.

The accord could provide a graceful way out for the Stephens family, which owns 25% of Worthen shares on a fully diluted basis. The Federal Reserve Board has been investigating ties between Worthen and the family, which also owns Little Rock investment bank Stephens Inc. Under federal law, it is illegal for an investment-banking firm to control a bank.

The Fed's formal investigation began 16 months ago, according to Worthen. "Frankly, I'm not sure where it stands," Curt Bradbury, Worthen's chairman, said yesterday .

Under the terms of the definitive pact, Worthen holders will swap each of their shares for one share in Boatmen's. The 17.3 million shares Boatmen's expects to issue in order to effect the acquisition represents a 14% stake. The Stephens family would get Boatmen's stock valued at $148.5 million.

This would put the family's stake in the combined company below the threshold that requires public reporting of ownership.

In Nasdaq Stock Market trading late yesterday, Boatmen's shares slipped 68.75 cents to $33.688; Worthen's shares also declined, 24 cents a share, to $30.75 on the American Stock Exchange.

The price Boatmen's is paying is nearly two times Worthen's June 30 book value of $17.22 a share. But the price provides little premium to Worthen's trading price, reflecting widespread investor anticipation that the Arkansas concern would shortly find a buyer.

Last month, Worthen hired PaineWebber Inc. to help it review its "strategic alternatives." But rumors that such a move might be in the works, fueled by a management change at the company, had pushed the stock up months before that announcement.

Joseph A. Stieven, an analyst at Stifel Nicolaus & Co. in St. Louis, said the Worthen transaction makes "strategic sense" for Boatmen's because it currently holds only a small market share in Arkansas. "They always like to have the dominant, or large, market position in every market they're in," he added. He called the price "fair, but not excessive."

Boatmen's said it expects the transaction to result in after-tax revenue enhancements and cost savings of about $13 million next year and $26 million in 1996. It will dilute per-share earnings in 1995 by about 1%, or four cents a share, but add to such earnings in the following year.

The transaction, which is expected to close during the first quarter of 1995, is subject to regulatory approval and the approval of Worthen shareholders, Boatmen's said.

If the transaction is approved, it could lessen federal scrutiny of the Stephens family. "This may have been the easiest way out" of the Fed inquiry, said Bill Baldwin, an analyst at Rauscher Pierce Refsnes Inc. in Dallas.

However, Worthen's Mr. Bradbury said that the company agreed to the merger because it was a good deal. Regarding the investigation, "I have no idea whether the merger will help, hurt or be neutral," he said.

The Stephens' holding in Worthen and the Fed investigation have been a focus of the Republican attack on President Clinton's financial dealings when he was Arkansas governor. Worthen and Stephens employees provided substantial financial support for Mr. Clinton's presidential campaign, among other Stephens ties to the Clintons.

Representatives of the Stephens declined to comment yesterday.

Albert R. Karr contributed to this article.

REVIEW & OUTLOOK

Whitewater Plugs

Democrats are trying to overturn the appointment of Kenneth Starr to replace Whitewater Special Counsel Robert Fiske and discredit David Sentelle, the chief federal appeals judge who appointed him. Even more ominously, the Resolution Trust Corp. has put on administrative leave the three Kansas City RTC officials most closely involved with the criminal investigation of Whitewater.

Our view of the offensive against Messrs. Starr and Sentelle is that it is partisanship blinded to its own interests. By all accounts, Mr. Starr's professional demeanor and work is fair-minded almost to a fault. We'd think the Democrats would want to take their chances with Mr. Starr's straight-arrow instincts rather than risk who might follow him. Unless, of course, a fair-minded interpretation of the facts is what they fear most.

Which brings us to the suspicious RTC action. Reports appeared Tuesday that Jean Lewis and two colleagues in the RTC's Kansas City office had been placed on paid administrative leave. Ms. Lewis is the investigator who led the Little Rock-based inquiries into the activities of Madison Guaranty S&L and the Whitewater land deals involving the Clintons.

After her office made criminal referrals on the matter to the Justice Department in September 1992, Ms. Lewis later became embroiled in a dispute with Clinton-appointed Federal Attorney Paula Casey in Little Rock over the disposition of the referrals. During the Whitewater Senate hearings, Arlen Specter suggested that Special

Counsel Fiske was investigating a U.S. Attorney for obstruction of justice. We discussed these matters Monday in an editorial, "Who Is Paula Casey?" The news reports of Ms. Lewis's suspension from her duties appeared the next day.

Indeed, most of the Kansas City RTC's Whitewater chain of command has been swept out. Also put on administrative leave were Ms. Lewis's supervisor, Richard Iorio, and their immediate superior, Lee Ausen. RTC spokesman Stephen Katsanos would say only that an internal investigation was on regarding "compliance with RTC policies and procedures."

This smells to high heaven. Set aside whatever "internal" case the RTC thinks it may have against these three. The action reeks of intimidation, an effort to muzzle a public official who's actually spent time with the original Whitewater and Madison documents. At the same time that Democrats are trying to destroy the credibility of a court-appointed independent counsel, a powerful federal agency is sending a signal across government that anyone who tells what he or she knows about Whitewater risks investigation and possible ruin. The action taken by Jack Ryan's RTC will have a chilling effect.

More broadly, this development points up one of our concerns about coping with the proliferation of official corruption globally, whether Whitewater, BCCI or party finance scandals in Japan, Italy and France. The FBIs of the world are good at chasing normal crooks, but it's difficult for law enforcement bureaucracies to carry out investigations of a nation's high officials. It's just too hot to handle. But we had better find a way to do it lest public cynicism also start to proliferate.

There was a time when the federal whistleblower law was supposed to protect officials such as Jean Lewis, but maybe someone ought to drop by the U.S. Office of the Special Counsel, which monitors that law, to see if Little Rock mores have arrived there, too. Suspicions of a cover-up will persist, and rightly so, as long as a public airing of Jean Lewis's case instead turns into a Star Chamber administrative leave. At the moment, they are getting away with it.

News Story

RTC Investigator Says Agency Officials Tried to Halt Madison Guaranty Probe

By ALBERT R. KARR

Staff Reporter of THE WALL STREET JOURNAL

WASHINGTON—A Resolution Trust Corp. investigator made new allegations that RTC officials in Washington tried to quash a regional office's inquiry into Madison Guaranty Savings & Loan.

The allegations were contained in a letter from the attorney for Richard Iorio, a criminal-investigations supervisor in the RTC's office in Kansas City, Mo. Mr. Iorio and two other investigators, who have issued 10 criminal referrals in the Madison Guaranty case, were placed on administrative leave last week while the agency's Human Resources Management Group looks into questions of "compliance with RTC policies and procedures."

In a letter to acting RTC chief Jack Ryan, the attorney, Joseph Bocock, asked that the compliance inquiry be turned over to the RTC's inspector general. Mr. Bocock said the RTC inspector general usually investigates allegations of wrongdoing by agency officials. The Human Resources Management Group is controlled by "key RTC management," he said, raising questions as to the impartiality of the personnel group's findings.

Mr. Bocock also said that the agency's Aug. 15 decision to put the three Kansas City investigators on administrative leave would prevent their continued assistance in several investigations by an independent counsel and others regarding Madison Guaranty and Whitewater Development Corp. The former owner of Madison

Guaranty was a partner of Bill and Hillary Rodham Clinton in Whitewater.

In the letter to Mr. Ryan, Mr. Bocock said that Mr. Iorio and his staff were warned "as early as" Feb. 18 of this year that "certain key RTC managers would take a 'dim view' of his office's investigation of Madison Guaranty." But Mr. Bocock said the office nevertheless pushed forward with the probe "to protect the public trust." He said, "These efforts must not be jeopardized by the very real possibility that the RTC will not independently conduct the current investigation."

Mr. Bocock expressed Mr. Iorio's concern that the RTC investigation of the three officials involves "a program of retribution" by politically motivated RTC managers.

RTC spokesman Stephen Katsanos said the agency has made "no allegations of wrongdoing" by the three investigators. He said he doubts that their absence from duty "for this brief period" will affect the RTC's civil investigation into Madison Guaranty or the criminal referrals that the three officials had made. A letter from the RTC to Mr. Iorio said the leave will last two weeks.

Mr. Katsanos also said the RTC inspector general isn't asked to investigate personnel performance unless there is first a determination that the inspector general needs to make such an analysis.

In a recent House Banking Committee hearing, April Breslaw, a Washington-based RTC attorney handling the civil investigation of Madison Guaranty, said that when she visited the Kansas City office she had been trapped into an informal discussion on Feb. 2 with Jean Lewis, the Kansas City investigator who wrote the criminal referrals. Ms. Breslaw has been quoted as saying in that conversation, which was tape-recorded without her knowledge, that top RTC officials would like to be able to conclude that Whitewater's financial troubles didn't cause any Madison losses.

Ms. Breslaw told the House panel that her comment to Ms. Lewis included a caveat that RTC officials wanted a favorable outcome only "if they could say it honestly." Ms. Lewis, who is supervised by Mr. Iorio, and Lee Ausen, who oversees both Ms. Lewis and Mr. Iorio, were the other officials placed on administrative leave. A lawyer for Ms. Lewis and Mr. Ausen said they haven't decided whether to ask that the inspector general investigate the matter.

Mr. Iorio had asked to testify at the House panel's Whitewater hearing, but was told by the RTC's senior counsel for legal services that the committee hadn't asked for testimony by additional RTC employees and that such testimony was "unnecessary."

News Story

Starr Takes Over Whitewater Probe as Decisions Must Be Reached On Batch of Possible Indictments

By ELLEN JOAN POLLOCK

Staff Reporter of THE WALL STREET JOURNAL

LITTLE ROCK, Ark.—The political thunder clouds are only just beginning to disperse over the appointment of Kenneth Starr as special Whitewater prosecutor. But he already is facing decisions that are likely to send him back into the thick of controversy.

Mr. Starr has assumed control of the Whitewater investigation at a critical moment. Former independent counsel Robert Fiske was expected to decide next month which Whitewater characters, if any, should be charged.

Those decisions now fall to Mr. Starr, who spent last week absorbing the myriad details of the investigation and recruiting new lawyers with prosecutorial experience. If Mr. Starr seeks indictments, the first charges aren't likely to deal directly with the Whitewater real-estate investment by President Clinton and his wife, Hillary Rodham Clinton, nor with Mr. Clinton's campaign finances when he was governor of Arkansas. Indeed, many elements of the wide-ranging investigation centering largely on events before Mr. Clinton was elected president have nothing to do with Mr. and Mrs. Clinton. The president says he did nothing wrong and has repeatedly expressed confidence that the lengthy investigation will prove his innocence.

Nevertheless, if there are charges, they could target some of the Clintons' friends and political associates; the repercussions would be felt as strongly in Washington as they would be here in Arkansas. A decision against seeking indictments would suggest that evidence of wrongdoing is much weaker than some early government investigators—and many of Mr. Clinton's political opponents—contend.

On the list of possible targets are two well-known political figures, former associate attorney general Webster Hubbell and Arkansas Gov. Jim Guy Tucker.

Mr. Hubbell is being vigorously pursued by the independent counsel staff because he allegedly charged personal expenses to the Rose Law Firm, where he was once a partner with Mrs. Clinton, according to people familiar with the investigation.

Gov. Tucker, who is likely to win an election this November (he was the lieutenant governor before Mr. Clinton became president), borrowed heavily from Madison Guaranty Savings & Loan and a company owned by David Hale that was only supposed to lend to disadvantaged businesses. Some of the loans are believed to have contributed to Madison's failure, and Gov. Tucker was named in a criminal referral from the Resolution Trust Corp. to the Justice Department. Madison's former owner, James McDougal, also has received intense scrutiny from investigators.

Mr. Hubbell was chosen for his top Justice post from the Clintons' circle of close Arkansas friends and any indictment of him would be a deep embarrassment for the White House. Although he resigned in March after his dispute with the Rose firm became public, he since has been invited back to the White House for social occasions.

Mr. Starr is in possession of records indicating that Mr. Hubbell allegedly billed the Rose firm for roughly $100,000 in expenses that he said were business-related but turned out to be personal, according to lawyers involved in the investigation. Mr. Hubbell, they say, used Rose firm checks to pay his credit-card bills. Possible felony charges against him could include mail fraud.

Mr. Starr's staff also has been trying to ascertain whether Mr. Hubbell billed the RTC for personal expenses. If he did, he could also be charged with making false statements to a federal agency. Mr. Hubbell represented the thrift agency in litigation. His attorney declined to comment.

At least two Rose Law Firm partners, including managing partner Ronald Clark, have spoken with the Whitewater prosecutors. Lawyers familiar with the investigation say Mr. Starr has substantial documentary evidence against Mr. Hubbell and that the investigation is likely to be wrapped up by late September.

Mr. Tucker, a Democrat, was never a close ally of Mr. Clinton's in Arkansas, but any legal problems for him would also present a sticky political situation. His opponent in November, Sheffield Nelson, has been one of President Clinton's most vocal critics on Whitewater. During Senate Banking Committee hearings earlier this month, Republicans worked hard to insinuate that the president was in a position to tip off Gov. Tucker to a pending investigation when they met in 1993, after Treasury Department officials told White House aides about the RTC's Madison probe. White House aides have said that President Clinton didn't know that Gov. Tucker was named in a criminal referral.

Some of Mr. Tucker's business deals resulted in serious losses to Madison and the governor could face charges if those losses can be attributed to malfeasance. Gov. Tucker's loans from Madison and Mr. Hale's firm are being aggressively scrutinized by the independent counsel's office. The RTC's criminal referral, which was transferred to Mr. Fiske, involved a $260,000 loan Gov. Tucker got from Madison to purchase a roughly 35-acre property for a shopping center near a trailer park being developed by Madison. The RTC alleged that about $130,000 was improperly diverted to pay off an unrelated loan the governor had guaranteed at another bank.

Gov. Tucker's lawyer, John Haley, says there was nothing improper about the diversion because Madison itself forwarded the money to the other bank. Gov. Tucker later sold the property to a company he partly owned. After Madison failed, Ikansa, a company set up and owned by Mr. Haley, acquired a $220,000 note for the remaining debt from the RTC on behalf of Gov. Tucker.

But the independent counsel office's interest in Gov. Tucker's business deals goes beyond the scope of that criminal referral. The team is also looking at a $1,050,000 loan from Madison to Castle Sewer & Water, a company partly owned by Gov. Tucker. Castle Sewer used the money to buy a sewer system from Madison, but the loan was written down by half, with the approval of federal regulators, after the company couldn't meet its loan payments.

As of 1987, Castle Sewer was owned by Gov. Tucker, R.D. Randolph, a businessman, and a firm owned by Mr. Hale, who has pleaded guilty to defrauding the Small Business Administration and is cooperating with the Whitewater prosecutor. Gov. Tucker transferred his share to Mr. Randolph. Madison's loans to Castle Sewer haven't been fully repaid, Mr. Haley said.

The investigators have subpoenaed thousands of pages of documents from Gov. Tucker and even from Mr. Haley, who complains that the government has been overzealous in demanding documents. The lawyer has turned over the records of Ikansa and recently was asked to turn over documents for Mikado Leasing, a company he set up that held shares in a cable-TV company the governor owned. The cable companies, which received loans from Mr. Hale, are also being scrutinized by investigators.

The political stakes are also high for Mr. Starr. He is standing firm despite calls for his resignation by those who say his appointment was sponsored by conservatives. But he may bend over backward to avoid the appearance of partisanship when he decides whom to indict. "It's going to be very difficult for him to make any close calls against the president," notes a lawyer familiar with Whitewater. "He'll have to satisfy a higher threshold of proof."

Mr. Starr, and Mr. Fiske, are mum on the direction of the investigation. How fast Mr. Starr can move will depend to some degree on whether he persuades Mr. Fiske's staff to stay on. Some are expected to leave this fall but are committed to staying until a transition is complete. That, says Starr staffer William Duffy, will minimize "whatever delay there is and I think in a number of situations will avoid a delay."

News Story

Former Madison Aide Tells Prosecutor He Recalls Clinton Signature on Loan

By ELLEN JOAN POLLOCK

Staff Reporter of THE WALL STREET JOURNAL

LITTLE ROCK, Ark.—Kenneth Starr, the new Whitewater prosecutor, has inherited plenty of unsolved mysteries from his predecessor. But few are as baffling as the suggestion that Hillary Rodham Clinton may have guaranteed a loan from Madison Guaranty Savings & Loan to Susan McDougal and her husband, Jim McDougal, the owner of the failed thrift.

If the loan guarantee's existence were proved, it might add credence to a potentially damaging allegation that President Clinton improperly pressured an Arkansas businessman into making a federally guaranteed loan to Mrs. McDougal. Mr. Clinton has denied the allegation, and the Clintons' lawyer says that Mrs. Clinton didn't guarantee a loan to the McDougals. More broadly, President and Mrs. Clinton have denied any wrongdoing in connection with their dealings with Madison or Whitewater Development Corp., a failed Arkansas land venture.

Don Denton, a former Madison senior vice president, has told members of the independent counsel's staff that he read through the McDougal loan file in 1986, and that when he looked on the reverse side of a loan document, he saw that it was guaranteed by Mrs. Clinton. Mr. Denton says he doesn't know if the loan documents still exist to support his eight-year-old memory.

Some of Mr. Denton's details are sketchy. For example, he recalls that the loan was for an amount between $100,000 and $300,000 and was made to a McDougal business interest, although he doesn't recall which one. He also admits that at the time he couldn't verify Mrs. Clinton's signature. David Kendall, the Clintons' lawyer, adamantly denies that such a loan ever took place.

But Mr. Denton says he remembers the guarantee by Mrs. Clinton, whose husband was then governor, because whoever documented the loan did not use the form usually used by Madison for guarantees. Also in the file, Mr. Denton recalls, was support material for a federally backed loan Mrs. McDougal received around the same time from David Hale, who has pleaded guilty to defrauding the Small Business Administration and is cooperating with the Whitewater prosecutor.

Mr. Hale claims that Mr. Clinton pressured him to make a $300,000 loan to Mrs. McDougal in 1986. Mr. Clinton has denied the charge. If Mr. Denton's memory is correct and Mrs. Clinton did guarantee a loan, it would seem plausible that President Clinton might want to make sure that Mrs. McDougal had enough funds to repay the loan guaranteed by his wife.

Rumors of a loan to Mrs. McDougal guaranteed by Mrs. Clinton have circulated in Little Rock for months, although Mr. McDougal remembers no such loan and Mrs. McDougal's lawyer won't comment. But investigators have spent many hours interviewing Mr. Denton about Madison deals.

Mr. Denton can't explain one puzzling aspect of his recollection. He remembers the signature "Hillary Rodham," but Mrs. Clinton added "Clinton" to her name in the early 1980s. That raises questions about whether the signature he remembers seeing is genuine.

Mr. Kendall puts it this way: "Any allegation that Mrs. Clinton guaranteed a loan in 1986 with the signature 'Hillary Rodham' has the unmistakable and clanging ring of falsity."

Editorial Feature

Jack Ryan
Presents a Chapter
Of His Adventures

By MICAH MORRISON

John E. "Jack" Ryan arrived at a new job back in 1985, leaving the Federal Reserve for the private sector and avowedly hoping to make some money. But within weeks, ESM Securities went under in a spectacular financial collapse, causing $250 million in losses. ESM was a principal client of Mr. Ryan's new employer, the Miami law firm of Arky, Freed, Stearns, Watson, Greer, Weaver & Harris.

"It wasn't clear from the outset that this wasn't going to subside," Mr. Ryan remembers ruefully when interviewed in his present job as acting head of the Resolution Trust Corp. But by the time the dust settled, Jack Ryan's new boss was dead, the state of Ohio was in the midst of a banking crisis, and his brief foray as a financial consultant was over.

The Miami episode long has intrigued aficionados of financial scandal, who experienced a shock of recognition when Mr. Ryan emerged from the Whitewater waves earlier this summer. In an Aug. 1 editorial on this page, "Who Is Jack Ryan?," it was noted that Mr. Ryan's previous posts often had put him at the switches of major political and fiscal imbroglios. From 1977 to 1985, for example, he was director of banking supervision and regulation at the Federal Reserve, when the Bank of Credit & Commerce International managed illegally to gain control of First American Bank in Washington.

Mr. Ryan won't talk much about Whitewater, or about the Fed and BCCI, but he did agree to discuss Arky, Freed.

The Miami firm became enmeshed in a loan repurchase scam run by ESM, an obscure Fort Lauderdale securities firm. ESM's downfall caused $100 million in losses in Florida and touched off a bank crisis in Ohio, where Home State Savings Bank lost $150 million and was shut down, signaling the beginning of the S&L crisis. Home State was owned by Marvin Warner, the father-in-law and business partner of Arky, Freed's lead partner, Stephen Arky. Mr. Warner was a Democratic Party financier and former Carter administration ambassador to Switzerland, a job he earned thanks to his early support of Mr. Carter's presidential bid and his friendship with Georgia banker Bert Lance.

Mr. Ryan had been hired away from the Fed by Mr. Arky in February 1985. "I had met Steve Arky a year or two earlier," Mr. Ryan said, "in connection with one of the cases that was before the Federal Reserve Board." At the time, Messrs. Arky and Warner were involved in a number of high-stakes takeover fights and mergers of Florida banks. "I had met Marvin Warner at the Fed when he was ambassador to Switzerland and his bank had made a couple of applications," Mr. Ryan said.

Florida, and the Arky firm's growing reputation as a powerhouse in the banking world, looked attractive to Mr. Ryan. "Steve Arky came to see me long after his case before the Fed was disposed of and talked about starting a consulting company, something like the one [former FDIC chairman] Bill Isaac started with Arnold & Porter."

Mr. Arky's world, however, was falling apart fast. In March 1985, ESM collapsed. In July, Mr. Arky committed suicide, leaving a note declaring his innocence in the deals that had brought down ESM and Home State. Mr. Warner went to prison on securities and bank fraud charges.

Mr. Ryan said he was not aware of the ESM situation when he joined Arky, Freed to form an affiliated financial consulting firm and "make money," as he told the press in 1985. "As events developed," he noted recently, "it became obvious that it was going to be more and more difficult to run a consulting firm under those circumstances." As to whether he found riches in the private sector, Mr. Ryan answered with a resounding "No!"

The Journal's Aug. 1 editorial noted that Mr. Ryan's recent biographies omit any mention of his sojourn with Arky, Freed. Mr. Ryan insisted the omission was not deliberate. "There were many fine people" at the Arky firm, Mr. Ryan said. "I was proud to be associated with them."

After 19 months in Miami, Mr. Ryan returned to government service in September 1986, filling a series of posts at the Federal Home Loan Bank of Boston and the Office of Thrift Supervision. This January, he started at the RTC as Roger Altman's deputy, along with the new general counsel, Ellen Kulka. At the Whitewater hearings, Bernard Nussbaum testified that both appointments had been vetted by the White House.

In February, RTC Washington attorney April Breslaw had her now famous conversation with RTC Kansas City investigator Jean Lewis. "April stated very clearly that Ryan and Kulka, the 'head people,' would like to be able to say that Whitewater did not cause a loss to Madison," read Ms. Lewis's notes to the conversation.

In a recent flurry of Whitewater-related RTC maneuvers, Ms. Lewis and two other Kansas City RTC officials involved in the Madison probe were suspended on undisclosed charges, then reinstated after Mr. Ryan received a letter from the chairman and ranking minority member of the Senate Banking Committee demanding "a detailed explanation." The investigation has been turned over to the RTC inspector general. The agency also has filed suit against the Rose Law Firm, seeking its client list for the past nine years in a conflict-of-interest investigation, and asked a federal court to enforce a subpoena against Arkansas Gov. Jim Guy Tucker for documents relating to his dealings with Madison Guaranty.

Mr. Ryan declined to discuss Whitewater matters. He did, however, indicate that he was open to sticking around Washington to become the RTC's permanent CEO.

Mr. Morrison is a Wall Street Journal editorial page writer.

Editorial Feature

No Juicy Clinton Stories Please, We're American

By CHRISTOPHER WOOD

Yesterday, I finished my second tour of duty reporting on America for The Economist. I return to Britain sorry to be leaving the many things that are admirable about the U.S. and the many things that are simply colorful and over the top. But I also leave a little puzzled by my colleagues in the American media.

For example, few stories could be juicier than the Whitewater saga. It has everything—dead bodies and death threats, allegations of drug smuggling, crooked speculation, looting of a federally guaranteed depositary institution, sweetheart land deals, abuse of municipal bond issuance and, of course, sex.

Yet much of the mainstream American press has kept a genteel distance from much of this Arkansas material, as if parts of the first couple's background are not fit conversation for polite company.

This attitude was most egregious during the 1992 campaign, when reporters by and large failed to alert their readers to many of the strange goings on in Arkansas during the 1980s. They failed to expose the real nature of the Clintons' rule over that tiny state, and the nature of the political machine of which they were a part.

The most charitable explanation of why many reporters failed to ask many of the awkward questions in Arkansas is that they were simply seduced by the candidate and his wife. Instead they focused on the Clintons' self-presentation and thus contributed to some of the most biased campaign coverage ever. Boredom with President Bush was already overflowing among media-types, and the Republicans ran the most feeble of campaigns. But in purely journalistic terms that is little excuse for the press corps choosing to look the other way when stories emerged that did not fit its preconceptions.

Thus the initial article on the Clintons' involvement in the Whitewater project was written in March 1992 by investigative reporter Jeff Gerth in the New York Times. Other reporters' excuse for not following it up more vigorously at the time is that the story was so "complicated" that they did not understand it and their readers never would. This is not quite as self-serving as it sounds. Many journalists' eyes glaze over at the first hint of a technicality. This is the by-now-familiar world of press coverage by sound-bite.

* * *

I was working in Japan during the 1992 presidential campaign, and even then it seemed odd that more was not made of the strange Whitewater-Madison affair, of which one read snippets of information. True, I had covered the U.S. savings and loan crisis in the latter part of the 1980s and had been amazed by the slowness of the American press in waking up to the reality of another "complicated" story—a $500 billion bill for taxpayers. But the Madison case read like a classic scam where the taxpayer was cynically ripped off.

If the Clintons had benefited at taxpayers' expense, that was surely an important story—even if only tens of millions of dollars was lost at Madison, rather than hundreds of millions as with so many other thrifts. Yet the press was all but silent. Its major concern during the campaign, regarding Bill Clinton, was the relatively unimportant one of Gennifer Flowers.

Recently the mainstream press has done more reporting on Whitewater as yet one new area of inquiry after another emerges. But some institutions still appear to be afraid of the story.

Terry Reed's book "Compromised: Clinton, Bush and the CIA" was ignored for months before a few reporters felt obliged to write about it. The continuing reluctance of the press to write about allegations made by a former fringe CIA operative is understandable. But its eagerness to dismiss the whole book as fabricated nonsense is not. For the most credible aspect of Mr. Reed's book is that it was not written with Whitewater in mind. It simply collided with Whitewater. If it is even a quarter true, it is as damaging in what it says about the Reagan and Bush administrations—since it reopens the old wound of

Iran-Contra—as in what it reveals about Bill Clinton's Arkansas.

* * *

If the press remains uncomfortable with Whitewater, many of its members are also quick to attack the motives of those trying to delve more deeply into the story. Accusations fly of using "biased sources" or of being in bed with the "Christian Right." This is bizarre. All sources are by their nature biased. It is true that the people who have assembled the most information about the Whitewater affair in all its many dimensions, be it Hillary Clinton's prescient commodity trading or the varied activities of the larger-than-life Dan Lasater, are political opponents of the Clintons. This is hardly surprising, especially as they are quite open about their motives. The issue that should count is whether the information is accurate.

There is now an active electronic mail network of Whitewater aficionados who disseminate material among themselves precisely because they are so indignant at the press's failure to probe more deeply. Talk radio is another vibrant outlet.

So here is a strange dichotomy. A media elite centered on Washington and New York talks to itself while the rest of thinking America listens to the radio and draws its own conclusion. If this administration ends in failure or worse, the blame will lie as much with the media that played such an important part in getting President Clinton elected as with the Clintons themselves. For this remarkable couple simply transferred to Washington the modus operandi they used so successfully in Little Rock. No realistic observer should have expected them to behave any differently. The failure of the American press to understand this at the time, let alone point it out, is simply extraordinary.

Mr. Wood was the New York bureau chief of The Economist until this week. His book "The End of Japan Inc." will be published by Simon & Schuster next month.

REVIEW & OUTLOOK

Whitewater Status Report

As Labor Day marks the traditional start of a fall political campaign, Whitewater hangs in a curious balance. Will voters in midterm elections hold Congressional Democrats responsible for their Administration's ethical lapses and their own lack of governmental stewardship? Or will the attempt at suppression, obviously under way on multiple fronts, succeed in covering up the issue at least through November 8?

The effort to bury Whitewater through the election was most obvious in the otherwise hilarious attacks on Kenneth Starr's appointment as special counsel. When the object of an investigation attacks the investigator, the ordinary citizen must figure the stars have moved into their proper places. But to hear Presidential mouthpiece Bob Bennett tell it, a special counsel probing

Kenneth Starr

White House conduct should be someone the President will like. Mr. Bennett, in charge of the Paula Corbin Jones case, complained that Mr. Starr actually expressed the view that a President is not above the law. And a group of incumbent Congressmen complained that Judge David Sentelle actually had lunch with two U.S. Senators, obvious subversives.

Now, having often expressed the view no one can be as objective

and wise as advocates of special counsel laws expect, we are not about to anoint Mr. Starr as above reproach. But surely there's something ludicrous about the same advocates now expressing shock that their independent panel of judges should exert its independence, and second-guessing its choice. What is fundamentally going on here is an effort to intimidate Mr. Starr, at least enough to avoid any pre-election indictments.

This effort may succeed. Mr. Starr is in fact anything but a boat-rocker, but rather an establishment figure attuned to the good graces of the Beltway bar and especially the press that covers it. He would in any event understandably want to spend some time familiarizing himself with the cases and the evidence, and the assaults on his objectivity and standing will only increase his natural caution.

The special counsel does however face a dilemma. Our Ellen Joan Pollock reported last week on two possible indictment targets developed by Robert Fiske. One was Webster Hubbell, resigned honcho at the Justice Department; this would be so politically explosive that postponement would be tempting. The other, however, is current Arkansas Governor Jim Guy Tucker, whose deep involvement with Madison Guaranty Savings & Loan was recently sketched in a series in the Arkansas Democrat-Gazette. Governor Tucker is running for re-election this fall, and Mr. Starr owes the voters of Arkansas a decision before they cast their ballots.

* * *

Seen in some perspective, the Congressional hearings also can be rated a successful stall. Roger Altman is of course well known along Wall Street, and the gang at Harry's watering hole now considers him a stand-up guy. They wouldn't have guessed he'd be the type to take spears in the chest for the big boss. In this perspective, he compares especially well with his immediate superior, Treasury Secretary Lloyd Bentsen, whose success was not taking responsibility for either defending or firing aides under fire.

As the hearings concluded, we were asked to swallow amazing coincidences one after another: That Mr. Altman changed his mind about recusing himself although no one pressured him to do so. That only by sheer routine did the Altman recusal meetings include Margaret Williams, Hillary Clinton's chief of staff, a death-night visitor to Vincent Foster's office and the aide in charge of storing Mr. Foster's papers in the White House family quarters before they went to the Clintons' personal lawyer. That when Mr. Altman wanted to announce his non-recusal at the White House, he chose to call Ms. Williams only because she's good at arranging meetings.

Also that Josh Steiner lied to his own diary. That Rhodes scholar George Stephanopoulos suffers memory lapses suggestive of attention deficit disorder. That Lloyd Cutler's redactions can always be trusted. That Treasury counsel Jean Hanson undertook on her own volition to brief the White House on criminal referrals. That White House and Arkansas confidant Bruce Lindsey knew of criminal referrals concerning Mr. Tucker before the President and the Governor met on October 6 to discuss the National Guard, but didn't tell the President until the following week.

Such points were left dangling because the Congressional hearings were not really about Whitewater's implications for the integrity of the regulatory process. The House hearings under Chairman Henry Gonzalez were a shameless farce. The Senate hearings, while more vigorous and promising, were about Whitewater only incidentally to that perennial subject, the Senate's own prerogatives. Mr. Altman's position became impossible because he shaded his Senate testimony, and Ms. Hanson's because she was somehow expected to correct him.

Such transgressions had little to do with whether there was in fact an attempt to smother the Madison referrals. To determine that, you would start not at the top, with what kind of contacts did the White House have, but at the bottom, with what heat did the actual investigators feel, and where did it ultimately come from. This was not done.

* * *

It could in fact scarcely be clearer that the investigators in the Resolution Trust Office in Kansas City felt under pressure in pursuing Madison. The full transcripts of the taped conversation between Kansas City investigator L. Jean Lewis and Washington RTC attorney April Breslaw tend to show Ms. Breslaw's discomfort with her role, but on how many other investigations did any such conversation take place? The RTC's reaction has been to investigate Ms. Lewis and her two supervisors, apparently asking whether she violated some rule or law in taping the conversation, and whether they may have made some mistakes in expense accounts.

The RTC put the three on paid administrative leave. They have now returned to work following a letter from Senate Banking

Chairman Don Riegle, who should be especially commended, and ranking Minority Member Alfonse D'Amato.

The Justice Department, meanwhile, is reported to be nearing an indictment of Billy Dale, former director of the White House travel office, whose abrupt removal was one of the first signs of the White House's brand of Arkansas mores. Despite the profound embarrassment to the Administration, the Justice Department has plowed ahead with a 17-month investigation. Mr. Dale's offense apparently is using pool money contributed by the press to bribe foreign officials, such as baggage handlers. Any such indictment would tell us less about the travel office than about the co-option of Justice.

* * *

The suppression effort has also run up some victories in court. Mr. Bennett has succeeded in getting a ruling that the Paula Jones case cannot proceed until his contentions of Presidential immunity are settled, a de facto postponement past not only the midterm election but probably the Presidential one. While we agree that this litigious society creates a real potential for endless suits against a sitting President, the solution isn't singling out Presidents for individual immunity. Part of Mrs. Jones's complaint concerns what was said about her by the President's appointed spokespersons; is defamation of a private figure privileged if it is uttered in the White House press room?

The RTC and other regulators, meanwhile, succeeded in stonewalling Rep. Jim Leach's demands for Madison documents from the RTC and other regulators. Empowering the minority party is in fact the cleanest way to inform the public on how its government is performing, but District Judge Charles Richey took refuge in the doctrine of "remedial discretion." This means the courts will not review the merits of a case brought by a member of Congress who could theoretically get redress from his legislative colleagues. The judge felt bound by D.C. Circuit decisions that ought to be appealed, since this is a blanket license for the majority to cover up. Under similar logic, Watergate Judge John Sirica could have refused to referee the dispute between Congress and the Executive Branch.

* * *

The point is well taken, though, that ultimately Whitewater is a political matter, as Watergate was as well. We are anything but keen to criminalize political differences. As the first to point a finger at

Webb Hubbell at Justice, let us say this: Indicting him for cheating his Rose partners through inflated expense accounts would only be a step above convicting Oliver North for accepting an illegal gratuity of a security fence. What we want to know about Mr. Hubbell is whether he maneuvered the firing of all U.S. attorneys to get Paula Casey appointed in Little Rock to tend to the likes of the Madison referrals. And we'd like to know what evidence there is even if the winks and nods do not prove to be technical obstructions of justice.

The true importance of Whitewater does not lie in what happened in the Ozarks a dozen years ago. It lies in what happened to Justice and bank regulation during Bill Clinton's tenure as President. Were those processes subverted to cover up what happened in Arkansas, and conceptually to do future favors for future friends of the President? And has Congress discharged its role in policing such abuse? About this no prosecutor or judge can render a verdict; voters will have to make their own decisions.

A Whitewater Chronology

1978

August: Bill and Hillary Clinton purchase a 230-acre land tract along the White River in Arkansas, in partnership with James and Susan McDougal. Mr. Clinton is Arkansas Attorney General.

October: Mrs. Clinton begins a series of commodities trades, earning nearly $100,000. The trades are not revealed until March, 1994.

November: Bill Clinton is elected governor of Arkansas. He makes James McDougal a top economic adviser.

1979

June: The Clintons and McDougals form Whitewater Development Co. to engage in the business of owning, selling, developing, managing and improving real property.

1980

November: Gov. Clinton is defeated by Republican Frank White. He joins the Little Rock law firm of Wright, Lindsey and Jennings.

1981

James McDougal purchases Madison Bank and Trust.

1982

James McDougal purchases Madison Guaranty Savings & Loan. It begins a period of rapid expansion.

November: Bill Clinton defeats Frank White, winning back the governor's seat.

1983

Capital Management Services, a federally insured small business investment company owned by Judge David Hale, begins making loans to the Arkansas political elite.

1984

January 20: The Federal Home Loan Bank Board issues a report on Madison Guaranty questioning its lending practices and financial stability. The Arkansas Securities Department begins to take steps to close down Madison.

March: Mrs. Clinton, a partner in the Rose Law Firm, receives the first payment of a $2,000-per-month retainer to assist Madison. Mr. McDougal later claims the payments were made at the request of Gov. Clinton.

November: Gov. Clinton wins re-election with 64% of the vote.

1985

January 16: Gov. Clinton appoints Beverly Bassett Schaffer, a long-time associate, to serve as Arkansas State Securities Commissioner.

March 1: Madison's accounting firm, Frost and Co., issues a report declaring the savings and loan solvent.

April 4:   Mr. McDougal hosts a fundraiser to help Gov. Clinton repay campaign debts. Contributions at the fundraiser later draw the scrutiny of Whitewater investigators.

April 30:   Hillary Clinton presents a recapitalization offer for the foundering Madison Guaranty to the Arkansas Securities Commission. Two weeks later, Ms. Schaffer informs Mrs. Clinton the plan is approved, but it is never implemented.

1986

March 4:   The Federal Home Loan Bank Board issues a second, sharply critical report of Madison, accusing Mr. McDougal of diverting funds to insiders.

April 3:   Judge Hale's Capital Management Services makes a $300,000 loan to Susan McDougal and a new company, Master Marketing; it is later alleged that about $100,000 of the loan ended up in a Whitewater Development Co. account. Indicted for fraud on an unrelated transaction in 1993, Judge Hale claims that Mr. Clinton and Mr. McDougal pressured him into making the loan; both deny the claim.

August: Federal regulators remove Mr. McDougal from Madison's board of directors.

November: Gov. Clinton wins re-election. Gubernatorial terms are extended from two years to four.

1987

According to Mrs. McDougal, all Whitewater records are brought to the Governor's Mansion and turned over to Mrs. Clinton sometime during the year.

1989

March: Federal regulators shut down Madison Guaranty Savings & Loan, at a taxpayer loss of about $60 million. Mr. McDougal is indicted for bank fraud.

Rose Law Firm attorneys Vincent Foster and Webster Hubbell obtain a Federal Deposit Insurance Corporation contract to help recover depositor funds from failed Arkansas savings and loans. Rose earns $400,000. A $10 million suit against Frost & Co., Madison's accounting firm, is settled for less than $1 million. Later, conflict-of-interest questions will be raised because of the Rose firm's previous work on behalf of Mr. McDougal, including the use of the Frost audit to aid Madison.

1990

Mr. McDougal is acquitted of bank fraud.

November: Gov. Clinton is elected to a second four-year term, promising to serve it out and not seek the presidency in 1992.

1991

October 3: Bill Clinton announces his candidacy for president and attacks, among others, "S&L crooks and self-serving CEOs."

1992

March 3: New York Times reporter Jeff Gerth discloses the Clintons' dealings with Madison and Whitewater.

March 20: Washington Times reporter Jerry Seper discloses Hillary Clinton's $2,000-per-month retainer from Madison.

March 23: In a hasty report arranged by the Clinton campaign, Denver lawyer James Lyons states the Clintons lost $68,000 on the Whitewater investment and clears them of improprieties. The issue fades from the campaign.

September: Resolution Trust Corporation field officers request that the Justice Department investigate Madison, forwarding Case #C0004 to the U.S. Attorney in Little Rock and officials in Washington. In the heat of the campaign, the issue is sidelined.

November 3: Bill Clinton is elected president.

1993

January 20: Bill Clinton is sworn in as 42nd President of the United States.

March 24: Year-old press clips about Whitewater are faxed from the office of Deputy Treasury Secretary Roger Altman to the office of White House Counsel Bernard Nussbaum. Mr. Altman also is serving as acting head of the Resolution Trust Corporation, an independent federal agency.

May 19: The White House fires seven employees of its travel office, following a review by Associate Counsel William Kennedy III, a former member of the Rose Law Firm. Mr. Kennedy's actions, which included attempting to involve the FBI in a criminal investigation of the travel office, are sharply criticized.

July 20: In Little Rock, the FBI obtains a warrant to search the office of Judge Hale as part of its investigation into Capital Management. In Washington, Deputy White House Counsel Vincent Foster drives to Ft. Marcy Park and commits suicide. (No direct connection between the two events has been established.) That evening, Mr. Nussbaum, White House aide Patsy Thomasson, and Mrs. Clinton's chief of staff Margaret Williams search Mr. Foster's office.

July 22: Mr. Nussbaum again searches Mr. Foster's office. During the two searches, documents are removed, including Whitewater files. Details on the removal of the files emerge months later.

July 26: A torn-up note is found in Mr. Foster's briefcase.

August 16: Paula Casey, a longtime associate of the Clintons, takes office in Little Rock as U.S. Attorney.

September: Ms. Casey turns down plea bargain attempts from Judge Hale's lawyer, Randy Coleman. Mr. Coleman had offered to share information on the "banking and borrowing practices of some individuals in the elite political circles of the State of Arkansas."

September 29: Treasury Department General Counsel Jean Hanson warns Mr. Nussbaum that the RTC plans to issue criminal referrals asking the Justice Department to investigate Madison. (The referrals are said to name the Clintons as witnesses to, and possible beneficiaries of, illegal actions. The current governor of Arkansas, Jim Guy Tucker, also is said to be a target of the investigation.)

Oct. 4 or 5: Bruce Lindsey, a top White House aide and Arkansas damage-control specialist, informs President Clinton about the referrals. Mr. Lindsey later tells Congress he did not mention any specific target of the referrals.

October 6: President Clinton meets with Arkansas Governor Jim Guy Tucker at the White House.

October 14: A meeting is held in Mr. Nussbaum's office with senior White House and Treasury personnel to discuss the RTC and Madison. Participants at the meeting later tell Congress that they discussed only how to handle press inquiries.

October 27: The RTC's first criminal referral is rejected in Little Rock by U.S. Attorney Paula Casey. Nine new criminal referrals are pending.

November 3: Associate Attorney General Webster Hubbell recuses himself from the Whitewater case.

November 9: Ms. Casey recuses herself from the Madison probe.

November 18: President Clinton meets with Gov. Tucker in Seattle.

December 19: New allegations of the president's sexual infidelities while governor surface in the American Spectator and The Los Angeles Times.

December 20: Washington Times correspondent Jerry Seper reports that Whitewater files were removed from Mr. Foster's office.

December 30: At a New Year's retreat, President Clinton asks Comptroller of the Currency Eugene Ludwig, an old friend, for "advice" about how to handle the growing Madison storm.

1994

January 20: Amid mounting political pressure, Attorney General Janet Reno appoints Robert Fiske as special counsel to investigate Whitewater.

February 2: Mr. Altman meets with Mr. Nussbaum and other senior White House staff to give them a "heads-up" about Madison.

February 24: Mr. Altman gives incomplete testimony to the Senate Banking Committee about discussions between the White House and Treasury on the Madison referrals.

February 25: Mr. Altman recuses himself from the Madison investigation and announces he will step down as acting head of the RTC.

March 5: White House Counsel Bernard Nussbaum resigns.

March 14: Associate Attorney General Webster Hubbell resigns.

March 18: The New York Times reveals Mrs. Clinton's 1970s commodities trades.

March 23: The Association of American Physicians and Surgeons files suit against Mrs. Clinton's health reform task force for violating the Federal Advisory Committee Act by holding secret meetings.

May 6: Former Little Rock resident Paula Corbin Jones files suit against President Clinton, charging he sexually harassed her while governor.

June 30: Special Counsel Robert Fiske concludes that Mr. Foster's death was a suicide and clears the White House and Treasury Department of obstruction of justice on the RTC contacts, opening the way for congressional hearings limited to the two subjects.

July 26: Congressional hearings open.

August 1: The White House reveals that the Whitewater files removed from Mr. Foster's office were kept for five days in the Clinton's residence before being turned over to their personal lawyer.

August 5: A three-judge panel removes Mr. Fiske and appoints Kenneth Starr as independent counsel.

August 17: Deputy Treasury Secretary Roger Altman resigns.

August 18: Treasury Department General Counsel Jean Hanson resigns.

Acknowledgments

Besides the writers whose bylines appear in this book, many others had a hand in producing the articles collected here. Following is a list of the writers, editors, secretaries and production people who put out The Wall Street Journal's opinion pages every day.

ROBERT L. BARTLEY, Editor
DANIEL HENNINGER, Deputy Editor of the Editorial Page

SHARON ALBURY	MANUELA HOELTERHOFF
APRIL ANDERSON	TAYLOR HOLLIDAY
DAVID ASMAN	HOLMAN W. JENKINS, JR.
MAX BOOT	MELANIE KIRKPATRICK
PAT BRODERICK	MAUREEN MCDERMOTT
DAVID BROOKS	JOHN MCGINNIS
VIRGINIA BUBEK	GEORGE MELLOAN
NED CRABB	MICAH MORRISON
KAREN M. CUDDY	CAROL MULLER
PAMELA M. DAIGLE	BARBARA D. PHILLIPS
KEN DEWITT	DOROTHY RABINOWITZ
ERICH EICHMAN	JOHNNA RICHARD
TIM W. FERGUSON	JOANN ROORBACH
JOHN H. FUND	LISA ROSSI
AMY GAMERMAN	JULIE SALAMON
PAUL GIGOT	AMITY SHLAES
KIRSTI HASTINGS	RAYMOND SOKOLOV
MARIAN HIEDA	MARK YOST

Index

Association of American Physicians and Surgeons et al. v. Hillary Rodham Clinton, 408-410

Association of Trial Lawyers of America, 387-388

Ausen, Lee, 404, 517, 519-520

B

Babcock, Bruce, 314-315

Bachus, Spencer, 316

Baird, Zoe, 39, 45-46, 49, 140, 217

Bakey, Tommy, 366

Baldwin, Bill, 514

Ball, Karen, 221

Ballot Access News, 503

Banca Nazionale del Lavoro (BNL)
  abuse of loans by, 105
  FBI investigation of, 74-75
  Iraqi armament financing by, 10-12, 21-23, 144-145

Bank Holding Company Act, 52-53

Bank of America, 26

Bank of Credit and Commerce International (BCCI)
  FBI investigation of, 74-75
  First American bought by, 271, 279, 469, 471, 527
  Justice Department settlement regarding, 427-429
  Kerry report about, 10-12, 196
  links with Whitewater scandal, iii, 154
  Morgenthau probe of, 82-84, 86-88, 133
  Orrin Hatch's link with, 419-420
  R. Tigert's role in monitoring, 167
  settlement of, 144-145, 154, 183
  SMERSH image of, 11-12
  Stephens Inc. links with, 2, 14-15, 24-26, 53-55, 68

Bank of New England, 28, 54

Banking regulations
  Madison Guaranty scandal and, 246-249
  securities business and, 16, 26-29
  Stephens Inc. and, 52-55

Banks, Charles A., 401-402, 499

Barclays Bank, 331-332

Bradbury, Curt
  named to American Bankers Association Board, 167-168
  Stephens Inc. and, 15-20, 54, 513-515
Bradley, Bill, 3
Brandon, David L., 335-339
Braun, Cheryl, 496-497
Breaux, John, 241, 305
Breslaw, April, 398, 405-407, 470, 519-520, 529, 535
Brinkley, David, 285
Brock, David, 123
Broder, David, 200
Brokaw, Tom, 56-57, 286
Bronson, Peter, 222
Brooks, David, 246
Brooks, Jack, 140
Brown, Hank, 10-12
Brown, Ron, 118, 134, 194, 278
Brownley, Christine, 504
Brummett, John, 378-380
Bryant, Ed, 44
Bryant, Winston, 424
Buchanan, Pat, 303
  presidential campaign of, 1, 3
Buckler, Arthur, 513-515
Buckley, James, 409
Buford, Doug, 79
Bumpers, Dale, 416
Bureau of Alcohol, Tobacco and Firearms, 281-283
Burger, Warren, 397
Bush, George, 303
  BCCI-BNI scandal and, 21, 153
  capital-gains tax cut proposal, 295
  drug traffic policies under, 447-449
  Iranian hostage crisis, 350-351
  Iraqi armaments questions concerning, 11
  Mena affair and, 361-363
  press's relations with, 2
  re-election campaign of, 1, 3, 6, 36, 457, 504
  Team 100 and, 13

Dunn, Leonard, 315-316

Durenberger, David, 295, 460

E

Easley, Charles, 292

Eastland, Terry, 2, 130, 134-137, 224-227, 332, 411-414, 509-512

Economic Regulatory Administration, 341

Economist, The, 288, 442, 530

Edwards, David, 140-141

Eggleston, W. Neil, 485-486, 488-489

Ehrlichman, John, 232, 453, 477

Eisenhower, David, 123

Elders, Jocelyn, 447

Eller, Jeff, 67-68, 92

Emmons, Garry, 426

Emshwiller, John R., 94-97

Engstrom, Stephen, 126

Entex, 34-35

Epstein, Edward Jay, 361-367

ESM Securities, 469-472, 527-529

Espy, Michael, 278

Ethics in Government Act, 323

Evans-Pritchard, Ambrose, 289, 442

Ewton, Ronnie, 470-471

"Eye on America," 361

F

Faircloth, Lauch, 183, 416

  Congressional Whitewater hearings, 455, 497, 506-508

  special counsel called for, 132

  Tigert nomination hearings, 162-168, 177-179

Falwell, Jerry, 441-443

Farris, Anne, 382-383

Farrkhan, Louis, 201

FBI (Federal Bureau of Investigation)

  BCCI investigation by, 74-75

  controversy surrounding Sessions' replacement, 70-75

G

Henry, Don, 443

Hertzberg, Rick, 2

Hesburgh, Theodore, 430

Heymann, Philip, 74, 77-78, 159, 180
  resigns from Justice Department, 160, 217-219, 274

Hill, Anita, 7, 31-32, 80, 267, 271, 326, 350, 384-391

Hills, Carla, 38-39

Holder, Eric, 194, 410

Hollings, Ernest, 430

Hollis & Co., 17, 28

Holly Farms, 17

Home Federal Savings and Loan of Centralia, 181-182

Home State Savings Bank, 471, 528-529

Horne, Wilson S., 278

Horner, Connie, 38-39

Horton, Odell, 44

House Banking Committee, probe of Madison
    Guaranty, 99-100, 103, 107-108, 131-133

House Small Business Committee, 99

Hoyer, Steny, 292

Hubbell, Webster, 14
  as associate attorney general, 58-60
  billing irregularities of, while at Rose, 204, 274, 522-524, 531, 536
  firing of William Sessions and, 74-75
  influence on presidential appointments by, 70-72
  Justice Department influence of, 47, 56-57, 59-60, 70-72, 118, 178,
      180-183, 492
  Madison Guaranty case, alleged conflict of interest
      in, 102, 181-183, 185, 187-190, 489
  recusal in Madison Guaranty case, 89-90, 103, 160, 163-165, 195
  resignation of, ii, 269-270, 273-275, 286, 369, 446
  role in Waco disaster, 56-58
  as Rose Law Firm partner, 380, 471
  suicide of Foster and, 77, 222, 496-497
  trial of Harold Ford and, 43-45, 47-49, 81, 103
  Vincent Foster and, 141
  White House travel office scandal and, 68-69

Huckabee, Mike, 504

Huggins, Stanley, 442

Ives, Kevin, 443

J

Jackson, Andrew, 343-344

Jackson, Fletcher, 208, 211

Jackson, Jesse, 8, 44, 51

Janensch, Ernst Paul, 349

Jaruzelski, General, 300

Jaworski, Leon, 22, 135

Jegley, Angela, 381

Jennings, Alston, 114-115

Jennings, Peter, 286

Jernigan, George, 504

Johnson Smick International Inc., 242-245

Johnson, Gary, 442

Johnson, Lyndon B., 225, 263, 294, 344, 346-350

Johnson, Manuel, 243-245

Johnson, Michael, 210-211

Johnson, Paul, 468

Jones, Earl, 380-381

Jones, Julia Hughes, 14, 502-504

Jones, Paula Corbin, 370, 375, 384-396, 399,
    411-414, 432, 455, 460, 536

Jordan, Barbara, 430

Justice Department (U.S.)
  alleged presidential intervention in, 331
  Bartley/WSJ suit against, 151, 156-161, 194, 220-222, 434
  BCCI/BNA scandal and, 21-23, 144-145, 427-429, 437-439
  Clinton's Whitewater files given to, 109
  Hale and Capital Management investigated by, 212-213, 499-500
  investigation of Foster suicide, 77, 151, 156-161
  Madison Guaranty investigated by, 98-99, 134-137, 212-213
  Office of Information and Privacy, 159
  Office of Legal Counsel, 431
  purge of U.S. attorneys in, 49-51, 103, 129, 132, 194, 369, 428

K

Kaiser-Permanente, 409

Kamillatos, Nicholas, 357

Karr, Albert R., 515, 518-520

Katsanos, Stephen, 517, 519-520

Katzenbach, Nicholas, 46

Kaye, Scholer law firm, 188-189

Keating Five, 35, 130-132, 173-176, 195, 267, 430

Keating, Charles, 10-11, 109, 131, 167, 173-176, 188

Keeney, John, 99, 212

Kefauver, Estes, 435

Keillor, Garrison, 358, 360

Keisler, William B., 147

Kelly, Michael, 501

Kelly, Virginia, 465

Kemp, Jack, 242

Kemp, Maurice, 6

Kendall, David, 218, 228, 359, 526

Kennedy anti-nepotism bill, 37-38, 46

Kennedy, Edward, 267

Kennedy, Robert, 273

Kennedy, Stephanie, 402

Kennedy, William III, 41, 62-63
  Arctic Alaska Fisheries Corp. and, 277
  Beverly nursing home deal and, 378-379
  influence on presidential appointments by, 71-72
  partnership in Rose Law firm, 102
  White House security passes controversy and, 264-265, 291
  White House travel scandal and, 67-69, 73, 81, 103, 229, 369

Kerr, William, 351

Kerrey, Bob, 4-5

Kerry, John, 10-12, 22, 195-196, 296, 507

King, Larry, 359

Kinsley, Michael, 80, 221, 223, 352

Kleindienst, Richard, 270

Koffsky, Daniel, 402

Koppel, Ted, 368

Koresh, David, 41

M

Meese, Edwin, 270, 341
  banking regulators links with, 444-447
  Justice Department and, 45, 48, 50, 60
  political influence of, 71, 80
"Meet the Press" program, 285
Melamed, Leo, 248, 374
Melloan, George, 246-249
Meloni, Robert S., 366-367
Mena, Arkansas, 361-367, 421-425
Mena, Arkansas Intermountain Regional Airport, 421-425, 443, 453
Merck Corporation, 329
Mercy Health Initiatives, 378-379
Merrill Lynch, 16, 26-29
Merrill Lynch Bank and Trust Co., 16, 26-29
Metzenbaum, Howard, 59
Mikado Leasing, 524
Milken, Michael, 196, 330
Miller, Cassidy, Larroca & Lewin, 270-271
Miller, Thomas A., 350-351
Mitchell, Dyone, 402
Mitchell, George, 31, 218, 241, 340-342, 398-400
  political clout of, 294-297
  resolution on Congressional Whitewater hearings, 415-417, 419
Mitchell, John, 303
Mitchell, Selig, Jackson, Tucker & White, 316
Mondale, Walter, 4
Money magazine, 81
Morgan Bank, 26
Morgan Guaranty, 182
Morgenthau, Robert
  BCCI investigation by, 10, 12, 22-23, 83
  settlement of BCCI case and, 130, 133, 144-145, 427-429, 437-439
Morrison, Micah, 377-383, 421-425, 443
Moynihan, Daniel Patrick, 49, 242-243, 295-296, 417
Munger Tolles & Olson, 430
Myers, Dee Dee, 204, 236, 263-264, 293, 331
Myers, Lisa, 286

N

Naqvi, Swaleh, 11, 144, 427-429, 437-439

National Archives, 61

National Bank of Georgia, 83, 135, 320-323

National Law Journal, 270

National Marine Fisheries Service, 278

National Security Council, 424

NationsBank, 28

Neas, Ralph, 59

Needles, Gene, 379

Neel, Roy, 217

Nelson, Sheffield, 17, 20, 502

Nesbitt, Patrick, 350

Neuringer, Felisa, 92-93

New Deal, 355

New Hampshire primary, 1

New Republic, 2, 80, 279, 352-353

New York Daily News, 221, 280-283

New York Post, 160, 228, 280-283

New York Times, 69, 109-111, 139, 212, 221, 240
  analysis of Arkansas politics, 501-502
  criticism of WSJ in, 384-385
  Hillary Clinton's commodities futures trading story, 317-319, 328
  Whitewater coverage of, 1, 345-346

Newcomb, John, 289-290

Newman, Frank, 168

Newsday magazine, 81

"Next American Frontier, The," 356

Nicaraguan Contras, 361-363, 366-367, 424-425, 443

Nichols, Larry, 441-443

Nixon, Richard, 128-130, 132, 231-238, 270, 286-287, 298, 303, 348-349, 456-458
  diaries and tapes of, 476-477

Nixon v. Fitzgerald, 411-414

Noonan, Peggy, 369

Noriega, Manuel, 196

North American Free Trade Agreement (NAFTA), 30-31, 501

North, Oliver, 65-66, 132, 196, 266, 348, 536

O

P

Q

R

S

U

V

Ventana Investments, 378

Vento, Bruce, 474

Volcker, Paul, 248

W

Wachtler, Sol, 50

Wade, Chris, 110

Wagman, Richard, 289

Walker, Jon, 442

Wallach, Robert, 45, 191

Wallop, Malcolm, 400

Walsh, Lawrence, 323, 424, 493

  BCCI and, 12, 22, 81, 83, 132-133, 154

  on Congressional testimony, 511

  on independent counsel, 240, 251

  on political vs. criminal investigations, 193

Walsh, Sharon, 427

Ward, Seth, 106-107, 111, 114, 489

Warner, Marvin, 471, 528

Warnke, Paul, 3

Warren, Gerald, 236

Washington Monthly, 501

Washington Post, 80, 92-93, 110, 114-115, 204, 281-282, 427, 445

Washington Times, 2, 79, 90, 110, 140-142, 182, 264-265, 288

Watergate scandal, Whitewater compared
    with, 132, 231-238, 435, 456-458

Watkins, David, 67-68, 408

  resignation of, ii

Watson, Thomas F., 127

Weaver, Vernon, 15

Weingarten, Reid, 476-479

Welch, Russell, 422-424

Wells Fargo, 28

Westbrook, Deborah, 402-403

Western Savings and Loan Association, 188

Weyrich, Paul, 59-60

Wharton, Clifford, 217

White House passes controversy, 229-230, 263-265, 291-293, 306